HOLY LAND
HOLLOW JUBILEE
GOD, JUSTICE
AND THE PALESTINIANS

HOLY LAND
HOLLOW JUBILEE
GOD, JUSTICE
AND THE PALESTINIANS

edited by
NAIM ATEEK and MICHAEL PRIOR

MELISENDE
London

First published 1999 by
Melisende
An imprint of
Fox Communications and Publications
39 Chelmsford Road
London E18 2PW
England

ISBN 1 901764 09 5

General editor: Leonard Harrow
Assistant editor: Alan Ball

Printed and bound in England by St Edmundsbury Press

CONTENTS

PALESTINIAN HISTORICAL PERSPECTIVES

JUSTICE AND RECONCILIATION: LIVING WITH MEMORY

PART 2: THE PRESENT—'DO JUSTICE' (MICAH 6.8)

RELIGIOUS FUNDAMENTALISM

PREFACE
Naim Ateek

Sabeel's Third International Conference was held on the campus of Bethlehem University on 10-15 February 1998. By holding the conference in Bethlehem, we at *Sabeel*, Ecumenical Liberation Theology Center wanted to express our solidarity with the Palestinian people of the West Bank, as well as to honour the Christian community of Bethlehem, Beit Sahour, Beit Jala, and throughout the Holy Land who have borne an uninterrupted witness to Christ over the last 2,000 years.

Unfortunately, many people in the world today do not anymore associate Christians with Palestine and the Middle East. For many of them, Christianity has become a Western religion. It is as if Jesus were born in Bethlehem, Pennsylvania. It was important, therefore, to hold the conference in Bethlehem, Palestine, where it all started, so that the international participants would meet and interact with the living Christians of the land.

Furthermore, we chose Bethlehem for political and theological reasons. It is the place from which the holy family, Joseph, Mary, and Jesus, left as refugees to escape the threat of King Herod. Herod, on the one hand, still represents people in power today who viciously use their power in order to terrorise and kill others. Joseph, Mary, and Jesus, on the other hand, represent the millions of refugees in the world, including Palestinian refugees who have been displaced as a result of injustice. At the same time Jesus Christ is, for us Christians, the incarnate Lord, born in Bethlehem, and the liberator who offers us new hope and life and the strength to struggle against all forces of injustice and oppression. Bethlehem, therefore, seemed an appropriate venue at a time when the Palestinians were going to commemorate fifty years of oppression and dispersion. Bethlehem stood for us as a symbol of hope, a better future, and renewed possibilities for liberation.

Having chosen as conference theme 'The Challenge of Jubilee: What Does God Require?', the words of the prophet Micah 6.8 seemed a fitting correlation and an important guiding principle. 'He has told you, O mortal, what is good; and what does the Lord require of you but to do justice, and to love kindness, and to walk humbly with your God.'

On the first full day of the conference, we invited the participants to take a hard and sobering look at the past fifty years. It was important to recall and evaluate the past, not to live in it, nor to dwell on it, but to learn from it, and to gain courage and wisdom in order to confront the future. As participants looked at the past, they were encouraged to lift constantly before their eyes the words of Micah, 'love mercy'. Admittedly, this is not easy for many Palestinians. It is difficult to feel merciful when one remembers the injustice. Many people find it difficult to forget and forgive. The challenge is ever before us to pray for grace to be merciful and forgiving while, at the same time, maintaining vigilance in the face of oppression and standing up against injustice. To be merciful as God is merciful does not mean to gloss over injustice. To be merciful means to be open always to the possibility of finding a resolution to the conflict that will be based on justice, a justice which will restore the humanity to both the oppressor and the oppressed. We live in a world where strict and absolute justice is not possible. Mercy must enter in without compromising the demand for justice.

On the second day, the participants were exposed to the present situation. They were encouraged to remember Micah's words, 'Do justice'. We felt it was impossible to give a comprehensive picture of life under occupation within the limited time of the conference. We organised, therefore, eight different sessions covering a whole range of topics that touch on the various aspects of Palestinian life. These sessions were conducted off campus in four community and church centres throughout Bethlehem. The participants were encouraged to attend only two of the eight, with the option of purchasing the audio cassettes for those sessions they could not attend. The topics included religious fundamentalism, Christian fundamentalism, Zionism, Christian-Muslim relations, jubilee and the biblical tradition, the Bible and Zionism, human rights issues, economics and jubilee, and pilgrimage alternatives.

On the third day, we planned to do something a bit unusual and innovative. We wanted the participants to experience some of the contemporary stations of the cross which have become part of the daily experience of our Palestinian people. In essence it provided the living and actual illustrations of the verbal, academic lectures which were presented in the morning. Ten buses transported the participants to different sites where they experienced first hand the ongoing injustice. The sites visited included checkpoints, demolished houses, destroyed villages, and confiscated land. At every station, participants were able to see, reflect, learn and pray. The day ended with Professor Edward Said's keynote address which knitted together the historical and political situation with a challenge to both local and international participants to become active in making history.

On the last day of the conference, we looked to the future with the motto of the day, 'Walk humbly with God'. We wanted to give some answers to questions such as, what contribution can we make to a just peace? How can we use the challenge of jubilee? How can our friends help us who experience injustice and pain? What is the vision of peace for the future, and what are the spiritual resources available to us as we move ahead? The conference was concluded at St Catherine's Nativity Church with a worship service of dedication and renewal for the work of justice, peace, and reconciliation.

Someone has said that our problem today is that we have reversed Micah's words. Instead of doing justice and loving mercy, we tend to love justice and do mercy. Many of us are more eager to engage in works of mercy, in lending a helping hand than in standing up for justice. Certainly people in power are more ready to be generous than to be just. They are keen on philanthropy but not on justice. In our Third International Conference, we wanted to emphasise the importance of doing justice, loving mercy, and walking humbly with God as we lifted high the challenge of jubilee.

This volume includes most of the papers which were presented at the conference. We hope that the reader will find them stimulating and instructive.

Al-Nakba and jubilee

The last fifty years have brought untold suffering upon the Palestinian people. Their only sin and crime was to say 'no' to the occupation of their country. For many people in the West, the success of the Zionists in 1948 was impressive. Within a few months, three quarters of a million Palestinians were displaced, and over three quarters of the land of Palestine was conquered. Some Palestinians fled in terror, like Joseph, Mary, and Jesus at the time of Herod, while others were forced out at gun point. More recent research by Dr Salman Abu-Sitta, former member of the Palestine National Council has shown that 531 villages and towns were depopulated, and that Palestinians were uprooted from over 662 other localities. In other words, the Palestinians were displaced from over 1,200 localities in Palestine. Many of us Palestinians today still recall the details of our catastrophe as children, or carry with us the memories of our parents who were uprooted from their homes. In those days the sufferings of the Palestinians did not really matter to many people in the world. What mattered was to find a home for the suffering Jews who had gone through the Holocaust, many of whom would have preferred to go to North America rather than come to Palestine, but it was to Palestine that the Zionists wanted them to come.

Approximately 35 per cent of the Jewish people in the world live in Israel today. Over the last fifty years, Israel has grown and developed tremendously. Its existence, however, has been maintained by two important factors, namely, its formidable military power, and the unflinching and uncompromising support of the United States. Undoubtedly, to a mere onlooker, Israel has developed in leaps and bounds, surpassing many other countries. Were it not for the basic injustice to the Palestinians, one could not help but be impressed by what Israel has accomplished for its people. It is the injustice that is the termite that eats at its core. It is the injustice to the Palestinians that exacerbates Israel's feeling of insecurity.

From an Israeli perspective, it is impossible to evaluate the last fifty years of Israel's history without a reference to the Holocaust. The Holocaust was a basic injustice done to Jews. The tragedy of the Holocaust, however, has been addressed rather adequately. The world has been continuously condemning it. The guilt has been admitted, the compensations have been and continue to be extended quite generously to the State of Israel, to the Holocaust survivors, and to the victims' children. Today, when the world looks back in greater objectivity on the events of the last fifty years, many people realise the tremendous injustice done to the Palestinians. But the tragedy of Palestine has not yet been dealt with properly and adequately. An increasing number of Jews is beginning to admit the guilt, and rewrite more accurately the history of the last fifty years; but the guilt has not been recognised by the government of Israel. In fact, for many Palestinians, the Oslo peace process was an attempt by the Americans and the Israelis to legalise and legitimise the injustice rather than to address it justly.

Nowadays, when the Zionist ideology and its claim to the land of Palestine seems flimsy, it is the appeal to the Holocaust that has become paramount. The Holocaust has been used as the most convincing argument in the rationale for the establishment of the State of Israel. Yet as classical Zionism wanes, biblical Zionism has become a formidable force among the right wing Jewish and western Christian Zionists in their apologetic for the state.

Be that as it may, we live today with certain important facts. The state and people of Israel are a reality, and the Palestinian people and their authority are likewise a reality. Both are here to stay. The Palestinians still seek justice and Israel still needs security. If Israel will give Palestinians justice, it will, in return, receive security. There is no other formula for a lasting peace.

As Israel celebrates its fiftieth anniversary, we, people of faith gathered in Bethlehem, who ostensibly have no political power or clout, and who seem weak and vulnerable, want to lift a prophetic voice and address the people and government of Israel. We simply say, 'all your outward and impressive celebrations will not hide your nakedness of injustice. We offer you this year the challenge of jubilee so that you may live and become secure; and so that the Palestinians may live also in justice and security.'

What then is the challenge of the jubilee? I would like to mention three points.

1. The sovereignty of God. At the heart of the biblical jubilee is the sovereignty of God. God is the creator and redeemer of the world. To God belongs the land of Palestine, as does the whole world. We are all tenants, aliens, and strangers (Leviticus 25.23). We all pay the rent to God, the real owner. Once we truly recognise the sovereignty of God, we know that it has moral, social, and political implications. For many of us, this concept carries with it the vital need for sharing the land under God. We are talking about an inclusive theology of land. At the heart of this theology is the one and only God who is the God of the Palestinians, the Israelis, and the whole world, and who is sovereign over all. If we accept the major premise that the land belongs to God, then, both Palestinians and Israelis have been placed by God on it, both must share it, and both are accountable to God for it. From the perspective of this contextualised Christian theology we can very well say that this land is God's gift to all the people of this land, namely, Palestinians and Israelis. This theology aims at peacemaking. The first challenge of the jubilee, therefore, is to accept the sovereignty of God over the whole of this land. We believe in the one God who loves and cares for all of God's children. God is colour blind, ethnic blind, and race blind. God sees us all as humans created in God's image.

2. The basic premise on which the jubilee is built is the fact that God is a God of justice, and wills that justice be done in the world. The jubilee year was ordained to set things right. The jubilee rationale is that, due to humanity's propensity to evil, God's will for the world can be thwarted and frustrated. In the jubilee year, God says to humans, stop the injustice,

stop the exploitation, free the oppressed, forgive the debts of the poor, return the land to its lawful owners.

In other words, at the basis of the jubilee is the proclamation of liberty to all the people of the land (Leviticus 25.10). True liberation comes when justice is done. No liberation or peace is possible if people live in oppression and under occupation. No liberation is possible if the land continues to be confiscated and monopolised by those in power. In this jubilee year, God asks us to take stock of where things have gone wrong and render justice to those it has been denied. The challenge is for justice to be tempered with mercy. This is clearly defined by calling on the State of Israel to withdraw from the whole of the 23 per cent of the land of Palestine which is the West Bank and Gaza, and allow the Palestinians to establish their own sovereign state on their own soil, with East Jerusalem as its capital. This is how most Palestinians today define justice with mercy. The challenge of jubilee is that justice must be done.

In order for Israel to live securely, it has to live justly. For the last fifty years, it has lived by the power of its gun and that of the United States. It can presumably continue to do so for many years to come, so long as the billions of dollars keep pouring in, and the military hardware is supplied. Israel, however, will never be really secure until justice is done to the Palestinians. Security will be achieved when Israel accepts to live justly with its Palestinian neighbours. This specifically means to stop all confiscation of Palestinian land and to withdraw its control from the whole of the West Bank and Gaza. It must stop all forms of humiliation, exploitation of, and discrimination against the Palestinians. Israel must treat the Palestinians as human beings who have rights to their land and to a life of liberty and peace. As we emphasise the importance of justice in the jubilee year, we denounce the use of violence or military force as a way of resolving conflicts anywhere in the world.

3. The challenge of jubilee implies the possibility of a new era, a new beginning between Palestinians and Israelis. In other words, when the oppressed are set free, their dignity and humanity is restored to them, and they become free human beings. When the land is returned to its legal owners, it means that people can cultivate it and live from the gift of the land and its produce which God has given them. When the debt of the poor is cancelled, they can have a fresh start with hope for a better future for themselves and their families. The jubilee allows for new attitudes to develop and new perceptions to be created. The Palestinians and Israelis will not perceive each other anymore as enemies, but as neighbours and

potential friends and partners. An inter-dependency would then develop because all the inhabitants of the land would see themselves working together under God and for a shared destiny. This is a realisable dream. The jubilee opens up the possibility of a better future for all of us.

This is the challenge of jubilee. This is what God requires of us. We came to proclaim the jubilee for the liberation of our land and all of its inhabitants. There is, however, an added note for those of us who are Christians. Our Lord Jesus Christ has given us an even higher calling whenever we think of the jubilee. Basically he says to us that the jubilee year should not be celebrated once every seven years, or only every fifty years—it should be our daily life and practice. God calls us to a life of perpetual jubilee. We are called to work for the abundant life, life lived to its fullest. This surely means the life of liberation and peace for all people. May we fulfil our calling as we stand in solidarity, and as we work together for the liberation of all the oppressed people of the world.

Jerusalem
Christmas 1998

ACKNOWLEDGEMENTS

Sabeel Ecumenical Liberation Theology Center wishes to express its deepest gratitude to all those who contributed to the success and fruitfulness of the Third International Conference held on the campus of Bethlehem University, 10-15 February 1998. It is difficult even to begin to name the many local and international friends who served on the different committees, and who came to our assistance in a variety of ways, working diligently and faithfully. We would like, however, to mention especially Jamal Abed Rabbu, Betty Bailey, Tom Getman, Hind Khoury, Anne Montgomery, Ghassan Nasr, Dianne Roe, Patty Shelly, and Brother Vincent Malham, FSC, the Vice-Chancellor of Bethlehem University for their significant contribution and help.

A sincere word of thanks goes to the *Sabeel* Board, Executive Committee, the Nazareth *Sabeel* Committee, Friends of *Sabeel* in North America and the United Kingdom, and the Jerusalem *Sabeel* staff, with a special recognition to Janet Lahr Lewis, conference co-ordinator; Laurel Nelson, assistant conference co-ordinator; Hilary Rantisi, photo exhibit co-ordinator; and Nora Carmi, administrator.

The front cover reproduces a painting by the Palestinian artist Suleiman Mansour, while the back cover carries the logo of our conference which was designed by Lori Hayes, a Global Mission Intern sponsored by the United Church of Christ and the Disciples of Christ, who is an art teacher at the Rawdat El-Zuhur school in Jerusalem. To both of these artists we are immensely grateful.

Equally, *Sabeel* would like to acknowledge the important contribution of a number of people who helped us in the editing and preparation of the papers for publishing. First and foremost we extend our gratitude to the Revd Dr Michael Prior, CM, for his invaluable contribution as co-editor, and without whom this volume would not have been completed. The computer work was done by our two Peace and Justice Interns of the Young Adult Volunteer Program of the Presbyterian Church, USA, Laurel Nelson and Catherine Gordon successively. We owe them a great debt of thanks. Our utmost appreciation goes to Cedar Duaybis for her meticulous editing skills, keen eye, and tireless endeavour in this project. Finally, a special thank you goes to Leonard Harrow and Alan Ball of Fox Communications and Publications, London, for publishing this important volume.

SPONSORS

Marilyn Borst
Edmond and Patti Browning
Church of Scotland
Episcopal Peace and Justice Network
Mission Covenant Church of Sweden
Mustard Seed Foundation
Paddock Foundation
Philanthropic Ventures
Presbyterian Church USA
Shepherd Tours and Travel
Stewardship Foundation
Osvaldo Vena
World Council of Churches
World Vision, Jerusalem

CONTRIBUTORS

Abu Lughod, Professor Ibrahim
Graduate Program of International Studies, Bir Zeit University

Ashrawi, Dr Hanan
Founder of 'Mifah'—Palestinian Initiative for the Promotion of Global Dialogue and Democracy
Elected member of Palestinian Legislative Council - Jerusalem District
Founder of The Palestinian Independent Commission for Citizen's Rights

Ateek, The Revd Dr Naim
Director, *Sabeel*—Ecumenical Liberation Theology Center

Bishara, Dr Azmi
Palestinian Member of the Israeli Knesset

Browning, The Most Revd Edmond L
Presiding Bishop of the Episcopal Church in the USA, Retired.

Brubacher, Dr Gordon
Associate Professor of Biblical Studies and Archaeology at Doane College in Crete, Nebraska

Chacour, The Revd Dr Elias
President and founder of Mar Elias College, Ibillin
Vice-President, *Sabeel*

Davis, Dr Uri
Director of External Relations and Chair of Study Programs in English at the Central Galilee Academic College, Sakhnin; Co-ordinator - Regional Editorial Group for the Middle East, Citizenship Studies; Chairman, Al-Beit

Ellis, Professor Marc H
Professor of American and Jewish Studies, J M Dawson Institute of American and Jewish Studies, Baylor University, Waco, Texas

Frayling, Canon Nicholas
Anglican Rector in Liverpool, UK
Chair of the Welfare Organisations in the City of Liverpool
Chair of the BBC Religious Advisory Panel in Merseyside

Gunner, The Revd Dr Göran
Senior Lecturer in the History of Religion at Stockholm School of Theology, Sweden

Isaac, Dr Jad
General Director, Applied Research Institute (ARIJ), Bethlehem

Khalidi, Professor Rashid
Professor of Middle East History and Director of the Center for International Studies at the University of Chicago
President of the American Committee on Jerusalem

Khoury, The Revd Dr Rafiq
Author, Parish Priest, Latin Church, Jifna

Kuttab, Attorney Jonathan
Palestinian human rights lawyer. Co-founder of Al-Haq (Law in the Service of Man) and the Mandela Institute for Political Prisoners. A member of both the New York and the Israeli Bar Associations. Board Member of *Sabeel*

Masenya, Dr Madipoane
Professor, University of South Africa, Pretoria

Milgrom, Rabbi Dr Jacob
Professor Emeritus of Biblical Studies, University of California at Berkeley

Nasser, Dr Yousef
Assistant Professor of Economics, Bir Zeit University

Prior CM, The Revd Dr Michael
Principal Lecturer, Department of Theology and Religious Studies in St Mary's College, University of Surrey, England

Rayan SJ, Dr Samuel
Professor, Faculty of Theology of Vidyajyoti, Delhi and Regional Theology Centre in Keralam

Reiss, Professor Moshe
Rabbi, Yale University
Guest Lecturer in Judeo-Christian Relations and Comparative Religion

Ruether, Professor Rosemary Radford
Georgia Harkness Professor of Applied Theology at Garrett Evangelical Theological Seminary and Northwestern University, Evanston, Illinois

Sabbah, His Beatitude Michel
Latin Patriarch of Jerusalem, President, Middle East Council of Churches

Said, Professor Edward W
Professor of English and Comparative Literature, Columbia University, New York
President of the Modern Language Association
Senior member of King's College, Cambridge University

Sandvik, Häkan
Pastor, Swedish Evangelical Lutheran Church, Finland

Sizer, The Revd Dr Stephen
Director, Highway Journeys, Vicar of Christ Church, Virginia Water, England

Seikaly, Dr May
Associate Professor, Department of Near Eastern and Asian Studies, Wayne State University, Detroit

Vena, Dr Osvaldo D
Ordained minister with the Reformed Church of Argentina
Assistant Professor of New Testament Interpretation at Garrett Evangelical Theological Seminary in Evanston, Illinois

Wagner, The Revd Dr Donald
Director, Center for Middle Eastern Studies, North Park University, Chicago
Co-ordinator for Evangelicals for Middle East Understanding, USA

Zaru, Mrs Jean
Presiding Clerk, Society of Friends, Ramallah
Vice President, *Sabeel*

INTRODUCTION
Michael Prior

The papers in this volume were delivered *viva voce* at the 1998 *Sabeel* International Conference. Each was followed by formal questions in the plenary sessions, and more intimate discussion in other gatherings. In most cases, the speakers took account of these exchanges as they prepared their papers for publication. However, in a small number of papers, the editors, wishing to retain the immediacy and intimacy of the spoken word, decided to publish texts with minimum concessions to the requirements of the academe.

The conference was structured around the biblical theme of jubilee and its possible relevance to current events in Palestine, fifty years after the Palestinian *Nakba* (catastrophe) of 1948. The papers in the first part comment on the biblical texts and reflect on the legacy of the past. The subsequent ones consider not only what happened, but how one deals with the consequent wounds, and discuss the interplay between memory, reconciliation and justice (Part 2). The papers in Part 3 project into the future and consider the political visions and spiritual resources for a lasting peace in Palestine.

This introduction reflects the flow of the conference. But even if it adequately encapsulated the lectures, it could never communicate the total spirit of the occasion. Worship, song, and prayerful reflection were at its heart, and were given quality time at the beginning, during and at the close of each session. A *Worship Program* accompanied the *Conference Program*, and, in addition, *Sabeel* had prepared a booklet, *Contemporary Stations of the Cross* for a modern *Via Dolorosa.* Visiting places of significance and listening to the testimonies of people who bear the brunt of Zionist colonialism and the Israeli occupation were an integral part of the convention.

*   *   *

Professor Edward W Said delivered the Keynote Address to a packed audience in the theatre of Bethlehem University on Friday evening, 13 February 1998, so packed in fact that several hundred people had to watch the proceedings, courtesy of closed circuit television. Earlier in the day, Professor Said had visited the former home of his family in West Jerusalem, which, ironically, is now the 'International Christian Embassy'. The conference participants for their part had spent the afternoon traversing a contemporary *Via Dolorosa*, whether in a refugee camp or a settlement.

Professor Said spoke freely, irrespective of what offence it might cause. He was resolute in classifying the 'peace process' as a further stage in the capitulation of the Palestinians to the advances of Zionism. He was dismissive of the United States' 'even-handedness', and scornful of the current Palestinian leadership. The Palestinians were worse off in every respect now than they were before 'the *misery* of Oslo'.

There could be no erasing of the historical truth that the existence of Israel is predicated upon the obliteration of the Palestinian people. The scars of the past and of recent times are still unhealed. But what of the future? How can the Palestinians co-exist peacefully with a state that has not declared its boundaries, and describes itself as the state of the whole Jewish people alone? How can they live in peace with Israel as long as it washes its hands of any responsibility for their plight, and pretends to seek peace, while persisting in their exploitation? The oppressive policies of the Israeli government repeat the original sin of the *Nakba*. Manifestly such actions are inimical to any real peace. But to aspire to remove Israel and its people is equally fanciful. The first challenge, indeed moral mission, for the Palestinian people, and for each individual, then, is to extract acknowledgement from Israel of its continued injustice towards the Palestinians. History will never excuse the Palestinians for failing in this enterprise.

Despite the odds, there is a way forward, one requiring a resolute national will and a mass movement determined to resist injustice. Some form of co-existence can be achieved, whereby both Israelis and Palestinians can live a better life, free of ethnocentricity and religious intolerance. Showing no sympathy for the customary descent into the rhetoric of lament and abject passivity, Professor Said stressed the capacity of people to make their own history. The tragedy that the Palestinians suffered was the result of human planning and endeavour. Equally the way forward lies in self-reliance and active resistance. However, one must win over international opinion.

The reality of Israel challenges the Palestinians to marshal their resources single-mindedly. This will require a massive campaign, in the United States and elsewhere, to dispel the Zionist nationalist myths, and undermine the morality of Israel's military occupation. Palestinians, like the ANC-inspired opposition to South African *apartheid*, must campaign in universities, churches, corporations and the media. History confirms that although the balance of power is unfavourable, the weaker side can overcome the stronger because of the *human* factor, the relentless will to resist injustice. If Palestinians make the case that they are prepared, with the Jews of Israel and Arab people in the surrounding region, to make a new kind of history, based on a new politics of integration and inclusion, they *can* carry the day.

Part 1: The Past—'Love Mercy' (Micah 6.8)

Three scholars reflect on biblical perspectives. **Gordon Brubacher** surveys the principles of jubilee in the Old Testament, and reflects on their significance in the contemporary world. Leviticus 25 enjoins a year of jubilee for every fifty years. The biblical narrative requires the ancient Israelites to set free those who had become slaves as a result of debt, and give back family land which had been sold, because of need, at any time over the previous fifty years. The jubilee was designed to protect vulnerable people, and flowed from the assertion that God owns both the land and the people. The Old Testament theology of jubilee demands justice, mercy, and proper conduct as a way of life before God. However, there is no clear evidence that the jubilee was observed after the time of the monarchy. Nevertheless, the principles of jubilee were appealed to constantly by the Hebrew prophets, outlining the benefits of observing them, and warning of the consequences of neglecting to do so. Brubacher sees little hope that the State of Israel will comport itself after the ideals of the jubilee, and appeals to the Palestinians, the party from whom the land has been taken, not to seek revenge.

Osvaldo Vena examines the New Testament with an eye to the theme of jubilee. Having surveyed the evidence he asserts that Jesus did not preach the Jewish Year of Jubilee, but something much more radical, namely, the reign of God, not for one year in every fifty, but forever. This new reality was not confined to one religious community. Moreover, Jesus did not provide a blueprint for the reign of God, but rather gave pointers. The early disciples would live by the jubilee principle of forgiving each other's debts, and would be generous with each other. Gradually the social demands of such discipleship were attenuated in a form of spiritualisation. Hence the importance of recapturing the radical message of Jesus in its original context, and giving it flesh within our own various cultures.

Michael Prior discusses the link between the Bible and the Zionist conquest of Palestine. In the view of many, the Bible provides the title-deed for the establishment of the State of Israel and for its policies since. This view is so pervasive that the very attempt to take issue with it elicits opposition. Indeed, in some Christian circles, anyone who opposes Zionism is considered to oppose God himself. But the biblical narratives of the divine promise of land pose fundamental moral questions, since they contain the divine mandate to exterminate the indigenous people. It is assumed widely that the literary genre of these narratives is history, even though this view runs in the face of all serious scholarly comment. Through its association with colonialist and imperialist nationalism, the potentially humanising function of religion has been corrupted. The communities which promulgate these biblical traditions must shoulder some of the responsibility for what has been done in conformity with the values contained in them.

On the political and social front, four contributors reflect on Palestinian historical perspectives. **Rashid Khalidi** contrasts the celebratory mood of some foreign governments congratulating Israel on its anniversary, with their neglect of the people which was displaced in order to found the Jewish state. Palestinians should move beyond the attitude of mourning, and work towards obtaining restitution for the damage done them. He calls on the Palestinians to assess their own narrative and acknowledge the part played in their catastrophe by bad leadership and lack of national cohesion. The Israelis, for their part, must acknowledge, and make restitution for what they did to the Palestinians in 1948. Broadly speaking, Khalidi settles for the creation of an independent state for the Palestinians alongside the State of Israel.

Reflecting on the Holocaust, **Uri Davis**, rejecting the concept of collective guilt, makes a sharp distinction between the guilt of this generation for crimes committed by generations before it, and its moral responsibility to set matters right now, insofar as it can. He focuses on the question, 'How was it possible for the Jewish people, victims of Nazi genocide, to subject the Palestinian people to war criminal policies of mass deportation, transfer and ethnic cleansing during, and around, the 1948-49 war?' He adduces examples from the practice of the labour Zionist leadership which subjugated everything to the Zionist goal. If the leadership could tolerate the annihilation of some of 'its own people' in Nazi-occupied Europe, in the interests of advancing its programme, what would deflect it from inflicting war crimes on 'another people' for the same purpose? The enormity of the Zionist crimes must be exposed, and owned up to. Because the war crimes, were, and continue to be committed by the successive governments of Israel in their name, present-day Israelis have a responsibility to protest, to act in defence of the Palestinian Arab victim, and insist on due reparation for the war crimes.

Three contributors deal with the theme of 'Justice and Reconciliation: Living with Memory'. **May Seikaly**, a diaspora Palestinian academic, reflects on the critical role of suffering, and in particular on the role which the memory of the suffering plays, both individually and nationally. She describes her field work of recording the memory of the distress of the Palestinians, in which the *Nakba* plays a controlling part. Formally recording the memories of the forgotten victims of injustice can become a means of their liberation.

Elias Chacour emphasises aspects of the Christian faith which his forefathers preached. A Jew no longer enjoys a privilege over a Gentile, man over woman, or master over slave. Secondly, Christians have a new vision of election: every man and every woman is invited to take part in the divine banquet. The Christian God is no longer a regional or tribal God.

Rosemary Ruether contrasts the relative success achieved in post-*apartheid* South Africa with what is called 'the peace process' in Israel-Palestine. The policy of the State of Israel, whether through its Labour- or Likud-led governments, is designed to consolidate Israel's interests, while leaving the Palestinians with only a series of Bantustan-like enclaves which bear no resemblance to an independent state. She inculpates the Christians of Europe and the USA in the genocide of the Palestinians, insofar as they legitimise the foundational injustice done to the Palestinians by regarding the prize of Zionism as due to the Jews, in virtue both of the biblical land claims, and as compensation for the Holocaust. Moreover, to salve their bad consciences regarding the past genocide of European Jews, Western Christians collaborate in creating a wall of silence around the injustice to the Palestinians. However, despite the obvious imbalance of power, the cry for even a minimally acceptable justice for Palestinians will not be suppressed indefinitely.

Part 2: The Present—'Do Justice' (Micah 6.8)

Three papers deal with aspects of the colonisation of Palestine. **Jad Isaac, Marla Schrader and Suhail Khalilieh** deal with the effects of Zionism over the last hundred years, marked particularly by the *Nakba*, and the extension of Israeli domination in the wake of the war of 1967. The expulsion of the majority of the Palestinian population, the seizure of their land and the destruction of their villages in 1948-49 was followed in 1967 by the expulsion of more Palestinians, more seizure of land and water resources, and systematic colonisation of the Occupied Territories through Israeli settlements. The Palestinians settled for the partial justice of the Oslo II Interim Agreement, but, despite the agreement, Israeli oppression continues, through the physical fragmentation of Palestinian communities, closure and restrictions on movement, and house demolitions. The authors analyse the conditions of Palestinians in Jerusalem and Bethlehem, and summarise the attempts to limit further their presence, for example, through confiscation of identity cards. They outline Israel's ongoing violations of the Oslo II Interim Agreement, and propose the minimum requirements for a lasting peace. Without Palestinian self-determination, and in the absence of conformity to UN Resolutions 242 and 338, there will not be a sustainable peace.

Yousef Nasser discusses the Palestinian economy, historically and at the present time, focusing particularly on the effects of the Israeli occupation, which, since 1967, has forced the West Bank and the Gaza Strip into subservience to the Israeli economy. He provides vital information on how the economy works, particularly in relation to underlying Zionist aspirations. Ironically, the economic conditions of the majority of Palestinians have deteriorated sharply since the inauguration of the 'peace process'. There has been no 'peace dividend'. The constraint on the movement of people and goods and other impediments which derive from the Israeli ideology of dominance are the major contributory factors accounting for this decline.

Jonathan Kuttab discusses issues of the human rights of the Palestinians. He shows how in practice the state systematically violates their natural rights, and how it deploys its legal system as an agent of such oppression. The Fourth Geneva Conventions, although signed by Israel, are not applied, since the Knesset has never incorporated them into Israeli law. The individual perpetrators of injustice to Palestinians, then, are merely carrying out the laws of Israel. Legal niceties, such as the pretence of justice through appeal to the Israeli High Court, lay a thin veil over a system of jurisprudence which contradicts the presumptions of justice with which the law is associated in the West. While Palestinians were in no doubt about the racist nature of the State of Israel and its attitudes to the Palestinians, it is only with the election of Premier Netanyahu that the full extent of its intentions has become brazenly overt.

The topic of religious fundamentalism is dealt with from a number of perspectives. In dealing with Jewish fundamentalism **Moshe Reiss** confines himself to the religious variety, which is well represented at both ends of the political spectrum. While *Haredi-ism* and *Gush Emunim* share the fundamentalist belief that each *knows* the direct word of God, they are poles apart. While for the *Gush* to 'give up' Greater Israel is a profanation of the name of God, for the others, Zionism is the ultimate denial of all the fundamentals of Jewish belief.

Göran Gunner discusses the different kinds of Christian Zionism in Scandinavia, drawing attention to changes in attitude over the last hundred years. Characteristically, 'End-Time' Christian Zionism takes its cue from a particular reading of certain biblical passages, leading to a distinctive theological interpretation of the State of Israel. It is insensitive to the human rights of the Palestinians, demonises Islam, and assists in the immigration of Jews to Israel. It supports Israeli governments indiscriminately, exclusively as a step in the direction of the coming of the millennium, while having little respect for Judaism as such. Institutional support for such views is on the wane. While less extreme forms exist with greater numerical support, the recognition of the sufferings of the Palestinians has stimulated a reassessment of popular views.

Stephen Sizer offers a British perspective on Christian Zionism. He judges that it has no place in the Middle East and should be repudiated by the Universal Church. He charges Christian Zionists with promoting an aberrant expression of the Christian faith and an erroneous interpretation of the Bible, which is subservient to the political agenda of the State of Israel. He views it as a distortion of the Christian faith, a devious heresy and an unwelcome intrusion into the culture of Palestine. Christian Zionism distorts the Bible and marginalises the universal imperative of the Gospel. It endorses the Israeli political right, and ignores the Palestinian tragedy. In doing so, it legitimises their oppression in the name of the Gospel.

Don Wagner's focus is on the alliance of the Likud Party with the American Christian right, whose theology he traces to the influence of the Dispensationalism of John Nelson Darby (1800-82) in evangelical

Protestantism in the USA. Realising that the mainstream Churches were showing more sympathy to the Palestinians, Israeli lobbyists in the USA worked on the evangelical constituency, particularly since 1977 when Menachem Begin became Prime Minister. The marriage of convenience has been particularly beneficial to the Zionist cause, whose interests have broken through to the White House, whose incumbent is dependent on the support of the Christian right.

Four papers focus on specifically religious aspects. **Rafiq Khoury** reflects on Christian-Muslim relations in the past and present, and suggests ways forward. He deals with the Middle East in general, as well as with Palestine. Christians and Muslims are bonded together in a cultural partnership, facilitated not only by physical proximity but by a common language and Arab culture. Muslim-Christian dialogue began in the earliest days of Islam. Relations between the two parties were not without difficulties from time to time, but, in general, the atmosphere was one of mutual respect. The dialogue in Palestine has unique features, related to the strategic and religious character of Palestine. The common experience of the *Nakba* has forged ever closer links between Muslims and Christians, a bond intensified by common suffering and striving together for a better future. Palestinian Christians do not consider themselves to be a minority. Rather, together with Muslims they constitute one Palestinian people. While being hopeful and optimistic about the future, the author is not insensitive to problems ahead. Each group should undertake to know more about the other, and avoid descent into sectarianism. The future dialogue must embrace religious and spiritual matters, and avoid being dominated by political considerations.

Two Jewish theologians offer perspectives on the jubilee, and its relevance to the contemporary situation. **Jacob Milgrom** confines himself to the Third World. Even though the simultaneous remission of all debts might inhibit creditors from lending, he adduces evidence that countries employing some of the jubilee provisions have experienced spectacular economic growth.

From the perspective of a new exile, that is, of separation from the prevailing Zionist reading of Jewish identity and history, **Marc Ellis** sees the ongoing destruction of Palestine as forcing a re-evaluation of the last fifty years and of Jewish history in general. Just as Auschwitz revealed the reality of Jewish weakness and Europe, Palestinians proclaim the reality of Jewish power and Israel. How can a Jew feel at home when those who were once at home have been displaced? The displacement of Palestinians constitutes the central question that accompanies the journey 'from Auschwitz to Jerusalem'. Palestinians, who suffer at the hands of some who survived the Holocaust, and of those who assert power in the name of its victims, are in fact the last victims of the Holocaust. The ongoing survival of the Palestinian people stands over against the Jews who commemorate the Holocaust as if Palestinians do not exist, and as if Jews were innocent of the crimes against them. It appears that forgetfulness has displaced memory as a distinctive, constitutive aspect of Jewish identity and history. The boundaries of Jewish destiny are being defined by Jews who have crossed over into a solidarity with the Palestinian people. What is called for is a new vision which will incorporate a shared future. The future should not be dictated by the desire to conquer and displace, but by a spirit of inclusiveness and reconciliation, suggested by some of the traditions within both Judaism and the other two religions, and in particular by that of the jubilee.

Häkan Sandvik reflects on the different modes of Christian pilgrimage to the Holy Land. In many cases, Western pilgrims do not engage the local communities, and seem to be determined to confirm the pictures of their imaginations. He stresses the value of engagement with the realities of peoples' lives, and suggests that a pilgrimage should challenge, rather than merely confirm one's theology and faith. He relates Christian pilgrimage to the central Christian message, the Incarnation, which presents God becoming a human being in a very ordinary setting. His examples show how a pilgrimage can expose one to the realities of the Holy Land, its people as well as its sites. Moreover, meeting local Christians enriches one's understanding of the worldwide Church.

Part 3: The Future—'Walk Humbly' (Micah 6.8)

Jean Zaru relates the struggle of Palestinian women to that of all women, indeed of all people, everywhere. She recognises the influence of religion, both in its progressive and reactionary forms: while it can support the poor and the oppressed, every religious tradition contains a narrowness which can ally itself with chauvinistic national movements. She looks to the Gospel to provide a message of liberation: the example of Jesus's dealings with women: the Samaritan woman, Martha and Mary, and the woman searching for the lost coin. The struggle for women's liberation begins in a woman's own heart, mind and actions. Palestinian women must acknowledge the reality of the structures, both within the Church and in society, which keep them 'in their place', and, empowered by (Christian) hope, continue the lifelong struggle to work for a new future, bringing about the liberation not only of all of the Middle East but of humanity in its totality.

Three participants bring the experience of other regions to the discussion, two focusing on places of contemporary struggle, South Africa and Northern Ireland. **Samuel Rayan,** coming from a tradition admired for its advocacy of non-violence in the face of social evil, invites one to consider different models of peace. The examples come from a variety of social and political contexts, including both those which, under the guise of working towards peace, continue to exploit the oppressed, and those which offer a more positive way forward. The reader is left to choose between the different modes as exemplified and evaluated by the author.

Madipoane Masenya discusses the transition in South Africa from the *apartheid* era, when 'peace' was achieved at the barrel of a gun, to living together today. She attributes it to two factors: the resoluteness of Nelson Mandela in promoting national unity and reconciliation, and the African concept of *botho/ubuntu* (humanness), which is rooted in the realisation that human beings depend upon each other. African humanism enabled the black South Africans to see even their former oppressors as created in the image of God. *Botho* inspired them to reach out to them, understanding that together they formed one humanity. Much remains to be done to advance the goal of togetherness. The whites in South Africa should admit their role in the dispossession of blacks from their land, and make restitution. While South Africa has not attained peace yet, great progress has been made. The vision of peace offered by Christ accommodates all, and has much to offer the nation in seeking its goal.

The contribution on Northern Ireland comes from an Englishman, an Anglican priest working in Liverpool. Speaking in February, while representatives of most of the political factions in the province were groaning through a process which ultimately achieved an historical compromise with the Good Friday Agreement,[1] **Nicholas Frayling** engages with the past. He cautions against the counsel, *forgive and forget*, and insists that the way forward is to *remember and repent*. He addresses the unhealed memories of both Britain and Ireland, and calls on the British first to acknowledge their responsibility for the injustices Britain perpetrated on the native Irish in the past. No true reconciliation is possible without sorrow and penitence, apology and symbolic restitution. True reconciliation can come only through the door of justice, and requires repentance for the past, and a new sense of trust for the future.

Two prominent Palestinian politicians propose a vision for the future. **Hanan Ashrawi**, a Member of the Palestinian Legislative Council, observes that, while history cannot be changed, it is essential not to be a captive to the past. It is necessary also to transcend the pain of the present, and to plan for the future, with creativity, imagination, boldness, and honesty. Peace is a right, rather than a privilege bestowed through the patronage of the strong. Since the Palestinian-Israeli conflict is one of the most complex conflicts in history its solution will require much effort and patience. The human dimension is critical, and its existence on both sides of the conflict, with two competing narratives, must be respected in an inclusive, rather than an exclusive manner. Parity and morality, rather than unbending, extremist absolutist ideologies must be at the heart of the search for peace. The widely ignored Palestinian narrative must not be denied, nor must Palestinian rights be surrendered to a pragmatism that has abandoned appeal to the legality of rights. There must be an acknowledgement of the injustice perpetrated on the Palestinians, and a recognition of the concomitant guilt. The source of Palestinian grievances and the cause of injustice must be addressed. Disputes must be solved in accordance with international law and the legality of rights, and in a fashion which brings real benefits to people. It will not be acceptable that peace discussions end with Palestinians repressing their own people in order to guarantee Israeli security. The Palestinian leadership derives its authority from its own people, rather than from the outside. It is essential, then, to

---

[1] In two referenda conducted later (22 May 1998), 'the Good Friday Agreement' was endorsed by over 70 per cent of the voters in Northern Ireland, and by 95 per cent in the Republic of Ireland, giving the 'green light' for elections to a Northern Ireland Assembly in June. Those elections duly took place, and, before the summer recess, the Assembly met and began its deliberations. As we go to press, however, progress towards a lasting peace is very slow.

guarantee democracy and human rights. Peace should liberate, rather than diminish people. To reach it, however, will demand international assistance as well as Palestinian steadfastness. Palestinians must shape their own future, rather than fall victims to the determination of others. Their resilience in the midst of all kinds of adversities suggests that together they shall achieve peace.

Azmi Bishara, a Palestinian Member of the Knesset has little interest in either the unthinkable or the unspeakable, preferring to dwell on what is achievable. 'Peace' for the Palestinians must include justice. Hence, the current refuge in an *apartheid* system cannot be sustained. In reality, there are only two viable solutions to the Israeli-Palestinian conflict: the national option (two separate states), or a bi-national option (the two peoples living with equality within one sovereign state). Despite the strength of the two nationalist rhetorics, neither is an ancient aspiration. Zionism is a product of 18th- and 19th-century European nationalisms, while the aspiration for a sovereignty Palestinian nation state is a by-product of the 1967 war. Prior to that, Palestinians spoke only of liberating Palestine from Zionist colonialism. After the war, they strove for sovereign statehood, an aspiration which by 1988 had accepted the partition of Palestine.

The Oslo accords, however, envisage only the demographic separation of the two peoples—an *apartheid* system—rather than two national sovereignties. What follows on the ground is the Bantustanisation of Palestine. In subscribing to the accords, the Palestinian leadership confused the tactic of Israeli recognition of the PLO with the goal of Palestinian sovereignty. The universal experience of liberation from colonialism presages that Palestinian sovereignty will never be achieved on the basis of a balance of power with the colonial power. Moral and economic constraints on Israel's power—through Israeli and American public opinion, as well as Arab struggle and pressure—will be required if one is to move beyond naked *apartheid*, which is the limit of the Israeli aspiration. However, *apartheid* is an unthinkable resolution to Palestinian aspirations in the long term, since it embraces inequality: a state for one people, with only autonomy for the other. It is at this point that the bi-national option emerges as a viable—and moral—alternative. It is also Bishara's preference. The Palestinian tragedy began with their expulsion in 1948. It was a refugee, rather than a national problem. The bi-national option makes it conceivable that the refugees could return from their camps, not to their ancestral homes within what is now the State of Israel, but within the borders of a bi-national Palestine. It holds out a viable future for the Jewish settlers also. They could remain, not as colonisers, but as citizens of a bi-national state. Without such an imaginative alternative the Jewish settlers, and Israel itself, face a dismal future, not least from a moral perspective.

Towards the end of the Conference, two prominent Christian leaders reflected on the unique contribution which spiritual traditions can bring to the current difficult situation in the Holy Land. The Latin Patriarch of Jerusalem, **Michel Sabbah,** emphasises the Christian vision which affirms the unique value of each person, whether Christian, Jew or Muslim. Both communities have to acknowledge that the past fifty years have not delivered peace for either the Israelis or the Palestinians. He outlines what needs to be achieved on the political front: the establishment of a Palestinian state, and an arrangement in Jerusalem which guarantees equality of place for all traditions. The Christian vision of God's love should propel the community to practise yet more love, and to seek more justice and more peace. Religion should not debase itself, and reduce God to our sinful ways, by aspiring to more military power, with its consequence of more death and destruction. Despite all the reverses along the way, Christians should be sustained by their hope, and be supported by the assurance that 'God builds with us'.

Edmond Browning, former Presiding Bishop of the Episcopal Church in the USA, was the last lecturer. He reflected on what he had heard and seen over the previous days, and under the shadow of the possibility of another Gulf War with Iraq. In his view, the major failure of the Christian Church in general has been its apathy in the face of human disasters in so many different places. Apathy towards the situation in the Holy Land was a feature of the citizens of the USA. The exposure of the tragedy of the region will go some distance, but it will not be sufficient merely to weep over the distress. Christians should look to the example of Jesus, who gave his life in the struggle 'to right the wrong'. Love was the spiritual weapon of Jesus, as it has been also of those pacifists who have followed his values. Christians are called to be the hands and the heart and the arms of the constant Christ. Hence, doing justice flows from our spiritual agenda, and if the participants leave the Conference with that commitment, we might make a difference in favour of peace in the Holy Land.

* * *

Since the date of the Conference (February 1998) events have moved on. The frustration at the lack of progress of the 'peace process' increased during the summer months of 1998, and was followed by the signing of the Wye Plantation Agreement in November. While the threat of the bombing of Iraq receded during the days of the Conference, it took place in December while the papers were being prepared for publication. The papers reflect the situation up to the time of the Conference.

The editing of the papers has been a collaborative enterprise between *Sabeel* in Jerusalem and myself in London. I am grateful to my co-editor, Naim Ateek, and to all who collaborated with him at *Sabeel* in Jerusalem. Not for the first time, I am extremely grateful to Leonard Harrow and Alan Ball of Fox Communications and Publications for the speed, courtesy and professional skill with which they undertook the publication of the volume.

St Mary's College
University of Surrey
Strawberry Hill
England
25 January 1999

INTRODUCTION TO EDWARD W SAID

Ibrahim Abu Lughod

First I should like to express my appreciation to *Sabeel* and particularly to the Revd Naim Ateek for making this evening possible. I am personally deeply grateful to him for honouring me with the very pleasant task of introducing someone who certainly needs no introduction. I am the one who is in such a need. But since I have that task, let me begin by saying that we welcome a native son, an esteemed native, and perhaps the most distinguished native son of Jerusalem. But Edward is certainly a native son of Palestine as well. But we all know, in a way that our adversaries the world over do not, that Jerusalem and Palestine cannot be separated from each other. Even while the UN suggested a *corpus separatum*, nature could not accept that division. So the first thing we should remind ourselves of is that Edward W Said is the esteemed, and loyal native son of Jerusalem, Palestine. Second, I must also say that it is both easy and difficult to introduce Dr Said. We have been friends for over four decades, going into our fifth. Can I have one minute for each year? Then in all probability you will not be out of here before midnight.

Now, who and what does Edward Said stand for? I will take a leaf from his own memoir and address an important issue. His name is both European/English and Arabic. It may appear odd to juxtapose those apparently conflicting identities. But those of us who have known Professor Said will find it quite natural. In fact, he has lived up wonderfully to both identities, and I cannot say with what difficulties. This tells us something about identity. Some time ago, in 1993, a profile of Edward Said in *Time* magazine stated that he was an envoy from one culture to another: he interpreted the Arab world to the West and the West to the Arab World. That has not been quite the case. Edward has combined two excellent, rich, rational cultural traditions which he identified with and assimilated, without seeing them as dichotomous. He has embodied the best in the two traditions: in intellectual breadth and interest, in artistic expressions, in food habits, and in affability. He has the values and perspectives, the sensibility and appreciation that both traditions entail. In that sense it was somewhat natural, and I say with ease that he has been the most authentic interpreter of the two traditions in the variety of his work.

Both cultures, in fact, aspire to include him within its fold. It is their appreciation of his contribution and standing that made it equally possible for both cultures to recognise his achievements and pay tribute to him. Without making invidious comparisons, he certainly was recognised first by Arab Americans, and then by the wider American society, to be followed by the world at large. Arab Americans paid their tribute in the mid-seventies when the AAUG recognised him as the most significant individual to contribute to humanistic studies. Birzeit University was the first institution of higher learning to award him an honorary Doctor of Letters in 1993. These were followed by innumerable prizes awarded to him in the United States, including honorary doctorates from the Universities of Chicago, Toronto, Michigan and others, and most recently his doctorates from Jawaharall University in Delhi. Next month he will receive the World Prize for literature awarded by Sharqa.

Clearly, the West and the East recognise his achievements and his profound contributions to the world of culture and learning. What are his seminal contributions? First, in literature and literary criticism, *Joseph Conrad, Beginnings, The World, the Text, and the Critic*, and so on, and *Orientalism*, which changed the entire discipline of Orientalism. Second, *The Question of Palestine*, followed by *The Politics of Dispossession*, and *Culture and Imperialism*. Defence not only of Palestine, but of the process of liberation, and the liberation of the mind. Edward speaks the same language, in all places. Because of his concern for the truth, with his clear method of analytic power, informed and honed by massive intelligence, disciplined by understanding, he and his work transcend national frontiers, directly or through translation. His discourse is universal. He shows concern for the Third World without taking a position against the First. It is appropriate that we hear him under the auspices of *Sabeel*, Liberation Theology, Truth and Justice.

Edward Said is the father of Wadi and Najla. He is a University Professor, a Fellow of the Royal Society of Literature, an Honorary Fellow of King's College, Cambridge, a Fellow of the American Academy of Arts and Science, the Vice-President and President-Elect of the Modern Language Association, which has some 60,000 members. He has honorary degrees from the Universities of Birzeit, Chicago, Toronto, Jawaharall, Jamiah Milliya Islamiyya. He has delivered the Rajeef Gandhi Memorial Lecture. He has written seventeen books, which have been translated into seventeen languages. One could go on, and on.

KEYNOTE ADDRESS

Edward W Said

I want to say that this occasion is very important to me for some of the reasons that Ibrahim has mentioned, and I am deeply grateful to all of you who came this evening. I have special greetings for the people in the auditorium beneath us, whom we cannot see, but who are watching the proceedings on TV. And particularly nice is the fact that I have seen so many friends and colleagues, and members of the community whose fortitude and persistence has kept the idea of Palestine going. Your fight here, against oppression on behalf of freedom and justice, is of enormous importance to those of us who do not live here, but who belong here. And you would be surprised. As Ibrahim says, I have travelled a lot, and wherever I have been, even when I was in South Africa in 1991, during the *Intifada*, that is what the people wanted to hear about! They knew very little about the history of our struggle, but they knew that the *Intifada* was an epoch, non-violent, unarmed rebellion of people, in the root sense of that word, and it was tremendously inspiring, and I felt so honoured to be able, in my own poor way, to speak about it.

I am also very grateful to the organisers of this conference, *Sabeel*, whose mottoes of truth, justice and liberation of the oppressed, have really been my principles for as long as I can remember, because that is really what it is all about. As you probably know, I am not a politician. I dislike most of them, maybe all of them! But I am also pleased that there are so many young people tonight and that we are in a university. I have spent most of my life in a university, and universities have been very good to me. I am the last one to complain about the state of the university, which is a fashionable thing to do, because the university gives one a unique opportunity to reflect and think, free of the normal pressures of everyday life. So to the administration and staff and students of Bethlehem University, thank you very much.

I also want to thank particularly, and express my admiration for Revd Naim Ateek, for whom I came, really—my health has not been very good. There are all kinds of connections between us, although we have not met that often, but I am a child of the Anglican community here—I have to tell you I am a lapsed child. I was baptised at St George's by Revd Mamoura, whom some of you may remember. His son Michel was my teacher at St George's, and later became my friend in Toronto. Anyway, I feel that Revd Ateek represents what has so often been left out of

Christianity, namely Christianity: dedication, the total absence of any egotistical, or personal kind of arrogance of any kind. It was perfectly embodied in his prayer this evening, and his dedication to what in effect is a cause that is not just the cause of the Church that he happens to belong to, but also of his people. And so, with many apologies to him for having had to change the order to the programme—I had a session of chemotherapy last week and I did not think I could make it at all—but I am so grateful for providing us all with the opportunity to be together and reflect on issues of importance connected to truth, justice and liberation.

Palestine, as Ibrahim said, has been for me for a long time an idea of freedom and diversity. What is it that distinguishes us as a cause from Israel and Zionism? It is not the people. It is the fact that we are talking about things that transcend ethnic, religious, and national boundaries. Palestine is also an idea of diversity; showing that people can live together without living in ghettos. And that, it seems to me, is something that we must not forget. Oslo and the whole period since 1993 have tended to dissipate that idea in the minds of many. We must hold to it, I think—Palestine as an idea of diversity and freedom.

Now I am going to take advantage of your kindness. I will not speak long, but I promise you I will speak freely—I do not know how to speak any other way. So if I offend people, well, that is just too bad I guess—and you can leave! But there will be a chance to have a discussion and questions afterwards. I think the importance of speaking freely is very central to us, especially in the Arab world. That is to say, we are a heavily censored culture these days, and we need not be. It is always done in the name of security and 'national this, that, and the other thing', but that is complete nonsense. This is one of the reasons we are in the state we are in today: people are afraid to speak out. But they do so anyway! That is the point. People speak out despite the restrictions, the press laws, the arrests, and so on. So we must fight for the right to speak our minds everywhere.

My subjects tonight are two. I want first to speak about the current situation on the heels of Yasser Arafat's visit to the United States, and then I want to spend a little time talking about, well, in a sense, the two halves of my life—Palestine and the United States.

The current situation

Immediately preceded by Benjamin Netanyahu, Yasser Arafat arrived in Washington for a meeting with President Bill on 22 January, the very day he was bombarded by the media about his relationship with Monica Lewinsky. Those of you who do not live in the United States may not be aware of the extent of the media hysteria. The media in the United States is generally hysterical, and to a degree of triviality and vulgarity I have never witnessed before, they went after President Bill Clinton. He is not somebody I tremendously admire, but I must say I felt rather with him for what he had to go through. But what was noticeable to me as a Palestinian, is that with the bewildered and obviously embarrassed Arafat sitting next to him quietly, Clinton stood off the press, vehemently denying allegations about having had sex with the twenty-three year-old intern in his office.

Two days before, on 20 January, Netanyahu went directly to members of the Christian right wing, to people like Jerry Falwell and Pat Robertson, who are unrestrained in their enthusiasm for Israeli territorial expansion, and similarly unrestrained in their condemnation of Clinton, whom they have accused of murder, dope-running, *etc.* This clammy embrace by Netanyahu of perhaps the worst element of a conservative movement in the United States, was designed to repay Clinton for an earlier snub of disapproval when, in November 1997, Clinton refused to meet Netanyahu, who was in the United States. This time, in January, President Clinton responded with customary delicacy, by pointedly refusing the Israeli leader a lunch at the White House, which is a major blow of course, as you know—that is meant to be a joke! That was the punishment: he did not get lunch! And so the speculation was that if he did have lunch, he probably would have had to pay $4.95 for a sandwich or something like that. But somehow Mr Netanyahu survived that handsomely by refusing to concede any further territory to the Palestinians, nothing more than the 3 per cent of the West Bank that had been given to them under the Oslo Agreement.

The irony of the whole thing was poignant. Arafat had filled the Arab media, before his arrival in Washington, with brave declarations about how this meeting with Clinton was to be the decisive one for the future of the peace process. Like every Arab leader, Arafat refused to believe that the USA—and not simply one or another president— has historically and invidiously refused to support any sign of Arab nationalism, or, in the case of Palestinians, any real movement toward our self-determination. In fact, the United States has been a *terrible* sponsor of the peace process, as it is euphemistically still called. It succumbs to Israeli pressure in everything, banning the principle of land for peace, pushing the Palestinian leadership into deeper and deeper holes, to suit Netanyahu's impossible demands.

The fact is that Palestinians are dramatically worse off everywhere than they were when Oslo began. Their annual income is less than half of what it was in 1992. They are unable to travel from place to place. More land has been taken than ever before, more settlements exist, and Jerusalem is practically lost. And still, Americans continue to subsidise Israel's profligacy, its land grabbing, its barbaric occupation practice, and what is the longest military occupation of the 20th century. At the same time that the USA enforces horrendously cruel sanctions and threatens bombing strikes at whom—not at Saddam Hussein, whom I do not like; I think he is a criminal—but at the people who are going to suffer, the Iraqi people! And the United States is doing it, it says, in the sonorous words of Madeleine Albright and William Cohen, and the others, to support the United Nations, while the United States is in arrears to the tune of $1.2 billion to the United Nations.

I am speaking now as an American. I am deeply ashamed that the United States has vetoed *any* United Nations Security Council Resolution censuring or condemning Israel—sixty times more than any other country has used the veto against human rights, against the most elementary principles of justice. And all of this to maintain a campaign against the people of Iraq, where 1.2 million have died since the Gulf War, through malnutrition, chronic illness, absence of medicine, and so forth, so that the United States could continue to be its macho self.

But to return now to here. The scars are still unhealed. The wounds fester. You all know this far better than I do. The past will not, and cannot be forgotten. And yet there is no overriding consensus in the Arab world as to what Israel represents, and how we should deal with it. Even using the collective pronoun 'we' suggests a unity of views that is more presumed than actual. At some higher level of politics and ideology Israel is an objective ally of some Arab policies and politicians, not all of them right wing Christian Lebanese. Jordan, for instance, has signed a peace treaty with Israel, as has Egypt and the PLO. Still, very few Arab writers—hardly any that I can think of, really—intellectuals, academicians, artists and even policy makers—will say that they are ready for normalisation with Israel, so long as it occupies Palestinian, Syrian, and Lebanese territory. An enormous grey area exists in our collective consciousness. Israel is there, but how are we to think about it, now at the end of the 20th century, after fifty years of dispossession? And above all, how are we to act toward it?

Everyone wants, and speaks about peace. Yet how, for Palestinians, whose entire territory was captured and society destroyed, is one to declare a statute of limitations and say, 'What is past is past. Let us reconcile ourselves to a future with Israel.' When it comes to the present, how are we to say that we want to co-exist peacefully with a state that still has not declared its boundaries, and still describes itself not as the state of its citizens, about 20 per cent of whom are Palestinians, but as the state of the whole Jewish people, entitled to the entire land of Israel.

As for the future, where is the glimmer—apart from a few individuals here and there, maybe a few small parties—where is the glimmer of a new Israel which is neither imperialist nor exclusivist, but somehow at one with the Arab world in whose midst it has been planted as idea and as reality since 1897? By posing the challenge of Israel, and the meaning of *Al-Nakba*, in this manner, a number of irreconcilable facts leap out at us. There can be no erasing of the historical truth that the existence of Israel is predicated, indeed imposed upon the obliteration of another society and people.

There has been far too much sustained damage to the Palestinian people to surmount this easily. Israel, in short, exists as a political fact, superimposed upon, and intertwined with another fact, the Palestinian people, whose existence in history is denied, and whose claims have never really been heard inside the discourse of Israeli life. Surely every Israeli knows this as much as every Palestinian does. The question is, how long can an intolerable situation of proximity and injury be endured by the victims, and how long can acknowledgement of it be deferred by the victors? Israeli policy, in my view, has always consisted of two parts. On the one hand, 'Strenuously absolve yourself of any responsibility for the existence of a Palestinian problem', and, on the other, 'Try to make compromises on the basis of that self-absolution with whatever Arab or Palestinian leadership exists at the moment, while *continuing* to settle the land.' The premise of both parts of this policy is the same. Given enough time and pressure, they reason, Palestinians will forget, give up, or variously accommodate themselves to the permanent loss of what was once theirs.

In the main, this policy has not been successful, despite the existence of a peace process, and two peace treaties with Arab states. Far from forgetting the past, Palestinians and other Arabs have been obliged to recall it because of Israeli insistence on endlessly repeating its original sin. By what preposterous logic can Benyamin Netanyahu proclaim to the world that he wants the peace process to continue, at the same time that he says that the West Bank, and Gaza, and Jerusalem are part of the land of Israel? Every house demolition, every expropriated *dunum*, every arrest and torture, every barricade, every closure, every gesture of arrogance and intended humiliation, simply revives the past, re-enacts Israel's offences against the Palestinian spirit, land, and body politic. To speak about peace in such a context is to try to reconcile the irreconcilable, which cannot be done.

But the fantasy of somehow removing Israel and its people is equally unthinkable. Yes, I think they could be made to withdraw from the Occupied Territories. But it is a dream to expect that they will all disappear. There is now an Israeli nationalism, and a society, independent of what we think, and autonomous also from Jews in the diaspora. Behind it are memories of the Holocaust, and centuries of Western Christian antisemitism, from which it would be folly for us to expect Israelis to disconnect themselves. Yet there is also a history of anti-Palestinian behaviour, that demands recognition as injustice and cruelty of the first order. Just as Jews require recognition from the world, we too must continue to make the same demands, not on the grounds of vengeance, but because *justice* requires it.

Thus the *misery* of Oslo is that our leaders simply brushed off our history, whereas it behoves us to remember what Zionism did, and no less important, what Britain, the United States, and other pro-Zionist Western governments have done to conspire in our dispossession. We hold them responsible too, along with Arab governments who today *still* discriminate against Palestinians. We are talking of *fifty years* of discrimination, of refugees, destitute refugees in Lebanon, Syria, and elsewhere. 150,000 refugees in Egypt today who have been there for fifty years and still have to register with the Egyptian government *every single month!* And this is a 'brotherly Arab country'. We must not forget that.

The first challenge, then, is to extract acknowledgement from Israel for what it did to us, and to other Arabs whose sons and daughters were killed in wars, conquests, military occupations, and settlements. This is a moral mission for each of us to pursue, by not forgetting, by reminding each other in the world, by testifying to the continued injustice against us. I simply cannot imagine that history will ever excuse us for failing in this task, or failing to fight for Palestinian rights wherever we live, and whatever our circumstances are.

But then I believe we must also hold out the possibility, even theoretical, of some form of co-existence, in which a new and better life, free of ethnocentrism and religious intolerance, could be possible. It is the present poverty of Zionism and Palestinian nationalism that accounts for the void in vision and moral energy that we suffer from today. I am certain that if we present our claims about the past as ushering in a new form of mutuality and co-existence in the future, a long-term positive echo on the

Israeli and Western side will reverberate. It is also evident to me that we cannot detach our views of Israel from our attitudes and policies toward the United States. Since 1949, America has poured about $140 billion into Israel. Not only is this a major financial investment, but the American political establishment has a long-term investment in the country as well. To expect the United States to lessen support for Israel, or even to become critical of it—these are real possibilities in my view and I will come back to that—requires a massive campaign in the United States on the part of Palestinian political and human rights activists.

Israel's successes on the ground have been prepared for and supported by assiduous propaganda about Arab intransigence, the Arab wish to drive Jews into the sea, the Israeli desire for peace and tranquillity, and central to all this, that Israel as a Jewish state was created by the National Liberation Movement of the Jews (Zionism), which found the place deserted, and made it a garden. A lot of the criticism and destruction of these malicious myths has been done obviously by Palestinians, but also by a group of Israeli revisionist historians, whom I am sure many of you know. Zionism, along with all the other successful mass movements of the 20th century, learned the lesson of propaganda: that the battle for opinion is the most important one to win. This is something that we Palestinians have still not completely grasped, and until we do, we shall always be on the losing end. In short, Israel can very often be seen as the measure of our failings and our incompetence. We have waited for a great leader for years, none came. We have waited for mighty military victory, but we were defeated roundly. We have waited for outside powers (the United States, or, in its time, the Soviet Union), but none really came to our aid. The one thing we have not tried in all seriousness, is, in the radical sense of the word, to rely on ourselves. Until we do that, with a full commitment to success, there is no chance that we can advance toward self-determination and freedom from aggression.

Take, as a simple case in point, the current Palestinian case today, where the failures seem the more glaring to someone like myself who lives abroad, and the remedy is more easily at hand than anyone has expected. We have been saddled with the constant problem—ever since I was a child I remember the complaints of my family and friends—that our leaders are inadequate. And still we persist in supporting the same type of leaders through all their mistakes and disasters. On the other hand, we justly pride ourselves on the many successes of our people: the doctors, lawyers, engineers, businessmen, entrepreneurs, intellectuals, academics, and artists. We claim that we want independence and statehood, yet few of the most basic institutions of statehood are on anyone's mind today. There is no basic law in the Palestinian Areas today. Our schools and universities are in a bad state, starved of money, desperately run and administered, filled with underpaid teachers and professors, who struggle to make a living, and, therefore, cannot do enough research and independent work for years.

We also have an extremely impressive group of wealthy business people, who simply have not grasped that the essential thing for any people trying to emerge out of servitude and oppression, is a massive, a really *massive* investment in education, the construction of a national library, and the endowment of the *entire* educational structure, as a guarantee that as a people we will have a real future. I have attended meetings for almost twenty years in which hundreds of little, extremely worthy projects are funded, but without a central vision of what it is as a society we need. The absence of a collective end to which all are committed has crippled Palestinian efforts, not just in the official realm, but even among private associations, where personality conflicts, outright fights, and disgraceful backbiting hamper our every step!

Looked at from this perspective, the fundamental challenge that Israel poses is to ourselves: our ability to organise, our ability to dedicate ourselves to a basic set of principles from which we do not deviate! Our ability to marshal our resources single-mindedly, our ability to devote all our efforts to education and competence, knowing how to do things right. And, finally, our ability to choose a leadership that is capable of this task.

It is no use blaming the failures of the current Palestinian leadership on a few inadequate and corrupt individuals. We now have the leadership we deserve, and until we realise that we are being driven further and further from our goal of self-determination and the recovery of our rights by that leadership, which so many of us still serve and respect, we will continue to slide. I am not saying our enemies are simple. They are not a pushover; they are the toughest enemies you could imagine. Sure! But they are not unthinkably strong. There are ways—and I am going to talk about this in a minute—of knowing how to plan for victory in the situation in which we find ourselves.

The Italian Marxist Antonio Gramsci put it very well: 'Pessimism of the Intellect; Optimism of the Will.' Yes, our situation *vis-à-vis* Israel is calamitous, and under Netanyahu the situation is getting worse. But we need to ask what it is that we can do, and then, by an act of collective will, we must do it! The rest is simply a waste of time.

The choice of better leaders is an imperative. But we must also improve our own conditions, so that our workers do not have to build Israeli settlements just to put food on their tables! And our students do not have to settle for an incredibly backward curriculum in an age when our opponents—500 metres from here—are sending people to the moon! And our people have to accept lamentable conditions of tyranny and oppression, which punishes dissent and bans books, and controls the media, and cows the citizenry, all in the name of national unity! Until we awake, we will continue to lose more land and power to Israel. But we cannot fight for our rights, our history, and our future, until we are armed with real weapons of criticism and dedicated consciousness. In this, we need the support of the Arab intellectual and cultural community, which has devoted too much time to slogans about Zionism and Imperialism, and the Protocols of the Elders of Zion, and all that kind of nonsense, and not enough to helping us fight the battle against our own incompetence. The challenge of Israel is the challenge of our own societies. We are unequal now to the task, because we are still chained to methods and attitudes that belong to an earlier time. The struggle of the 21st century is a struggle to achieve liberation and self-decolonisation.

Humans make their history

And now I want to talk about what I consider to be the alternative to what we are now. I want to begin by talking about two philosophers of history who have meant a great deal to me over the years, and about whom I have taught. They are separated from each other by well over 300 years, and the Mediterranean Sea. Ibn Khaldun, the Arab philosopher who died in 1406 at the age of 74, and Giambattista Vico, the Neapolitan philosopher who died in 1744. Although separated by 300 plus years, they held astonishingly similar views of history, both of which have great relevance today. Vico's *The New Science* was published a year after his death, that is, in 1745, and it remained relatively unknown until the late 18th century, when it was discovered by the French historian Jules Michelet, who translated it from Italian into French.

Since that time, numerous major figures in European thought—Hegel, Marx, Nietzsche, Freud, James Joyce, Beckett, Crochet, and many others—were in some way indebted to Vico's profound insight, that *human beings make their own history*, a history that, therefore, can be understood by human beings scientifically, and according to laws of context, development, and understanding. This is extremely important, and, even though it sounds very simple, it is really very complicated. Thus it would be wrong, Vico said, to judge the primitive world of Homer by the advanced rational world of Aristotle some 900 years later. One cannot use the mentality of Aristotle to understand the world of Homer. Humankind, Vico said, begins in barbarism, moves to sociability, when the family is invented, and then achieves social solidarity—what Ibn Khaldun in the *Muqaddima* calls *al-'Asabiya*—social solidarity; which is an advanced stage.

The essential point for both these two men, independent of each other, is that the world of human beings is neither the world of nature, nor the sacred world which is made by God, but the world of history, a secular world, that can be understood rationally as a result of transformations, instabilities, and upheavals that are governed by observable laws and human actions. Historical understanding is the comprehension of what human beings do and what they cannot do. In a famous passage in the *Muqaddima*, Ibn Khaldun makes fun of an earlier, very well known historian, Mas'udi, who had an entirely fanciful idea of how Alexander of Macedon first descended into the Mediterranean to frighten the sea monsters so that he could come back up again and build the city of Alexandria by keeping the sea monsters at bay. Ibn Khaldun makes fun of this—this is not history, this is *khurafat.* In other words, historical truth has to be plausible. It must be able to place events in their proper context, it must be free of exaggeration, it must not be partisan, it must focus on what human beings did, and so on.

Although this brief summary makes these two great thinkers appear simple enough to accept, the fact is that we are still struggling with the consequences of their insights, especially in the Arab world, but elsewhere too. Notions of conspiracy, divine intervention, and heroic individuals impede our capacity for understanding that history is made by human effort, not magic, or mysterious forces that act mysteriously. This may seem like an unarguable reality, but if we pay close attention to some of the explanations that are passed out today as explanations for, let us say, American and Israeli behaviour, we will conclude that these explanations are really quite far from being rational, secular, or even plausible. In its dealings with the Arab world, the United States has been governed by pressures and interests, and not simply by a Zionist plot, or an immoral disregard for Palestinian rights, which is certainly there!

As I have said frequently, it is one of the most illogical things for Arab leaders, including Palestinian leaders (well, especially Palestinian leaders), to throw themselves on the mercy of the United States, just because it is powerful, and seems to speak a language of official morality! That, in my opinion, is an example of 'magical thought'—the assumption that some leaders, somewhere, will overturn the logic of interests and pressures, jump out of historical context, and, perhaps as a result of a sudden illumination (*ilham*), embrace the Arabs. A recent study, by a distinguished Arab political scientist, chronicles the distressing history of American one-sidedness when it concerned Israel—the massive amounts of money and arms that have been poured in, and so forth. Oslo, he says, was simply the result of the balance of power (thanks a lot!), as if the balance of power were something we did not know about, but, more important, as if the balance of power were a fact of nature, like a tree, or a mountain. Nowhere in these accounts that say 'it is just a balance of power' do we find an account, first of all, of how Israel constructed its image of itself in the United States, so as to gain support. Nor do we find any effort expended on trying to find out what could be done about the situation now. Balance of power is not a historical phrase. It is magical thinking, inclining us to think that it just happened, that there was nothing that could have been done that would have made a difference, and to feel badly.

The missing factor here, is the role of *will* (*al-irada*) in the creation of power and human affairs, which both Ibn Khaldun and Vico well understood. Will operates aggressively, as well as defensively. The core idea of Zionism, as the Israeli historian Zeev Sternhell shows in his important new book, *The Founding Myths of Israel,* was conquest. This is clear in Ben-Gurion's rhetoric. It is also clear in the language of Berl Katznelson, the major theorist of Labour Zionism, who openly proclaimed that, 'the Zionist enterprise is an enterprise of conquest.' He then adds, 'that it is not by chance that I use military terms when speaking of settlement.'

To this end, the Zionist movement sought, consolidated, and deployed power consistently. This was as true in Palestine as it was after 1948 when it was clear that the new state of Israel required sustained support from abroad, especially from the United States. This will to power and conquest must be understood as the conscious, systematic creation of men and women, dedicated to keeping hold of a conquered territory. Far from it being a matter of luck or coincidence, or conspiracy, it was and still is announced as the goal of every major Israeli leader, of the right or the left. In this respect, Netanyahu is cruder, but really no different than Ben-Gurion, or Rabin.

One of the main misunderstandings of those Palestinians who

negotiated Oslo was not that they were not aware of the balance of power. Of course they were, all *too aware*! But that they were ignorant of the detailed circumstances of the Israeli military conquest and occupation of the West Bank/Gaza, the Golan Heights and Jerusalem. If they had known them, they would have seen clearly that, as it was drafted, Oslo was designed to get Palestinian approval for an *extension* of those circumstances into the very heart of a formal peace agreement between Israel and the PLO. Everything we now know about what happened at Oslo suggests that the Palestinian leadership believed it was getting a state, whereas the Israelis, in fact, were planning exactly the opposite. In such circumstances, will, conscious effort, preparation, and co-ordinated effort played a predictable role. And the absence of those things resulted in the state of affairs we have before us, in which Israel has conceded only 3 per cent of the West Bank without sovereignty, and states openly that it plans to annex most of the rest.

The point to be made here is that Israel and the United States planned deliberately to use power and will to perpetuate injustice against the Palestinian people. The question, then, is that if this situation was made by human beings, and was not an act of God, or a fact of nature, is there any way of dealing with it that does not perpetuate the injustice? I think the answer is 'Yes', but once again, by conscious, secular and rational means, not by waiting for a miracle, or a great leader, or some unforeseen intervention, none of which can be expected in what Vico and Ibn Khaldun studied as the world of the nations—the secular world, which is governed by human effort that can be analysed and understood rationally and historically. And I ask you to notice that in Canon Ateek's prayer, there was nothing about miracles. There was only a prayer for dedication, for humility, for discipline, for collective love, and working with others. Not for something big to happen, a big army to appear suddenly, or any of that stuff.

The influential English critic Raymond Williams once said that no social system, no matter how oppressive, can exhaust every social alternative that might contradict or resist it. The same is true of the United States. I am talking to you now after thirty years of speaking and writing on the United States, in the media and in the universities—I mean everywhere! And if I could do more of it I would, but I have done as much as I can, to tell you where, despite the power of the Israeli lobby, and the converging interests of that lobby with the strategic aims of the United States as characterised by the corporate and defence communities, there is an important sector of the population that is perplexed and angry that Israel should be getting away with so many infractions of what are stated US policies.

The United States openly says that we are against human rights abuse, and the proliferation of weapons—we are willing to go to war with Iraq because we do not want weapons of mass destruction to proliferate. We are against the illegal annexation of territory, and so on. So people ask, 'Well, why is Israel doing that?' But we spend all our time having conversations with the policy makers and the senior officials—the Dennis Rosses of this world—and leave the rest of the population completely unattended to! As I said earlier, the Zionists grasped the importance of opinion in the modern world and sought to influence the largest number of people in the West by bombarding them with images of Israel as a pioneering democratic state, built on empty, neglected, or uninhabited land, surrounded by violent Arabs who wanted to drive them into the sea. Ninety per cent of the Western electorate still does not know otherwise.

In nearly every lecture I give, in the United States and elsewhere, I talk about the Law of Return, and I am always surprised that most people have never even heard of it! That there is a Law of Return that says that only Jews can return to Palestine, and that Palestinians such as myself, and many of us who were born here, cannot. And—another thing that most people do not know—that Israel was built on the ruins of Palestinian society, and that only Jews, at the expense of the indigenous inhabitants, can benefit from the institutions of the state, especially so far as landowning is concerned. As Israel Shahak has said many times, 'How many Americans would accept the idea that only white Protestants could buy land in the United States; that Jews would not be allowed to buy land?' Well, they would not stand for it for a second. Somehow, most people do not even know that, but when they do, and we do not say anything about it, nothing happens. The importance, therefore, of holding onto our land is crucial—and you are doing this by staying. But no less crucial is the need to undermine the morality of Israel's military occupation, which is opposed by many Israelis as well as supporters of Israel in the West.

The enemies of South African *apartheid*—the ANC—did exactly that. They did *exactly* what I am talking about. They organised and campaigned—in universities, churches, corporations and in the media—and I can guarantee you there were not that many Black South Africans in America! There are far more Arabs than there are Black South Africans in the United States. But they went out into the community—that was the plan! To get the United States to move, you cannot just whisper in the ear of Bill Clinton or Madeleine Albright! It is not going to happen! You have to talk to the people who vote, and make characters like Jesse Helms and Tom Lantoss, and all those guys aware. Jesse Helms is a guy who was proud of the fact that he never left the United States! Indeed 35 per cent of the Congress of the United States has never had a passport! And these characters *run the world!*

Two weeks ago I was ill, and sitting watching television, which is a horrible thing to do. I was watching an interview with Jesse Helms. He is the Head of the Senate Foreign Relations Committee—he is one of the most powerful men in the Congress! He is a Southerner, and is completely up to his neck in debt to the cigarette companies. I mean, he is about as crooked as they come! Even though he has never been abroad, and does not give a damn about the rest of the world, he has his ideas. So one of the interviewers said to him, 'Senator Helms, what do you think about the Iraq crisis? Is the President handling it well?' He said, 'I want that guy Saddam Hussein outta there—I want him out!' Well what about Cuba? 'Fidel Castro's gotta go!' I mean the guy is sitting in North Carolina and he can run the world! Now the reason is that his electorate does not challenge him on these points, but he can be challenged! I will come back to that in a minute, I will tell you how.

The task ahead

So the South Africans campaigned in universities, churches, and organised a campaign to show the Americans that discrimination against non-whites was not just a South African cause, but a public, moral cause! We have never even *tried* to organise such a campaign on a mass level. Partly we have not understood its importance, partly also because some of us still refuse to see the connection between power, will and injustice, and refuse, therefore, to see the reverse: that power and will can be harnessed to resistance and to the cause of justice. There is nothing else on the horizon, which is more bleak than it ever has been. We are getting weaker, we are slowly being overtaken and forgotten, our resolve is in danger of succumbing to the solemn silence of other defeated native peoples.

And yet a proper reading of history teaches us that even though the balance of power is unfavourable, the weaker can overcome the stronger because of the *human* factor, that is, the will to resist, to seek new and ingenious ways to fight injustice, to be relentless in energy and hope. I think we should draw support—you know, we tend to push each other down, we hit each other all the time, especially when we are down, because it is very easy. But I think we should draw support for the future from the fact that despite years, fifty years of oppression and dispossession, we continue to exist as a people, and our voice can *still* sometimes be heard. That should encourage us to go on critically, consciously, creatively.

Above all, we must always remember to read history as the record of what men and women did and what they did not do. Like success, failure is made. It is not simply an automatic thing. Failure has to be constructed, and worked at until it becomes a habit and a commitment, the way most Arab regimes have been working so hard. It is neither a matter of our genes—sometimes Ibrahim says that 'It is in the Arab genes. We are committed to failure'—I do not believe it—and it is not a matter of destiny. By the same token we can commit ourselves to changing the situation, not by force of arms which we do not possess, and cannot foreseeably possess in requisite strength, but by a *mass movement* of people determined by political, moral, non-violent means to prevent our further ghettoisation and drift.

There are hundreds of thousands of Palestinians everywhere—in the diaspora, in the Arab world, everywhere—who are in principle prepared to sound the message, the message that men and women will listen to and are interested in understanding. I will give you just one simple example. I was telling my friends about it last night. I am a recent devotee of e-mail (just the last two months), but one of the most striking things is that every single day, I get something like six messages from the same person, and that person is a young man who was a classmate of Wadi's at Princeton, called Ali Abunimah. He is a Palestinian boy. His father, I think, is the Jordanian ambassador at the United Nations, but that does not matter. And this guy has done something which I have never seen done, and of course what I am talking about now is also the next generation, it is not my generation, it is the generation of my son and his friends. I will tell you about this. What he does is this: he seems to have an insatiable capacity to listen to all the important newscasts on television and radio and read all the major newspapers. I mean, you can make yourself do that if you are a masochist! But that is not just what I mean. A lot of us read the newspapers, right? But what he does is he always responds! So every day, for example, in the morning there is a famous programme across the entire United States called, 'National Public Radio'. And this guy has a comment to make every single day! He writes letters to ABC, 'That was a good program, or, that was a bad program.' He is on top of the thing, and he then—which you can do with e-mail—he can then copy the message to hundreds of different people! One person can do that, right?

I also want to give an example of my son, who is here—and you will forgive parental pride! Now, he is an American kid, right? He grew up in New York, and is interested in basketball and all kinds of revolting things like that. But, somehow, you know—I do not recall ever telling him to do this—he taught himself in the University, and went and studied Arabic. He then got himself a Fulbright, and spent a year in Egypt, and then he spent a year here on the West Bank. His Arabic now is perfect! He can read it, write it, speak it, and translate from one language to another, and, of course, he has read everything there is to be read on Palestine. He is a law student now. What is he writing his major law paper in the second year on? On the abuse of the rights of the Palestinians in Lebanon, which is one of the most heart-rending, appalling, examples of human cruelty in the annals of the 20th century. It is these kids who really provide an example to the likes of us fossils and dinosaurs, who think, well, balance of power, right? But it is not! You can make a difference by individual effort that, you know, without waiting for people to say, 'Well listen, let me give you a scholarship, or do you want to travel first class, or, ...' None of that, they just do it on their own! And because there is a belief—to go back to Ibn Khaldun and Vico—that history is made by human beings, and these people are making history, and it is *that* that we need to remember, and that that we need to focus on.

In conclusion, I say that there are hundreds of thousands of Palestinians everywhere who are in principle prepared to sound the message everywhere that men and women will listen to, and are interested and understanding. Because of its historical, cultural, and religious significance, Palestine is a perennially renewed, open-ended symbol of a possibility of diversity, pluralism, and not balance of power—a creative balance. To have expected Zionism to rise to Palestine's challenge on human and political grounds was an idealistic thought, maybe even ingenuous and naïve. But I remain convinced that if, as Palestinians, we make it clear that we are prepared, with the Jews of Israel and Arab people in the surrounding region, to make a new kind of history, based on a new politics of integration and inclusion, we *can* carry the day! It is slow, hard work, but it is doable, and, I think, achievable in the best sense. To settle for less, as our leaders have, to settle for less would be a terrible mistake, whose consequences are already evident all around us. Thank you!

PRINCIPLES OF JUBILEE IN THE OLD TESTAMENT, AND FOR THE ENDURING COMMUNITY OF FAITH

Gordon Brubacher

Introduction

Leviticus 25 presents a startling idea: the year of jubilee. Every fifty years the ancient Israelites were required to do two things:

1. Set free those who had become slaves as a result of debt;
2. Give back family land which had been sold, because of need, at any time over the past fifty years.

In some ways this idea was as crazy as it sounds, for it runs completely counter to human nature. But this is precisely why the instruction was given. It was needed to protect vulnerable people, in a world where too many take what they can get unless they are restrained.

Jubilee was one such restraint, and it actually made sense, in the socio-economic structure of its time and place, if people could be persuaded to do it. That structure included the following. The smallest socio-economic unit in ancient Israel was the extended family, called the *bet 'ab* (father's household). Most of these families made a living working their own inherited portion of land, and depended almost entirely on that land.[1] In the modern world, many people have jobs, go to work, take wages home, and buy what they need to support family and self. But in the time visualised

---

[1] Wright, C J H, 'Jubilee, Year of', in *The Anchor Bible Dictionary*, edited by David Noel Freedman, New York, Doubleday, 1992, vol. 3: 1025-1030, pp. 1025, 1029.

by Leviticus 25, the equivalent of gainful employment was working the family land.[2] As a result, losing the family land meant becoming homeless and unemployed. Taking someone's family land meant causing that result. Causing enough of that result, of course, would inflict social and economic chaos, which would be bad for everyone, including the minority who had acquired the land. So, preventing that result would in fact be a practical thing to do, if it were possible.

It would have been nice if no household ever lost its land, but this was impossible to prevent. For example, people had bad years with their crops and fell into debt. One possible solution was to sell oneself, as an indentured servant or slave, in return for food and shelter. Another was to sell the family land. And in a difficult world, that need certainly arose. As a natural result, some people would acquire other people's land, and also their living bodies as indentured servants.

Leviticus 25 steps in with the year of jubilee to prevent such a result. Moreover, it does so in the form of 'God requires' certain things, and even gives divine reasons. Because of divine involvement, it is possible to speak of a theology of jubilee in the Old Testament.

Basic theology: jubilee in the Old Testament

Based primarily on Leviticus 25, a core theology of jubilee in the Old Testament includes five main parts or aspects.

General principles

The following permeate the Old Testament, and need no elaboration.

1. God is sovereign, that is, in control.
2. God cares what humans do, and has standards for human behaviour.
3. God sometimes intervenes in human activity, based on one and two above.

---

2 Wright, 'Jubilee ...', p. 1028; cf. Fager, Jeffrey A, *Land Tenure and the Biblical Jubilee: Uncovering Hebrew Ethics through the Sociology of Knowledge.* JSOT, Supplement Series, no. 155, Sheffield: JSOT Press/Sheffield Academic Press, 1993, pp. 27-34.

Explicit principles

Jubilee is based on two explicit principles, both found in Leviticus 25.

God owns the land. That is, humans do not own it: 'The land shall not be sold in perpetuity, for the land is mine; with me you are but aliens and tenants' (Lev 25.23).[3] The point: one cannot buy or sell land which already belongs to someone else—in this case, to God.

God owns the people. 'For to me the people of Israel are servants; they are my servants whom I brought out from the land of Egypt: I am the LORD your God' (Lev 25.55). The point, again: one cannot buy or sell people who already belong to a powerful ruler—in this case, to God. The message is: 'Hands off. They're mine. They are under my protection.' This picture of God acquiring the people of Israel as slaves from their former owner—the emperor of Egypt— is used consistently throughout the entire cycle of Egyptian bondage, Exodus, Sinai, desert, and land entrance stories.

Main elements

The following primary elements, or components, are found in the jubilee instructions of Leviticus 25.

Liberty. Do not control or use other people. Set them free: 'And you shall hallow the fiftieth year and you shall proclaim liberty throughout the land to all its inhabitants' (Lev 25.10a). This needs no explanation. It proclaims a very big concept in few words.

Restoration. Restoration includes returning land to its family, and people to their land:

> 'It shall be a jubilee for you: you shall return, every one of you, to your property and every one of you to your family' (Lev 25.10b).

[3] Bible quotes are from the *New Revised Standard Version*, 1989.

> 'In this year of jubilee you shall return, every one of you, to your property' (Lev 25.13).

> 'If anyone of your kin falls into difficulty and sells a piece of property, then the next of kin shall come and redeem what the relative has sold. If the person has no one to redeem it, but then prospers and finds sufficient means to do so, the years since its sale shall be computed and the difference shall be refunded to the person to whom it was sold, and the property shall be returned. But if there is not sufficient means to recover it, what was sold shall remain with the purchaser until the year of jubilee; in the jubilee it shall be released, and the property shall be returned' (Lev 25.25-28).

Note that this transaction does not actually buy ownership. It only buys, or actually rents, *use* of the property (to raise crops) until the property returns to its family, whether by redemption or jubilee.

Justice. The jubilee instructions repeatedly insist on fairness when calculating the price for a temporary sale: 'When you make a sale to your neighbour or buy from your neighbour, you shall not cheat one another' (Lev 25.14). Details are given on pro-rating the price to the next jubilee year. Then, 'You shall not cheat one another, but you shall fear your God; for I am the LORD your God' (Lev 25.17). These instructions stress fair prices. They forbid charging the maximum that the market might bear on the one hand, or taking advantage of the seller's need on the other. Exploiting the other party apparently is viewed as cheating God. Another word for fairness, of course, is justice. Justice is an explicit element of jubilee.

Options for consequences

Finally, there are three main options, plus their guiding principle, for the consequences of observing jubilee, or not observing it.

Security and prosperity for obedience. If the society keeps jubilee, God commits to providing security and prosperity in return: 'You shall observe my statutes and faithfully keep my ordinances, so that you may live on the land securely. The land will yield its fruit, and you will eat your fill and live on it securely' (Lev 25.18-19). In addition, Lev 26.1-13, which immediately follows the jubilee instructions and relates directly to them, provides a detailed description of the security and prosperity with which God will reward the society for obedience.

Severe punishment for disobedience. On the other hand, Lev 26.14-43 (immediately following the above) gives a detailed description of the disasters which God will bring for disobedience. These disasters come first as warnings, then as punishments, all in forms which match the land-related offence and which ensure the opposite of security and prosperity. They include: no crops; defeat by enemies; and ultimately scattering the people among other nations so the land can have rest from human exploitation. Examples:

> 'But if you will not obey me, and do not observe all these commandments, if you spurn my statutes, and abhor my ordinances, so that you will not observe all my commandments, and you break my covenant, I in turn will do this to you: I will bring terror on you; consumption and fever that waste the eyes and cause life to pine away. You shall sow your seed in vain, for your enemies shall eat it. I will set my face against you, and you shall be struck down by your enemies; your foes shall rule over you, and you shall flee though no one pursues you' (Lev 26.14-17).

> 'And you I will scatter among the nations, and I will unsheathe the sword against you; your land shall be a desolation, and your cities a waste. Then the land shall enjoy its sabbath years as long as it lies desolate, while you are in the land of your enemies; then the land shall rest, and enjoy its sabbath years' (Lev 26.33-34).

Divine mercy for repentance. Nevertheless, if the offenders or their descendants repent as a result of this discipline, God will restore them to the land:

> 'But if they confess their iniquity and the iniquity of their ancestors, in that they committed treachery against me and,

> moreover, that they continued hostile to me ... then will I remember my covenant with Jacob; I will remember also my covenant with Isaac and also my covenant with Abraham, and I will remember the land' (Lev 26.40, 42).

Governing principle. In the three consequences listed above a vital governing theological principle is found. The road to security lies *not* through military power, and *not* through controlling others by force, but only through observing the principles of jubilee, by actions, in the life of the society.

Summary

In summary to this point, an Old Testament theology of jubilee contains the three major elements of justice, mercy, and proper conduct as a way of life before God. Does that sound familiar? Jubilee tells the people of God what is good—what God requires. It anticipates the theme passage for this conference:

> He has told you, O mortal, what is good; and what does the LORD require of you
> but to do justice, and to love kindness, and to walk humbly with your God? (Micah 6.8)

Jubilee provides a concrete example of what God requires, of what God has told humans to do—how to walk with God in the Old Testament. But the question, of course, still remains: 'Did they actually *do* it? How did things work out?' This brings us to the story of jubilee observance in the remainder of the Old Testament.

Keeping jubilee

Time passed. Eventually the Israelites insisted on having kingship as the solution to a series of security crises (1 Sam 8.4-20). For this they received two main results in return:

1. Continued lack of security, except for brief interludes such as David's rule.
2. A major change in socio-economic structure, for the worse. Kings took freedom and land from their citizens, and created a ruling class which did the same. Words in the mouth of the prophet Samuel gave warning and description:

> He said, 'These will be the ways of the king who will reign over you: he will take your sons and appoint them to his chariots and to be his horsemen, and to run before his chariots; ... and some to plough his ground and to reap his harvest, and to make his implements of war and the equipment of his chariots. He will take your daughters to be perfumers and cooks and bakers. He will take the best of your fields and vineyards and olive orchards and give them to his courtiers ... and you shall be his slaves. And in that day you will cry out because of your king, whom you have chosen for yourselves; but the LORD will not answer you in that day' (1 Sam 8.11-14, 17-18).

These permanent changes made a literal jubilee almost impossible, and certainly unrealistic. As a result, there is no clear evidence that the jubilee was ever kept after kingship began.[4] It became a lost cause. Instead, the main indications are the opposite, and they are found in prophetic oracles like Micah 6, quoted above. This is no surprise.

Prophetic voices

The Old Testament would be a great deal shorter if the jubilee had been observed. The prophets, for example, might have been virtually unemployed. But they had plenty of work, and apparently they did not give up. If their preserved oracles are any guide, the prophets still applied the ethical principles of jubilee, even though the literal legal mechanism seemed impossible to enforce. In short: circumstances could change, but principles did not.

---

[4] Wright, 'Jubilee ...' , p. 1028.

Violation of jubilee principles

The prophets repeatedly denounced their ruling class for violating the jubilee principles of justice and mercy as the proper 'walk with God', especially regarding the use of land. Two such examples are:

'They covet fields ... and take them' (Mic 2.2). Micah 2 defines wickedness and evil deeds as seizing fields and houses by force ('because it is in their power,' v. 1), and thus oppressing householders and their inheritance:

> Alas for those who devise wickedness and evil deeds on their beds!
> When the morning dawns, they perform it, because it is in their power.
> They covet fields, and seize them; houses, and take them away;
> they oppress householder and house, people and their inheritance (Mic 2.1-2).

As a result, warns the prophet, God will invoke and enforce the sanctions of Leviticus 26—the punishment for failure to observe jubilee principles of conduct. The punishment will fit the offences (relating to land seizure) by sending the offenders into exile and giving their land to others (Mic 2.3-4).

'You who ... add field to field' (Isa 5.8). Similarly, Isaiah 5—in a sequel to the celebrated Song of the Vineyard—describes how God looked for justice and right actions ('righteousness'), but found only bloodshed and cries of pain. Here too, the offence is in terms of exploiters taking fields and houses until the population no longer has a place to live.

> For the vineyard of the LORD of hosts is the house of Israel,
> and the people of Judah are his pleasant planting;
> he expected justice, but saw bloodshed; righteousness, but heard a cry!
> Ah, you who join house to house, who add field to field,
> until there is room for no one but you, and you are left to

live alone
in the midst of the land! (Isa 5.7-8).

Again the prophet warns that God will punish these violations of jubilee principles with the sanctions described in Leviticus 26. The result will be the opposite of security and prosperity: God will entirely remove divine protection (Isa 5.5), the land will become untended (v. 6), and the offenders will be deported by foreign armies into humiliating exile (vv. 13-15).

Repent!

Nevertheless, divine threats of punishment were not cast in bronze. Prophetic voices also held out hope that catastrophe could be averted if, but only if the people would repent. For example, in Isa 58.9-12, *if* the offenders are sorry, and apologise to God publicly for their violations of jubilee ethics ('call [to] the LORD'), and *if* they halt the oppression ('remove the yoke'), *and* make restitution ('offer your food to the hungry'), *then* God will restore the divine protector relationship with Israel.

> Then you shall call, and the LORD will answer; you shall cry for help, and he will say, 'Here I am.'
> If you remove the yoke from among you, the pointing of the finger, the speaking of evil, if you offer your food to the hungry and satisfy the needs of the afflicted (Isa 58.9-10a).

Indeed, the people will experience a reversal of fortunes leading to a new era ('your light shall rise in the darkness,' v. 10b), characterised by divine guidance, prosperity, and restoration of the country (vv. 11-12):

> then your light shall rise in the darkness and your gloom be like the noonday.
> the LORD will guide you continually, and satisfy your needs in parched places,
> and make your bones strong; and you shall be like a watered garden,
> like a spring of water, whose waters never fail.

> Your ancient ruins shall be rebuilt; you shall raise up the foundations of many generations;
> you shall be called the repairer of the breach, the restorer of streets to live in (Isa 58.10b-12).

But it never happened. The result, according to the Old Testament, is that God destroyed the Northern Kingdom of ancient Israel, and sent the Southern Kingdom of Judah into Babylonian exile. According to 2 Kings and Jeremiah, both disasters resulted from failure 'to do justice, and to love kindness' (Mic 6.8) when dealing with the vulnerable people of the land. That is to say, the consequences of failing to observe jubilee principles were very tragic indeed.

Consequences

End of the Northern Kingdom

Warnings. Unheeded warnings from prophets to the Northern Kingdom are mentioned in 2 Kgs 17.13-15: 'Yet the LORD warned Israel and Judah by every prophet and every seer ... They would not listen ... They despised ... the warnings that he gave them.'

For example, warnings from Amos and Hosea show that persistent actions which violated jubilee values were high on the list of offences:

> Thus says the LORD: For three transgressions of Israel, and for four,
> I will not revoke the punishment; because they sell the righteous for silver, and the needy for a pair of sandals (Amos 2.6).

> But let justice roll down like waters, and righteousness like an everflowing stream (Amos 5.24).

> Hear the word of the LORD, O people of Israel; for the LORD has an indictment against the inhabitants of the land. There is no faithfulness or loyalty, and no knowledge of

> God in the land.
> Swearing, lying, and murder, and stealing and adultery break out; bloodshed follows bloodshed (Hosea 4.1-2).
>
> For I desire steadfast love and not sacrifice, the knowledge of God rather than burnt offering (Hosea 6.6).
>
> In all this, God is merely holding them to the same standards which apply to other nations (Amos 9.7-8).

Catastrophe. Tragically, the prophetic warnings were correct, and the Assyrian empire destroyed the Northern Kingdom, in two stages. First, in 733 BC Tiglath-Pileser III (744-722) carried out a punitive campaign which destroyed much of the Northern Kingdom (leaving a remnant around its capital, Samaria). He deported the population to Assyria and annexed the territory as the Assyrian provinces of Megiddo and Gilead. This disaster is summarised in 2 Kings 15.29, and also listed in the Assyrian royal annals.[5]

Second, in 722 his successor, Shalmaneser V (726-722) finished the job. To punish a final and futile rebellion by the pathetic Israelite king, Hoshea, Shalmaneser captured and destroyed Samaria, deported the population to other parts of the empire, imported immigrants from other provinces, and turned the region into the Assyrian province of Samaria. This final catastrophe is described in 2 Kings 17.3-6, and also in the Assyrian royal annals.[6] The terrible consequences of that catastrophe are still evident in the archaeological remains (see Appendix below).

In this way the Northern Kingdom came to a resounding end, with its epitaph recorded by the prophetic editors of the Books of Kings:

---

[5] Oppenheim, A L, 'Babylonian and Assyrian Historical Texts', in *Ancient Near Eastern Texts Relating to the Old Testaments*, edited by J B Pritchard, Princeton, Princeton University Press, 1969 (third edition with supplement): 265-317, 556-67, p. 283. Tadmor, Hayim, *The Inscriptions of Tiglath-Pileser III, King of Assyria, Critical edition, with Introductions, Translations and Commentary*, The Israel Academy of Sciences and Humanities, Jerusalem, 1994, pp. 80-84, 141, 189, 203, 279-82; convenient summary with maps in Rainey, Anson, and Safrai, Ze'ev, *The Macmillan Bible Atlas*, Carta Jerusalem: and Macmillan General Reference/Simon & Schuster, New York, 1993 (Completely Revised Third Edition), pp. 110-13.

[6] Oppenheim, 'Babylonian ...', pp. 284-85, where the annals attribute this action to his successor that year, Sargon II; convenient summary with maps, Rainey and Safrai, pp. 114-15.

> This occurred because the people of Israel had sinned against the LORD their God ... until the LORD removed Israel out of his sight, as he had foretold through all his servants the prophets. So Israel was exiled from their own land to Assyria until this day (2 Kings 17.7, 23).

Fall and exile of the Southern Kingdom

Warnings. Unheeded warnings from prophets to the Southern Kingdom are recorded as well. Soon after the destruction of the north, the rule of King Manasseh of Jerusalem (687-642) earned the following assessment and warning:

> The LORD said by his servants the prophets, 'Because King Manasseh of Judah has committed these abominations, has done things more wicked than all that the Amorites did ... I will stretch over Jerusalem the measuring line for Samaria ... I will cast off the remnant of my heritage, and give them into the hand of their enemies ...' Moreover Manasseh shed very much innocent blood, until he had filled Jerusalem from one end to another ... (2 Kings 21.10-11, 13-14, 16).

But, apparently, warnings like this were insufficient. As a result, it became the prophet Jeremiah's primary task to warn repeatedly the last kings of Jerusalem, watch unhappily as his message generally fell on deaf ears, and finally witness first-hand the dreadful tragedy that resulted.

Jeremiah's warnings included the major jubilee idea of justice as God's requirement—or else. For example:

> Hear the word of the LORD, O King of Judah ... Thus says the LORD: 'Act with justice and righteousness, and deliver from the hand of the oppressor anyone who has been robbed. And do no wrong or violence to the alien, the orphan, and the widow, or shed innocent blood in this place. For if you will indeed obey this word, then through the gates of this house shall enter kings who sit on the throne of David, riding in chariots and on horses, they, and their servants,

> and their people. But if you will not heed these words, I swear by myself, says the LORD, that this house shall become a desolation' (Jer 22.2-5).

Jeremiah's specific warning to King Jehoiakim (607-598), who presided over the beginning of the end, contained the same themes:

> Woe to him who builds his house by unrighteousness, and his upper rooms by injustice;
> who makes his neighbours work for nothing, and does not give them their wages ...
> Did not your father eat and drink
> and do justice and righteousness? Then it was well with him.
> He judged the cause of the poor and needy; then it was well.
> Is not this to know me? says the LORD.
> But your eyes and heart are only on your dishonest gain,
> for shedding innocent blood, for practising oppression and violence (Jer 22.13-17).

Like its northern counterpart, Jerusalem also fell in two stages. First, King Nebuchadnezzar II (604-562) of the newly-triumphant Babylonian empire made King Jehoiakim a vassal in 604. But he rebelled in 601 (thinking Egypt was on the rise), so Babylon captured and plundered Jerusalem, and deported its aristocracy. As Jehoiakim apparently died during the siege, Nebuchadnezzar deported his successor Jehoiachin (brief reign in 598), and set Zedekiah on the throne instead. This event is also told in a Babylonian royal annal.[7]

According to 2 Kings 24.1-4, this happened under divine control. God followed unheeded verbal warnings with a severe warning through action. Violating jubilee principles, by using force for injustice and oppression, is here labelled 'the sins of Manasseh' (v. 3), Manasseh being a king who was famous for his violent oppression (2 Kgs 21.16).

At this point Babylon set Zedekiah (597-586) on the throne, but essentially he repeated the mistakes of his predecessors. Rebelling against his Babylonian overlord, he soon saw Jerusalem besieged again. Jeremiah then delivered a similar warning, followed by a call to repent:

---

[7] Oppenheim, 'Babylonian ...', pp. 563-64.

> To the house of the king of Judah say: Hear the word of the LORD, O house of David! Thus says the LORD: Execute justice in the morning, and deliver from the hand of the oppressor anyone who has been robbed, or else my wrath will go forth like fire, and burn, with no one to quench it, because of your evil doings (Jer 21.11-12).

Tragedy. What followed was a fascinating and complex historical and spiritual drama involving the jubilee principle of release from indentured slavery. It unfolded in several tragic steps:

—In a desperate attempt to gain divine favour, Zedekiah made a deal with Jerusalem's leaders to free all the Hebrew slaves, because such slavery was forbidden in the Mosaic covenant in Deut 15.12-18 (Jer 34.1-10).
—Then the resurgent army of Pharaoh Apries (Hophra) approached from Egypt, so Nebuchadnezzar of Babylon had to cease temporarily the siege of Jerusalem in order to face the Egyptian threat (Jer 37.5).
—The Jerusalem rulers apparently thought they were rescued, possibly recalling the deliverance of Hezekiah's Jerusalem from Assyria 110 years earlier under similar circumstances (2 Kgs 18-20).
—They immediately took all their slaves back. It became evident that they were just trying to shed responsibility for feeding their slaves during the siege, when food was running out (Jer 34.11; 37.6-10).
—For Jeremiah, this was the last straw. The covenant was entirely broken and God would certainly punish them by destroying Jerusalem and sending them into exile (Jer 34.12-22).

Jeremiah 34 merits careful reading in this sequence. The jubilee idea in the phrase, 'make a proclamation of liberty to them, that all should set free their Hebrew slaves' (vv. 8-9), is of special note.

Tragically, Jeremiah's warnings came true as the drama continued through its final acts. The Babylonian army returned, breached the wall, destroyed the Temple and city, executed Zedekiah, and carried off much of the population to exile. Only the poorer people were left to work the land (2 Kgs 25.4-21; Jer 39.1-40.6). Again, these catastrophic consequences can be seen in the archaeological remains (see Appendix: below).

Prophetic visions

Although the practice of jubilee fell flat on its face, the prophets did not give up. The Book of Isaiah in particular preserves later oracles which keep the subject alive.

'Justice to the Nations' (Isaiah 42.1-7)

Isaiah 42 describes a divine servant of the future, who will universalise the principles of jubilee justice by bringing them to all nations. For example:

> Here is my servant, whom I uphold, my chosen, in whom my soul delights;
> I have put my spirit upon him; he will bring forth justice to the nations ...
> He will not grow faint or be crushed until he has established justice in the earth;
> and the coastlands wait for his teaching (Isa 42.1, 4).

The kind of power required to create such an extraordinary social order—a virtual new order—must come from God the Creator, 'the LORD, who created the heavens ... who spread out the earth ... who gives breath to the people upon it ...' (v. 5).

The resulting new era of universal social justice, if brought about, is described in terms of a new creation, with the light of Genesis 1.3 ('let there be light') bursting into a violence-darkened world of chaos. The new era includes not only general justice, but also the specific jubilee principles of release and return:

> I am the LORD, I have called you in righteousness, I have taken you by the hand and kept you;
> I have given you as a covenant to the people, a light to the nations,
> to open the eyes that are blind, to bring out the prisoners from the dungeon,
> from the prison those who sit in darkness (Isa 42.6-7).

'Good News to the Oppressed' (Isa 61.1-11)

Isaiah 61 describes the divine servant and mission in even more detail. The mission is clearly central to divine plans for salvation because the call of the servant is described in terms of endowment by the 'spirit' of God, and also as being 'anointed':

> The spirit of the Lord GOD is upon me, because the LORD has anointed me;
> he has sent me to bring good news to the oppressed, to bind up the brokenhearted,
> to proclaim liberty to the captives, and release to the prisoners;
> to proclaim the year of the LORD's favour, and the day of vengeance of [punishment by] our God (Isa 61.1-2).

This vocabulary typically is used in conjunction with a call and mission central to divine plans for the chosen people, so here it indicates the same idea for the divine servant.[8]

No less important is the mission itself, described as good news and bad news respectively to a pair of selected audiences. On the one hand, for the underdogs, good news indeed—bondage turned into liberty and release (Isa 61.1), funeral mourning turned to celebration (vv. 2-3a), people flourishing like forests, ruins rebuilt (vv. 3b-4). In short, a whole new order of justice setting an example for the world (vv. 9, 11), using a special phrase—'the year of the LORD's favour' (v. 2)—which was almost certainly a name for the jubilee year.[9]

On the other hand, bad news for oppressors. Embedded in the good news is a reaffirmation that God will not turn a blind eye to those who wield force in violation of the jubilee standards for action, which would prevent the good news from taking place. The message is two-sided. The servant comes,

> to proclaim the year of the LORD's favour, and the day of vengeance of [punishment by] our God ...
> For I the LORD love justice, I hate robbery and wrongdoing;
> I will faithfully give them their recompense, and I will make an everlasting covenant with them (Isa 61.2, 8).

---

[8] Matthews, V H, 'Holy Spirit', in *The Anchor Bible Dictionary*, 1992, vol. 3: 260-80, pp. 262-63; Jonge, M de, 'Messiah', in *The Anchor Bible Dictionary*, 1992, vol. 4: 777-88, pp. 777-81.

[9] Wright, 'Jubilee ...' , p. 1028.

Recompense promises appropriate consequences, whether for justice or wrongdoing (v. 8). Covenant (8d) simply means a contract—the terms are set. That God will faithfully do all this (8c) is a good news promise to one group, and an unveiled threat to the other. At this point, two roads diverge in the yellow wood of that which God requires. Choosing which road to take will make all the difference.

These are very strong ideas indeed. It is no accident that 600 years later a prophet from Nazareth caused a riot when he claimed that the mission applied to himself (Luke 4.16-30). Such ideas would cause a similar stir if they were attempted in the same land today.

Second Temple Period and diaspora

The return from exile which began the Second Temple Period (539 BC—70 AD) provided an opportunity to start over in the land, a second chance or new beginning to keep covenant with God.

According to the Books of Ezra and Nehemiah, this idea was taken seriously. For example, in Neh 10.32 the people committed to observing the sabbatical year, which had stringent requirements entailing considerable self-sacrifice. It required that, every seven years, they allow agricultural land (including vineyards and olive orchards) to lie fallow, and that all debts be cancelled (Exod 23.10-11; Lev 25.1-7, 18-22; Deut 15.1-11). The original reasons resembled the values of jubilee, for they included justice and care for the underprivileged: 'So that the poor of your people may eat' (by gleaning free-growing food, Exod 23.11); 'a year of complete rest for the land' (Lev 25.5); and generosity with 'the poor and needy neighbour in your land' (Deut 15.11).

Nevertheless, the returnees from exile did not include jubilee in this commitment, for a simple reason. As Shmuel Safrai, p. 580, describes it:

> That the jubilee did not apply during the period of the Second Temple was deduced from the verse 'unto all the inhabitants thereof' (Lev 25.10) with the corollary that 'from the time that the tribes of Reuben and Gad and the half-tribe of Manasseh were exiled the jubilees were discontinued (Sifra, Be-Har 2.3).[10]

---

[10] Safrai, Shmuel, 'Sabbatical Year and Jubilee Year. Jubilee in the Second Temple Period', in *Encyclopaedia Judaica*, Keter Publishing House, Jerusalem (vol. 14), 1971, 580.

As a result, this rationalisation, of course, applied to the post-Second Temple period as well. The long centuries of diaspora, after the Roman empire expelled so many Jewish people from their ancestral land in 135 AD, meant no literal practice of the jubilee. But return during the past century, and especially the establishment of the modern Jewish State of Israel in 1948, has started a fifty-year countdown again bringing the Jewish people face-to-face with the idea of jubilee.

Modern period and relevance

Principles

The prophetic message that the principles of jubilee constitute 'a light to the nations' means that these values apply to all humanity—to us, today. And one look at the world which we moderns have made suggests they are badly needed.

The principles of jubilee are a biblical answer to the sin of Cain. The sin of Cain (Genesis 4) was not only the sin of violence against his brother. It was also his failure to heed God's prior warning about the very impulse to use force and his failure to resist that impulse.

Humans need warnings, and also need the will or help to resist, because, the moment they have power, the sin of Cain is a demon crouching at the door. All too often people fail to resist. This failure is shared by all. That is, virtually all people come from a culture or heritage which has failed to keep jubilee values one way or another. Hopefully, there is still the opportunity to do better. Local examples come readily to mind.

The State of Israel

The modern State of Israel, whose ancestors provided and preserved the texts which contain the idea of jubilee, yesterday (11 February 1998) began to celebrate a fifty-year anniversary which is being called a 'jubilee year' by the Israeli government and press. Indeed, this is quite a thought. It presents a special opportunity for the institutional practice of jubilee values carried into action by the State of Israel itself.

Until now, however, little along this line has been heard, and instead the notion of jubilee is regarded in Israel primarily as a fiftieth anniversary celebrating the founding and triumphal progress of the State.

But for many Palestinian people, 1998 marks fifty years of Israeli oppression which has contradicted every element of jubilee in the Bible. What do we think and feel about this? Is it proper to hope for or expect divine judgment on the State of Israel? After all, what if God still holds the Jewish people accountable for their failure to live by jubilee principles? It is a chilling thought. Might God remove them from the land into diaspora again?

In light of Isaiah 58.9-11, is it too late for Israel to repent? Let us pray that it is not.

Do we love mercy? Let us pray for God's mercy on this erring nation.

Counting the cost

A word about counting the cost. The radical idea of jubilee always had a price. On the one hand, for the modern State of Israel the cost of 'doing justice' would be immense. Carrying out the idea of restitution and return for Palestinian land and refugees would take tremendous political will and huge sums of money. From where will the courage and sacrifice come?

On the other hand: to 'love mercy' might mean that Palestinians who *could* claim the jubilee right of restoration from Israel or individual Israelis should be generous with those who have wronged them. For Palestinians, this would prove very costly as well.

Future Palestinian State

If a future State of Palestine ever has power over the Israeli colonies called 'settlements,' what will the State of Palestine do? Dear Palestinian friends, the biblical jubilee says:

> Love mercy! No revenge!
> Walk humbly with your God!

Finally, it is always surprising how quickly the oppressed can become the oppressor when given a chance. Dear Palestinian friends: Let us join in praying that the future State of Palestine will always heed the jubilee warning: 'Do not give in to the impulse to use force for what we want.'

Conclusion

Dear friends of *Sabeel*: The word 'liberation' in Palestinian liberation theology includes freedom *from* bondage to the sin of Cain. In addition, it provides freedom *for* something: freedom to do justice, to love mercy, and to walk humbly with our God.

And so, in closing: through the magnificent, daring, radical, relentless, costly, difficult, challenging idea of jubilee, scripture sets before us the way of death or the way of life. Ladies and gentlemen, let us choose *life*. Let us choose the principles of jubilee as the guiding path, in all that we do, into the next millennium and beyond.

Appendix: Archaeology and the Fall of the Kingdoms

A. Archaeological evidence for the conquest of the Northern Kingdom by the Assyrian campaigns ending in 733 and 722 BC is summarised in Barkay, Gabriel, 'The Iron Age II-III', in *The Archaeology of Ancient Israel*, edited by Amnon Ben-Tor, Yale University Press and The Open University of Israel, New Haven and London, 1992: 302-73, pp. 327-28, and is found, e.g., at the following sites:

Tel Dan, Stratum II (Biran, Avraham, *Biblical Dan*, Israel Exploration Society, Jerusalem, 1994: 245-46, 253, 260-61; Biran, Avraham, 'Dan' in *The New Encyclopedia of Archaeological Excavations in the Holy Land*, edited by Ephraim Stern, Simon & Schuster, New York, 1993, vol. 1: 323-32, pp. 330-31).

Hazor, Stratum V, Areas A, B, G (Yadin, Yigal, 'Hazor. Excavation Results: First Four Seasons (1955-1958)', in *The New Encyclopedia of Archaeological Excavations in the Holy Land*, 1993, vol. 2: 594-603, pp. 601-603; Ben-Tor, Amnon, 'Hazor: Fifth season of Excavations (1968-69)', in *The New Encyclopedia of Archaeological Excavations in the Holy Land*, 1993, vol. 2: 604-606, p. 606).

Tel Chinnereth, Stratum II (Fritz, Volkmar, 'Chinnereth, Tel', in *The New Encyclopedia of Archaeological Excavations in the Holy Land,* 1993, vol. 1: 299-301, p. 300).

Megiddo, Stratum IVA (Shiloh, Yigal, 'Megiddo: The Iron Age', in *The New Encyclopedia of Archaeological Excavations in the Holy Land,* 1993, vol. 3: 1012-23, pp. 1021, 1023).

Beth-Shean, Upper Stratum V (Mazar, Amihai, 'Beth-Shean. Tel Beth-Shean and the Northern Cemetery', in *The New Encyclopedia of Archaeological Excavations in the Holy Land,* 1993, vol. 1: 214-223, p. 222).

Tirzah/Tell el-Far'ah (North), Stratum 2*, Period VIId (Chambon, Alain, 'Far'ah, Tell el- (North). Late Bronze Age to the Roman Period', in *The New Encyclopedia of Archaeological Excavations in the Holy Land,* 1993, vol. 2: 439-40, p. 440).

Shechem (Tell Balatah), Stratum VII (Campbell, Edward F, 'Shechem. Tell Balâtah', in *The New Encyclopedia of Archaeological Excavations in the Holy Land,* 1993, vol. 4: 1345-54, p.1353).

Samaria, Period VI (Avigad, Nahman, 'Samaria (City)', in *The New Encyclopedia of Archaeological Excavations in the Holy Land,* 1993, vol. 4: 1300-10, pp. 1301, 1303).

B. Archaeological evidence for the destruction of Jerusalem by the Babylonian campaigns ending in 597 and 586 BC is summarised in Mazar, Amihai, *Archaeology of the Land of the Bible, 10,000-586 B.C.E.*, Anchor Bible Reference Library, Doubleday, New York, 1990, pp. 458-60); and in Shiloh, Yigal, 'Jerusalem: The Early Periods and the First Temple Period. Excavation Results', in *The New Encyclopedia of Archaeological Excavations in the Holy Land,* 1993, vol. 2: 701-12, 709. It is found, e.g., at these sites:

City of David, Stratum 10A, Areas E1-E3 and G (Shiloh, 'Jerusalem ..., pp. 701, 704, 709; Cahill, Jane M, and David Tarler, 'Excavations Directed by Yigal Shiloh at the City of David, 1978-1985', in *Ancient Jerusalem Revealed,* edited by Hillel Geva, Israel Exploration Society, Jerusalem, 1994: 31-45, pp. 37-40).

Ophel, Buildings C and D (Mazar, Eilat, 'The Royal Quarter of Biblical Jerusalem: The Ophel', in *Ancient Jerusalem Revealed,* 1994: 64-72, p.

65; Geva, Hillel, 'Jerusalem: Recent Discoveries Within the City', in *The New Encyclopedia of Archaeological Excavations in the Holy Land,* 1993, vol. 2: 715-16, p. 715).

Jewish Quarter of Old City, Tower (Barkay, Gabriel, 'The Iron Age II-III', in *The Archaeology of Ancient Israel,* 1992: 302-73, p. 368; Mazar, Amihai, *Archaeology of the Land of the Bible ...,* 1990, pp. 420-22; Shiloh, Yigal, 'Jerusalem ...', in *The New Encyclopedia of Archaeological Excavations in the Holy Land,* 1993, vol. 2: 709).

THE NEW TESTAMENT UNDERSTANDING OF THE BIBLICAL JUBILEE

Osvaldo D Vena

I am overwhelmed by the historical moment in which this Conference is being held. Therefore I approach the subject at hand, the New Testament understanding of the biblical jubilee, with complete humility and awe. I am aware of the repercussions that some of the things we will say might have here in Palestine/Israel, and also in the communities we serve back home, as we try to share with our people some of the issues we will explore during these days. Quite simply, this conference may change our lives forever.

Introduction: revolutionaries and revolutions in 1st-century Palestine

We know from the writings of Josephus that there were messianic movements operating in the countryside during the time of the Jewish uprising in 66-70 AD. In his *Jewish War* he left us a vivid account of what a group of rebels did at the beginning of the war in 66 AD:

> The others then set fire to the house of Ananias the high priest, and to the palaces of Agrippa and Bernice; after which they carried the fire to the place where the archives were reposited, and made haste to burn the contracts belonging to their creditors, and thereby dissolve their obligations for paying their debts. (2.426-427)

This can only be interpreted as the revolutionaries' desire to free the peasantry from the heavy burden of debt and oppression, to which they had been subjected for a long time in a social system that evidently did not abide by the jubilee provisions spelled out in Leviticus 25. Their violent action aimed at correcting years of wrongdoing by those who possessed the land and who had the right connection with the Roman administration.

Forty years before, a Galilean peasant by the name of Jesus of Nazareth did something similar. He also entered the Temple in Jerusalem where he disrupted the worship by overturning the tables of the money-changers and the seats of those who sold pigeons, not allowing anyone to perform any of the daily rituals. Jesus' action was truly revolutionary because it was an indictment of the temple as an oppressive system. Jesus attacked the temple institutions because of the way they exploited the poor.[1] But unlike the rebels' actions in 66 AD, Jesus' action was largely symbolic. Next day the temple continued with business as usual.

Perhaps the most revolutionary action performed by Jesus was his sermon in the synagogue at Nazareth as recorded in Luke 4.16-30, a sermon some have called the 'Nazareth Manifesto'.[2] This and other passages in Jesus' teaching have been interpreted as Jesus' intention to call Israel as a whole to celebrate the jubilee, that time every fifty years when debts were cancelled, slaves were released and the people were allowed to return to their patrimonies. One of the main proponents of this view has been John Howard Yoder in his book *The Politics of Jesus.*[3]

The purpose of this paper, then, is to probe into Yoder's, and others' argument. The main issue that I will be exploring is: What is the relationship between the jubilee and the reign of God as proclaimed by Jesus? Was Jesus' message a jubilary proclamation? Or was it to be understood in some other way?

The jubilee in the Hebrew Bible

When one thinks of the jubilee, the text that comes to mind almost immediately is Leviticus 25. This chapter spells out the legal provisions of the jubilee, and is made up of several traditions coming from different historical situations, '... probably woven together as part of the Holiness Code by a priestly editor of the late exile or post-exilic period.'[4]

---

[1] Myers, Ched, *Binding the Strong Man. A Political Reading of Mark's Story of Jesus,* Orbis Books, Maryknoll, New York, 1988, p. 299.

[2] Wright, N T, *Jesus and the Victory of God,* Fortress Press, Minneapolis, 1996, p. 294.

[3] Yoder, John Howard, *The Politics of Jesus. Vicit Agnus Noster,* Eerdmans and The Paternoster Press, Grand Rapids, Michigan/Carlisle,UK, 1994 (2nd ed.).

[4] Ringe, Sharon, *Jesus, Liberation, and the Biblical Jubilee,* Fortress Press, Philadelphia, 1985, p. 26.

Some of the traditions that underlie the legislation of Leviticus 25 denote an agricultural situation prior to the establishment of the monarchy. For example, Exodus 21.2-6 concerning the release of slaves, and Exodus 23.10-11 concerning the fallow year. Some traditions come from a time when the society seems to have been under the jurisdiction of a central administration and with a fairly complex economy, a period of transition from an agricultural setting to a more urban, commercial one.[5] One example of such a time would be Deuteronomy 15.1-18, where we find legislation about release of debts, the poor and manumission of slaves, though not concerning the fallow year.

A third group of traditional materials comes from the so-called royal proclamations of release, such as the decree of Zedekiah in Jeremiah 34.8-22 and the decree of Nehemiah in Neh. 5.1-13. These are not related to the Sabbath year, as the previous ones, but to instances of royal favour on the occasion of an important event. The Hebrew word being used in these passages is not *semittah*, as in Exodus and Deuteronomy, but the word *deror*, meaning 'release' or 'liberty'. This word is related to similar words found in secular documents of Israel's neighbours where they are used in connection with the prohibition to transfer real estate permanently, and with reference to the release of people from their economically forced servitude.[6] Therefore, even though the particular provisions of Leviticus 25 echo the Sabbath-year laws of Exodus 21-23 and Deuteronomy 15, the language links it with the royal decrees of release as found in Jeremiah 34 and Nehemiah 5 since the word for 'release' and 'liberty' used in both instances is *deror.*

Leviticus 25, then, was compiled during the exile in the event of the imminent return of the Hebrews to Palestine. It was meant to solve problems related to the allocation and subsequent management of the land. Sharon Ringe has affirmed that, 'If they had actually been observed, the collection of jubilee laws would have had a sweeping impact on the social and political life of any community governed by them.' But she suggests that there is no proof, either in the Hebrew Scriptures, or in the Second Temple literature, or in any secular account, that this legislation was ever implemented in Israel.[7] Many other scholars have arrived at the same conclusion.

Jubilee language in the prophetic books fulfils a different function. Isaiah 61.1-2 is one of the best examples and one which was readily noticed

---

5 Ringe, *Jesus* ..., p. 21.

6 Ringe, *Jesus* ..., p. 23.

7 Ringe, *Jesus* ..., p. 27.

by the New Testament writers. This oracle was produced by a group of visionaries who did not see the return of Israel to Palestine as God's final word for the people. Because they felt excluded from the specific plans of the leadership redistributing the land and creating the legislation to ensure its possession, they were more concerned with eschatology than with history. Their understanding of the people of God was more inclusive, in contrast to the more hierarchical understanding of the editor of the Holiness Code, or the writers of the prophecies of Haggai and Zechariah.

In this oracle, Third Isaiah portrays an eschatological event. It is the proclamation of a royal edict of release on behalf of the divine sovereign whose reign is at hand. It is not the announcement of a historical event such as the return of the Jews to Palestine, but the proclamation of God's eschatological reign which will culminate in a new creation, new heavens and a new earth (Isaiah 66.22).

All these traditions associated with the jubilee appear to affirm two things. First, that God is sovereign over Israel both in actual fact and in eschatological hope. Second, that the structures of economic and social life must embody the people's affirmation of God's sovereignty. As Ringe puts it, God's reign and humankind's liberation go hand in hand.[8]

Jubilee passages in the New Testament

The temptation exists to find references to the jubilee whenever the idea of preaching good news to the poor appears. In that regard, Sharon Ringe warns us of the danger of reading into the New Testament jubilee imagery based on similarities of language or concepts.

One of the problems is that the Septuagint translates the Hebrew words *deror* and *yobel* with the Greek word *aphesis*, which has a broad range of meaning beyond the jubilee traditions. In other words, there is no distinctive jubilee vocabulary in Greek. Because of that, Ringe suggests that we have to limit ourselves to those passages in the New Testament where it is clear that the author is quoting or paraphrasing an actual jubilee tradition. In the Gospels these traditions constitute a limited semantic field outside of which it is neither valid nor responsible to claim the presence of jubilee texts. For example, it would be wrong to assume that every reference to 'proclaiming good news' is a citation of Isaiah 61.1. Ringe would

---

8 Ringe, *Jesus ...*, p. 31.

therefore question Yoder's work by saying that even though it constitutes a provocative piece it is still less than convincing, for it fails to engage in careful literary and historical criticism of the alleged jubilee passages.[9]

The clearest reference to the jubilee is found in Luke 4.16-30.

> The Spirit of the Lord is upon me,
> Because he has anointed me to bring good news to the poor.
> He has sent me to proclaim release to the captives
> And recovering of sight to the blind,
> To let the oppressed go free,
> To proclaim the year of the Lord's favour.

Grammatically speaking, three things are significant about this text. First, it is really a composite text made up of Isaiah 61.1-2 and 58.6. Second, the last two phrases of Isaiah 61.1-2 are omitted. Third, the quotation is closer to the Septuagint than to the Hebrew text.

Sharon Ringe suggests that all these things point to the Early Church's shaping of the quotation. Jesus could not have read from the Isaiah scroll in that manner, nor could he have altered the reading intentionally in order to set in motion his ministry at Nazareth. The quotation as it stands reflects the way in which people in the primitive Church were used to hearing the Scriptures. The quotation was already in that form when the evangelist incorporated it into his Gospel.

But the significance of the addition of Isaiah 58.6 is not examined by Ringe. It is Thomas D Hanks in his book *God So Loved the Third World* who, after noting how this insertion has not been adequately explained by biblical scholars, goes on to propose that 'the insertion of Isaiah 58.6 in Isaiah 61.1-2 is best explained by recognizing that both of them reflect the teaching of Leviticus 25 concerning the Year of Jubilee, and that the originality and boldness exemplified in relating the two texts is best accounted for as reflecting Jesus' own exegetical insight and passion for liberation.'[10]

Therefore, when Jesus inserts this passage from Isaiah 58 into the quotation of Isaiah 61.1-2 he does so intentionally because he understands this passage to be charged with jubilee imagery. He then omits the reference to 'the day of vengeance of our God' in Isaiah 61.2, not because he wants to negate the reality of divine judgement, but because

---

9 Ringe, *Jesus ...*, p. 103.

10 Hanks, Thomas D, *God So Loved the Third World: The Biblical Vocabulary of Oppression*, Orbis Books, Maryknoll, NY, 1983, p. 99.

he wants to place 'all possible stress on the programmatic nature of the Jubilee Year for his own ministry of liberation.'[11]

The obvious difference between Hanks and Ringe is that whereas Hanks attributes the composite quotation from Isaiah 61 in Luke 4 to Jesus himself, Ringe attributes it to the Early Church. She is sceptical about the possibility of tracing this sermon to the actual ministry of Jesus, but believes it reflects some specific social, political and ecclesiastical contexts in the life of the Early Church.[12]

What can we say about this? Did Jesus attribute jubilary significance to his ministry, or was this the Early Church's doing? The solution to this dilemma is not an easy one, and we might not find a straightforward answer to it. Sharon Ringe puts it this way.

> Even when one has proceeded with the greatest possible care in identifying jubilee traditions in the Gospels, questions about the motives, intent, or purpose of the Gospel writers, the Early Church, or even Jesus himself cannot be answered with certainty. One simply cannot know for certain whether these traditions were incorporated because they are jubilee traditions, or because of particular points which they make (such as the proclamation of good news, or the declaration of *aphesis*).[13]

But, perhaps, we can say that the sermon in Nazareth reflects a tradition that goes back to an actual incident in Jesus' life, and not merely a Lucan construction intended to give his own version of Mark 6.1-6a. Then we may ask ourselves what the elements are in that tradition which proved to be of importance to the Early Church for a correct understanding of Jesus' ministry.

The quotation from Isaiah

If this passage was understood as a prophetic rendering of the jubilee traditions emphasising the reign of God as an eschatological reality, then what Jesus is saying here is that in his ministry the reign of God is being inaugurated. He is the one who has been anointed by the Spirit of God to

---

11 Hanks, *God So Loved ...*, p. 103.

12 Ringe, *Jesus ...*, p. 35.

13 Ringe, *Jesus ...*, p. 35.

set in motion God's reign. He is the herald who announces that God is drawing near and that this reality of God's reign changes every other reality: the poor, for a change, hear good news, the captives are promised release, the blind sight, and liberty is announced to those under the yoke of oppression.

By utilising a prophetic, rather than a legal text, Jesus is showing the eschatological and inclusive nature of his ministry. He is not just announcing the implementation of the Year of Jubilee for the people of Israel but rather announcing God's perpetual jubilee for all peoples, of which the historical jubilee was only a precursor, a shadow. As Dr Naim Ateek has said,

> God's jubilee, at long last, has come to be fulfilled in the coming of Jesus the messiah. It is now to be proclaimed not once every 50 years as was envisioned in the old jubilee concept in the Torah but as a perpetual jubilee that must become the pattern of daily life and practice of those who believe. People of faith should proclaim perpetual jubilee and should try to work constantly and persistently for its implementation. In other words, God is calling us to work for justice and liberty for all the oppressed people of the world.[14]

Jesus' affirmation concerning the scripture being fulfilled

Jesus is saying that this prophecy, born in the imagination of the visionaries who produced the Isaiah text, was being actualised in unprecedented ways. This can only be interpreted as his way of saying: 'Something new is happening here, something that is going to change the old order forever.' The Early Church understood Jesus' ministry as God's new and final word for humankind. Therefore it was interested in highlighting those traditions which would convey this idea.

This idea of the scriptures being fulfilled is reinforced by Luke 7.18-23, where Jesus, after having cured many people of a number of diseases (v. 21), answers the disciples sent by John to ask whether he was the one who was to come, by saying that, 'the blind receive their sight, the lame walk, the lepers are cleansed, the deaf hear, the dead are raised, the

---

[14] *Cornerstone,* Christmas 1997, p. 2.

poor have good news brought to them.' The present tense of all these verbs conveys the idea of continuous action in the present. The promises are being enacted, the reign of God has began!

Elijah and Elisha

The mention of the Elijah and Elisha traditions puts the emphasis on God's freedom to bless those whom God wills in the way that God wills.[15] The townspeople learn from Jesus' mouth that they do not hold a place of privilege in the fulfilment of God's promises. The Messiah has come for everyone, Jews and non-Jews. His mission transcends racial and ethnic barriers.

The people's wrath can then be interpreted as their astonishment at Jesus' daring rereading of Isaiah 61.1-2. The eschatological promises that were directed to Israel in the text of Isaiah are now universalised, and said to apply to any of God's children. God does not have a chosen people. Rather, God has chosen the whole human race to receive God's mercy and favour. The message thus understood ceased to be a promise, and became a threat for Jesus' audience: the poor to whom the good news would come, and the captives who would be set free, could be any of God's children, even some of those considered enemies. No wonder, then, that when they heard Jesus' reversal of the prophetic proclamation of Isaiah 61.1-2 they wanted to get rid of him in such a violent way. They considered him a false prophet.

In the Early Church such a teaching would warn believers of claiming ethnicity or first-hand knowledge of Jesus as grounds for privilege. It would legitimise the mission to the Gentiles, and it would also provide the Church with a programme for social action, following Jesus' concern for the poor and the outcast, in anticipation of the reign of God soon to arrive. The description of the early community's social practices narrated in Acts 4.32-37 seems to correspond to this belief.

Therefore, if we decide that the quotation of Isaiah 61.1-2 in Luke 4 reflects a tradition that goes back to an actual event in Jesus' ministry, but that its positioning in the Lucan context shows a reworking by the Early Church to fit some specific ecclesiological need, then we should ask ourselves, 'What are the chances that Jesus really intended to summon the nation as a whole to observe a jubilee year?' J H Yoder is one of the main proponents of this idea. He writes:

---

[15] Ringe, *Jesus ...*, p. 44.

> It is really a jubilee, conformed to the sabbatical instructions of Moses, that Jesus proclaimed in AD 26: a jubilee able to resolve the social problems in Israel, by abolishing debts and liberating debtors whose insolvency had reduced them to slavery. The practice of such a jubilee was not optional. It belonged to the precursors of the kingdom. Those who would refuse to enter this path could not enter into the Kingdom of God.[16]

N T Wright, in his *Jesus and the Victory of God*, has given three reasons why Jesus did not proclaim the need for a Jubilee Year. First, it is not clear that a Jubilee Year had ever been celebrated. Probably the Leviticus legislation was held more as an ideal than as a reality. Second, the fact that Jesus quotes from Isaiah rather than from Leviticus may suggest that he was interested, as was Isaiah, in the imagery, the symbolism of the jubilee rather than in the legislation itself. Third, we do not find such an agenda in the rest of Jesus' ministry. Actually, we find agendas that go further, beyond even the most radical social or cultural reform.[17]

Besides Luke 4.16-30, the other passage that clearly refers to Isaiah 61.1-2 is Luke 7.18-23/Matthew 11.2-6, where John the Baptist sends two of his disciples to ask Jesus whether he was indeed the one who was to come, or if they should wait for another. Sharon Ringe thinks that even though the passage shows that it has been edited by the Church (cf. 'Christ' in Matthew 11.2, and 'Lord' in Luke 7.19), the fact that Jesus does not answer John's question in a direct way, and the fact that John does not make any affirmation about Jesus, are proofs that the Early Church did not invent this story. It must have come from a real event in Jesus' life, just as the incident in the synagogue at Nazareth.[18]

There are many other passages in the Synoptic Gospels where these jubilee images are elaborated, but none of them represents a direct quotation from a jubilee tradition as Luke 4 and 7 do. Nevertheless, the fact that expressions like 'proclaiming good news to the poor' and 'the poor', as well as other expressions, such as 'release' or 'forgiveness', became part of the Church's confession about Jesus is important, because it shows how jubilee images were used to define Jesus' ministry from the beginning.

Consider, for instance, the image of 'forgiveness' of debts and

---

[16] Yoder, *The Politics of Jesus*, pp. 68-69.

[17] Wright, *Jesus and ...*, pp. 294-95.

[18] Ringe, *Jesus ...*, pp. 46-47.

'release' of slaves. The Septuagint translates this aspect of the jubilee proclamation with the words *aphiemi* and *aphesis.* These words, which convey in the Greek the idea of release from bonds, debts, or other legal requirements, are also used in the Septuagint to translate verbs of remission, verbs that express sin and guilt in relationship to God. By so doing, these verbs, which were previously associated with the secular world, are now being used in a religious context. Thus, the Greek words *aphiemi* and *aphesis* take on the meaning of forgiveness in a religious sense, and the vocabulary of forgiveness in the Hebrew scriptures is broadened beyond its primarily religious, cultic usage into a more contractual, covenantal usage.[19]

When we get to the New Testament we find that *aphiemi* and *aphesis* are the most common words to express forgiveness of sins (Matthew 6.14-15; 18. 21; Mark 2.5-10, etc.) but also forgiveness of monetary debts (Matthew 18.27,32) and release of captives (Luke 4.18). Even though ethical and cultic concerns can usually be distinguished, they cannot be separated. Sharon Ringe concludes, then, by saying that:

> Both are means of talking about the effect of the advent of God's reign in breaking the tyranny of evil in all its forms. In that context, 'release' is more than a metaphor for God's work of redemption and reconciliation, and the economic image of the cancellation of debts is not simply another way to speak of God's forgiveness of humankind. Rather, 'forgiveness' or 'release' in all arenas of human life is portrayed as one of the principal characteristics of humankind's encounter with God's reign.[20]

Jubilee and the reign of God

I do not believe that Jesus preached the Jewish Year of Jubilee, but rather something much more radical: the reign of God. Jesus was not announcing a specific, historical jubilee to be celebrated every fifty years, but a perpetual, eternal one. This new reality would affect not only Israel, but the whole world. And people's preparation for this new order would be an attitude of genuine conversion, a true turning to God, a true repentance.

---

[19] Ringe, *Jesus ...,* p. 65.
[20] Ringe, *Jesus ...,* p. 66.

> The time is fulfilled, and the kingdom of God has come near; repent, and believe in the good news (Mark 1.15).

The gospel as outlined by Jesus at the synagogue in Nazareth, rather than providing a blueprint for the reign of God, points at what happens whenever humankind encounters the fact of God's sovereignty.[21] It also constituted an invitation to people to join the proclaimer in the act of proclamation. For those who, like John the Baptist, were not sure if this really was God's *kairos*, the liberating acts seen in Jesus' ministry were to be enough proof that the reign of God had been set in motion.

The disciples first, and the early community later, are examples of people who decided to follow the proclaimer of the kingdom and became themselves proclaimers of good news to the poor. It has been suggested that, perhaps, Jesus expected his followers to live by the jubilee principle among themselves as a way of showing their belief that the kingdom of God was indeed at hand.[22] They were to forgive each other's debts and forgive each other's sins; they were not to accumulate wealth on earth, but rather were to be generous with each other, giving to the ones who asked from them, and lending to the ones who could not repay them. This lifestyle, marked by forgiveness and compassion, seems to have been essential for Jesus' followers, since the book of Acts describes the early community as doing precisely that.

But whoever reads the New Testament attentively will notice that this lifestyle of the Early Church did not continue for long. One reason is that as the Church became increasingly Gentile the relationship with Israel and its institutions lost historical, as well as ethnic continuity, and became a purely theological one. A second reason is that the need for a jubilee was not felt in the urban society of the Greek world. Thus, some of the images of the jubilee legislation—release of captives, forgiveness of debts, proclamation of good news to the poor—were reinterpreted in a world in which the provisions of the jubilee could not have been realised. This legislation made sense in a Palestinian, agricultural setting, but not in the cities of the Graeco-Roman world.

Therefore, a process of hellenisation and spiritualisation began to happen which took away from the jubilee vocabulary its socio-political bite. Forgiveness of debts became just forgiveness of sins; the captives to be released were those enslaved by sin; the poor to whom the good news

---

[21] Ringe, *Jesus ...*, p. 36.

[22] Wright, *Jesus and ...*, p. 295.

was proclaimed were the spiritually poor. When the Church realised that it would stay on in this world longer than initially expected, it began to build ideological walls around itself, and became more concerned with creeds, clergy, and canon, than with social ethics. Accordingly, the coming reign of God was connected with the *Parousia* (Second Coming) of Jesus Christ, which, in turn, was pushed into an indefinite future.

That is why it is important to go back to the original message of Jesus and the earliest recollection of it by the Church. I am not advocating for the reconstruction of Jesus' true, authentic words. All I am saying is that we have to read again the Gospels, especially the Synoptic Gospels. We have to take a second look at Jesus' message, and avoid being too influenced by later Christological readings. We have to be aware of centuries of Christian theology which have domesticated Jesus' radical message of liberation.

Jesus, the proclaimer of God's perpetual Jubilee

I believe that Jesus was a visionary, not a lawyer, a prophet, not a priest. He envisioned a society based on just human relations. He believed himself to be living at a boundary moment, a point of change from the old order to the new.[23]

I believe Jesus was a revolutionary, not a rebel, a revitaliser of the society of his time, not a maintainer of the *status quo*. But he was a shepherd—the 'Good Shepherd'—not a Zealot. His summary of the Law in the love principle included the jubilee provisions. In Jesus' mind, if you love God with all your heart, and your neighbour as yourself, is there a need for a jubilee year?

But Jesus was also a realist. He knew what was in the human heart. His radicalisation of the Law aims at showing the true intent of the Law. Just as divorce was a divine provision to protect women from excessive and unnecessary hurt so also the jubilee legislation was provided so people would not forget the poor. These laws were provided because of people's hardness of heart. 'But from the beginning it was not so,' said Jesus.

Therefore, Jesus' ethics is a return to the beginning, to God's

---

[23] Ringe, *Jesus ...*, p. 84.

original plan in creation. His preaching was taking place at that boundary moment between the old order and the new. Consequently, he saw himself as the messenger of God's eschatological age who stood at the threshold between two different orders. The old was passing away, the new was dawning.

Conclusion

I would like to suggest that as we re-consider the value and pertinence of the jubilee tradition as it is re-interpreted by Jesus and the New Testament writers, we should keep in mind the following points:

—Jesus preached at a boundary moment ... and so do we! That boundary moment is not chronologically 'bound', but it responds to the rhythms of the Spirit's liberating purposes. Jesus' eschatological awareness did not result in the historical establishment of God's reign, but it opened for many the possibility of true historical liberation. We can say, then, that this boundary moment happens even today '... whenever human institutions and designs to enable business as usual are met by the proclamation of God's reign.'[24] At this moment what is required from us is a change of allegiance from the old order to the new. But, like the man in the parable of the unforgiving servant of Matthew 18.23-35, who, even though he was forgiven a great debt, was not himself merciful toward his fellow servant, we can choose to live with double standards, and exclude ourselves from God's reign. God requires from those who have experienced mercy to be merciful.

—Jesus' radicalisation of the Law represents a return to God's original plan in creation. We should not try to re-establish a jubilee that is ethnically or religiously conditioned, but rather try to spread a jubilee mentality that is based on God's original intention for humankind. That is, as Mitri Raheb has said, '...that all human beings, no matter what their religion or nationality, are created in the image of God. To protect a human being's rights is therefore a divine law.'[25]

—Jesus' proclamation of the good news to the poor had deep political

---

[24] Ringe, *Jesus ...*, p. 97.

[25] Raheb, Mitri, *I Am a Palestinian Christian*, Fortress, Minneapolis, 1995, p. 44.

implications. John Howard Yoder sets out to test the hypothesis that 'the ministry and the claims of Jesus are best understood as presenting to hearers and readers not the avoidance of political options, but one particular sociopolitical-ethical option,'[26] and, as we discussed earlier, he believed Jesus was proclaiming a specific jubilee year. But even if we conclude, as we have, that Jesus was proclaiming something more final and more inclusive than a historical, Jewish jubilee, we can still see how his actions were considered politically dangerous. N T Wright has observed that anyone announcing the kingdom of God, but opposing an armed resistance, was engaging in a doubly serious political action. He was enraging not only the Romans but also those who gave allegiance to the resistance movement.[27]

—We need to re-appropriate the jubilee tradition from our own contexts. I believe in the power of symbols and images to convey truth, and generate change in people and in the institutions on which we build our lives. In that sense, Jesus' message is truly revolutionary, because it has the power to evoke those symbols that bring us to a new relationship with God, creation, and our fellow human beings. Such symbols as 'forgiveness of debts', 'release to the captives', 'sight to the blind', 'liberty to the oppressed', and 'proclamation of the acceptable year of the Lord', need to be embodied in concrete historical situations. The people of God around the world need to come to terms with the implications of these symbols in their particular social locations. And, especially, the vision, the dream, has to become incarnate in a concrete legislation, in a concrete historical project.

May God help us to be able to find the answers to these questions and, having found them, to act accordingly.

---

[26] Yoder, *The Politics of Jesus*, p. 11.
[27] Wright, *Jesus and* ..., p. 296.

ZIONISM AND THE BIBLE

Michael Prior

Whatever the intentions of its various supporters, Zionism is responsible for the dispossession, dispersion and humiliation of the indigenous Arab population of Mandated Palestine, west of the Jordan, over the last fifty years. While such devastation is by no means unique in the history of human civilisation, the Zionist colonisation does have distinctive features, both when measured against prevailing attitudes in our post-colonialist world and in terms of the resistance of the indigenous people.[1]

The critical role of the Bible

What is particularly striking from a moral perspective is the widespread support in the Western world which the Zionist enterprise enjoys. Whereas elsewhere the perpetrators of colonial plunder would be charged with war crimes and crimes against humanity, the Zionist conquest is widely judged to be a just and appropriate political accomplishment, and, in some quarters, is accorded unique religious significance. Much of the rationale for such benevolent appraisal of the Zionist colonial plunder derives from engagement with particular traditions of the Bible, and with a literalist interpretation of the biblical traditions of land and of some of its messianic texts. In most Western Christian and Jewish theological and religious circles the Zionist prize is viewed as being no more than what the Jewish people

---

[1] The establishment of the State of Israel in 1948 ran in the face of the trend towards the independence of indigenous peoples, signalled by the independence of India in 1947, and of some forty-nine African countries in the years after World War II. While many other peoples eventually shook off their colonisers' control, the indigenous Arab society in Palestine was destroyed, and was largely replaced by the influx of Jews from all over the world. Although the Palestinians resisted the colonisation of their land from the beginning, the last decade witnesses to how its leadership has capitulated to the colonial occupation *before* that occupation had been defeated and forced to leave. In the judgement of Edward Said, what the Oslo and subsequent agreements call 'compromise' is 'a massive abandonment of principles, the main currents of Palestinian history, and national goals' ('Preface', in Mikhail, Hanna, *Politics and Revelation. Mwardi and After*, Edinburgh University Press, Edinburgh, 1995, pp. vii-xv, p. vii).

deserve in virtue of the promises of God outlined in the Bible.

The link between the Zionist conquest and the Bible is reflected widely, whether in propagandistic claim of Ben-Gurion that the Bible is the 'Jews' sacrosanct title-deed to Palestine ... with a genealogy of 3,500 years,'[2] in the mainstream theology of the Jewish religious establishment, or in much Christian ecclesial and theological opinion. Indeed, some Christians see Zionism as the instrument of God promoting the ingathering of Jews, and, in such circles, anyone who opposes Zionism is considered to oppose God himself. The view that the Bible provides the title-deed for the establishment of the state of Israel and for its policies since 1948 is so pervasive, not only in Christian Zionist and Jewish Zionist circles but even within mainstream Christian Theology and university biblical studies, that the very attempt to raise the issue is sure to elicit opposition.

Western Christian support for the restoration of Jews to Palestine antedates Herzl's Zionism, and can be traced back to views which surfaced at the Reformation period. These views depended virtually solely on a literalist interpretation of some of the biblical traditions.[3] Ironically throughout the Reformation period, and right up to the emergence of political Zionism, Jews themselves viewed the biblical texts promoting a culture of restoration as requiring divine, rather than political intervention. The Orthodox establishment continued to hold to the traditional position for several more decades, while Reform Judaism rejected the notion of Jews as constituting a nation, and any special attachment to Palestine. Nevertheless, the ground had been laid in Reformed Europe, and later yielded a steady stream of supporting literature.

More recently Western Christian support for Zionism is facilitated by various forms of the Jewish-Christian dialogue. In promoting an asymmetry of responsibilities, this unique ecumenical pact infects the noble ideal of inter-religious discourse. With a virtual Orthodox Jewish veto on discussion of theological matters, much of the dialogue's energy focuses

---

2 *The Rebirth and Destiny of Israel*, Philosophical Library, New York, 1954, p. 100.

3 See Sharif, Regina S, *Non-Jewish Zionism. Its Roots in Western History*, Zed Press, London, 1983, for details from the past. More recently, successive Israeli governments have been quick to latch on to Zionist Christian circles whose ideology derives from an unique, literalist interpretation of apocalyptic and prophetic biblical texts. In line with the precedent of courting the support of Christian evangelicals established by Premiers Begin, Shamir and Rabin, in his recent visit to Washington Prime Minister Netanyahu attended a reception hosted by the Christian evangelicals. Afterwards, Revd Jerry Falwell pledged that he and the Southern Baptists would mobilise '200,000 evangelical pastors ... to go into their pulpits and use their influence in support of the State of Israel and the Prime Minister' (Martin Sieff, *Jewish Chronicle*, 30 January 1998, p. 3).

on support for Zionism. It does this by a crude process of fuelling guilt in contemporary Christians for sins for which they themselves have no responsibility, while ensuring that they will not intervene in an area for which they have some. With contemporary Christians wallowing in cheap guilt for the outrages committed against Jews in the past, and mute on the injustice perpetrated by Israel on the Palestinians in our own day, all moral response is suspended. Silence on the oppression of the Palestinians, in spite of the presence of overwhelming evidence, appears to be a compulsory element of the dialogue in order to maintain good relations between the two parties.

Invariably in such circles, consideration of the origins of Zionism and of the birth of the State of Israel betrays either ignorance, naiveté or dishonesty, and contradicts both the theory of Zionism and the reality of the expulsion of the Palestinians. Reflecting an irredentist benevolent Zionist interpretation of events, it distorts facts of history, omits core elements of the discourse, and makes claims that lack substance. While promoting ecumenical cosiness, it does little to advance truth and justice.[4] Silence in the face of contemporary violations of human dignity is unworthy of adherents of any worthwhile religion. It should not be tolerated by people concerned with the integrity of Judaism and Christianity, and with the relations between their believers. If we allow others to suffer, and even be killed without protesting, we become 'accomplices by omission'. Protesters against the virtual annihilation of Palestinian society must stand in the face of the cheap jibes, abuse, and the predictable, organised intimidation of such pro-Israeli lobbies.

Despite the shifting claims to the contrary and the protestations that Zionism was from the beginning a secular, and even anti-religious enterprise, the Bible is a *sine qua non* for the provision of alleged moral legitimacy. The Zionist claim 'to return' and expel 'the Canaanites' rests with the Bible, since there is no other convincing moral ground to support it. The expulsion of an indigenous people and their replacement by invading settlers is not a programme that commands moral approval in our day. However, a straightforward reading of the biblical narrative of 'Israelite origins' offers an example showing that an earlier, equivalent Israelite enterprise had not only alleged divine support, but was in fulfilment of the alleged express command of God. The Bible read at face value, then, provides not only a moral framework which transposes Jewish claims into a divinely sanctioned legitimacy, but postulates the taking possession of

---

4 The general tone of the discourse is reflected in Harrelson, Walter, and Randall M Falk, *Jews and Christians: A Troubled Family*, Abingdon, Nashville, 1990. See further, Prior, M, *Zionism and the State of Israel: A Moral Enquiry*, Routledge, London, 1999.

the Promised Land and the forcible expulsion of the indigenous population as the fulfilment of a biblical mandate. Without the Bible Zionism would be a discourse in the conquest mode, as against a moral one. While some religious Jews are embarrassed by the obvious conflict between the Bible's mandate and decent human behaviour, most of them ever do little more than bear guilt for their prudent silence.

Although Zionism was a secular ideology and enterprise from the beginning, and was bitterly opposed by the religious establishment, some of its proponents, when it suited their purposes, could point to the Bible in support of its achievement. In particular, the narratives of the promise of land to Abraham and his descendants and the execution of the promise in the conquest as narrated in the Book of Joshua were available. Although apologists for Zionism appeal to a number of other factors also (the *Shoah*, endemic antisemitism in Europe, etc.) there is no doubt that it is the appeal to the Bible that is the most convincing to the Western world, since its witness can be skilfully deployed to argue that the Zionist conquest is merely restoring the land to the Jews in accordance with the clear intentions of the God of the Christians as well as of the Jews.

The influence of the biblical narrative in the secular intentions of Zionism is reflected even in the 'father of Zionism', the religiously indifferent Theodor Herzl (1860-1904).[5] It was the testimony of the Bible above all which allowed him to insist that Jews world-wide constituted one people and a *distinctive nationality* (pp. 76-79), the solution of whose problem could be achieved only through the *restoration* of the Jewish state (p. 69). He insisted that 'Palestine is our ever-memorable historic home', and that its very name 'would attract our people with a force of marvellous potency' (p. 96). Herzl ended his pamphlet by promising that 'a wondrous generation of Jews will spring into existence. The Maccabeans will rise again.' Furthermore, fearing that the option of Jews settling in Uganda, discussed at length at the Sixth Zionist Congress at Basle (22-28 August 1903), might split the Zionist movement, Herzl emphasised that Uganda would only be a staging post to the ultimate goal of Palestine, and, lifting his right hand, he cried out, '*Im Yeshkakhekh Yerushalayim ...*' ('If I forget you, O Jerusalem, may my right hand wither'), quoting Ps 137.5.[6] Moreover, on the day of Herzl's burial Israel Zangwill compared him with Moses, who had been given only a sight of the Promised Land.

---

5 The page numbers refer to *The Jewish State*, Dover Edition, New York, 1988, a translation of Herzl's *Der Judenstaat* (1896).

6 Laqueur, Walter, *History of Zionism*, Holt, Rinehart and Winston, New York, Chicago, San Francisco, 1972, p. 129.

But all was not lost, since, after Moses, Herzl 'has laid his hands upon the head of more than one Joshua, and filled them with the spirit of his wisdom to carry on his work.'[7] The exploits of Joshua would be appealed to again.[8]

The changing face of Zionism

As an ideology, Zionism is difficult to tie down in a definition. Like a chameleon blending its colour with that of its changing environment, it is a most versatile ideology, capable of being adapted to diverse contexts.[9]

Labour and Revisionist Zionism

Out of the variety of conceptions of a Jewish state in the history of Zionist thought over the last hundred years, one can discern two contrasting emphases, which, since the foundation of the state, are reflected in the

---

[7] Zangwill, Israel, *Speeches, Articles and Letters of Israel Zangwill, Selected and Edited by Maurice Simon*, Soncino Press, London, 1937, pp. 131-32.

[8] US Televangelist Pat Robertson considered Israel's 1982 Israeli invasion of Lebanon to be a modern Joshua event, and urged American viewers to phone President Reagan offering encouragement to Israel's war. Moreover, according to a report in the *Washington Post*, on the night before the signing of the Declaration of Principles on the White House Lawn on 13 September 1993, President Clinton, fearing that his speech required more work, had not been able to sleep. He woke at 3.00 am and reread the entire Book of Joshua. The religious-political link was illustrated further when President Clinton introduced Prime Minister Rabin and President Arafat, and announced to the world that both people pledged themselves to a shared future, 'shaped by the values of the *Torah*, the Koran, and the Bible'. Clinton's address mixed Bible-based exhortation in the Baptist tradition with shrewd political manoeuvring. The late Premier Rabin's speech also referred to the Bible. One hopes that it was not the traditions of Clinton's nocturnal reading which would shape the shared future.

[9] I define Zionism as the movement founded to establish a state for Jews in Palestine, as outlined in Theodor Herzl's programme at the First Zionist Conference in Basle in 1897. Zionism has the quality of a rainbow ideology, with distinctive aspirations, sometimes mutually exclusive: to establish a utopian socialist society, a utopian religious society, a homeland for a renaissance of Jewish culture, a haven from oppression, a state in which Jews could rule themselves, and so on. Some formulations required the expulsion of the indigenous population, rather than aspired to co-existence with it on mutually agreed terms. While reflecting an awareness of the polychromatic character of the enterprise I focus on the impact which its triumphant form (the State of Israel) have had on the indigenous people.

two major streams of Israeli political life:[10] the Zionism of the Labour movement, and the Revisionist Zionism pioneered by Vladimir Jabotinsky (1880-1940) and represented today by the Likud party. While Labour aspires to establish a Jewish version of a European-style democratic socialist republic (with as few Arabs as are necessary to hew wood and draw water), Likud, true to its Revisionist roots, is more concerned with expanding the present boundaries, than with what kind of polity obtains within the state. But neither of these major strands manifests a distinctively religious complexion.

Forms of Religious Zionism

To these two one must now add a third tendency, broadly termed Religious Zionism, which has grown steadily since 1967, and has significantly influenced the Israeli polity ever since. The war of June 1967 came to the rescue of a jaded secular Zionism and helped to revive an old vision and identify a new set of priorities. The conquest of vast territories was achieved so spectacularly as to suggest, at least to those unaware of the military imbalance between the contending parties, some form of miraculous intervention. The scene was set for the realisation of another step in the capture of 'biblical Israel'.

In addition to its ideology being represented by the three avowedly religious parties,[11] its influence suffuses many other areas of the Israeli political mosaic. With respect to its expansionist ideals, Religious Zionism matches and sometimes exceeds even the Revisionist tendencies of the Likud and the parties of the secular Right. In general, the religious parties and other groups of Religious Zionism invest the Zionist enterprise with distinctively (messianic) redemptive significance, and view the establishment of the State of Israel as a critical stage in speeding up the advent of the Messiah. Since 1967 in particular Religious Zionism has

---

[10] I single out these two tendencies because of their popular support. One must remember, however, that there is an intense, ongoing inner-Jewish debate about the nature of Zionism and the state, and a very broad spectrum of opinion on the subject. Some of the ideological standpoints have sought electoral representation, while others have functioned as extra-parliamentary movements and opinion formers.

[11] Currently Shas has 10 MKs, the National Religious Party has 9, and United Torah Judaism has 4.

transposed the rhetoric of Zionism from having been a secular aspiration to create a state for Jews to the apocalyptic one of redeeming *Eretz Yisrael.* Even though the Zionist conquest in 1948 and the period since 1967 have been catastrophic for the indigenous Arab population, in the view of religious Jewish Zionists, and not a few foreign Christians, this is a small price to pay for the benefits of messianic redemption—especially when someone else is paying.

From occupation to universal redemption

I focus here on Religious Zionism because of its overt appeal to the Bible and because it constitutes a core element in the ideology of Zionist imperialist colonialism, whose supporters are a major obstacle to bringing about some accommodation with the Palestinian Arabs. Religious Zionists saw the war of 1967 as a turning point in the tortuous process of messianic redemption, and since then religious values have renewed the ideological drive and pioneering zeal of secular Zionism that had become 'routinised'. Without appeal to religious values, Greater Israel would be little different from the fruits of old fashioned colonial plunder. But clothed in the pure garment of religious rectitude, religious Zionism could appeal to its divine provenance and be fuelled by eschatological fervour. Its theological underpinning was provided by father and son Kook, and the *Merkaz HaRav*, the centre for the training of rabbis established by the elder Kook in 1921.

When Rabbi Avraham Yitzhak Kook (1865-1935) immigrated to Palestine in 1904 Orthodox Jewry was vehemently opposed to Zionism. They rejected it because of its secular inspiration and values, and regarded Zionists as heretics and sinners who presumed to usher in the messianic era without waiting for God. Rav Kook, however, saw secular Zionism as an instrument of God to further the messianic redemption not only of Jews, but of all humanity through Jewish restoration. He was convinced that God was leading Jews, whether secular or religious to return to the Holy Land, after which the nation would return to its faith. God was bringing about redemption through the 'Divinely inspired' Balfour Declaration that 'mirrored the Dawn of Salvation'. In Rav Kook's view, practical activities were inseparable from spiritual aspirations: stirrings 'down below' were a necessary preamble to evoking messianic grace 'from above'.[12]

It was only after his death that he became a cult hero and an idolised spiritual guide in the 1970s after the settler movement, *Gush Emunim*, claimed him as its forefather, and devoted itself to carrying out his legacy, under the authoritative guidance of his only son. Rabbi Zvi Yehuda Kook (d. 1982). The link between the two Kooks is the key to understanding *Gush Emunim.* While the father's view that the messianic era had begun was not taken seriously in his own day, his son now supported it with a programme of messianic political activism. The younger Kook saw in the rebirth of the Jewish state the first step towards the coming of the Messiah. All its institutions were means to a messianic end: its government and army were *Kadosh* (Holy).[13]

In the wake of the June 1967 War, nobody was more prepared to build on what they believed God had handed them than a group of rabbis who had come under the son's influence in the rabbi's centre. For them, the biblical texts constituted a living title-deed. Every advance of the army recalled the promise, 'Every place on which you set foot shall be yours,' anticipating some future time when 'Your territory shall extend from the wilderness to the Lebanon and from the River, the river Euphrates, to the Western Sea' (Deut 11.24). On the final day of the war some of these rabbis carried their mentor to the Western Wall, where Rav Kook declared, 'We announce to all of Israel, and to all of the world that by a divine command we have returned to our home, to our holy city. From this day forth, we shall never budge from here'. Since the dimensions of *Eretz Yisrael* were those of Genesis 15, rather than of pre-1967 Israel, Jews were obliged to fulfil the 'commandment of conquest', by settling in the whole land and defending Jewish sovereignty over it.[14] Since such settlement had redemptive and messianic meaning, and would mark a Jewish renaissance, the indigenous population could be pushed aside. It was a sacred activity, and those engaged in such a holy enterprise had

---

12 Many of the Rav's rich and varied writings were published only after his death in 1935, and some remain unpublished. The main ones are *The Letters of Rabbi Kook*, 4 vols. (1985), *The Offering of Rabbi Kook* (1985), *The Lights of the Holy* (1985), and *The Lights of Repentance* (1987), all published in Hebrew by Mosad HaRav Kook in Jerusalem.

13 Kook, Zvi Yehuda, *Torat Eretz Yisrael. The Teachings of HaRav Tzvi Yehuda HaCohen Kook.* Commentary by HaRav David Samson, based on the Hebrew *Sichot of HaRav Tzvi Yehuda,* Eng. trans. by Tzvi Fishman, Torat Eretz Yisrael Publications, Jerusalem, 1991, p. 353.

14 See Heilman, Samuel C, 'Guides of the Faithful: Contemporary Religious Zionist Rabbis', in Appleby, R Scott, *Spokesmen for the Despised. Fundamentalist Leaders of the Middle East*, University of Chicago Press, Chicago and London, 1997: 328-62, pp. 329-30 and 306-12.

'souls equal to the most righteous Jew'. Under their influence, the superficial nationalism of secular Zionism was giving way to a religious Zionism, issuing in the popular slogan, 'There is no Zionism without Judaism, and no Judaism without Zionism.' The settlements dotting the landscape of the West Bank in every direction are a testimony to the success of their enterprise. However, in addition to being a violation of international law and of the rights of the indigenes, they are a major obstacle to peace in the region.

For the indigenous inhabitants, participation in the universal redemption associated with 'Kookist' settlement of the land is somewhat down the line towards the eschaton. The example of Joshua's divine mission is eternally true: the Palestinians are *gerim* (non-Jewish residents) who according to the *Torah* are to be treated with tolerance and respect, but not more. More seriously, they are perceived to be an obstacle to the redemptive process. Since the universal principle of self-determination is no match for God's mandate, it does not apply in *Eretz Yisrael*. Hence, talk of human rights and demands for national self-determination are meaningless. Palestinians have three choices: to acknowledge the legitimacy of 'Kookist' Zionism and receive full civil rights; to obey the laws of the state without formal recognition of Zionism, and be granted the rights of resident aliens; or, to accept incentives—including the inducement of force—and emigrate.

In his later years, the younger Kook identified redemptive Israeli politics with a particular brand of nationalism: he vehemently opposed withdrawal from conquered territories, and equated settlement and annexation of the Occupied Territories with truth, justice and religious fulfilment.[15] The new Religious Zionism has given Political Zionism an opportunity to survive the erosion which has been the fate of so much of the political idealism of the 19th century (e.g., communism and socialism).

In addition to Labour Zionism which attempts to justify its achievement in the stereotypical language of colonialists, and Kookist Religious Zionism which veils it in the rhetoric of eschatological redemption, there is a 'moderate Religious Zionism' which tries to have it both ways. While its proponents pay lip service to Western post-colonial values, they bypass the foundational injustice done to the Palestinians, and accord the establishment of the state a religious significance. There is no shortage of silver-tongued Jews, usually of North American provenance,

---

[15] See Aran, Gideon, 'The Father, the Son, and the Holy Land: The Spiritual Authorities of Jewish-Zionist Fundamentalism in Israel', in Appleby, R Scott, *Spokesmen for the Despised*, pp. 294-327.

who, while shying away from according redemptive qualities to the State of Israel, nevertheless clothe the Zionist enterprise in the garment of piety.

During my tenure as Visiting Professor in Bethlehem University, and Scholar-in-Residence in Tantur Ecumenical Institute (1996-97) I was treated a number of times to the special pleading of silver-tongued, invariably American Jews clothing Zionism in the garment of piety. In the estimation of Professor David Hartman, for example, it marks the high point of biblical spirituality in that its secularity brought new energies to Jewish life, unleashing its human capacities to influence the whole of life, and not just the religious aspect which Rabbinic spirituality focused on. Zionism was a great Liberation Movement, restoring the legacy of biblical spirituality in the modern world.[16] When questioned by a Palestinian as to whether covenantal sharing would include Jabal Abu Ghneim, Hartman retorted that Jews have the right to build anywhere in their Jerusalem. I suggested to Hartman that Zionism, both in its rhetoric in history and in its practice, was not an ideology of sharing, but one of displacing. When pressed on the moral issue of the expulsion of the indigenous Arab population he took refuge in the litany of Zionist propaganda: Zionism never intended to disturb the Arabs; what happened was only the result of having been attacked by the Arab nations in 1948; the real problem was that the Arabs had not welcomed Jews back to their homeland, etc. To clinch his argument, he reminded the audience that great developments in history sometimes require initial destruction: the USA's defeat of totalitarianism was preceded by the displacement of the Indians.

Conclusion

The Jewish religious establishment, although late in embracing Zionism, today fully supports its achievement. What others perceive as old-fashioned, 19th-century colonialist plunder has been metamorphosed into the eschatological 'redemption of the land' through the hands of millions of Jews who have ascended to *Eretz Yisrael.* The civic religion of Jewish nationalism has been refracted into a veritable Jewish religious nationalism,

[16] 'The Future of Religious Zionism' was the title of the Tantur Public Lecture delivered by Professor Hartman on 6 March 1997, from the podium of Tantur Ecumenical Institute for Theology, situated just across the valley from Jabal Abu Ghneim, and above the checkpoint which cuts off Arab Jerusalem from its hinterland in Bethlehem, Beit Jala and Beit Sahour.

which has displaced the high ideals of secular, universalist democratic values, and substituted in their place a distinctive religious nationalism which is reminiscent of fascism and totalitarianism. The Bible, read in a naive literalist fashion, provides the moral foundation for such a metamorphosis.

The Bible and ethnic cleansing

Let us review some of the traditions of the books of Exodus, Deuteronomy and Joshua. The Book of Exodus portrays Yahweh as having compassion on the misery of his people, and as willing to deliver them from the Egyptians, and bring to a land flowing with milk and honey (Exod 3.7-8). But the biblical text notes that the promised land belongs to 'the Canaanites, the Hittites, the Amorites, the Perizzites, the Hivites, and the Jebusites'.[17] Manifestly, while the promised land of the narrative flowed with milk and honey, it had no lack of indigenous peoples. The conventional use of the Exodus model of liberation, whether in the Christian liturgy, or in the works of liberation theology, does not rise to the challenge of reading the narrative 'with the eyes of the Canaanites'.[18] Combining the Exodus from Egypt with the *Eisodus* (entry) into the land of the Canaanites and others, as the narrative requires, the biblical paradigm would more appropriately justify the behaviour of the *conquistadores* of Latin America, than support the indigenous population.[19]

In the narrative of the Book of Deuteronomy, after the King of Heshbon refused passage to the Israelites, Yahweh gave him over to them, and they captured and utterly destroyed all the cities, killing all the men, women, and children (Deut 2.33-34). The fate of the King of Bashan was

---

[17] See the discussion of the ambivalence of the Exodus paradigm in my *The Bible and Colonialism. A Moral Critique*, Sheffield Academic Press, Sheffield, 1997, pp. 273-84. As one of many examples from liberation theology, the title page of Esther and Mortimer Arias' study, *The Cry of My People. Out of Captivity in Latin America*, Friendship Press, New York, 1980 reproduces Exod 3.7-8, but ends with, 'a land of milk and honey ...'

[18] In *The Bible and Colonialism* I deal with the liturgical censoring of the offensive genocidal traditions and the naive use of the Exodus paradigm by liberation theologians (pp. 273-84).

[19] In an essay written in 1917, Ben-Gurion considered Zionist settlers to be 'a company of conquistadores', conquering, rather than merely working the land (*The Rebirth and Destiny of Israel*, 1954, p. 9). He compared their efforts with those of the European

no better (Deut 3.3). We learn how the invaders are to behave religiously:

> When Yahweh your God brings you into the land that you are about to enter and occupy, and he clears away many nations before you—the Hittites, the Girgashites, the Amorites, the Canaanites, the Perizzites, the Hivites ... and when Yahweh your God gives them over to you and you defeat them, then you must utterly destroy them. Make no covenant with them and show them no mercy ... Break down their altars, smash their pillars, hew down their sacred poles, and burn their idols with fire. For you are a people holy to Yahweh your God; Yahweh your God has chosen you out of all the peoples on earth to be his people, his treasured possession (Deut 7.1-11; see also 9.1-5; 11.8-9, 23, 31-32).

In the rules for the conduct of war, when a besieged town surrenders, all its inhabitants shall serve at forced labour; if not, the Israelites shall kill all its males, and take as booty the women, the children, livestock, and everything else in the town (Deut 20.11-14). The narrative presents 'ethnic cleansing' as not only legitimate, but as required by the divinity:

> But as for the towns of these peoples that Yahweh your God is giving you as an inheritance, you must not let anything that breathes remain alive. You shall annihilate them —the Hittites and the Amorites, the Canaanites and the Perizzites, the Hivites and the Jebusites—just as Yahweh your God has commanded, so that they may not teach you to do all the abhorrent things that they do for their gods, and you thus sin against Yahweh your God (Deut 20.16-18).

The book ends with Moses' sight of the promised land before he dies (Deut 34.1-3). Although Moses was unequalled in his deeds, he left a worthy successor, Joshua, who, after Moses had laid his hands on him,

---

settlement in America, in which the white Europeans fought against 'wild nature and wilder redskins' (p. 6). For his part, Weizmann preferred the models of the French *colons* in Tunisia, and the British settlers in Canada and Australia, as well as the settlers in South Africa (*Trial and Error: The Autobiography of Chaim Weizmann*, Harper and Row, New York, 1949, pp. 191, 27).

was full of the spirit of wisdom (Deut 34.4-12).

The Book of Joshua presents its hero as the divinely-chosen successor of Moses, who is destined to complete his work (Josh 1). The first part (2.1-12.24) describes in epic style the conquest of the land, concentrating on the capture of a few key cities, and their fate in accordance with the laws of the holy war. After its wall had collapsed, all the men and women (excepting Rahab's family), oxen, sheep, and donkeys of Jericho were slaughtered, and Joshua pronounced a curse on anyone who would try to rebuild the city (Josh 6.21-27). The marauding party moved on to Ai at Yahweh's command, to do to it what was done to Jericho: not one of the twelve thousand inhabitants survived or escaped, and Joshua burned it, and made it forever a heap of ruins (Josh 8.2, 19-29). The Israelite elders complained at the lapse in fidelity to the mandate to destroy all the inhabitants of the land when the Gibeonites were to be spared, to become 'hewers of wood and drawers of water for all the congregation' (Josh 9.21-27). Chapter 10 describes the campaign in the south, and chapter 11 that in the north, in each case ensuring the rigorous enforcement of the ban (*herem*). The author summarises Joshua's destruction of everything that breathed, as Yahweh commanded (Josh 10. 40-43). Chapter 11 describes the northern campaign. Israel left no one remaining: Joshua took all the land, utterly destroying its inhabitants (Josh 11.1-23). The whole achievement is summed up: Yahweh gave to Israel all the land that he swore to their ancestors he would give them (Josh 21.43-45).

A straightforward reading of these traditions presents God as demanding, and not merely sanctioning the genocide of the indigenous population of the land. It is widely, if naively assumed that these biblical texts narrate what happened in the past. Moreover, because of the religious authority of the Bible we find that many readers approve of the alleged behaviour of God who mandates genocide. Moreover, in addition to presenting God as demanding that the land of Canaan flow with the blood of its inhabitants, as well as with milk and honey,[20] these traditions have fuelled virtually every form of Western colonialism, including the colonisation of Palestine in our own time.

The contradiction between what some claim to be God's intentions and ordinary civilised behaviour, poses the question as to whether God is a chauvinistic, nationalistic and militaristic xenophobe. What does

[20] I chose *A Land flowing with Milk, Honey and People* as the title of the 1997 Lattey Lecture, which I delivered at Cambridge University on 26 November. The text is published by the Von Hügel Institute, St Edmund's College, Cambridge, and appears also in *Scripture Bulletin* 1998: 2-17.

one do with these traditions that portray God as gloating over the destruction of the crown of his creation, and what does one do in the realisation that they have been deployed as a blunt instrument of oppression? One wonders to what extent the Book of Deuteronomy, the Book of Joshua, and, in particular, the Book of Esther may have contributed to the world view of Dr Baruch Goldstein and Yigal Amir. And what influence did the reading of the Bible have on a number of rabbis who insisted that any Jewish leader who would give back land should be killed?[21] And these are merely the vulgar tip of the iceberg of religious Zionism for whom the biblical mandate justifies the displacement of the indigenous population. Although the zealotry of the religious nationalist movement in Israel offends the liberal views to which Western society has become accustomed, they are in strict conformity with the ideals of certain traditions in the Bible.

Towards a solution: a moral reading of the Bible

I can only indicate here some ways forward for a moral reading of the biblical narratives we have discussed. For Palestinian Christians, biblical hermeneutics, and the relation between the Old and New Testaments are not mere matters of interesting speculation. Palestinian theologian Canon Naim Ateek sharply focuses the problem with two questions: how can the Old Testament be the Word of God, and how can a Palestinian Christian read it in the light of its use to support Zionism?[22] Both he and the Latin Patriarch of Jerusalem, Monsignor Michel Sabbah, themselves victims of Zionist colonialism, provide some guidelines. They search for a hermeneutic of the Bible that will be valid both biblically and theologically, and they find it in the person of Jesus Christ.[23] Ateek insists that if a passage fits in with what one knows of God through Christ, it is valid and authoritative, and, if not, it is invalid. He detects in the later Prophets, and more especially in Jonah, greater emphasis on the universalism of God, and sees this third

---

[21] See Hertzberg, Arthur, 'The End of the Dream of the Undivided Land of Israel', in *Journal of Palestine Studies* 25 (1996): 35-45, p. 37.

[22] Ateek, Naim Stifan, 'A Palestinian Perspective: The Bible and Liberation', in Sugirtharajah, R S (ed.), *Voices from the Margin: Interpreting the Bible in the Third World*, SPCK, London, 1991: 280-86, p. 283. See also his *Justice and Only Justice. A Palestinian Theology of Liberation*, Orbis, Maryknoll, NY, 1989, pp. 77-78.

[23] Sabbah, Michel, *Reading the Bible Today in the Land of the Bible*, Latin Patriarchate, Jerusalem, 1993, pp. 25-31.

strand raised to a new intensity in the universalism of Jesus and the New Testament. On that basis, he judges the Zionist movement to be a retrogression to most elementary and primitive forms of the concept of a tribal God.[24]

In his Pastoral Letter, written only a couple of months after the Rabin-Arafat handshake at the White House in 1993, Latin Patriarch Sabbah discusses the problems of the Old Testament for Palestinian Christians for whom it is an integral part of faith and religious heritage. In general he allows those passages which abhor violence to correct those which promote it, and rejects the notion of a 'holy war' and of any kind of violence which seeks justification in the biblical text (pars. 44-46).

Of course, Christians are accustomed to reading the Old Testament in the light of the life and paschal mystery of Christ. Under the influence of the Holy Spirit, they recognise in the New Testament the fulfilment of the Old Testament. The Christian vision redefined the biblical concepts of election and covenant.[25] Although this modality of reading the Old Testament—seeking its 'spiritual sense' in the light of its movement towards Christ, the completion of the Law—reduces the impact of the more embarrassing traditions of the Old Testament concerning occupation and war, it is not satisfactory, especially when one insists on the divine provenance of the whole Bible and of each of its parts.

Although the allegorical method employed by the Fathers of the Church is very much out of vogue today, it represented one way of confronting texts which were scandalous. Another mode of dealing with the unacceptable elements in the biblical tradition is to assert that 'the Bible reflects a considerable moral development, which finds its completion in the New Testament.' The writings of the Old Testament contain certain 'imperfect and provisional' elements (Vatican II's *Dei Verbum* 15), which the divine pedagogy could not eliminate right away.[26]

In its liturgy, the Roman Catholic Church employs another means of dealing with scandalous biblical texts. When it comes to the land traditions of the Bible, one observes that the liturgy deals with the problematic of divinely mandated ethnic cleansing by a combination of omission of unsuitable narratives, or by excision of offending verses.[27]

---

[24] *Justice and Only Justice*, pp. 80-82, 101.

[25] See Prior, Michael, *Jesus the Liberator. Nazareth Liberation Theology (Luke 4.16-30)*, Sheffield Academic Press, Sheffield, 1995, pp. 48-60, 141-48.

[26] Pontifical Biblical Commission, *The Interpretation of the Bible in the Church*, St Paul Books & Media, Boston, 1993, pp. 113-14.

[27] See Prior, *The Bible and Colonialism*, pp. 268-74.

The view that the Bible can be understood in a straightforward way—a popular tenet of the Protestant Reformation—must be abandoned, since it produces erroneous interpretations. It concludes that the narratives which purport to describe the past are in fact accurate records of it; that is, that their literary form is historiography. Moreover, at the other end of the chronological scale, those texts which speak of the future are customarily considered to be fulfilled in a literalist fashion; that is, their literary form is considered to be prophecy in the sense of foretelling the details of the future. These two common misperceptions, springing from a failure to appreciate the distinctive literary forms—of legend, fabricated myths of the past, prophecy and apocalyptic, etc.—are the source of the most obvious excesses of biblical literalism, which continue to have harmful social consequences.

Modern scholarship and the biblical narratives

Happily, there is a way of reading the texts which reduces the injury to sensitive consciences. This mode takes seriously the different literary genres and contexts of the texts, and the intentions of the human authors. Biblical scholarship has shifted from viewing much of the biblical narrative of the past as simple history to concentrating on its authors as historiographers, whose reconstruction of the past reflected their own religious and political ideologies.

The questions concerning what, or whether God's promise of land to an Abraham and his descendants actually happened are of critical importance. There is a virtual consensus that the patriarchal narratives of the Book of Genesis do not record events of the patriarchal period, but are retrojections into a past about which the writers knew little and reflect the authorial intentions at the period of composition. For that reason, it is unacceptable to cleave to the view that God made the promise of progeny and land to Abraham after the fashion indicated in Gen 15. To abandon one's attachment to the historicity of the events of the narrative in the light of compelling contrary evidence is not to forsake belief.

We have seen that the Exodus narrative poses particular difficulties for any reader who is neither naive nor amoral. It is the entrance *(Eisodus)* into the land of milk and honey which keeps the hope of the wandering Israelites alive. It is high time that Christians faced into the two-sidedness of the Exodus motif, and read the narrative with sensitivity to the innocent third party about to be exterminated, even if they cannot quite bring themselves to read the text 'with the eyes of the Canaanites'.

Readers of the Book of Deuteronomy should not forget that the dream of colonisers invariably exacts a nightmare for the indigenous population. They should not be seduced by the clothing of genocidal conquest in the garment of religious language, insisting that the land was not stolen from its original inhabitants but came into the possession of the Israelites 'by the grace of God'. It is no small comfort to be rescued from a literalist reading of Deuteronomy, since such a reading predicates a god who shares the predictable dispositions of a ghetto community in an exclusivist, ethnicist, xenophobic and militaristic fashion.

Although modern biblical scholarship is united in concluding that the narrative of the five books, Genesis to Deuteronomy, does not correspond to what actually happened, it is not acceptable to allow the narratives to escape an evaluation based on criteria of morality, especially in the light of the use to which they have been put.

There is virtual unanimity among scholars that the model of tribal conquest as narrated in Josh 1-12 is untenable. Leaving aside the witness of the Bible, we have no evidence that there was a Hebrew conquest. Moreover, there is in effect a scholarly consensus that the biblical narratives which describe the conquest-settlement period come from authors writing many centuries later than the 'events' described (whether in the exilic, or post-exilic periods), who had no reliable information about that distant past. No amount of special pleading is sufficient to justify the classification 'history' for the biblical narrative of Israelite origins. History proper must be distinguished from a series of ideologically motivated assertions about the past.

The Exodus-Settlement accounts reflect a particular genre, the goal of which is to inculcate religious values of a particular group at the time of composition, rather than merely present empirical facts of history. The modern historian must distinguish between the actual history of the peoples and the history of their self-understanding. The archaeological evidence points in an altogether different direction from that suggested by Josh 1-12. It suggests a sequence of periods marked by a gradual and peaceful coalescence of disparate peoples into a group of highland dwellers whose achievement of a new sense of unity culminated only with the entry of the Assyrian administration. There was neither invasion from outside, nor revolution within.

Moreover, the 'Israel' of the period of the biblical narrative represented a multiplicity of 'ethnic' identities, reflecting the variety of provenances in the Late Bronze-Iron Age transition, and that brought about by three waves of systematic, imperial population transfer and admixture (Assyrian, Babylonian and Persian). The predication of Israelite 'ethnic' distinctiveness prior to the Persian period is illusory, and the unity of the biblical 'children of Israel' is a predilection of the biblical authors, rather than the reality reflecting a commonality of ethnic identity or communal experience.[28]

The contemporary needs of the final redactors of the biblical narrative determined and dominated their ideological stance. If we excuse the biblical writers for their misrepresentation of the past on the basis of their paraenetic motives for their own circumstances, we ought not to be equally indulgent with theologians and Church-Synagogue people for whom the evidence of what happened in the past is more reliable. The legendary account of Josh 1-12 offers no legitimising paradigm for land plunder in the name of God, or by anyone arrogating to himself His authority. Indeed, the extra-biblical evidence promotes a respect for the evolution of human culture, rather than for a process that can deal with adjustment to changed circumstances only by way of violent destruction.

While generations of religious people have derived both profit and pleasure from the retelling of the biblical stories, victims of the colonialist plunder such as the Palestinians are likely to be less sanguine in their attitude to the texts, and would welcome any attempt to distinguish between the apparent ethnocentricity of the God of Genesis-Kings, and the paranaetic and political intentions of authors writing much later.

Conclusion

As we have seen, the biblical claim of the divine promise of land is integrally linked with the claim of divine approval for the extermination of the indigenous people. It is assumed widely that its literary genre is history, even though this view runs in the face of all serious scholarly comment. These land traditions pose fundamental moral questions, relating to one's understanding of the nature of God, of His dealings with humankind, and of human behaviour. They have been deployed in support of barbaric behaviour in a wide variety of contexts for close on two thousand years. All too frequently the ideological underpinning for European colonialism is traced back to biblical paradigms of 'ethnic cleansing' and 'belligerent

---

28 See Thomas L Thompson's 'Hidden Histories and the Problem of Ethnicity in Palestine', in Prior, Michael (ed.), *Western Scholarship and the History of Palestine*, Melisende, London, 1998, pp. 23-39.

settler colonialism', the legitimisation of which have the authority of Sacred Scripture. The communities which have preserved and promulgated those biblical traditions must shoulder some of the responsibility for what has been done in conformity with the values contained within them.

Altogether the two stages of Zionist achievement, 1948 and 1967, cast a dark cloud over the aspirations of the ethnocentric dream of 19th-century Jewish nationalist colonialists. The rhetoric of the sacral discourse of the achievement of Zionism, which since 1967 has been transposed from the secular aspiration of Zionism to create a state for Jews to the apocalyptic one of redeeming *Eretz Yisrael,* is undermined by the reality of the catastrophe for the indigenous population. Redemption of *Eretz Yisrael* has required 'the spilling of the blood' of the indigenous Palestinian population—in most contexts, however, 'spilling the blood' of the other is better described as atrocity, rather than redemption.

What is most distressing from a moral and religious perspective is that the major ideological support for Zionist imperialism and the principal obstacle to treating the indigenous people with respect come from religious circles for whom the biblical narratives of land, understood in a literalist fashion, are normative. This was seen at its starkest in the assassination of Premier Rabin by a religious zealot acting in God's name.

The alignment of religious mythology with aggressive and militant nationalism has resurrected a type of religious piety that had been dormant since the Bar Kochba revolt of 135 AD. Since the entry of *Gush Emunim* and the late Rabbi Kahane's *Kach* into the body politic of Israel a new type of holiness has developed, propelled by some of the more ignoble elements of the religious tradition, particularly those underpinned by a naive-literalist reading of the land traditions of the Bible, especially of the book of Joshua. Sadly, this extreme interpretation has infected virtually the whole body of the Orthodox Jewish establishment, in Israel and abroad, and is supported by many Christians and much of Christian theology. The potentially humanising function of religion, through its association with a form of nationalism that was ineradicably colonialist and imperialist, has been corrupted, and a naive-literalist interpretation of the biblical narrative is the source of this corruption.

From a religious perspective the 'transfer' of the indigenous population, which the Zionist enterprise required, was a small price to pay for 'scaling the wall', and foreshortening the coming of the Messiah. In the spirit of contemporary moral discourse, it is a matter of concern that religious Jews have little regard for the indigenes who have paid the price for the establishment of Israel. But then, neither did Joshua in the biblical narrative. The cultural Zionist, Ahad Ha'am, saw dark clouds in the future: as early as 1913, the behaviour of Zionists towards the Palestinians made him fear for the future if Jews ever came to power. In a letter to a settler in Palestine, he wrote 'If this be the "Messiah": I do not wish to see his coming.'[29]

[29] In Smith, Gary, *Zionism, the Dream and the Reality*, Harper and Row, New York, 1974, p. 32.

FIFTY YEARS AFTER 1948: A UNIVERSAL JUBILEE?

Rashid Khalidi

As might be expected, the fiftieth anniversary of the establishment of Israel is being treated as an occasion for universal jubilation, whether in Israel, in the American Jewish community, in the American political sphere, or among world leaders who have been involved in symbolic celebrations of the event.

It should surprise no one that the devastating impact of the events of 1948 on the Palestinian people has been generally forgotten in the rush to observe the fiftieth birthday of Israel. Indeed, this latest episode fits well into the larger pattern of the repression of history which, since the beginning, has characterised the struggle between the two peoples, each trying to come into being at the expense of the other. Such a pattern was natural given that this was a struggle to establish a Jewish state in a land with an Arab majority, and to impose the fact of Israel's existence on the stubborn reality of Palestinian people-hood in Palestine. While Israelis and their friends have much to celebrate in 1998, which marks their victory in this struggle, Palestinians and those who know their history have much to mourn. For them, the fiftieth anniversary of Israel's establishment marks what since 1948 has been universally known in Arabic as *Al-Nakba*—the catastrophe—meaning the disappearance of Arab Palestine in 1948.

The year 1948 has many meanings for Palestinians. It means the year in which they lost their country. As the entity called Palestine disappeared, for several decades the Palestinians' hopes for self-determination and statehood receded. It means the year in which about 750,000 of the total Palestinian population of 1.4 million became refugees, some fleeing the violence and chaos of war, others driven out of their homes by the forces of the nascent Israeli state. Of these, some ended up in refugee camps, although the majority of them have since left the camps over the past two and a half generations, achieving prosperity, mobility and success elsewhere. It means the year in which the two cities with the largest Arab populations in Palestine, Jaffa and Haifa, the centres of the country's Arab economic and intellectual life, together with many other cities and towns, and a total of 418 villages, were overrun and emptied of most of their Arab inhabitants. It means the year in which the vast bulk of Palestine's land and huge amounts of other property passed out of the hands of the country's Arab population and into that of the new state of Israel. Finally, it means the year in which the Palestinians disappeared from the world stage as a people, instead becoming a 'refugee problem', losing their voice to the Arab regimes, which purported to speak for them, until the Palestinians wrested back the right to represent themselves in the 1960s.

Clearly, Palestinians have little cause to celebrate anything in 1998. Indeed, it marks a collective trauma in their national history of the order of Sedan in 1870 for France, or Pearl Harbour in 1941 for Americans. Of course, both France and the United States eventually turned the tables, and overcame the humiliation of defeat on the battlefield. This is highly unlikely, to say the least, in the Palestinian case. In this respect, the trauma of the Palestinians is much more akin to that of the Armenians and the Kurds, who, like the Palestinians, were victims of brutal campaigns of what we have learned to call ethnic cleansing. For these two peoples, to the injury of losing their respective national homelands, and with them the prospect of an independent national existence, was added the insult of decades of non-recognition of the hurt which had been done to them. The denial that the Armenians were the victims of genocide, and the curtain of silence drawn over several generations of repression of the Kurds by three different Middle Eastern governments, those of Iraq, Turkey and Iran, constitute close parallels to what has happened to the Palestinians.

For the Palestinians, this non-recognition of their national agony has been in some ways the unkindest cut of all. Not only did they correctly feel that they were the victims in 1948, losing their country, most of their property, and seeing 13,000 of their fellow citizens killed. (It is worth noting parenthetically that 6,000 Israelis died in the conflict, and in each case these death tolls amounted to about 1 per cent of the respective total populations. The differences were that most of the Palestinians killed were civilians, while most of the Israelis were combatants, and, most importantly, that the Israelis won the war, got their nation-state, and ended up with all that property.) Beyond this, because the Palestinians were the victims of victims, and were defeated and dispossessed by the survivors of the modern era's greatest human atrocity, the Holocaust, their own suffering was forgotten or ignored. Even worse, as the history came to be written, they were depicted as the villains of the piece, the latest incarnation of a sequence of tormentors who have persecuted the Jewish people throughout their history.

In light of the enormity of the evil done to the Jews—albeit elsewhere and at the hands of others—the specificity of Palestine, of what had actually happened in this small Mediterranean country in the years leading up to 1948, quickly faded in the international imagination. This specificity was replaced by a narrative in which Israel and the Jewish people figured predominantly, and in which the centrepiece was not the tragedy of the Palestinians, but rather the greatest trauma in Jewish history, and one of the greatest in modern human experience: the Holocaust. This powerful narrative, which described what was happening in Palestine in terms of Jewish national redemption and resurrection, firmly reoriented Jewish history on a completely new axis, with the birth of Israel serving as the bright counterpoint to the black horror of what had happened in the death-camps of Europe only a few years before. In this grand scheme of things, the Palestinians could only be an annoying complication, to be written out of the history, painted out of the pictures, the names of hundreds of their ancestral villages erased as new Hebrew names were concocted or resurrected, and their very name and that of their country becoming almost embarrassing epithets in polite company.

As if all of this were not enough, an insidious process of blaming the victims ensued, ensuring that even if a few inconvenient facts about what had happened in 1948 did come out, they could be laid at the door of the Palestinians themselves, or of their fellow Arabs. Thus the scandalous canard that 'their leaders told them to leave' was concocted, which assiduous research has shown to have been an essentially false story devised and propagated by Israeli apologists, and which untold multitudes in the West have come to believe to be gospel truth in the intervening decades. Thus, we had the self-delusion and comforting argument that while the Zionist leadership was willing to share Palestine and live in peace with the Arabs before 1948, it was the Arabs who refused accommodation, started the war, lost it, and deserved all the consequences. From this premise followed logically the conclusion that 1.4 million Palestinians and their descendants unto the third generation and beyond somehow deserved everything that happened to them in 1948 and afterwards because of the sins, or the stupidity of their leaders.

Like all successful big lies, each of these embodied some element of truth, however small. Thus, in beleaguered Haifa in the spring of 1948, some Arab League representatives did tell the population to leave, although other Arab leaders told them to stay. In fact, the Arab leadership all over the rest of the country futilely tried to keep the Palestinian population from fleeing their homes. They did this as the refugee tide turned into a flood as defeat turned into rout in Spring of 1948 under the hammer blows of Plan Dalet. This was the Zionist master plan for the conquest of the coastal strip, including Jaffa and Haifa, and other key strategic regions of the country, which was implemented before the Mandate ended on 15 May 1948.

Thus, while a very few important individuals of integrity and courage, like Judah Magnes and Martin Buber, sincerely called for sharing Palestine with the Arabs, the hard pragmatists who led the Labour Zionist parties, like Ben-Gurion, and their even harder rivals among the Revisionists, like Jabotinsky and Begin, knew from at least the 1930s onwards that this was a fight to the finish over who would dominate the country. These leaders intended to win the whole country for the Jews exclusively, and knew from the mid-1940s onwards that the big battalions were on their side.

By the time the Arab armies entered Palestine on 15 May 1948, the miserably disorganised Palestinians had been crushed by the victorious military forces of the nascent Jewish state, which had already turned into refugees perhaps half of the 750,000 Palestinians who ultimately fled their homes. The Palestinians and the Arab states were hamstrung by crippling internal divisions and appallingly bad leadership at the local and national levels. This is not to speak of scrupulously respected secret commitments to restrict the sphere of action of his forces made to the Zionist leadership before and after 15 May by King Abdullah, who controlled the two best Arab armies in the field, Jordan's Arab Legion and the Iraqi contingent. There is much still to be told of the events of 1948, and little of it will reflect favourably on any of the actors on the Arab side.

The 1948 war was nonetheless a closely fought affair, at least at the outset, and was very costly to the new state of Israel. Coming in the wake of the Holocaust, the losses which the nascent state of Israel incurred were particularly painful. But these losses, combined with the sweet intoxication of victory as a new Jewish national polity arose in the ancestral homeland of the Jews, and with the vindication of the central premises of Zionism which the atrocities of the Nazi era appeared to provide, blinded Israelis and those who sympathised with them to the losses involved in the dispossession of an entire people.

From the celebratory frenzy which has just begun moving into high gear in Israel, the United States and other Western countries this year, it is clear that little has changed since 1948, as far as the international representation of this event is concerned. We are told that this is Israel's jubilee birthday, a holiday, an occasion for universal rejoicing. We do not hear the heads of state or governments the world over phoning one another to commemorate the simultaneous passing of Palestine in 1948, nor are there plans anywhere in the world for a solemn observance of the dispossession of the Palestinian people. Just as they have been for the past fifty years, the Palestinians are forgotten in all the festivities.

But a genuine celebration, one which would commemorate the establishment of a Jewish state at peace with its neighbours, cannot take place until two things happen. The first is a realisation that in the zero-sum terms in which both communities understood reality in 1948, the birth of Israel necessarily involved the bloody infanticide of Palestine. The second is the righting of the wrong, insofar as this is possible, via the much-delayed birth of a state of Palestine. This state will not be born, and peace will not come, until the reality of what happened in 1948 has been confronted. For there can be no progress towards the reconciliation which is necessary to resolve this conflict unless we can get out of the closed box which posits Israeli innocence regarding what has happened to the Palestinians, and which places the primary onus for their own victimisation on the Palestinians themselves.

In other words, history—meaning history which is not obsessively self-reflexive as so much of Israeli and Palestinian history is—has to be let back in. While neither people should be expected to change its national narrative, it will be necessary for both to take account of elements of that of the other. For Palestinians, this does not require acceptance of the idea of Israeli innocence. It requires rather coming to understand the oppressive weight of the European context which drove Jews to Zionism—and drove many of them to Zion—and to doing what they did in Palestine to the Palestinians. We know, or should know, of the direct impact of these events in Europe on the balance of power in Palestine: thus, the proportion of Jews in the total population of Palestine had grown from under 10 per cent in 1918 to 19.4 per cent by 1926; however, from 1926 until 1932 this proportion actually *declined*, to 18.3 per cent. After the rise of Hitler in 1933, however, the number of Jewish immigrants shot upwards, until Jews were a full 30 per cent of the population only five years later, with more Jewish immigrants arriving in Palestine in 1935 alone than the country's entire Jewish population in 1918. This was the critical demographic mass which made Jewish statehood in Palestine possible, a critical mass which very possibly would not have been reached but for the impact of the rise to power of the Nazis.

Edward Said has stressed recently that if the Palestinians are ever to comprehend and come to terms with what has happened to them over the past half century and more, they must understand fully the European context which drove Jewish refugees to the shores of Palestine, and then drove them to do grave deeds here. Palestinians must understand why a narrative centred on the Holocaust is so compelling, which they cannot do unless they understand in detail the history of the Holocaust, and how it affects Israelis, Jews and others in the West. I agree, and as I have argued elsewhere, in order to come to terms with their own history, it will also be necessary for the Palestinians to accept some responsibility for their own failures in the 1930s, 1940s and afterwards, as a few Palestinian historians have begun to do. Specifically, Palestinians must confront sensitive issues like the mistakes of their leadership in the 1930s and 1940s, and why their society fragmented so rapidly and so totally under the blows of Plan Dalet in 1948. This means doing something Palestinians have thus far been reluctant to do: accept at least partial responsibility for their fate. For, however powerful were imperialism, Zionism and the hostile Arab regimes before 1948, it must also be accepted that the Palestinians were an independent actor, one which had agency and had choices in the difficult circumstances of the 1930s and 1940s.

On the other hand, taking account of elements of the narrative of the other will require Israelis to do a number of things. Foremost among them is the need to accept and atone for the fact that, however pure their motives and intentions may or may not have been in the 1930s and 1940s, and however pressing their circumstances at the time in view of the Nazi threat, in the process of constituting their nation-state they did grievous harm to a weaker people which had done nothing to them before this conflict began, harm which has continued and multiplied in the succeeding half century. This will require confronting a potent and well-entrenched reading of Jewish history (one embodying profound distortions of Palestinian history) which is relatively new, but which will not surrender the hegemony it has attained over the past fifty years without a struggle.

None of this will be easy. Both Palestinians and Israelis are accustomed to viewing themselves as victims, and to seeing the other as no more than one of a series of accessories involved in inflicting suffering on them. Rather than granting the Palestinians agency and accepting that they may have had honourable, or at least rational, motivations for their actions, many Israelis and Jews see the Palestinians as motivated by the same blind hatred which has driven so many persecutors in Jewish history. There is no room in such a scheme for the idea that Israeli actions may have some bearing on, or could even cause, Palestinian behaviour: by definition, Israelis are victims, no matter what they do, and their adversaries are oppressors, no matter how weak they may be by contrast with Israel.

Similarly, for Palestinians, Israel and Zionism are only part of a vast concatenation of forces including Britain, the United States and the Arab regimes, which has conspired throughout this century to deprive them of self-determination, and ultimately of their very land and homes in many cases. And since the Palestinians are by definition victims, they are not responsible for their actions, and these actions are invariably justified, even if they cause great suffering to Israelis, since the suffering the Israelis have inflicted on the Palestinians has generally been even greater.

The fact that there is some truth in the world view of both only makes each more stubborn. To underline these similarities, however, is not to say that the two are the same: historically, in the conflict between the two sides in Palestine over the past century, one side eventually grew far stronger and became the winner, while the other grew far weaker and ended up the loser. In this conflict, one became the victimiser and the other the victim. And yet this is not the way in which these two peoples are regarded by the world, or at least in the United States. As I was writing this talk, a debate was raging in the United States about whether Yasir Arafat should, or should not, be invited to visit the United States Holocaust Museum in Washington DC, and learn about a crime committed against the Jewish people on another continent by another people when he was a thirteen-year old boy. Completely different though the events were in scale, scope and universal historical importance, there is no museum, no memorial, no notice anywhere which records what Israel did to the Palestinians in 1948. Nor would Benyamin Netanyahu visit one if such did exist, even though he is head of government of a state which stands today on the ruins and in the place of Palestine.

While 1948 therefore does *not* mark a universal jubilee, it could still provide a valuable occasion for reflection on the differing meanings of the events of that climactic year for these two peoples, which in turn could be a stepping-stone to something else more substantial. However, if instead of sober reflection, this anniversary is used by Israel and its friends for the kind of triumphalist crowing of which we have already heard so much, and which rubs more salt into the wounds of the Palestinians, it will take us further away from the possibility of peace and reconciliation between the two peoples.

Nor is it acceptable that this occasion be used solely to mourn the sad fate of the Palestinians. In fact, after fifty years it is time for the Palestinian people to put mourning behind them, and to move on to attempting to achieve restitution for the wrongs done to them. Certainly, if the Palestinians are ever to put forth a credible demand for recognition of the injury done to them, and atonement and restitution for it, they will have to do two things. The first is to shed the passive attitudes associated with mourning, and the second is to see their own history in a broader context. Specifically, they must attempt to understand why the awful course of Jewish history in Europe led Zionism to do what it did in Palestine, unjust though this was to the Palestinians, and why that same history might lead some to celebrate this outcome, tragic though it was for the Palestinians. Moreover, it is vital to understand fully why and how recognition, atonement and restitution were achieved in the case of the Holocaust, since, as the most horrific crime against humanity in modern times, this is the paradigmatic case for all of these things.

If there is ever to be a universal celebration which Palestinians and Israelis can share, much will have to change in the way of attitudes, and it is clear that today we are very far from such changes—much farther away today that we were five or six years ago. Among many other things, the Palestinian historical narrative will have to be explained more fully and less apologetically and diffused more widely, and the Palestinian attitude towards Jewish history will have to evolve. However, such an evolution is exceedingly difficult to expect today, while the Palestinian people rightly feel themselves to be oppressed by the overwhelming power of the Jewish state, more than half of them living in exile from their homeland, and the rest under military occupation or living as second class citizens within it.

Most importantly, however, if such a celebration, such a jubilee, is to be truly universal, the Palestinians must have something concrete, such as independent statehood and national self-determination, to celebrate alongside the Israelis. For this to happen, Israelis and their supporters must recognise and make restitution for the grievous harm that was done to the entire Palestinian people in creating the state of Israel in 1948. After half a century, such a process is long overdue.

RE-EXAMINING HISTORY: ISRAEL AND THE HOLOCAUST

Uri Davis

As I had occasion to write to the organising committee of this Third International *Sabeel* Conference, I doubt that I am qualified to address the latter part of the title 'What God requires?', but I am, perhaps, qualified to make a critical contribution to the former part, 'The Challenge of Jubilee', meaning, I assume, the challenge of the jubilee of the establishment of the State of Israel as a Jewish state, in the Zionist sense of the term, and the mass expulsion of the Palestinian Arab people from such parts of their homeland, Palestine, as came under the control of the Israeli army in the course of the 1948-49 war.

It is in order to establish at the outset the universal distinctions, moral and conceptual, that underpin this contribution. First, the distinction between Judaism (a confessional preference) and Zionism (a political programme). Judaism is not Zionism. Judaism, as a confessional preference, is strictly an individual matter, and, generally speaking, like other individual preferences (e.g., musical, culinary, or sexual preferences) ought not be the concern of the law.

Zionism as a political programme is a matter of public debate. The aims of Zionism include the establishment and the continued existence in historical Palestine of a state, the State of Israel, with a secure, guaranteed, ethnic majority of people classified as 'Jews'. Such individuals and bodies, who are committed to the values of an open society, of democracy, and of the separation of religion from the state, and who, therefore, disagree with the political aims of this particular political programme, who indeed regard this programme to be a racist political programme, are anti-Zionists, in the same sense that those who had for many decades opposed the political programme of *apartheid* for South Africa (since 1994 thankfully ended) were anti-*apartheid.*

Second, the distinction between guilt and responsibility. There is no collective guilt. Children are not guilty of the crimes of their parents; Germans in general are not guilty of the crimes of the Nazi occupation of Europe; Western Christians in general are not guilty of the genocide of the Holocaust; and Europe in general is not guilty of what it did to the Jews. Only anti-Jewish racists are guilty of what they did, and continue to do to Jews.

And, by the same token, children of Zionist settlers in historical Palestine are also not guilty of the crimes of their parents. Responsibility, however, is a different matter. Whereas children of Zionist settlers in historical Palestine are not guilty of the crimes of their parents, citizens of the State of Israel have a responsibility, a duty, which citizens of other states do not have in the same way, to raise their voices against such crimes, act in defence of the victims of these crimes, and work for due reparations to the Palestinian Arabs. This is the case because these crimes were committed, and continue to be committed by the successive governments of the State of Israel in their name.

Many of us have spent a good part of our lives in defence of human rights; defence of the weak against the abuses of the powerful; defence of humankind against cruelty. And in this connection, many of us have been involved in the defence of the Palestinian people against the violation of their human rights; against the abuses of Zionism; against the cruelty of the Israeli occupation. On the basis of truth and integrity we have needed often to address the fallacious, misplaced and misleadingly simple question of, 'How was it possible for a people, the Jewish people, victims of Nazi genocide during the occupation of Europe in the World War II by the Third German Reich, to subject the Palestinian people to war criminal policies of mass deportation, transfer and ethnic cleansing during, and around the 1948-49 war?'

Occupation is occupation. Occupation is the military presence of a state on the territory of another state, with the result that all or part of the territory comes under its control. Occupying armies and occupation governments can commit terrible crimes against the occupied population. Not all occupation governments commit the same war crimes under the cover of war. The occupation governments of the State of Israel clearly have not committed the crime of mass murder in killing centres of the Palestinian people in the same way as the Nazi occupation government of the Third German Reich, where two thirds of the Jewish people under Nazi occupation, one half of the Gypsy people under Nazi occupation, and untold tens of thousands of Slav people, homosexual people, mentally challenged people and more, were mass murdered under Nazi occupation.

But the Israeli occupation of 1948-49 of 77 per cent of the territory of historic Palestine clearly did commit the war crime of mass ethnic cleansing of the Palestinian people, mass transfer resulting in the depopulation of nearly 85 per cent of the Palestinian Arab population resident in the territories that came under Israeli control, dispossessing them of their vast rural and urban real estate and financial properties, illegally appropriating this huge wealth for the colonial settlement of Jews and only Jews, stripping some three quarter of a million Palestinian Arabs (today numbering over three million) of their right to citizenship in Israel, thereby manufacturing the Palestine refugee problem.

The Israeli mass ethnic cleansing operations, under the cover of the 1948-49 war, and the manipulation of the 1948-49 war and Israel's alleged security concerns, as a veil to cover the war crime of the mass transfer of the Palestinian people from the territories that came under Israeli control, have been the subject of extensive re-examination by a range of Israeli scholars in the past decade, and their work is now widely available. Less critical work has been done on the Zionist and Israeli manipulation of the Nazi occupation of Europe and the Holocaust to cover-up and veil Israeli and Zionist war crimes against the Palestinian people in Palestine and beyond.

But it is in this context that I wish to consider on the occasion of the jubilee commemoration of the Palestinian catastrophe of 1948, the question of re-examining established Israeli and Zionist history, and I propose to begin my enquiry into the intellectual, as well as the political implications of the Nazi occupation of Europe for the question of Palestine by quoting a letter.

I should note that, in order to be able to quote this letter before you today, a small band of people, including myself, associated with the publication of *Perdition: A Play in Two Acts* by Jim Allen, had to defend ourselves against libel proceedings in London and Tel Aviv for the entire decade of 1987 through 1997. That we have won our case, as well as all of our costs (well over £40,000 sterling) is due to our tenacity and perseverance, and notably to the tenacity and perseverance of David Wolton, the publisher of *Perdition* at Ithaca Press, London.

The letter I propose to quote below was written by Nathan Schwalb, representative of the Zionist *He-Halutz* (The Pioneer) organisation in Geneva, and addressed to the Jewish rescue Working Group in Bratislava. It was sent in or about the Autumn of 1942 in reply to the repeated and pressing appeals of the said rescue Working Group for money to bribe senior Nazi officials with the view to delay, suspend or otherwise obstruct the Nazi mass transport of Czechoslovakian Jewry to Auschwitz and other centres of genocide. The original letter was lost in the war. A copy may exist in the classified archives of Nathan Schwalb (Dror). The text quoted here was reconstructed by one of the recipients of the original letter, Rabbi Michael Dov Weissmandel, a leading member of the said Working Group, in his book *Min ha-Metzar* (From the Depth of Distress), as follows:

> Since a messenger has been found, he [Schwalb] writes to the Group that they must always remember that the most urgent issue, the main issue which must always be in front of us, is that in the end the Allies will win. After the victory they will divide the world again among the nations as they did at the end of the First World War. Then they paved the way for us to take the first step.
>
> Now, at the end of the war we must do everything so that Palestine will become the State of Israel. There have already been important steps made in this direction. And, as for the outcry coming from our country, we should know that all the Allied nations are spilling much blood. If we shall not make sacrifices, with what shall we buy the right to sit at the table when the division of the nation and the countries takes place after the war?
>
> And therefore it is nonsense and even impudent on our part to ask from the nations who are spilling their blood that they permit their money to be brought into the land of their enemy to defend our blood—because only in blood shall we have the land.
>
> This is as far as the community as a whole is concerned. As for your members of the Group, you take a walk [namely, escape], and for this purpose I provide you with money illegally by means of this messenger.[1]

Schwalb's letter is an accurate representation of mainstream Labour Zionist thinking at the time. Consider, for instance, the statement by the Labour Zionist leader Yitzhaq Gruenbaum, head of the Rescue Committee of the Zionist settler community in Palestine at the time at the meeting of the Zionist Executive on 18 February 1943:

> Meanwhile a mood swept over Eretz Israel that I think is very dangerous to Zionism ... How is it possible ... people will call: 'If you don't have enough money [for rescue] you should take it from *Keren Hayesod* [Zionist settlement foundation fund] ... I thought it obligatory to stand before this wave ... When some asked me: 'Can't you give money

[1] Michael Dov Weissmandel, *Min ha-Metzar.* Private Edition by the Sons of the Author, Jerusalem, 1960, p 92, and Jim Allen, *Perdition: A Play in Two Acts*, Ithaca Press, London, 1987, pp. 62-63, 77.

> from *Keren Hayesod* to save Jews in the Diaspora?' I said no! And again I say no! ... we have to stand before this wave that is putting Zionist activity into the second row ... Because of this, people called me an anti-Semite, and concluded that I am guilty, because we do not give priority to rescue ... I think it is necessary to say here: Zionism is above everything.[2]

And David Ben-Gurion, addressing a meeting of Labour Zionists on 7 December 1938, a bare few weeks after the notorious Nazi anti-Jewish pogroms of Kristallnacht throughout the German Reich in the night of 9-10 November 1938, said:

> If I knew it would be possible to save all the [Jewish] children in Germany by bringing them to England, and only half of them by transporting them to Eretz Israel [Palestine], then I would opt for the second alternative. For we must weigh not only the life of these children but also the history of the people of Israel.[3]

In the light of these representative quotes, the answer to the question, 'How was it possible for a people, the Jewish people, victims of Nazi genocide during the occupation of Europe in the World War II by the Third German Reich, to subject the Palestinian people to war criminal policies of mass deportation, transfer and ethnic cleansing during and around the 1948-49 war?', then, becomes possible. A political elite, that opted politically, intellectually, morally and emotionally to hold back and deny much of its financial and other resources from rescue actions of 'their own people', 'the Jewish people', under Nazi occupation, because they gave priority to Zionism and Jewish state building, and thereby made themselves accomplices by default, sometimes by deliberate design, to the mass murder of Jews by the Nazi annihilation machinery, would have little political, intellectual, moral and emotional hesitation in manufacturing by design and by default the mass 'transfer' of the majority of the Palestinian

---

2 Yitzhaq Gruenbaum, *Bi-Mei Hurban ve-Shoah* (In the Days of Destruction and Holocaust), Haverim, Tel Aviv, 1946, pp. 68-69, quoted in Lenni Brenner, 'Zionism and Rescue', in *Perdition* ..., p. 78.

3 'Zionist Policy and the Fate of European Jewry (1939-1942)', *Yad va-Shem Studies*, Vol XII, p. 199, quoted in Akiva Orr, 'One Hundred Years of Zionism—A Critique', unpublished manuscript, 1997, p. 5.

inhabitants from the territories designated for the projected Jewish state. In order to understand 'How was it possible for a people, the Jewish people, victims of Nazi genocide during the occupation of Europe in the Second World War by the Third German Reich, to subject the Palestinian people to war criminal policies of mass deportation, transfer and ethnic cleansing during and around the 1948-49 war?' It is first necessary to identify correctly the players in this equation. It is not 'the Jews' in general who committed the war crime of mass expulsion of the Palestinian people under the cover of the 1948-49 war, nor 'the victims of the Holocaust' in general—rather, it was the Israeli army and the Israeli provisional government who are responsible, the same people who, until 1948, constituted the leadership of the World Zionist Organization and the Jewish Agency, whose real choices in the face of the Holocaust are reflected in the statements of Nathan Schwalb, Yitzhaq Gruenbaum and David Ben-Gurion above.

The Zionist leader, David Ben-Gurion, and his like, who would opt to see half of the Jewish children in Germany murdered in order to have the surviving half transported to Palestine in the name of Zionism, would have little moral qualm, as prime minister of the provisional government of the newly established State of Israel, to effect by design and by default the mass expulsion of the Palestinian people from such territories that came under the Israeli control in the course of the 1948-49 war.

I suggest that the re-examination of official Israeli historiography over the past half century of the role of the Haganah, IZL and LEHI, and, since 1948, of the Israeli army, in manufacturing the mass expulsion, the transfer of the Palestinian people under the cover of the 1948-49 war, is intimately connected to the official denial by Zionist historiography of the real choices effected by the Zionist leadership in the face of the Nazi occupation of Europe and the Holocaust.

The theme of this presentation echoes what I understand to be the theme of Jim Allen's *Perdition*, namely, that a people under occupation, all peoples under occupation, by and large respond to occupation by developing two basic alternatives, with a lot of grey areas in between: collaboration or resistance; that the Jewish people under Nazi occupation, like the Gypsy people under Nazi occupation, like the Norwegian people under Nazi occupation, like homosexual people under Nazi occupation, responded to the Nazi occupation in similar ways: some among each people opted for resistance, and some for collaboration, and that the Jewish people was not unique in this respect in that some Jews resisted and some Jews collaborated. The official Zionist and Israeli claim that being classified 'Jew' under Nazi occupation was uniquely different from being classified as 'Gypsy', or 'homosexual', in that a Jew under Nazi occupation of Europe could, by definition, not be a collaborator, was historically incorrect, morally false, intellectually bankrupt and politically a brazen lie, a denial of an important aspect of Holocaust history.

The theme of this presentation also implies a statement about Zionism which I wish to make explicit. Zionism and European anti-Jewish racism meet politically, intellectually, morally and emotionally at one crucial point: both Zionism and European anti-Jewish racism, for different, overlapping or parallel reasons, believe that Jews have no place on an equal footing as minorities in predominantly non-Jewish societies. At this point of meetings, mainstream Zionism has historically collaborated with anti-Jewish racism. By way of highlights, one would mention the Transfer (*Haavarah*) agreements between the World Zionist Organization and the Nazi government of the German Reich of 1933; the case of Rudolf Kastner's collaboration with Adolf Eichmann in Nazi occupied Hungary in 1944-45 (of which *Perdition* is a dramatisation); and the Memorandum submitted by the Zionist LEHI paramilitary organisation to the Nazi officials in Beirut in 1941 suggesting that

> The establishment of the historical Jewish state on a national and totalitarian basis, and bound by a Treaty with the German Reich, would be in the interest of a maintained and strengthened future German position of power in the Near East.[4]

It is in order to note that a leading member of the LEHI, Yitzhaq Shamir, was to become a prime minister in Israel, succeeding Menachem Begin. It is also in order to note that it was the LEHI together with the Irgun (headed by Menachem Begin) who were the primary perpetrators of the Deir Yasin massacre of some 250 men, women and children in April 1948.

I submit to you that it is only when we include these, and related historical records into our narrative of the jubilee commemorating fifty years of the 1948 Palestinian catastrophe that we are able to understand

---

4 Quoted in David Yizraeli, *The Palestine Problem in German Politics, 1889-1945*, Bar Ilan University, Ramat Gan, 1974, pp. 315-17, and Lenni Brenner, *Zionism in the Age of the Dictators: A Reappraisal*, Croom Helm, London, 1983, pp. 267-68.

the historical inter-relations between the Palestinian catastrophe, on the one part, and the Jewish Holocaust under the Nazi occupation of Europe on the other, and begin to answer the question, 'How was it possible for a people, the Jewish people, victims of Nazi genocide during the occupation of Europe in the World War II by the Third German Reich, to subject the Palestinian people to war criminal policies of mass deportation, transfer and ethnic cleansing during and around the 1948-49 war?' with a measure of truth and integrity, thereby making a modest contribution to preventing such a catastrophe to befall any people anywhere again.

To re-cap, the mainstream of the Labour Zionist leadership, having made criminal choices regarding 'its own people' in the name of Zionism and Jewish state building, such as the choices expressed in the quotes above, would not hesitate to make war criminal choices with regard to 'another people', the Palestinian Arab people for the same purpose.

It was Hisham Sharabi who pointed out to me that, though the Israeli ethnic cleansing of 1948-49, and the Israeli occupation of 1967 to date are no less barbaric than, for instance, the mass ethnic cleansing that had taken place in India and Pakistan at about the same time, or the French occupation of Algeria, the tragedy of the Palestinian Arab is that his persecutor and occupier is identified in Western narrative, not as 'Zionist', nor as 'Israeli', but as 'Jew'. This means that, so long as the Israeli occupation does not mass transport the Palestinian people into killing centres and concentration camps, gas them, and dispose of their bodies in crematoria, the cruelty of the Israeli occupation and the suffering of the Palestinian people remain invisible to enlightened public opinion in the West.

It is our responsibility to make the Palestinian suffering visible.

JUSTICE AND RECONCILIATION— LIVING WITH THE MEMORY LEGITIMACY, JUSTICE AND NATIONHOOD

May Seikaly

Human memory is unique among memories of all other beings, because it is complex, extensive, varied and multifaceted. It is also essential to rational existence, giving individuals and groups reference and significance to their roots, experience and identity. Memory is the repository of human experience, individual and collective, and the measure of what one treasures from the past. While flexible and evolving, it reflects the holistic experience of the carrier, informed by cultural, social and historical events. By remembering, people are involved in the most intimate and secret communion with the essence of human life, where life's experience and the values of existence are confronted and interpreted. It is in that process that people are drawn to introspect, review, criticise and evaluate their experience in terms of the present.

Memory provides the historical parameters of identity, and identity reinforces and feeds memory. It is through recall and communicating shared experiences that the sense of sameness and collectivity is sustained. The struggle of groups to preserve their self-identification and their social honour is an existential need. It is a need that explains the bonds of collective memory and the group's interpretation of historical events, positive and negative. The attachment to identity is sharp and dramatic among people whose historical experience has been shrouded by a sense of injustice, and the infringement of their human rights. Similar to the Jewish and Armenian experience of holocaust and genocide, Palestinians are haunted by their memories of injustice, fragmentation and extensive loss of life. Injustice is felt by victims in exactly the same intensity, irrespective of social, ethnic, religious or national affiliation. Furthermore, memories of injustice are remembered, communicated and reconstructed more vividly and trenchantly than others, due to their emotional impact and long-lasting effects.

By utilising recall, historians capture the many dimensions of 'Truth' in order to expand and solidify their means of recreating the reality of the past. Human memory gives history and its writing the voice of the *live* experience, the humane and passionate aspect of facts, and the sensitive channel to document the subtleties of social change and transformation. Today many social scientists face the challenge of humanising their fields, by drawing in the oral narratives from memory, and so verify and enlarge the myriad interpretations of the past. Through this method, genuine historical consciousness is developed.

When these memories are given historical expression they democratise the historical narrative by inputting the voice of the common person, and particularly the voice of individuals and groups who are suppressed and ignored. While the truths of the official and established political frames and vested interests are recorded, as well as those of the victors, the many other truths, and their potential to inform and rectify are ignored. These are the truths of the unrecorded, the unrepresented, the vanquished and the marginalised; it is the experiences of those whose voices are made invisible, veiled and unknown. Addressing this injustice is the burden of the conscientious and courageous. Furthermore, to expose and publicise these voices of memory will only enlarge and improve peoples' understanding, compassion and the means at their disposal to resolve global dilemmas.

The need that has impelled Palestinians to use oral recording of their memories is not limited to their particular experience; societies with similar histories of uprooting, dislocations, beleaguerment and colonisation have used the same. Along with peoples of the Third World, aborigines and natives of many continents, as well as uprooted and maligned ethnic communities, Palestinians feel that their history has been expropriated.

After the passing of fifty years to the *Nakba* of 1948, and the dispersal of its people, Palestinians are involved, more than ever before, in the process of recall, and in setting the record straight by rebuilding their historical legacy. It is a tribute to the spirit of justice and fair-play among a new breed of scholars, that we see the proliferation of literature on peoples and issues previously ignored. Scholars have become aware of the necessity to salvage the story of the 'other', the 'invisible' Palestinian. The need to repossess all aspects of the national collective memory, to search for grass-root indicators of its identity, and to make its documents available, has a growing number of advocates. It is only recently that the Israeli version of a corroded, falsified and manipulated Palestinian historiography has been seriously contested and questioned by a new generation of Israeli New (revisionist) historians, including Benny Morris, Avi Schlaim, and Ilan Pappé. Their version has vindicated the claims of the *eye-witness* and *memory narrative* of the unheard voices and experiences of Palestinians, voices that had been relegated to oblivion (see, for example, the works of Walid Khalidi, and others.) It is obvious, however, that only with continuous retelling will the Palestinian story achieve recognition and the plight and injustice borne by its people acquire attention.

I would like to share with you some results of my on-going research on Palestinian collective memory, on Palestinian perceptions of themselves, of the world around them and of the future. Through oral interviews, informed by memory, I have studied the life histories of individual Palestinians—people of all walks of life, living in all corners of the universe, and during different junctures of Palestinian history. For over twenty years I have tried to record their subjective memories, and to encode them into the frames of objective historiography. It is through the many pieces of Palestinian life that the mosaic of their experience is verified and recognised. Also, by viewing the whole matrix of society in an integrated form, the individual experience makes sense at the level of its broad association with the ethnic community, its ideology and political beliefs.

In these trips of rediscovery and reminiscences, the significance of being a Palestinian was reflected as an anchor in a past-present dialogue. It is a past that is ever present, powerful and gripping; but it is also a past that promotes introspection, criticism and a search for solutions. These memories are multi-faceted mirrors of Palestine's social and political past that are held and passed on from one generation to the next. In these recollections, Palestinians contextualised the present in relation to Israeli occupation, to dispersal, unending strife and suffering, and to their aspirations for self-determination.

For Palestinians, this memory, which is socially articulated and maintained, is defined by flashbacks of crisis, trauma and suffering. Remembrance takes place in a socio-political chain of emotionally wrenching experiences, on-going and accumulative, resulting in the construction of a memory-laden identity and its outward form of national expression. Emotion is an important bonding agent for memories which affect the process of retention and realistic retrieval. In the case of Palestinians, the severity and depth of the emotional injury inflicted, and the vividness of communal experiences associated with pain, indignity and impotence, have sharpened and moulded their identity.

In these interviews, two paramount issues were repeatedly remembered and pondered. They are: the impact of recurring tragedies, with strong focus on 1948 and its aftermath, and the strong attachment to the homeland, villages, towns and cities of Palestine, particularly to Jerusalem. Both issues are interrelated and based on group self-identification. They were expressed in the overwhelming sense of injustice, dispossession, dispersal, vulnerability and persecution.

A very high percentage of responses registered a sense of betrayal. The experience of betrayal had started early in their politicisation process. Even though respondents came from varied socio-economic and religious backgrounds, all those who experienced the dramatic events of 1948 as adults or children with clear recall have similar impressions and deep, trenchant memories. The sense of loss, dislocation, fear, panic, misery and betrayal were remarkably similar and continued to colour the interviews in varying intensity. It is clear that these early experiences had left an impact on the later life of each. Even those to whom the experience came secondhand—from parents—1948 stood as a landmark in their lives.

The memories of pre-1948 and the event itself released a flood of enlightening information. Males and females from villages and towns who recalled that period had clearly relived it often since it happened. Names of victims, descriptions of incidents and personal contributions, reactions and analyses were vivid and cathartic. The dispersal of 1948 and what accompanied it, in communal misery and degradation, seem to be the primal base for the development of a pervasive ethno/national identity among disparate people. Subsequent history and a legacy of hardship and injustice were also relayed in a continuum, which strongly suggest the psychological basis for the development of a Palestinian ethos, characterised by adamant attachment to ethnicity as a last refuge.

The personal memory, which had become that of the group, has had climactic influence on the path their lives took and the quality of that life. It is an experience etched on their memory and persona, and, whether consciously or otherwise, it has constantly affected their subsequent dealings, as was made clear in their accounts. A respondent summarised this condition when he said: 'We are a nation which labours under feelings of suffering and a central heroic theme that have colored our view of ourselves and our relations to others.'

Most of the respondents defined their lives as a series of events and junctures correlated to the history of the Palestinian problem. These life-histories were relayed in stages punctuated by events related to Palestinian highlights: the massacres of Deir Yasin, the fall of Haifa and Jaffa, the atrocities in Lod and Ramlah, the exodus to Jordan and Lebanon, the snipers and bombings, the death of Nasser, the massacres of Sabra and Shatila, Sadat's visit to Jerusalem, Oslo and the Gulf War—and it goes on. The retelling contextualised individual encounters with these events which were also restructured through retrospective assessments of each.

The period prior to 1967 was recalled by some as periods of rebellion, of struggle to construct an identity opposed by Arab alienating policies and Israeli retaliation. 1967 solidified their bitterness and feeling of despair. While 1948 had left a deep wound on the Palestinian psyche, 1967 seems to have left a similar impact on their lives, with new waves of expelled people and recurring catastrophes.

Attachment to cultural ethnicity was persistently expressed as a defining feature of the group. It is clear that in view of such a history, a certain political ideology emerged that reflected a Palestinian world- and life-view. It was an emphatic attachment to the primary unit of political identity, the ethnic culture, and to the structures that support its expression. As expressed again and again by many, the reproduction of culture with its ethnic particularities is emphasised. It is the constant—the refuge—in a world of flux. The condition of homelessness, exile, harassment and defeatism is offset by finding refuge in one's ethnic setting. Furthermore, social, religious and political structures that assure the survival of this group identity, became paramount to most. By constant recall many tried to impress and confirm a strong attachment to an identity that even the young, who have never known Palestine, claim as their own.

The political status of the homeland and the ongoing events surrounding its future keep Palestinians alert and expectant. Transformation of the territorial and demographic character of the homeland over time is still very graphically recalled, and more recent violations in that regard are watched with alarm. Jerusalem, the latest city subjected to this pattern of occupation, evoked a strong renewal of bitterness and feeling of doom, which is compared to past Israeli tactics of de-Palestinianising the land. In the memory of many respondents, the Old City of Jerusalem has been a refuge; historically it had taken in Jerusalemites and Palestinians after the exodus of 1948, and had been a source of permanence and belonging. Today, the rooted and established society in Jerusalem is challenged by the onslaught of forces to uproot and disperse it. The feeling of claustrophobia is strong; encirclement of the Old City is intensified by visible indications of encroachment within its walls.

Jerusalem has also contributed to all stages of the Palestinian saga; a city of refuge, a centre of resistance, and a symbol of Palestinian continuity in the land. As such it was remembered and associated with what is close to the heart and soul: traditions, ancestors, family friends, religion, business and future generations. Attachment to Jerusalem is expressed by reliving its heroic stance and remembering its martyrs of 1948, 1967 and the *Intifada.* It is also remembered for its communities and their relationships and inter-dependence.

Conclusion

The Palestinian story has left among its people a strong residue of painful frustration which remains unresolved. Through their memories, they had rewoven the experience of Palestinian hope and despair, and shown its impact on their thoughts and actions today. As such, the remembering and retelling, while cathartic, has also activated the process of analysis, criticism and the seeking for a dignified and just solution. Memory plays an important part in Palestinian self-esteem and dignity, in the urgent need to unveil the truth, to acknowledge the pain, and recognise the injustice, and, in that process, to seek recovery.

At this time, a global movement of soul-searching is calling for reopening the files of human injustice as a first step to recognise the past and rectify its effects, thus opening the way towards world peace. It can be called a movement of memory which is reminding people that it is essential to look on the past with an open mind and with objectivity and humanity, in order to reach compromises and living solutions. It is only by opening old wounds that healing can begin. Victims and victimisers need to meet with their bags of memories, meet on an equal basis, and, face to face, discover channels of reciprocal recognition of wrongs, for the sake of healing and co-existence. They need to come together to discuss, debate and negotiate the past, and through that process define the future.

It is the duty of all peace-loving and democratic societies to publicise memories and identities of people subjected to protracted injustice and humiliation. Only then can memory become a means of liberation, rather than of enslavement.

RECONCILIATION AND JUSTICE: LIVING WITH THE MEMORY

Elias Chacour

It is a great pleasure to be present with you at the *Sabeel* Conference, and it is also a very special privilege for me to thank all of you who came from so far, just for once, to listen to Palestinian Christians expressing their identity, their fears, and their hopes. Whenever we stand before you, we remember so many things. Our memory goes back to 2,000 years ago when our forefathers were unable to keep to themselves what they had shared with their children, namely the life of the man from Galilee, the Nazarene, Jesus Christ. And the message went all over the world, with people sharing their experience, and their faith.

When we see that you have come from so far away, we say to ourselves, 'Our forefathers have done a good job!' It is in the name of these forefathers that I would like to welcome you wholeheartedly to Bethlehem, supposedly the City of Peace. In reality the city has been crucified for such a long time. We pray, and hope, and act that this crucifixion of Bethlehem, as well as of other Palestinian cities—indeed of all the Palestinian people, who are on their *Via Dolorosa* (the Way of the Cross)—that this suffering will be brought to an end, and that the Resurrection will shine very soon, so that there will be not only peace, but justice as a step toward reconciliation. Thank you for being with us.

Palestinian Christians—I am one of them—are very proud to be Palestinian Christians. I am also an Arab. I am a Christian Palestinian Arab, and, as much and as strongly, a citizen of Israel. However, I was not born a Christian. I was born a baby, created in the image and with the likeness of God—no more, no less. In this perspective, the human family consists of Muslims, Christians, Jews, and everyone else, all together, created babies in the image of, and with the likeness of God.

As Palestinian Christians, we have a particular place to show you. Moreover, we have someone particular to introduce to you. Both are absolutely unique. The place we have to show you is an empty tomb. Not because it is empty, but because it has been emptied. And the person we like to introduce to you is a Risen Lord. This is for us Palestinian Christians the newness of the New Testament, and the uniqueness of Jesus Christ. We call it the Good News. I wish to consider four points that constitute that Good News for us Palestinian Christians, and I hope for you, Christians from overseas, also.

The first of the four points of our faith, which we have been preaching consistently since the discovery of the empty tomb, is the Risen Lord; that there is not any longer privilege for Jew over Gentile, for Man over Woman, for Master over Slave. This applies also to our socio-political status, and our situation in the Holy Land (Israel and Palestine). We have lots to do still to do away with the old distinction between Jew and Gentile (*Yehudi va Goy*), between Jew and Palestinian.

The second aspect of the Good News concerns the notion of election. My forefathers, the first Christians, proclaimed that Christians have a new vision of election, a renewed understanding of the calling of God to take part in the divine banquet in the heavenly land. This is what they preached, and we have followed them. We have been taught for centuries that the Jews are the Chosen People. We do not believe anymore that they are the Chosen People of God, since now we have a new understanding of that Chosenness. Who is chosen? Man and Woman—every man and every woman—are invited to take part in the divine banquet.

What, then, do we do with our Jewish brothers and sisters? We can simply ask them if they are 'men and women'. If they answer positively, then they are invited to the divine banquet in heaven, as much as you are. If they are no longer 'men and women', there is a serious problem—and we Christians, at least, know what being no longer 'men and women' implied: we summed it up in the saying that 'outside of baptism there is no salvation.' So far, so good.

But then we start discussing what kind of baptism? The reborn, the reformed-, or the not-yet-reformed-baptism. Of course, religious wars followed all that extravagance of faith. I am so happy to be sure that in heaven there will be no Judaism, no Christianity, and no Islam, and I pray for, and act upon the principle that many Muslims, many Christians, many Jews, would be considered worthy to enjoy the Kingdom of Heaven.

The third point of the Good News is this. My forefathers preached all over the world that their God is no longer a regional God. We remember the wonderful prophet Jonah, who fled from the land of God. He was a good, orthodox Jew, who did not want to obey God's directive to go to Nineveh, and so he fled. In the depths of the ocean, and not only in the land of Israel, he recognised the lordship of God. But not only in the ocean, but even in Nineveh, where there were no Jews—the Ninevites, too, were children of God.

I think we have done away with the old distinction between Jews and *Goyim*, and with the notion that God reigns only in his own territory. He also lived among the Syrians. One of them, too, was healed of his leprosy through the prophet Elijah.

When it comes to worship, we need not confine ourselves to the land of Israel—it is possible to worship God in Damascus also. No longer do we need to go to Jerusalem, or to Samaria, to worship our God. We need to go there in Spirit, and in truth. This theological perspective, of course, does not in any way undermine the just claims of the Palestinians, whether Christians or Muslims, to share Jerusalem, and to reject a unilateral domination and control over the city of the King of Justice. Together we need another king of justice, so that Jerusalem becomes again 'Yerushalim', the city of integrity, the city of wholeness, the city of perfection and of peace.

The fourth point that my forefathers preached, and that still meets so much resistance in our society, is that our God is not a tribal God. God is not Christian—we know that very well. At least, I hope we do. But God is not a Jew, either, or a Muslim. We three peoples are called to be God-like, and that requires an effort, from birth to second birth. More than that, my forefathers prepared us so well, but not merely for 'tolerance', to tolerate the Jews in the land of Palestine. It should not be a question of tolerating any other religion. Tolerance is the lowest policy we can practise toward each other—Hitler himself tolerated the Jews, at least until he was able to find the *Endlösung*, the final solution. However, he never accepted the Jews as part of the German community.

And if we, Palestinians and Israeli Jews, offer resistance today, we should resist the notion of mere 'tolerance', and try to accept each other as partners who belong to the same land, without discrimination, without any master-slave relationship. And, after all, do we not all, Christians, Muslims, and Jews—all members of monotheistic religions—do we not claim so strongly that we are the children of an Iraqi citizen? That sounds awkward today, with the conflict with Saddam Hussein. But we are! We are the children of a man from Iraq, from Mesopotamia—Abraham. And who was he? I hope that we agree that before Abraham there was no Jew, and Abram could not have been a Jew; he was a Gentile living among a Gentile nation. He was commissioned to behave in a new way, commissioned to burn the bridges behind him. And when he heeded God's call, he did not hesitate to set about burning even the bridges in front of him, to sacrifice his own son, for his own mission, to reveal the invisible God, not to the Jews—they did not exist yet—but to the nations (*Goyim*). His descendants, whether Jews, Muslims, or Christians, carry the same mission to reveal this invisible God to outsiders. But today, we need to reveal that God to the insiders also.

Abraham's behaviour was not sufficient to remind the Gentiles of God's Lordship. If the behaviour of the Israelis today—no matter how many weapons they have, or how strong their lobby in Washington, or how righteous they are—is no longer a reminder of the Lordship of that one invisible God, the land where they are shall vomit them out. This is not just the teaching of Father Chacour. It is in the Old Testament (Lev 18.24-30), and in the Talmud. And the Talmud is not a Christian teaching, but a very venerable Jewish one.

I do not wish that Israel, the Jews, be vomited out—the Jews are beloved to us. We are sorry that they have been persecuted in a barbarian way somewhere else—far away in Europe. I feel responsibility for the Jews, in virtue of what happened to them. I feel the same grave responsibility for the Armenians, the Cambodians, the El Salvadorans, and the Bosnians, and the Palestinians in virtue of their sufferings. However, I do not in any way feel guilty for what happened to these noble peoples. But to feel that I am responsible means that I must make a common front with Jews, Palestinians, and others, to ensure that such horrors are never repeated.

While I was in Washington not long ago, I was invited to visit the prestigious Holocaust Monument. I refused, because there is no mention of any other Holocaust there. No mention of Tal Al-Zatar, of Sabra and Shatila, of Bosnia, of Rwanda, of El Salvador, of Cambodia, or elsewhere. I said to my host, 'I am going back home and I will build my own Holocaust Monument.' I invite you to come to Galilee, to Ibillin, to Prophet Elias College, where the first Holocaust Monument has been built by a Palestinian community. It is very simple, unpretentious monument. It consists of two semi-circular walls that face each other, with a statement engraved on each one. One reads, 'This is a memorial for Jewish martyrs.' And, on the opposite wall, 'This is a memorial for Palestinian martyrs.' The place is named 'Listening Post'.

Come and listen to the martyrs. They will say with one voice, 'No more martyrs.' The tragedy is that one's martyrs are considered terrorists by the other side, whether one is a Jew or a Palestinian. Nevertheless, the memory is there. Only death can kill our personal memory. I am a native of Bi'ram. I gave my home to what we thought were simply the survivors of a certain devil called Hitler. But we became the deportees, the refugees, despite two resolutions of the Supreme Court Justice of Israel. We have the right, but we do not have the might. That is why we are still deportees in our own homeland.

I had the pleasure three years ago of welcoming at the college and at my home the then Foreign Minister of Israel, Shimon Peres. I reminded him that although Bi'ram and Iqrit have been destroyed, the inhabitants are still alive, and that we want our right to return. He answered spontaneously, 'Father Chacour, when you left Bi'ram you were a little baby. It was fifty years ago! Have you not yet forgotten? When will you start forgetting?' I answered him, 'You are making our lives miserable because you were here 2,000 years ago. Tell me, when will you start forgetting?'

JUSTICE AND RECONCILIATION

Rosemary Ruether

Reconciliation is a problematic concept for oppressed people. Too often the demand for reconciliation is put forward without regard to genuine change in the oppressive situation of power. The victimised are called to forgive and be reconciled in a way that perpetuates, rather than rectifies, the causes of alienation and division. It is my contention that reconciliation is only possible when there is genuine conversion on the part of those who are divided from each other, and a transformation of relations that promotes justice. Both personal and social conversion is required for real reconciliation.

The powerful often expect that victimised people can be made to be reconciled to their bad situation, to accept passively that nothing better is possible. Since the collapse of the former communist regimes in Eastern Europe, the Western capitalist neo-liberal market economy has been demanding this kind of reconciliation from the whole world, including the majority who are disadvantaged by it. They are saying to the poor, the under- and unemployed, those who are experiencing cutbacks in basic social services and the pollution of their environments: 'This is it. This is the best, indeed the only possible, economic system. Accept it as the best of all possible worlds. Give up any dream of an alternative.'

So far those who profit from the neo-liberal economy have got away with this silencing of hope, but hopefully not for long, for human beings cannot be made to be reconciled with hopelessness, with hollow promises that are contradicted by a worsening reality for the majority of humans on this planet. It is in the nature of humanness that one cannot live without a vision of a better future, of a redemptive transformation. This is why the demand for reconciliation as passive acquiescence to an unjust fate must finally fail. If not the defeated generation, then their children, will recreate resurgent protest against injustice, resurgent visions of alternative futures.

But what are the ways of creating genuine reconciliation, through conversion of hearts and conversion of unjust social relations? How is this possible, given the endemic tendency of those who are advantaged to cling to their unjust advantages and to refuse to repent and change? This is what the Christian tradition has called 'sin'. I think that the feminist liberation theologies have some insights into this process of transformation that need to be learned by a dominant perspective that recreates the cycle of violence through endless efforts to win at the expense of others.

I want to illustrate the problem of authentic and inauthentic reconciliation by two contemporary examples of peace-making: the first example is that of South Africa, with the victory over *apartheid* and the conduct of the Truth and Reconciliation Commission; the second is the Israel-Palestinian 'peace-process'. I want to ask what has led to imperfect but real change and reconciliation in the case of South Africa, in contrast to the Israeli-Palestinian case, where injustice is actually being worsened through what is euphemistically called 'the peace-process'. I taught in South Africa for several months in 1989 shortly before the release of Nelson Mandela from prison, during the final stage of protest against *apartheid* called the 'defiance campaign'. At that time, the *apartheid* legal, political and economic system, which had been built for over eighty years, seemed intractable. The fiction of the African homelands were still in place; martial law made public protest meetings illegal, and even to hope for a change in the political system that would give the African majority equal votes seemed utopian. Yet in less than five years this system unravelled. The banned African National Congress is now the ruling party; Nelson Mandela is president and a new constitution giving all South Africans equal citizenship has been put in place. With the Truth and Reconciliation Commission, chaired by Bishop Desmond Tutu, a process is in place by which those who perpetrated the crimes of *apartheid* are asked to disclose fully the truth, with a promise of amnesty.

The work of this Commission is far from creating full reconciliation. On the white side, it has become apparent that, while lesser white police and military personnel might admit their misdeeds, those in top political office, specifically former President De Klerk, are not willing to admit that the permission for these misdeeds was general policy well known to the top leaders. On the other hand, the families of those who were tortured and killed are not happy when their persecutors receive amnesty only in exchange for full disclosure.

Moreover, although political equality is now established for all South Africans, the economic consequences of white monopolisation of land and resource wealth is far from changed. The black majority is still desperately poor and lacks basic amenities. In addition, gender relations, especially endemic violence against women, has hardly been touched. Yet because there was some genuine change, political equality, the election of a black majority government accepted by whites, the basis for some real reconciliation is present.

Because the criminals were so many, one can hardly punish them all, the Commission reasons. Let there just be full disclosure of the truth; let the criminals publicly admit their crimes before the whole nation; and have to live with being thus known; let the record be set straight, and then let us go forward to create a new South Africa where political equality may blossom into more equally distributed social and economic means of life. In the South African case, reconciliation is built on real change toward greater justice, coupled with amnesty for those who make a public admission of guilt. This is repentance and forgiveness translated into legal, political terms.

In the Israeli-Palestinian case there were hopes of similar change that would lead to some real justice, allowing for reconciliation and peace, but these conditions are being undermined and betrayed as the peace-process shows its actual face as a strategy by which the Israeli government consolidates its victory over the Palestinians in terms of demography and land. Like South African *apartheid*, with which it is being increasingly compared, the Israeli conquest of Palestinian land and people was shaped from the turn of the century, but especially since the 1948 war.

The shaping of a Jewish state in Palestine at the expense of Palestinian residence and land-ownership over the last fifty years can be summarised as a three-fold process: occupying as much of the land as possible, eliminating Palestinian landownership and residence as much as possible, and increasing Jewish population and their spread across as much of the land as possible. In short, creating what the Israelis call 'facts on the ground'; that is, a process of continuing demographic shift from a Palestinian majority population and land ownership to a Jewish majority population and landownership.

In 1947 Palestinians were over 1.5 million, three times the Jewish population. Jews were 600,000 and had purchased less than 10 per cent of the land. Yet the United Nations partition plan of that year gave the Jews 55 per cent of the best land, leaving 45 per cent for a Palestinian state. In the 1948-9 war Israel expanded to another 20 per cent of the territory, drove out close to a million Palestinians and took control of 90 per cent of the land in this expanded territory for exclusive Jewish use. More than 400 Palestinian villages were destroyed, and the land given for a Palestinian state was divided between Israel and Jordan, with the Gaza Strip occupied by Egypt.

Then in 1967 Israel took control of the Golan Heights, the West Bank and the Gaza Strip (also the Sinai, later negotiated back to Egypt).

Since that time it has confiscated about 78 per cent of the West Bank and 44 per cent of the crowded Gaza Strip. (A current Knesset bill would transfer this land to Israeli law, effectively putting it under Israeli sovereignty.) From 1987-91 Palestinians rose in protest (the *Intifada*) against these intolerable conditions of continuing repression, displacement and land confiscation. Some 1,500 mostly young people were killed and 135,000 injured, many permanently.

Outcry over this situation finally brought enough pressure both outside and within Israel that the Israeli political leaders, under the government of Yitzhak Rabin and Shimon Peres agreed to what appeared to be a reverse of this historic policy, conceding the possibility of a Palestinian 'entity' in the West Bank and Gaza, in exchange for peace. Former enemies, PLO Chairman Arafat and Israeli Prime Minister Rabin, shook hands on the White House lawn. The world was amazed and rejoiced.

However, the design of the peace process as conceived by Rabin and Peres soon showed its limitations. Basically, the Labour government had no real intention of allowing a sovereign Palestinian state to emerge in the whole of the West Bank and Gaza, with its capital in East Jerusalem, the minimal demand of Palestinians. Rather their intention was to create conditions for the ratification of a new partition of this 25 per cent of Palestine, allotting about a third of it to Jewish settlers in regions to be annexed to Israel, another third to Palestinians and a third zone that would be negotiated.

At best Palestinians might receive about 12 per cent of historic Palestine or less than half of the West Bank and Gaza, but these Palestinian zones would be divided from each other into enclaves surrounded by the Israeli military and settlers and with little access to adequate land for farming or other means of making a living, and without access to roads linking them with each other and, most of all, with Jerusalem. These separated enclaves would be administered by a Palestinian authority charged with keeping the Palestinians under control, but under Israeli military supervision which could intervene at any time. In short, not an autonomous state, but a system of *apartheid*, similar to that constructed by white South Africans for blacks, only with less land and more crowded conditions.

Most of all, the Labour government shaped a plan, continued with even more gusto by the succeeding Likud government of Netanyahu, to eliminate as many Palestinian residents from East Jerusalem as possible, while increasing Jewish landholding and settlements in this occupied territory in an expanded Jerusalem area. The purpose of this judaisation of greater Jerusalem is to turn the Palestinian majority population in this area to a minority, thereby undermining the demographic basis of a Palestinian claim to East Jerusalem as the capital of a unified Palestinian state.

These policies clearly do not represent conditions of minimally acceptable justice for Palestinians. They are in fact the continuation of occupation and its final consolidation under the cover of what is misleadingly called a 'peace-process'. The Israelis have counted on the sympathy of Western Europeans and North Americans for Israel, fuelled by a combination of: 1) their alliance with Israel's hegemonic presence in the Arab world, 2) their need to compensate for their guilt for the genocide of European Jewry, and 3) their inability to care enough about Arab Palestinians to understand the details of this process of ongoing injustice, to prevent an effective outcry against this deception.

Real repentance and a desire to create minimal justice for Israeli-Palestinian coexistence are lacking in this policy, one that is as much that of the Labour government as the Likud. Sadly, the good desire of Western Christians to repent of their crimes toward Jews has been turned into the destruction of Palestinians, by making Western Christians feel that they should pay for their guilt to Jews by turning a blind eye to their unjust treatment of Palestinians. Palestinians have been made to pay for Western Christian sins against Jews.

This is really the key issue that European and American Christians need to confront. We need to understand not only what is happening there to promote justice or injustice; we need to understand *our own role*, as European and American Christians, in the promotion of the ethnocide of the Palestinian people. In effect we have created the historical framework in which this process of ethnocide goes on. And we have done it and continue to do it in the name of reconciliation with the Jews. It is Americans particularly who provide the money and arms through our government that allows this to happen. But Western Christians generally have constructed the historical framework of legitimisation of this process.

We legitimise it as something due to the Jews, both by biblical land claims and also as compensation for the Holocaust. We also collaborate in creating a wall of silence around the resulting injustice to the Palestinians that prevents this from being seen and understood. And we imagine that, by doing it, we salve our bad consciences for our past genocide of European Jews.

Why are Western Christians so unable to recognise what they are doing? Why is injustice to Palestinians so invisible or unimportant to them? Why do they imagine they are rectifying an injustice to one people, the Jews, by destroying another people, the Palestinians? Perhaps a key problem is that Christians are still not able to accept Jews as ordinary human beings. They still need to construct them in archetypal scheme as paradigms of either exemplary virtue or exemplary vice.

Seeking to escape from the evil consequences of making Jews the paradigms of vice, we flip to the opposite pole of seeing Jews as incapable of wrong, paragons of folk wisdom and founders of a messianic state. To recognise that great evil is being done by Israeli Jews to Palestinians in the construction of this state makes us feel anxious that we are falling back to the other pole of the dualism; i.e., Jews as evil. Jews are not allowed to be ordinary people, with a range of capacities, good and bad, in different contexts of power and powerlessness. This myopia is bad enough in personal relations, but fatal in world politics.

The critical question for any discussion of reconciliation is, how does one nurture the growth of a breakthrough community of friends that crosses boundaries, deconstructs the dominant ideology that normalises sin and injustice, and shapes an alternative praxis of mutuality that can touch and transform both personal consciousness and social structures? This is not easy. The pathway to conversion, transformation and justice that grounds reconciliation is filled with pitfalls. But the first step is taken when persons across broken relations glimpse one another as friends, and are no longer able to affirm themselves without affirming the other at the same time. In other words, the ground and fruits of conversion is love, for it is love that melts the heart of stone and gives us hearts of flesh by which we begin to experience what it means to love the neighbour as oneself.

THE COLONISATION OF PALESTINE

Jad Isaac, Marla Schrader and Suhail Khalilieh

Background

Due to its strategic location at the crossroads of Africa, Asia and Europe and to its religious significance, geographical Palestine has witnessed a parade of conquerors throughout its long history. Likewise, the indigenous inhabitants of the land, the Palestinians, have witnessed and been subjected to foreign occupiers. Most recently, Zionists have claimed that Israel was a 'land without a people for a people without land'. The indigenous people of this part of the world, the Palestinian Canaanites, were living here long before the early Hebrews came. For the purposes of this presentation, we shall not go back to the early history, but, shall focus on the period from the late 1800s to the present.

By 1850 there were 11,000 Jews living in Palestine alongside 400,000 Palestinian Arabs. At that time, Jews were living with their fellow Christians and Muslims in the main cities, most notably Jerusalem, Tiberias and Safed. Only in 1878 did Jews establish Petah-Tikvah as the first exclusively Jewish settlement. By 1900, there were less than twenty Jewish settlements in all of Palestine.

By 1908, the number of Jewish settlements increased to 32. In 1918 the number of Jews in Palestine was 56,000, compared to 644,000 Palestinians. At the beginning of the British Mandate in 1922, 97.5 per cent of the land was owned by Arabs who numbered 660,641, compared to 88,000 Jews. However, between 1932 and 1938, 213,000 Jewish immigrants came to Palestine.

By 1939, there was 445,457 Jews and 997,498 Arabs in Palestine. Jewish-owned land increased from 416,000 *dunums* (c. 100,000 acres) in 1914 to 1,231,000 *dunums* by 1936, which amounted to 4.5 per cent of the country. By 1940, while the Jewish population comprised 30 per cent of the population it controlled only 6 per cent of the land. Despite efforts to purchase more Palestinian lands, the Jews owned only 7 per cent of the total land area by the year 1942, and since that percentage did not give the Jews any legitimate claim over Palestine, the Palestinians rejected the Partition Plan proposed on 29 November 1947.

The latest tragedy for the Palestinians, which left them a displaced and uprooted people, began with the establishment of the State of Israel on the land of geographical Palestine in 1948. As a result of the 1948 War, approximately 714,000 of the 800,000 Palestinians lost their lands, homes and properties, and at least 418 villages were depopulated and/or demolished.

Between 1948 and 1967, Israel began to seize control of the Arab shares of water resources, especially those in the Jordan River Basin. This, in spite of the fact that the longest part of the Jordan River system lies with the West Bank, to which Palestinians are a riparian. The Israeli National Water Carrier was constructed in the late 1960s, and currently diverts approximately 400-500 MCM (million cubic metres) of water from the Jordan River system to most parts of Israel and the Negev. To this day, the land and water resources of Palestinians living inside Israel continue to be used inequitably by the State of Israel, as they are allowed to utilise only 2 per cent of the water and 5 per cent of the land. Furthermore, their full social and political rights have yet to be secured. Soon after its occupation in 1967, Israel seized absolute control over the West Bank and Gaza's land and natural resources. Since that time, Israel has either confiscated or declared as closed areas over 55 per cent of the West Bank and 22 per cent of the Gaza Strip, thereby placing it out of Palestinian reach. Palestinians are permitted only less than 15 per cent of the total water resources available to them.

Israel has continued to expand its civilian colonies and their infrastructure on illegally confiscated Palestinian (mainly agricultural) land, further degrading the Palestinian environment. Furthermore, a devastated Palestinian economy is still controlled largely by Israel, as is access to medical facilities and educational institutions.

To reverse this unjust situation, the Palestinian people, by and large, accepted the discourse of peaceful negotiations based on the grounds outlined in the Madrid Conference of 1991. The guiding principles of these negotiations were 'Land for Peace' and the United Nations Resolutions 242 and 338.

Likewise, the Oslo II Interim Agreement was accepted by the Palestinian Authority as an interim step towards the establishment of a Palestinian state. It is interim in nature and should therefore be applied as such by the concerned parties. That is, 'neither side shall initiate or take any step that will change the status of the West Bank and the Gaza Strip pending the outcome of the permanent status negotiations.'[1] Yet, in reality, Israel has violated, and continues to violate and manipulate the Interim Agreement by creating *de facto* realities on the ground which have severely fragmented the West Bank and the Gaza Strip. This will not only affect the outcome of the final status negotiations, but will render a future sustainable Palestinian entity unattainable and, more immediately, cause intolerable hardship and suffering.

The ongoing fragmentation of Palestinian land and communities into disconnected cantons, combined with the frequent collective punishment of closures, house demolitions, withdrawal of identity cards, and the confiscation of private property will impose only a physically unsustainable and brittle peace.

A lasting peace can be based only on UN Resolutions 242 and 338, in which a fully sovereign Palestinian state will be established on the whole stretch of Palestinian land occupied by Israel in 1967, neighbouring a secure and independent Israeli state. In this respect, the international community is required to secure such an outcome, and only then can the currently stalled peace process be set back on track. More immediately, the international community is asked to intervene and lift the immediate hardships of the Palestinian people, imposed upon them by means of collective punishment.

The physical fragmentation of Palestinian communities

In Palestinian society, which is predominately agricultural, the loss of land is similar to the loss of life. Agriculture contributes approximately 24 per cent to the Palestinian gross national product. The confiscation of land by Israel has not only led to the loss of income, but has also led to the dissolution of Palestinian agricultural society, its culture, traditions and family systems. Furthermore, it has forced many Palestinian farmers to rely upon day labour inside Israel. Therefore, the fragmentation and loss

[1] *The Israeli-Palestinian Interim Agreement on the West Bank and Gaza Strip (Oslo II)*, Washington, DC, 28 September 1995, Chapter 2, Article 31, Item 7.

of land has weakened the Palestinian economy, making it dependent upon Israel.

According to the Oslo II Interim Agreement, the West Bank has been divided into three main areas. The jagged distribution of Areas A, B, and C has partitioned the West Bank into isolated cantons of Areas A and B, which are physically separated from each other by Area C. Only Area A, less than 2.3 per cent of the total West Bank area, is under the complete control of the Palestinian Authority. Although this arrangement was intended to be temporary, Israeli unilateral expansion and construction of colonies and by-pass roads is transforming it into a permanent reality. A special case involving the Israeli colonists residing in Hebron City led to a division of the city into two sectors, H1 (Palestinian Control) and H2 (Israeli Control). According to the Hebron understanding, 85 per cent of the city of Hebron is under Palestinian control, while the remaining 15 per cent will be subjected to Israeli rule. No further redeployment of the Israeli army in Hebron will take place in the Interim period, leaving the city to exist under Saxon law. The 85 per cent that falls under the Palestinian control are just part of Hebron City, but not the Hebron District.

In conjunction with the above described land scheme, Israeli by-pass roads further fragment Palestinian communities. A cross-examination of the overall geographic extension of both the existing and planned by-pass roads in the West Bank, totalling over 700 km in length, with the various previously prepared plans for the separation lines between Israel and the West Bank, uncovers the true nature and purposes behind the construction of these roads.

It is worth mentioning that the by-pass roads so far built in the West Bank exceed 276 kms in length, while the planned roads are estimated at 452 kms. With the safety buffer zone they enjoy, the construction of these by-pass roads requires the confiscation and destruction of approximately 109,200 hectares of Palestinian land, most of which is agricultural. Many farm lands were totally destroyed by the construction of by-pass roads, depriving owners of their main source of income. Other farm lands were split into several pieces, rendering it impossible to cross from one side of the land to the other.

Israeli colonies further fragment Palestinian communities, and illegally confiscate much of the remaining land on which these communities can grow and develop. Presently, there are 18 Israeli colonies in the Gaza Strip, housing an estimated 4,000 Israeli colonists and another estimated 270 colonies in the West Bank with a population of approximately 340,000 colonists, of whom over 170,000 reside in East Jerusalem. Colonies in the occupied Palestinian territories are environmentally unsustainable, incongruent with indigenous land use. Furthermore, their existence is in direct violation of international law, especially the Fourth Geneva Convention, which states that, 'The occupying power shall not deport or transfer part of its own civilian population into the territory it occupies' (Article 49, item 6).

The fate of Israeli colonies was not mentioned in the articles of the Oslo II Interim Agreement. Rather, it was left for the final status negotiations, provisional upon the understanding that no unilateral steps be taken by either side that might alter the status of the final negotiations. Moreover, the full implementation of the Oslo II Interim Agreement demands that Israel freeze settlement activities in the Palestinian territories pending the outcome of the permanent status negotiations.[2]

Palestinian objection to the existence of Israeli colonies in the West Bank and the Gaza Strip is not limited to the issue of their illegality. These colonies impose a serious threat to the Palestinian environment and to Palestinian religious and archaeological sites. Firstly, most colonies are built on confiscated Palestinian agricultural or grazing lands, which has led to the uprooting of thousands of fruit trees, and, as a direct result of the drastic reduction in land cover, has increased soil erosion. According to *Al-Haq*, an estimated 227,661 fruit trees have been uprooted by Israeli soldiers and colonists between 1987 and August 1997.[3]

Second, Israeli colonists in both the West Bank and the Gaza Strip consume unsustainable amounts of scarce Palestinian water resources. While the average per capita Palestinian water consumption, for all sectors, is 107-156 cubic metres per year, an Israeli colonist uses 640-1,480 cubic metres per year. While Palestinians are often not supplied with enough drinking water during the summer months, Israeli colonists extravagantly fill their swimming pools, and water their green lawns.

A crucial, yet often overlooked, fact is that the geographical distribution of Israeli colonies in the Palestinian territories severely restricts the growth of Palestinian communities. In most cases, colonies either

---

[2] Chapter 2 Article 31, item 7 of the Agreement states that, 'Neither side shall initiate or take any step that will change the status of the West Bank and the Gaza Strip pending the outcome of the permanent status negotiations.'

[3] *Al-Quds* Newspaper, 'Over Two Hundred Thousand Fruit-Bearing Trees Uprooted by The Israeli Occupation in the Last Decade', Jerusalem, 29 August 1997.

surround Palestinian communities, and, therefore, prevent their natural growth, or, they confiscate huge tracts of Palestinian land, ensuring that the land is available for future expansion of the colonies.

In sum, colonies are a focal point for land destruction and the pollution of the Palestinian environment. Their existence creates a major political dilemma for the Palestinian Authority and the Israeli government, and their further expansion will not only render Palestinian geographic integrity impossible, but will also adversely affect the environment and the quality of life today as well as for future generations.

The closure and restrictions on movement

In addition to the continuous closure of the West Bank and the Gaza Strip to Israel and East Jerusalem since March 1993, Israel frequently imposes internal closures on these areas. During times of internal closure, Palestinians are not allowed to enter Area C. Thus, movement between most Palestinian communities is forbidden. Also, during these times the few labourers and the other Palestinians who have permission to work in, or visit Israel and East Jerusalem are not allowed to travel for any reason.

Recently and most notably during 1997, the internal closures have been combined with the sealing of international ports of entry to and from the Occupied Territories. Goods and supplies, including medical supplies, are also subject to this comprehensive travel ban. On a micro-level, this has translated into critical shortages of fresh produce, dairy products, medicine, fuel and other basic staples. Likewise, Palestinians are not guaranteed unobstructed access to medical care, schools and universities and places of worship, located mainly in the sealed urban areas.

Around 33,000 students and 15,000 teachers have been denied access to universities and other institutions of higher learning during times of internal closure. The Vatican-supported Bethlehem University reported on 27 August 1997 that 70 per cent of its students and 30 per cent of its staff who reside outside of Bethlehem's Area A had been unable to reach the university. Consequently, all academic and cultural activities were brought to a standstill. Although the Oslo Accord states that Israel must provide free access between the West Bank and the Gaza Strip, many students from Gaza are denied free access to and from their universities in the West Bank by the Israeli authorities.

As of 10 September 1997, 50 per cent of the medical supplies in the West Bank and the Gaza Strip have been depleted. Human rights organisations have reported many cases of Israeli soldiers delaying, or not permitting the passage of critical medical cases to the appropriate hospitals. Over the years, this has resulted in the death of hundreds of Palestinians, the denial of necessary treatment for kidney failure, heart attacks, complicated deliveries and other cases.

Each day of total closure results in a loss of US $1.35 million in household income, and a loss of US $1.5 million in direct export revenue. During the most recent closure in 1997, the budget deficit of the Palestinian Authority increased dramatically from US $52 to US $300 million. The accumulated Palestinian losses for the month of August 1997 totalled US $258 million. Also, during this same period, the unemployment rate rocketed to 60-80 per cent, and the tourism industry in the Bethlehem district reached a virtual standstill. The economy of the Occupied Territories cannot regain stability under such unpredictable circumstances, which, in turn, deters international investors from investing in Palestine's economy.

House demolitions

Israeli demolition of Palestinian homes increases dramatically during times of total closure, and during times of larger regional crisis, such as the United States-led February 1998 near-war with Iraq. Although currently accelerated, this policy has been enforced since 1968. For example, between 1992 and 1995, approximately 539 Palestinian houses were demolished in the West Bank, including East Jerusalem. Between 1 August 1997 and 10 March 1998, 141 houses, 75 Bedouin structures and 1 elementary school were demolished. The list of Palestinian houses slated for impending demolition presently exceeds 3,400.

Regrettably, geographical Palestine has witnessed the demolition of Palestinian homes by Israel throughout the past 49 years. By the end of the 1948 war, more than 400 Palestinian villages had been depopulated, and their houses either blown up or bulldozed. Furthermore, between 1948 and 1958, a series of laws and legal instruments was created by the State of Israel to refuse authorisation, among other things, of zoning plans for Palestinian villages inside the 'green line'. Through this 'legal' device, hundreds of Palestinian homes have been declared illegal, tagged for demolition, and demolished.

Since the 1967 Israeli occupation, destruction for a similar purpose has taken place in the West Bank. Usually, house demolitions are justified by Israel by one of three reasons: security violation, zoning violation, or the lack of a proper building licence. Currently, and in violation of international law, the demolition of West Bank Palestinian homes has reached a crisis level. This is due not only to the prolonged effects of house demolitions on communities and the family unit, but also because never before have demolitions made way for such extensive environmental degradation and unilateral political implications. Ironically, this latest wave of demolitions has been escalated in the name of peace.

Indeed, house demolitions are a human tragedy with grave political and environmental consequences. The policy of house demolitions is not directly related to the lack of building permits. Rather, it fulfils the Israeli designed Allon Plus Plan which was devised by the Israeli Inner Ministerial Cabinet, and published in the Israeli press during the autumn of 1997.

According to this plan (which is more moderate than other proposals), Israel will retain under its control over 55 per cent of the West Bank, and return to the Palestinians only 45 per cent of their land. The implementation of the Allon Plus Plan will bring a catastrophe to the Palestinian people and will seriously threaten their existence. According to the Allon Plus plan, the mere 45 per cent of the West Bank land which is to be returned to the Palestinian Authority not only deprives Palestinians of most of their agricultural and natural grazing lands, but it fragments Palestine into nine disconnected entities. It also deprives Palestinians of the Eastern Slopes and the fertile and water-rich Jordan Valley and border areas of their natural resources.

The implementation of this plan requires the eviction and demolition of thousands of Palestinian houses in the West Bank in order to empty the land of its native inhabitants. This measure, which is presently in process, is creating a new wave of Palestinian refugees and uprooted people. The Allon Plus Plan will have a detrimental impact on the sustainability of the development of the Palestinian economic sectors and render the Palestinian aspiration to a Palestinian state an unattainable dream.

Jerusalem

Jerusalem is a holy city for Christians, Muslims and Jews where all faith communities should be guaranteed unrestricted freedom of worship. In addition to serving as a spiritual capital, Jerusalem must also serve as the political capital of both the State of Israel and the emerging state of Palestine.

The issue of Jerusalem was postponed until the final status negotiations which have been stalled since their initiation in May 1996. Aspects of Jerusalem to be discussed include: sovereignty over the city, legal structure, religious freedom, and cultural rights. However, in the meantime, the Israeli government has not stopped its unilateral practices in Jerusalem by which it creates *de facto* realities on the ground.

These *de facto* realities, clearly favouring Israel, affect the outcome of the negotiations on the final status of Jerusalem. This action is in total violation of UN's resolutions, particularly 298 and 242, as well as the standing Palestinian-Israeli Oslo Agreements. Recently, Israel decided on expanding the Jerusalem municipality boundaries so as to ensure enduring Jewish majority in the city. The new expansion will embody several Israeli neighbourhoods which will raise the Jewish population up to 70 per cent of Jerusalem. This decision follows Israel's other unilateral steps to create facts on the ground, including the E-1 plan adjacent to the Ma'ale Adumim colony, the initiation of a colony in the Ras al-Amoud neighbourhood of Jerusalem, and the continued construction of Har Homa colony on Jabal Abu Ghneim.

Measures leading to strong demographic shifts have been staged by Israel in order to create an exclusive Jewish population in Jerusalem, while de-development strategies have been adopted to restrict expansion of the city's Palestinian communities. In this de-development process, the provision of infrastructure and services for this group of residents by the Israeli Jerusalem Municipality have been altogether inadequate, and do not provide a healthy living environment. Overcrowding has become the norm, and the pressure on Jerusalem's land and natural resources also has been devastating. Palestinian houses built without a licence have been, or are threatened to be demolished by the Israeli government. Presently, over 2,800 houses in East Jerusalem alone are slated for demolition by the Israeli Jerusalem Municipality.

Confiscation of identity cards

To further the Jerusalem Municipality's efforts to cleanse East Jerusalem of its Palestinian residents, a policy of cancelling the Identity Cards (IDs) of Palestinian Jerusalemites has been put into practice. This policy has led to the withdrawal of approximately 3,800 IDs between 1967 and 1996. In 1996 alone, 689 Palestinians were deprived of their IDs. An additional 358 were confiscated in the early part of 1997. These figures do not include the approximately 10,000 Palestinian infants born in Jerusalem, whom the Israeli Ministry of the Interior has declined to register in their parents' identity cards.

A similar policy has been applied to Palestinian residents of the West Bank and the Gaza Strip. To date, approximately 92,000 Palestinians have lost their IDs and, consequently, the right of return to their homeland.

Violations of the interim agreement

The Israeli violations of the Oslo II Interim Agreement are numerous. They start with the indefinite delay of 'redeployment' of Israeli troops from the occupied Palestinian territories, the opening of the Palestinian airport in Gaza, the seaport in the Gaza City, the release of political prisoners, and many others. Other violations are related to the changing of the map of Palestine through land confiscation, demolition of houses, and building of colonies. One of the peculiar violations, however, is the unjustifiable delay in the construction of a 'safe passage' between the West Bank and the Gaza Strip.

This issue has impacted directly on the economies of both the West Bank and the Gaza Strip, and made them vulnerable to Israeli hegemony, as no physical connection exists between these two geographic entities: one must pass through Israel. The delay in the designation of the safe passage is in direct violation of Annex I, Article X of the Oslo II Interim Agreement, which states that, 'Israel will ensure safe passage for persons and transportation during daylight hours (from sunrise to sunset) or as otherwise agreed by the Joint Steering Committee (JSC), but in any event not less than 10 hours a day.'

The lack of a safe passage between the West Bank and the Gaza Strip intends to break the geographic integrity of these two entities of Palestine. The Israeli control over the passage between these complementary geographic entities of Palestine has been used by Israel as a tool of economic sanctions against the Palestinians and furthermore prevents freedom of travel to educational institutions and places of worship.

The case of Bethlehem

On 28 June 1967, extensive tracts of land from the Bethlehem district were annexed to the Jerusalem municipality by Israel. Approximately 16,000 *dunums* (16 square km) of land from the tri-city area of Bethlehem, Beit Jala and Beit Sahour were confiscated by Israel, which thereby rendered them unavailable for use by the owners. This annexation has drastically restricted future expansion and development of the area and its communities.

More recently, the tri-city area (Bethlehem, Beit Sahour and Beit Jala) has been hit hard by the designation of Areas A, B, and C, and by internal closures. Bethlehem's Area A is the smallest among all Palestinian cities in the West Bank, with a land area of approximately 18 square km. As it contains very little agricultural land, most of its residents depend for employment on jobs inside Israel, or on the tourism sector. During times of strict closure, the unemployment rate reached a record high, as Bethlehemites were denied entry into Jerusalem, and tourists were denied entry into Bethlehem. This severe blow to the Bethlehem economy has detrimental effects on family and community life. Due to this hardship, many families have emigrated.

The ability of Bethlehem to absorb its natural population growth declined dramatically after the 1967 annexation of 16,000 *dunum*s of its land, and even further after massive Israeli confiscation of land, and the building of by-pass roads and colonies. Whereas, the nascent Har Homa colony will draw the northern boundary of the Bethlehem area, the Gush Etzion bloc of colonies limits Bethlehem's southern expanse. From the west, Bethlehem is surrounded by Bitar colony, as well as by two by-pass roads. From the east, by Taqoa colony and a by-pass road. The building of Har Homa and the fenced military by-pass road, which will connect it with the neighbouring Gilo colony, will deprive Bethlehem of the only land left for its future development.

Construction on Har Homa colony began in March 1997 and has continued uninterrupted since. The construction not only violates international laws, but also threatens the Christian holy sites located on Jabal Abu Ghneim, and places them under the control of Israeli Jewish colonisers.

The Har Homa colony will ensure that Israel deprives Bethlehemites of their main source of income: tourism. The project includes the building of a tourist village to attract Christian tourists who come to visit the Church of the Nativity in Bethlehem. To this end, Israel is working hard to complete the settlement before the year 2000.

Therefore, Israel, rather than the local Palestinian community, would benefit from the potential development of the tourism sector. It is worth mentioning here that the Paris Economic Protocol between Israel and the Palestinian Authority stipulates that both sides should allow free movement of tourist buses and vehicles between the two sides.

The fact that large portions of the community live outside of Area A is a further devastating factor for Bethlehem. Thus, many neighbourhoods in a town or village are physically separated from the core part of their communities. In times of internal closures, children of these neighbourhoods are not allowed to reach their schools, sick people are denied access to hospitals, and it is impossible to visit relatives or friends.[4] For example, several neighbourhoods in the towns of Beit Sahour and Beit Jala are excluded from Area A, and classified as Area C. The mayor of Beit Sahour, who happens to live in one of these excluded neighbourhoods, is denied access to the municipality, and, therefore, is not able to serve his community adequately during the harsh times of Israeli closure. Also, Talita Kumi Lutheran Secondary School, one of the most prominent and largest schools serving the Bethlehem area, is located in Area C. On several occasions since the signing of Oslo II, Talita Kumi's over 1000 students were not allowed to reach their school and carry on with their education.

What it takes for a lasting peace

The major challenges in Palestine at this stage are not a direct result of the content of the Oslo II Interim Agreement. Rather, they are a result of Israeli noncompliance with, and only partial implementation of the agreement itself. A renewed commitment by Israel to the full and immediate implementation of the agreement is absolutely necessary to restore Palestine's geographical integrity. By halting the confiscation of land and the expansion of Israeli colonies, by ceasing further construction of by-pass roads, by eliminating the restrictions on their use by Palestinians, Israel would not only begin to fulfil its obligation to a just and

---

4 *Al-Hiyat* Newspaper, '245 Villages are Deprived of Health Services', Friday, 15 March 1996, p. 4.

comprehensive settlement, but also demonstrate its foresight and wisdom by safeguarding the sustainable future of Palestine and its peoples. In order to reach a political environment conducive to a sustainable final status agreement of the Israeli-Palestinian conflict, both parties not only need to implement the terms and spirit of the Oslo II Interim Agreement, but should also maintain a high level of consultation on issues left to final status negotiations, such as Jerusalem, water, Israeli colonies, and Palestinian refugees. These requirements are the recipe for a lasting and comprehensive peace process, without which tension will remain in the area, and the peace process may fall into real jeopardy. The violation of the above two principles for a lasting peace agreement, however, has become the norm, and the Israeli appetite for a genuine peace has disappeared. Unless the international community exerts pressure on Israel to abide by the standing agreements, it will be impossible to put the stalled peace process back on the right track.

If such a situation continues beyond the intended interim period, maintaining the stability and the environmentally sustainable and progressive economy required for an independent Palestinian state will be impossible. This will not only deny the right of Palestinians to self-determination, but also directly contradict international resolutions, namely UN Resolutions 242 and 338, which are the essence of the peace process begun in Madrid in 1991.

In sum, regardless of the titles of the agreements to be signed between the Palestinian Authority and Israel, the agreements should not violate the terms of international conventions, such as Fourth Geneva Convention, and the inalienable rights of the Palestinian people stated by the many UN Resolutions, especially 242 and 338. Unless these agreements respect Palestinian rights which have been violated throughout the past fifty years, they will be unable to deliver a sustainable and lasting peace.

THE ECONOMICS OF PALESTINE AND JUBILEE

Yousef Nasser

The subject of jubilee and that of economics have much in common. Both jubilee and economics deal with humankind's resources, the question of ownership of these resources, how they are utilised, and for whom they are allocated and produced. The subject of Israel's jubilee this year, concurrent with the continued occupation of Palestinian lands and control over Palestinian resources and movement of people and goods, brings into focus the necessity of the fulfilment of the essence of jubilee. According to scripture, 'In the jubilee year, among other things, the slaves were to be set free, the debts of the poor were to be forgiven, and the land was to be returned to its original owners.'[1] The essence of jubilee is justice, the essence of the Palestinian plight has been the absence of justice, and the essence of Israeli existence and its jubilee is injustice. The fact that Israel exists is also the fact that the Palestinian predicament exists. One 'nation's' establishment and existence has required the oppression and exploitation of another 'nation'.

Modern day 'pragmatic economics' does not consider issues of justice when it comes to the distribution of income, or to the ownership of the means of production—these are taken as given. However, these issues were high on the agenda of classical economics and modern day political economists. When dealing in a scholarly fashion with the economics of Palestine, in the past, in the present and in the future, 'jubilee' takes on significant meaning regardless of one's spiritual disposition. I will even venture to say that jubilee is crucial in the Palestinian-Israeli quest for peace. Throughout this paper, the relationship between the concept of jubilee and the economics of Palestine (and the Palestinians) will be disclosed.

The first part of this paper will distinguish between the specific and concrete historical economic conditions of the Palestinian people. The aim is to identify the particularity of the Palestinian case in terms of prospects for economic development. The second part will attempt to

---

[1] See Leviticus 25, *Cornerstone* 10 (Christmas 1997), *Sabeel*, p. 1.

identify the necessary and sufficient conditions that need to be addressed for a brighter and peaceful future for the Palestinians as well as for the Israeli people.

The historic and concrete condition of the Palestinian economy

Historically the Palestinian economy and the economic conditions confronting the Palestinian people have been influenced, and in most instances determined by external forces. The most significant force to impact on and determine the history and shape of Palestinian society has been Zionist colonisation and the establishment of the State of Israel. By 1948 the Zionist movement had become powerful enough to establish the State of Israel on over 70 per cent of historical Palestine, expel and scare-off over 700,000 Palestinians to surrounding areas, expropriate their material possession, and then systematically destroy over 350 towns and villages. For the Palestinians remaining within the boundaries of the new state their day to day lives were extensively controlled by the military authorities of the Zionist State. Until 1964 they were controlled by draconian military laws, and since then they have been subjected to institutionalised third class status and treatment (the second class being oriental Jews).

Those areas of historical Palestine not falling under Israeli control, the West Bank and Gaza Strip, came under Jordanian and Egyptian authority respectively. In addition to alien rule over these areas, the flooding of over 200,000 Palestinians into Gaza, and over 350,000 into the West Bank aggravated the already limited economic resource base of the inhabitants. In addition to this, the new rulers over these areas implemented policies designed to benefit themselves, and not to serve the interest and well-being of the Palestinian people under their control. In 1967 Israel occupied the remaining parts of historical Palestine and until 1995 controlled every aspect of Palestinian life in these areas by means of military dictate, justified on security grounds. With the establishment of the Palestinian Authority, control over civil matters was handed over to the Palestinians, whereas control over resources (land and water), movement of goods, and people remains under Israeli jurisdiction. Yet, despite the commencement of the peace process in 1991, the most detrimental aspects of Israeli occupation continue to this day. These include land confiscation, restricted use of water, imprisonment, torture, collective punishment and the unnecessary harassment and delay of the movement of people and goods from one location to the next, let alone to the outside world.

Zionist ideology and policy: politics over economics

Israeli policy towards the Palestinians has been shaped primarily by ideological, political and security considerations, and secondarily by the interests and needs of the Israeli economy. Expropriation of Palestinian land and possessions, the denial of a Palestinian national entity are based on the essence of Zionist ideology. According to Zionist ideology the land of Palestine belonged exclusively to the Jewish people by divine and historical right. The portrayal of the backwardness of the indigenous population led to the conclusion that the native population should make way for the civilised settlers. Unable to cleanse the land of Palestine of its native population, although the intent and design to do so was, and still is there,[2] the necessity of denying the existence of a people with legitimate rights to self-determination was imperative. This required sophisticated and efficient forms of political oppression. The consequent economic exploitation of the Palestinians by Zionist Israel, and the prevailing economic structure of the Palestinian entity are, therefore, a consequence, and not an objective of Zionist aggression. Unlike classical colonialism and classical occupations, Zionism did not aim at economically exploiting the native population. It did not see the Palestinians as a steady supply of cheap labour for their factories (although this did happen).

Since 1967 Israeli policy has also been influenced by differing political tendencies within and between ruling parties. Within the Labour Party there were those, such as Defence Minister Moshe Dayan in 1967, who advocated a policy of integration. At the same time, others advocated territorial compromise, such as government minister Yigal Allon, who feared that the incorporation of over one million more Palestinians would harm the Jewish character of Israel. The Likud Party, on the other hand, which came to power in 1977, ruled until 1992, and was re-elected in 1996, has always been united in its ideological commitment to 'Greater

---

[2] Masalha, N, *Expulsion of the Palestinians: the Concept of 'Transfer' in Zionist Political Thought, 1882-1948*, Institute of Palestine Studies, Washington DC, 1992.

Israel'. This position implied the incorporation of the West Bank land but not its people. In an effort to achieve this, the Likud government established over 100 settlements in the late 1970s and early 1980s. The aim was to isolate physically Palestinian-inhabited areas from each other, and connect Jewish settlements to Israel proper. These settlements and their ongoing expansion today are the major obstacle to peace. Physically this was to be achieved by a carefully constructed infrastructure (roads, electricity, and communications) system. Legally it was to be achieved by applying Israeli law only to Jewish settlements.

The 1968 decision to allow Palestinians from the Occupied Territories to work in Israel on a daily basis was made both out of security considerations and economic necessity. The Israeli position was that it would be dangerous to allow the Palestinian population to endure economic deprivation, arising from the serious dislocation after the war, for a prolonged period. Such a situation could lead to political unrest and provide a catalyst for active resistance.[3] Allowing employment of Palestinians in Israel was to be a means of defusing such a situation. Economically, the employment of Palestinians in Israel satisfied an emerging Israeli need. The post-war economy of Israel was experiencing an economic boom, as well as an acute labour shortage, particularly for unskilled manual labour. Palestinian labour satisfied this demand at less than half the cost of Israeli labour.

The decision to open the labour market was consistent with the Labour movement's politically hawkish tendency led by Moshe Dayan. The opening of the labour market and settlement building contributed to the political aim of integrating, or merging the Occupied Territories with Israel. The aim of these policies is to make a political settlement harder to negotiate, since it will involve dividing the country.[4]

In line with this thinking, which, although political in motive, primarily served Israeli economic interests, was the decision to open the West Bank and Gaza Strip markets to Israeli commodities, thus expanding the market for Israeli manufacturers. Soon after 1967 these two markets became the second largest importers of Israeli goods, after the United States.

Another major policy decision was that of the 'open bridges'

---

[3] Shabtai, T, *The Cursed Blessing: The Story of Israel's Occupation of the West Bank*, Weidenfeld and Nicolson, London, 1969, p. 95.

[4] Tamari, S, 'The Dislocation and Re-constitution of a Peasantry: The Social Economy of Agrarian Palestine in the Central Highlands and the Jordan Valley, 1960-1980', PhD thesis (September 1983), pp. 74-75.

between the West Bank and Jordan. This was aimed first at providing an atmosphere of normality, by allowing the inhabitants to retain some form of contact with relatives, business interests, and the Jordanian government, and, secondly, to provide an outlet for Palestinian agricultural commodities. The open bridge policy did contribute to a semblance of normalcy, helped limit dissatisfaction, and allowed the king of Jordan some form of influence over his supporters in the West Bank. The king was viewed by the Israeli leadership as having a moderating influence over Palestinian politics.

Two other Israeli policy actions that shaped the structure of the Palestinian economy were the closure of all the major financial institutions on the West Bank, and the application of Israeli property laws and regulations. All banks, Arab and foreign, operating in the West Bank were closed just after Israeli rule was established in 1967. Israeli banks that were allowed to open branches in the territories were not able to fill the gap, and have only been used by Palestinian businessmen and businesswomen to facilitate their transactions with Israeli and foreign suppliers. Although an Arab bank (the Cairo-Amman Bank) was allowed to open branches in Ramallah and Nablus in 1986/87, the conditions imposed on its operations did not allow it to fill the void existing in the credit (and capital) market.

Since the signing of the Oslo Agreement numerous banks opened in the Palestinian territories, with much greater freedom, and with three legal tenders, the US dollar, the Jordanian dinar and the Israeli shekel. Yet, although the banks are allowed to function as a conduit for savings to become investment, this has not happened. The main stumbling blocks include high interest rates, and the lack of stability. The absence of stability is mainly a product of the stalled peace talks, and the continued control of trade routes by the Israeli authorities. The operation of storefront moneychangers that have been allowed in the West Bank has also been unable to fill this void. Moneychangers concentrate on changing money from one currency to another (primarily US dollars, Jordanian dinars, and Israeli currency). What little credit they offer is short-term (one month usually), and is determined by non-market familial and personal relations. The very high interest rates they charge (3 per cent per month) have limited their development as an alternative credit market.[5]

At the core of the Palestinian-Israeli conflict is the question of

[5] For a detailed and comprehensive account of the financial regime in the West Bank see Laurence, H, 'Money and Finance with Undeveloped Banking in the Occupied Territories', in Abed, G T, (ed.), *The Palestine Economy: Studies in Development under Prolonged Occupation*, Routledge, London, 1988, pp. 191-222.

land. By 1985, over 52 per cent of the land-mass of the West Bank was under Israeli control and over 50 per cent of the land mass of the Gaza Strip. According to Benvenisti, 'This was achieved through elaborate mechanisms and quasi-legal procedures ... The system was so well developed [over the years] that land alienation became routine ...'[6] A number of methods are used to expropriate land including absentee-owned land laws, government lands policies, the Declaration of State Land, and land expropriation for public use. The first law derives from an Israeli law first imposed in 1948, placing the property of absent owners in the hands of the Custodian of Abandoned Property. Thereafter the burden of proof of ownership rests with the claimant. The second method transferred land owned by the Jordanian government to the military government; the last two are derived from the Ottoman Land Code of 1855 and the Jordanian law (No. 2, 1953), respectively, and have been amended by military orders.

The first law, the absentee land law, combined with the structure of land ownership and the attitude towards land, has constrained any development in a land market. The character and structure of land ownership in Palestine derives from the *mesha'* (communal) system, which both parcelled the land and fragmented ownership. Thus, an individual may own ten *dunums* of land, composed of 15 to 20 parcels, and own one share in the first, 20 shares in the second, 30 shares in the third, 6 shares in the fourth, and so on. Many Palestinian property owners were absent during 1967, and could not return afterwards. Many more have lost their residency status since 1967 and have become absentee property owners. Their partners in the land (brothers, sisters, other kin) would not dare attempt to sell the land, because it would entail exposing the absence of one of the co-owners to the Israeli authorities, who would claim the share as absentee land.

Impact on the structure of the West Bank economy: change within parameters

Although this section will focus on the impact of occupation on the West Bank economy, the same policies and practices apply to the Gaza Strip. However, given the nature of the geographic size and the demographic

---

6 Benvenisti, M, '1986 REPORT: Demographic, Economic, Legal, Social and Political Developments in the West Bank', West Bank Data Project, Jerusalem, 1986, p. 25.

characteristics of the Gaza Strip, the consequences of Israeli actions on the economy and the people of the Gaza Strip have been much more detrimental and profound.

Within the political-security parameters set by the Israeli authorities, the introduction of labour and commodity markets modified the structure of the West Bank economy without expanding or developing the resource base that prevailed in 1967. Israel's occupation of the West Bank brought together by force two distinct, asymmetric social formations under one rule: on the one hand, the West Bank, an agrarian, capital poor, low income economy, described by Graham-Brown as 'an agricultural hinterland'[7], and, on the other, an industrial, capital rich, high income economy, with a combination of private enterprise, and substantial state enterprise. The relationship between these two social formations, like any other relationship, is unique. But also like other relationships there are features which are common to the experiences of other countries. Examples of economic relationships between capital rich, high income regions and labour surplus, low income regions are many. Among these are the relationships between South Africa and its neighbouring states, North Africa and the French economy, the historical relationship between England and Ireland, and America and Puerto Rico.

Depending on the conceptual formulations utilised, and on political position, differing interpretations and conclusions have been reached about the outcome of this encounter.[8] However, there is agreement that the consequences of the occupation on the economies of the Occupied Territories have been profound and far-reaching. It would be difficult for either side to challenge Brian Van Arkadie's observation that although there was no:

---

[7] Graham-Brown, S, 'Agriculture and Labour Transformation in Palestine', in Glavanis, K and P (eds.), *The Rural Middle East: Peasant Lives and Modes of Production*, Zed Books, London, 1990, p. 56.

[8] From among the favourable conclusions, see Ater, M, 'Autonomous West Bank is Poor Economics', *Jerusalem Post* (30 October 1975); Bergman, A, *The Economy of the Administered Territories 1974-1975*, Central Bank of Israel, Jerusalem, 1976; Bull, V, *The West Bank, Is It Viable?*, Lexington Books, Lexington Mass., 1975; Zakai, D, Economic *Development in Judea-Samaria and the Gaza District*, Central Bank of Israel, Jerusalem, 1988. And, from among the negative conclusions, see: Hillal, J, *The West Bank: its Economic and Social Structure, 1948-1974*, PLO Research Center, Beirut, 1975 (in Arabic); Tamari, S, 'Building Other People's Homes: The Palestinian Peasant's Household and Work in Israel', *Journal of Palestine Studies*, XI (1981): 31-66; and Sayigh, Y, 'The Palestinian Economy under Occupation: Dependency and Pauperization', *The Journal of Palestine Studies* XV (1986): 46-67.

> ... Israeli master-plan for changing the external economic relationships of the two Occupied Territories or a long-range vision of a preferred economic future for them ... what happened after 1967 was more complex and no less profound than if such a master-plan actually existed.[9]

Eighteen years after occupation, and ten years after the observation made by Van Arkadie, an Israeli observer reached a similar conclusion. He noted that after examination of the facts, Israel's economic policy seems to be clear and consistent, aimed at,

> ... freezing the economic development of the Palestinian sector along with encouragement of improvements in the standard of living, based on income from work in Israel; economic prosperity for individual residents alongside economic stagnation at the communal level; discouraging independent economic development that would enter into competition with the Israeli economy, and prevention of independent economic development that could enable Palestinian political forces to establish power bases, and eventually a Palestinian state.[10]

After further investigation he found that Israeli policy,

> has actually been ... a haphazard *post factum* consequence of decisions made without forethought, in response to pressures, or as compromises or concessions to Israeli pressure groups ... [however] ... in actual fact, economic policy is inseparable from political and security policies, and derives from them.[11]

The Israeli decisions to open the labour market to Palestinian workers and the Palestinian markets to Israeli commodities exposed the

---

[9] Van Arkadie, B, *Benefits and Burdens: A Report on the West Bank and Gaza Strip Economies Since 1967*, Carnegie Endowment For International Peace, New York, 1977, p. 37.

[10] Benvenisti *et al., The West Bank Handbook: A Political Lexicon*, West Bank Data Project, Jerusalem, 1986, p. 67.

[11] Benvenisti *et al.* (1986), p. 65.

Palestinian economies to powerful market forces, forces which were further intensified by the differences in the economic structures and wage levels between the two. However, market forces in the West Bank were not allowed to operate under conditions of *laissez-faire*, but were under the sway of Israel's political, security, and economic interests. For example Van Arkadie notes,

> Israel channelled and controlled the basic market forces while, at the same time, limiting severely the role of public investment and comprehensive development programs in the territories.[12]

Since 1967, whether by design or by default, Israeli occupation has warped the Palestinian structure and forced the West Bank and Gaza Strip into subservience to the Israeli economy. They serve the Israeli economy in two important ways: first, by being a reserve for cheap labour; and, second, by providing a 'captive market' for Israeli commodities. The market for Palestinian labour in Israel and the market for Israeli commodities in the West Bank have been crucial in determining significant changes in the structure of the West Bank economy in general, but they also have been the central forces altering the conditions of production and reproduction of the economy. In the process, the occupation of a population of over 2.5 million people has been a profitable venture for the Israelis, rather than a burden.[13]

Structural changes within the economy

The makeup of gross domestic product (GDP) has gradually shifted over the years. The trend has been a move from agriculture to services, a decline in the share of industry, and a rise in the share of GDP from construction. These changes have been directly and indirectly related to the developments of the market for Palestinian labour in Israel and the emergence of the

---

12. Van Arkadie (1977), p. 38.

13 It has been estimated that between 1967 and 1986 the net capital transfer from the West Bank to Israel was in the range of $600 to $700 million (US dollars), or almost $39 million per year. See Benvenisti *et al.* (1986), p. 92. This does not include the benefits of lower wages paid to Palestinians working in Israel, nor the deductions of income tax, social insurance, national insurance, and Histadrut fees taken out of gross wages.

West Bank as a protected market for Israeli commodities.

The West Bank economy remains based largely upon agriculture as the productive base. Within agriculture, there has been no investment in physical infrastructure, no agrarian reform, and no support systems such as marketing and credit. On the contrary, since 1970 government assistance to agriculture has decreased, loans were eliminated by 1986, and the number of agricultural advisers has declined.[14] The share of agriculture in GDP has steadily declined from an average of 30 per cent, in the period 1970-1982, to just above 20 per cent thereafter. Although the share of GDP from agriculture and the number of employed have declined, the total output has increased significantly, reflecting rising productivity within the sector. However, the value of agricultural output has not risen as fast as output, and during some years the value of total output has declined. Prices of agricultural goods have been restrained by competition from subsidised Israeli produce. Agriculture has also experienced a total shift in the make up of output. The share of use value crops, such as wheat, barley and pulses has been declining the most; and the cash crop, mainly olive, has been rising the most. The output of vegetable cash crops has increased significantly, but this has been concentrated in irrigated farming areas. In the dry farming hill region vegetable output levels have declined, and what continues to be cultivated is for use value. Even though the proportion of labour involved in agriculture has fallen significantly, now ranging between 26 and 29 per cent of total employed in the West Bank (down from over 40 per cent), its proportion remains greater than agriculture's contribution to GDP, indicating the labour intensive traditional nature of agricultural production.

The decline in the share of agriculture in GDP has not been due to a rise in the contribution of industry. Industry continues to account for an insignificant share of GDP (and GNP), with the bulk of establishments continuing to consist of small-scale, labour intensive workshops. Industrial contribution to GDP has been and remains meagre, accounting for less than 8 per cent of GDP after 1975, falling from a high of 9 per cent of GDP in 1971. Although the share of GDP from industry has declined, the absolute value of output of this sector has grown. By 1980 the real value of industrial output increased by almost double its level in 1970, and by 1987 it had increased by almost three times the 1970 level.[15] Yet the total

---

[14] Benvenisti *et al.* (1986), p. 1.

[15] Israel, CBS, *National Accounts of Judea, Samaria and Gaza Area: 1968-1986*, CBS, Jerusalem, 1988, Special Series No. 818, p. 90.

value of industrial output in 1987 (around $100 million) accounted for less than 17 per cent of imported manufactured goods, and less than 6 per cent of GNP. Today, the share of industry to GNP continues to be less than 10 per cent of GNP.

The growth in the contribution of construction has been the most significant, consistently rising from just under 6 per cent in 1971 to over 16 per cent in 1987 and around 18 per cent in 1997. This is a reflection of the growing demand deriving from population growth financed by rising household incomes, primarily derived from wage income in Israel and remittances. The major investment activity over the past two decades has been in construction.

A major shift within the economy has been towards services, primarily non-government services. The contribution of the service sectors has shown significant growth, and by 1987 accounted for over 57.7 per cent of GDP. This growth has primarily been in the private service sector. The contribution of private services ('other services') to GDP has grown from around 34 per cent in 1970 to 47 per cent in 1987. The contribution of this sector is pronounced, and is not common for an economy with industrial and agricultural sectors at this level of development.

On the other hand, services provided by the Israeli occupation government have shown a consistent decline, falling from just over 15 per cent in 1970 to around 10 per cent in 1987. The rise in the share of public services between 1981 and 1985 was primarily due to the political decisions deriving from the Camp David peace accords. These decisions include imposing a 'civil administration', and establishing and financing 'Village Leagues'[16] as an alternative leadership to the PLO. The drive to create facts on the ground by building more settlements also contributed.[17] However, since the coming of the Palestinian Authority (PA), this figure has increased substantially, given that over 75 per cent of the PA budget goes to wages. And given that the number of government employees has grown to around 80,000 from around 20,000 during the previous period, the share of public expenditure has increased significantly since 1995.

---

[16] The Village Leagues were sponsored, financed, and armed by the military authorities as an alternative leadership to the PLO. Between 1981-83 the Village Leagues received $20.8 million from the public budget—see Benvenisti *et al.* (1988), p. 220.

[17] By 1986, a total of 109 Jewish settlements had been built on the West Bank, 60 of which had been established between 1980 and 1985. The building of roads, and electrical and telephone grids serving these settlements is partially financed by the military government.

Growth of income

The shift in the sectoral distribution of West Bank GDP, shown above, is primarily a consequence of the introduction of a wage labour market that increased per capita incomes. Initially this induced spectacular growth in GDP and GNP, then high growth, and finally faltering growth. During the five-year period 1971-1975, West Bank GDP grew by an average of 14.5 per cent per annum (GNP grew at 17.5 per cent per annum). In the next four years (1976-1979) average GDP growth per annum fell to less than 5 per cent (GNP growth was a little over 4 per cent per annum), and finally during the six year period 1980-1985 GDP growth per annum was 2.25 per cent (GNP was 1.5 per cent per annum).[18] However, if we exclude the year 1980 (which witnessed a bumper olive crop), and look at the five year period 1981 to 1985, average growth of GDP per annum was negative at -1.6 per cent.

Part of the explanation for the spectacular growth in the early 1970s was the low baseline from which growth was measured. The West Bank economy between 1967 and 1969 was still recovering from the shock and dislocation in economic ties caused by the war. A low level of economic activity prevailed immediately after the war, when economic activity within the given parameters was not near its potential, and, once the economy adjusted to the new conditions and new relations were established, it took off. Taking the 1967-1969 period as a baseline, which was relatively low, partially explains the spectacular growth rates as simply being a recovery. This recovery seems to have lasted into 1976. It was not until sometime between 1975 and 1976 that the West Bank economy regained its old base, or its pre-war estimated level of GDP (around $166 million in 1966). Gross domestic product in 1975 was around $135 million, and around $180 million in 1976.

Another important explanation for this growth rate in GDP and GNP was the growth in income earned from employment outside the economy, mainly in Israel. Van Arkadie estimated that between 1968 and 1973,

> ... *over one third* of the increase in gross national product is accounted for directly by the increase in wage earnings in Israel. [And calculating the indirect effects of] ... the

[18] Various Issues of CBS, *Statistical Abstract of Israel.*

> contribution of employment earnings outside the territories [at] somewhere around one half of the total growth seems reasonable.[19]

At the time, Van Arkadie doubted that employment of Palestinians in Israel would continue to grow in the numbers and at the rate of its contribution to net earnings from abroad as it did between 1968 and 1973. The conclusion was that the growth of employment in Israel would not play the same role as a source of growth in the West Bank in the future as it had done in the past. For it to do so, Van Arkadie estimated that net factor payments from abroad would have to grow by 17 per cent per annum, in real terms, during the next five years.[20] He thought the probability of this was highly unlikely. According to available data, employment of Palestinians from the West Bank in Israel rose from 38,600 in 1973 to 48,100 in 1983 and to 62,900 in 1987.[21]

Corresponding to this we find that real factor payments from abroad grew, but not at the 17 per cent per annum necessary to maintain the high growth rates. Between 1973 and 1978 real net factor payments from abroad increased by around 50 per cent, representing an average growth per annum of 9 per cent. And during the next ten years (1978-1987), real net factor payments grew by 54 per cent (or around 5 per cent per annum), this growth being concentrated in the period 1986-1987. With the slow-down in growth of factor payments from abroad, we see a slow-down in the growth rates of domestic GDP. Van Arkadie predicted a fall-off in GDP growth, which did happen.

Employment in Israel has not been the only source of growth for the economy of the West Bank. Other external sources of income growth have been from transfer payments and capital movements. Transfer payments amounted to $58.2 million in 1987 and included the cash transfers of UNRWA, still a major employer in the West Bank, and transfers made by the Jordanian government. Net capital movement was equal to $134.2 million in 1987. Both of these items were equal to 47.5 per cent of wages earned in Israel in 1987. Thus, the total contribution to West Bank economic growth of external factors (wage employment in Israel, transfer payments, and capital movements) would rise significantly. Between 1970 and 1985 direct contribution to growth from all three sources would rise

---

[19] Arkadie (1977), pp. 120-22.

[20] Arkadie (1977), p. 122.

[21] Various issues of CBS, *Statistical Abstract of Israel.*

from 27.3 per cent to around 40 per cent, and total contribution (direct and indirect) to growth would rise from 41 per cent to around 60 per cent.

Trade imbalance and Israeli hegemony

The trade pattern of the West Bank economy exhibits characteristics of underdeveloped regions. The West Bank was before 1967, and continues to be primarily a producer of agricultural goods and an importer of manufactured goods. It has always run a large trade deficit, and since 1967 the deficit has expanded. After 1967 the direction of trade changed dramatically. From the early years of the occupation a pattern of trade was enforced and maintained, with Israel emerging as the dominant trading-partner of the West Bank, followed by Jordan, and finally 'other countries'.

The volume of West Bank trade has grown significantly since the early 1970s. Imports rose from \$64.9 million in 1970 to \$639.1 million in 1987,[22] increasing by a factor of 8.8. The value of imports has, on average, been equal to over 65 per cent of what the domestic economy produces. During many years it has been above 70 and 80 per cent of domestic production. Exports also rose dramatically, from \$30.5 to \$228.2 million between 1970-1987. However, the value of exports was equal to 26 per cent of GDP, increasing to 34 per cent in 1981, but declining afterwards to 20 per cent of GDP in 1987. The West Bank trade deficit has grown from \$34.4 million in 1970 to \$410 million in 1987.

Trade with Jordan

Jordan accounted for less than 2 per cent of total imports in 1987, falling from 11 per cent in 1969, and for 29 per cent of exports in 1987, falling from 59 per cent in 1969. Trade with Jordan has reflected the only positive trade balance; however, it has steadily declined since 1982 from its maximum of \$81 million, falling to \$32.2 million in 1988. Exports to Jordan declined from a high of \$90 million in 1982 to \$24.5 million in 1990. At

[22] Trade data between Israel, the West Bank, and Gaza Strip have not been published since 1987 by the Israeli authorities; one explanation for this is that the Israeli authorities do not want to reveal the extent of the success of the boycott of Israeli goods which was enforced by the *Intifada* in December 1987.

the same time, imports increased and have remained above 9 million dollars since 1986, thus decreasing the trade surplus of $57 million in 1987 to $12 million in 1990.

Trade between Jordan and the West Bank is restricted by both Israeli and Jordanian policy, as has been shown above. The fall in exports to Jordan since the early 1980s is a reflection of the Jordanian policy of decreasing agricultural imports from the West Bank, so as to protect its own agricultural sector, which started to exhibit increased output after a concerted development scheme was implemented in the late 1970s. This was further compounded by Jordan's policy of disengagement from the West Bank, implemented in 1988, whereby Jordan renounced any claims of sovereignty over the West Bank in favour of the PLO. The price for this has been greater restrictions on goods crossing to Jordan.

Trade with other countries

The low level of trade with 'other countries' is explained by the Israeli protectionist policy and Israeli-imposed barriers on West Bank exports to other countries. Tariffs and fees on imported commodities from abroad increase the international market value of these goods by around 60 per cent.[23] This not only allows Israeli merchandise to compete successfully with imported merchandise, but also allows Israeli merchants to sell their products at high prices (almost two thirds above net import prices).[24] Thus imports from other countries have never accounted for more than 16 per cent of total imports, and since 1983 they have been less than 10 per cent of total imports. Exports to other countries have never reached above 4 per cent of total exports and since 1977 have been below 1 per cent of total West Bank exports.

Trade with Israel

That the trade with Israel has become the most important component of West Bank trade is obvious from the figures. However, the available data only allow for the presentation of a gross picture. Trade figures between

[23] Benvenisti *et al.* (1986), p. 95.

[24] See Van Arkadie (1977), p. 89. Here net imported prices equals import prices minus customs duties and taxes.

the West Bank and Israel do not provide a commodity breakdown. The data do not expose the degree to which imports from Israel are re-exports from other countries, nor do they indicate if exports to Israel are re-exported. The delineation between industrial and agricultural goods is obscured by inclusion of agricultural goods processed to some degree in the industrial category.

The most striking feature of the trade pattern has been the opening of the West Bank market to Israeli commodities. Since the early 1970s the West Bank has become the second most important export market of Israel; only the United States is more important. On its own the West Bank is the third most important export market for Israel, after the US and British markets.[25] During the late 1960s and early 1970s, imports of goods and services from Israel accounted for around 80 per cent of total imports. By 1973 they had approached 90 per cent of total imports, remaining around this level until 1987 when they surpassed the 90 per cent mark to equal $580.5 million. However, the reported trade deficit with Israel is an underestimate. Official statistics do not, and practically cannot, account for all the individual purchases made by Palestinians from Israeli businesses across the Green Line. These include the over 60,000 workers crossing daily into Israel who do much of their shopping in Israel before returning to the West Bank. This was evident on the many trips to Israel I made with workers.

The bulk of imports from Israel are manufactured commodities, accounting for 90 per cent of imports in 1986 and worth $381 million. The rest are agricultural goods worth over $69 million. It is significant to note that the value of manufactured imports from Israel in 1986 was equal to 3.8 times the value of West Bank industrial output (around $100 million in 1986). Furthermore, the value of agricultural imports from Israel, although less significant than manufactured goods, was equal to over 15 per cent of agricultural output in the West Bank. If the olive crop is excluded from West Bank agricultural output, the value of the share of agricultural imports from Israel rises to 23 per cent in 1986 and 29 per cent in 1987. Agricultural imports from Israel are subsidised on average by 50 per cent,[26] although this has benefited local consumers it has unfairly competed with West Bank agriculture, which also contributed to the significant fall in cultivation, primarily in the dry farming hill regions.

---

25 Israel, CBS, *Statistical Abstract of Israel 1988*, CBS, Jerusalem, 1989, No. 39, Table VIII/6.

26 Benvenisti *et al.* (1986), p. 95.

Israel has also become the major destination for West Bank exports, rising from 39 per cent in 1969 to 70 per cent of total exports in 1987. However, the absolute value of imports is significantly greater than exports to Israel. Exports from the West Bank to Israel grew nine-fold between 1970 and 1987, rising from $16.3 to $160.5 million; yet this was far from offsetting the deficit of over $420 million. It must be noted that the growth of exports to Israel is a reflection of the growth in subcontracting firms in the West Bank, mainly in the textile industry, whose share to value added is minimal. To a lesser extent it is also due to the increased exports of agricultural goods (such as grapes) that Israel has stopped supporting, consequently reducing the subsidies granted to its farmers.

The dominance of Israel over West Bank trade is mainly due to the restrictions and barriers placed on imports from other countries, and the 'free' access Israeli manufacturers are given to the West Bank markets. Thus, it is not surprising to find that the West Bank (and the Gaza Strip) economy has been described as a 'captive market'[27] for the '... shoddy Israeli industrial [and agricultural] products which could not compete with the local manufactures of the industrialised countries of Europe and North America.'[28] For example, agricultural commodities such as avocados, which do not meet the standards of the export market, are channelled to the West Bank (and Gaza Strip) markets.[29]

A number of conclusions can be drawn about the pattern of trade since 1967. First, trade has generated a significant and heavily-protected market in the West Bank and Gaza Strip for Israeli commodities. Second, trade with Jordan has steadily declined, and no alternative trading links have been established in other parts of the Middle East, or elsewhere. Third, the absence of protection and support for West Bank industry has meant that local industry in general has not developed. Only those sectors which complement Israeli industry (such as textiles and quarried materials) have grown, and those only marginally. Finally, the most prominent feature of trade links with Israel has been the persistent and growing trade deficit.

---

[27] Sayigh, 'The Palestinian Economy ...', p. 47.

[28] Ryan, S, 'The West Bank and Gaza: Political Consequences of Occupation', *MERIP Reports*, No.74 (January 1979), p. 3.

[29] This has also hampered recent attempts by farmers in the Tulkarm district to expand and develop the cultivation of avocados.

Labour and exploitation

One of the most attractive characteristics of the Palestinian labour force for the Israeli employer is its mobility—geographical, seasonal, and structural. Geographical mobility is particularly important in the construction industry. Given that the Palestinian worker cannot live in Israel and must travel a distance which on average takes two hours round trip to his place of work, in such a case an extra travel time of ten or fifteen minutes would not make too much difference. On the other hand, it is difficult to attract Jewish workers to jobs that are far from their homes, where twenty to thirty minutes travel time is considered long. Seasonal jobs, such as weeding, fruit-picking, citrus-packing, and industrial food-canning are virtually all filled by Palestinian workers.[30] These workers are hired on the spot and dismissed once the task is completed.

The structural mobility of Palestinian labour is another advantage. The majority of Jewish workers have security of tenure, and cannot be dismissed without receiving considerable severance pay. They are protected by the Histadrut (General Federation of Hebrew Labour). Although the Palestinian workers employed through the *leshka* (the [Work] Agency, from *Leshkat Avodah*) have a Histadrut fee deducted from their pay check, they are not considered members, and thus do not enjoy Histadrut protection. While it is very difficult and costly to dismiss a Jewish worker, it is very easy to dismiss a Palestinian worker, and it costs nothing. According to Histadrut regulations, a worker employed continuously for the same employer for ten years is entitled to job tenure and a pension. A common practice, which is illegal according to Israeli law, is to lay off the worker before this period and re-hire him after a short period has elapsed. This is simple to achieve with Palestinian workers, but impossible with Israeli workers.

Another advantage of Palestinian labour is that virtually all the Palestinian workers from the Occupied Territories are employed on a daily basis. Thus their income depends on the number of days actually worked; they receive no sick pay or vacations. The average number of days worked by workers from the territories has historically been in the range of twenty days per month. While reviewing one worker from Zatar's pay slips for the previous year, I found the number of days he worked varied each month between a minimum of eleven and a maximum of nineteen days.

---

30 Farjoun, E, 'Palestinian Workers in Israel: a Reserve Army of Labour', in Rothschild, J (ed.), *Forbidden Agendas*, Al Saqi Books, London, 1984, p. 109.

This was not because he was sick, or lazy, but because whenever the employer did not need him, he was simply told not to come for the following day or two.

Yet by far the most advantageous aspect (and the determining factor) in the demand for Palestinian labourers is the low wages they are willing to accept. Palestinian labour power is purchased at a cost below its value (the value of goods and services needed for the production and reproduction of the worker); thus, it is much more attractive than Jewish labour. Palestinian labour is also profitable for Israeli society as a whole. As pointed out by Meillassoux, the means of subsistence paid to labour is made up of two parts: one is the direct wage paid to the worker during employment, and the other is the indirect wage he receives in the form of social security benefits, (i.e., unemployment benefits, family allowances, health services, and so on).[31] The vast majority of Palestinians employed through the *leshka* who pay income tax, social insurance tax, health insurance, pension payments, and Histadrut fees do not receive these benefits. By 1987, only 700 workers were receiving retirement pensions, a very small number according to the ILO.[32] Palestinians are excluded from the following: old age and survivor's invalidity, unemployment, child allowances. The excuse is that they are non-residents of Israel.[33]

Whether they were employed through the *leshka* or not, Palestinian workers performing similar jobs on average received the same net wages. Although Israeli authorities claim that employment through the *leshka* ensures that they receive the benefits they are entitled to, Palestinian workers have lost faith in this claim through bitter experience. Those workers who choose not to go to the *leshka* explain that they avoid red tape this way, and that it is faster to find a job on one's own than to wait for assignments through the bureaucracy. Today, with the security limits, there are only around 50,000 Palestinians from both the West Bank and Gaza employed in Israel. These workers compete with around 300,000 foreign workers (200,000 of whom are considered illegal) in Israel today. Palestinian workers in Israel today feel lucky to have a job, let alone ask for equal rights as workers.

---

[31] In Wolpe, H, 'The theory of Internal Colonialism: the South African Case', in Oxaal, I, *et al.* (eds), *Beyond the Sociology of Development: Economy and Society in Latin America and Africa*, Routledge and Kegan Paul, London, 1975, p. 247.

[32] International Labour Conference, 'Report on the Situation of Workers of the Occupied Arab Territories', *Report of the Director General*, Appendix III, ILO, Geneva, 1988, p. 23.

[33] International Labour Conference, *Report* ..., Appendix III, p. 143.

It has been reported that the average wage received by Palestinians in 1972 for performing the same work in the same location as Jewish workers is 40 per cent lower than those of the Jewish workers.[34] However, it has been found that in sectors where Jews and Palestinians performed the same jobs such as in the textile industry, and small private businesses, the difference was 100 per cent. The Jewish worker was paid double the average wage of the Palestinian worker. In other sectors, especially construction, it was difficult to compare, because there were no Jewish workers performing the same jobs. Today, it is either Romanian or Thai workers performing similar work, and in some cases they are making less than Palestinian workers.

Conclusion

Israeli policy directed by ideological/political imperatives, namely the 'Greater Israel' syndrome, required denial of Palestinian self-determination. This required, and continues to require land confiscation, settlement building and expansion, and integration of these with Israel. To undermine the success of Palestinian self-determination, all institutions private or public were attacked, harassed and hampered from becoming bodies that would promote Palestinian nationalism. These policies did not mean that Israel would not take advantage of its military strength, and maximise its economic exploitation of Palestinian resources, mainly human labour.

Palestinian-owned land continues to be confiscated for the purpose of building new settlements (Jabal Abu Ghneim, or Har Homa), the expansion of existing settlements, and for the purpose of by-pass roads that connect (integrate) them to Israel 'proper'. Water is strictly controlled by Israel, and its use by Palestinians is highly restricted. For example, the Palestinian population has since 1967 been permitted access to only 30 per cent of the total water resources available under the West Bank and Gaza, despite an over 2.5 fold increase in the Palestinian population.

Today, some aspects of life faced by the Palestinians have deteriorated. The constraint on movement of people and goods between, and within Palestinian inhabited areas is one of the major difficulties faced. Prior to the peace process, movement of people and goods between Palestinian areas disconnected by Israel (the West Bank and Gaza) was possible on a routine basis; this was so even during the height of the

[34] Farjoun, 'Palestinian Workers in Israel ...', p. 99.

Intifada. Today, this is impossible without a permit from the Israeli military authorities. Travel to Israel, for purpose of work, business, and transient travel through Lod Airport requires a permit, which is expensive and time-consuming (at least a full day) to obtain. When Israel feels that a community deserves to be punished, because an act of violence against the settlers or army takes place, the area is placed under curfew for days on end, or the major town (which is area A and under Palestinian Authority control) is closed off. This deprives between 45 and 179 villages access to their major commercial, health, education, and supply centres. One such closure in 1996-97 around the city of Ramallah lasted for sixteen days, and another around Nablus lasted for around fourteen days.

Palestinians on the West Bank and Gaza continue to live under the threat of arrest and imprisonment by the Israeli authorities. Some are tried and sentenced, and others are placed in jail under 'Administrative Detention', which is imprisonment without charges or trial, for up to six months, renewable at the whim of the military authorities (the longest stretch lasting for seven years). Today, Israel holds over 2,500 Palestinians in their jails accused of security offences. Furthermore, Israel continues to practise torture, as verified by the most recent report of Amnesty International, and others, who criticised Israel for its torture of Palestinian detainees.

Another major form of punishment that continues to be implemented by Israel is the demolition of the homes of the families of individuals convicted, or suspected of security offences. This is also a form of collective punishment, for the whole family (average of six persons per family) is left homeless. The elderly, as well as the children, suffer.

At present, daily life for the majority of Palestinians in most of its aspects, and in particular the economic aspect, is worse than it was before the peace process began. The reality of the situation is that the Israelis have inserted a Palestinian face on the bureaucracy that controls their daily life. Today, the people face two bureaucratic monsters to fulfil necessary transactions: the Palestinian Authority, which is inefficient, overstaffed, and at times incompetent, and the second, the Israeli military, which continues to be the ultimate decision maker, for it must approve all activity related to movement of people and goods. What makes matters worse is that the Israeli military continues to behave according to its pre-Oslo mindset, that of an occupying force facing a 'hostile' native population. As a result, transactions which once required one week to complete now need two weeks, or more, to accomplish (not to mention the added cost).

Over the past hundred years the Palestinian people, in their day-to-day struggle to satisfy their basic wants and needs, have been subjected to continuous oppression, expulsion, dispossession, and untold injustice. This has primarily been at the hands of the Zionist colonisers of Palestine, and, since 1948, at the hands of the Zionist government of Israel. Throughout modern history, there has been no jubilee for the Palestinians, yet, as noted above, during 1998 Israel is celebrating its first jubilee, and Zionism its second jubilee as an organised movement in Palestine. The question of undoing the wrong, and of returning the land to its rightful owners is being implemented today in Europe for the injustice carried out against the Jewish faithful, prior to, during, and after the Second World War. These same questions, when it comes to the injustice carried out against the Palestinian people, are at present taboo among the Jewish faithful of Israel and the world, not to mention the Zionist faithful. Unless the Jewish people will do unto others as they demand be done unto them, there can be no jubilee in Palestine, and there can be no real peace in the area.

HUMAN RIGHTS ISSUES

Jonathan Kuttab

It is always a pleasure to speak to a group like this at *Sabeel*. What we are about at this conference is not simply documenting, or informing, or educating a group of people who do not know, but rather engaging with committed individuals who are quite knowledgeable and are wrestling with the current issues pertaining to the Palestinian-Israeli conflict, specifically from a Christian point of view. Also the occasion of the jubilee, the theme of this conference, is an occasion for rethinking, re-examining, and for seeking. I believe that new insights and comprehensions will allow us to continue in the struggle. In this sense I very much feel like the Apostle Paul, who said, 'Ours is a fight with Powers and Municipalities'—Principalities, I mean!

The struggle for human rights in this part of the world is unique. Human rights, of course, is a secular concept, and perhaps its very essence is that it is universal. It is inscribed in a number of documents and reflects certain values that were promulgated most clearly in the Declaration of Human Rights of 1948, which people who promote human rights believe should apply everywhere, to every country, in every situation. In dealing with human rights in Palestine, we must also recognise that while the same human principles apply, the violation of these human rights that occur here is distinctive. I am almost tempted to say that they are unique.

I will not catalogue for you what these human rights violations are—I am sure you are very familiar with them. Moreover, there is a lot of literature, Palestinian, Israeli and international, that describes these violations which are ongoing. Instead, I would like to treat the subject a little bit more from a philosophical, even religious, perspective, knowing that we are in fact dealing with issues of institutional evil. Secular people do not like to use the term 'evil'. They correctly point out that there is good and bad in everybody, and they are very reluctant to make such a harsh moral judgement. But the reality is that the Zionist movement, from its very beginning, has at its very core, and of its very nature led to violations of the human rights of Palestinians, of the indigenous people, that are different from violations that we see throughout the world. They are not necessarily the worst. I am sure there are some countries in the world where there are more frequent and perhaps more bloody incidents of torture, more outrageous abuses of due process, imprisonment, deportation, (house demolitions I do not think), but certainly detentions, other violations and/or restrictions on freedoms. Here, however, it is a little bit different. First, because it is not necessarily sadistic in nature. This is very important. At the beginning of the *Intifada*, for example, when many Palestinians were tortured, abused, and beaten by soldiers, one organisation that expressed its lack of comfort with what was happening, was the Shin Bet (the domestic section of the Israeli secret service). They thought that the process of interrogation—torture—should be left to the professionals. You should not allow eighteen-year-old recruits who do not know what they are seeking, what they are after, to beat up Palestinians and get confessions out of them. That way you get confessions but you do not get information! That way you break up their bodies but you do not necessarily break their spirits! You should leave it to the professionals, who know how to do it.

I submit that within the Israeli system, human rights violations are first and foremost utilitarian in nature. They are intended to achieve a specific result within the ideology of Zionism and for the political interest of the state, and not to give vent to personal individual venom. There is venom, there is racism, there is sadism aplenty, but that is not the purpose or the driving force behind human rights violations by the State of Israel.

A second aspect of human rights violations in Israel is that the State of Israel, having set for itself a certain standard, a certain goal, a certain vista, a certain appearance that it wanted to present to the outside world, is very careful to maintain that outward appearance. The session this morning (Michael Prior's lecture on 'The Bible and Zionism') was very interesting in that it laid bare the religious basis, or the religious justification for much of what is happening here in terms of the conquest of the land, displacement, and abuse of its indigenous population. I submit to you that the Israeli establishment has never acknowledged such a motivation. In fact, they have often fought against it.

To return to 'municipalities': former Jerusalem mayor, Teddy Kollek, who was as interested as any other Zionist in the judaisation of Jerusalem and making it a Jewish city, was one of the greatest and most vehement opponents of the *Ateret Cohanim* settlers. These settlers are the extremists, who, under the religious guise of wanting to rebuild the Temple, are taking a building here or a building there in the midst of the Muslim quarter. Mayor Kollek did not want that! It was problematic for him! He did it in a more subtle, organised, consistent, comprehensive, and secular fashion: through zoning and planning! Through major confiscation of all 'empty' plots around Jerusalem; through prohibition of building permits to the Palestinians; and through massive building for Jews, with state funds that would, in fact, achieve the racist goal of Judaising Jerusalem, without necessarily attracting all that negative publicity, and giving it the religious connotation as would the provocative actions of the *Ateret Cohanim* settlers.

In order to achieve that goal, one of the instruments that has been least acknowledged is the principle of legal positivism. This describes the idea that the law has nothing to do with justice. Apart from the fact that there is no constitution in the State of Israel, there is a tradition that the law is what the 'black letter of the legislation' says. That means that in a democratic society, where 51 per cent of the elected legislators pass a law in the Knesset, that law becomes binding on everyone else, and it is the duty of all the citizens, certainly of the police, of the courts, of the establishment, to fulfil the letter of the law. Whether the law is just or unjust becomes an academic issue of discussion for the political arena and is not the business or the concern of those who fulfil the law.

The idea that we are only obeying laws, that we are only obeying orders, and that this is the law of the land, etc., is not unique to Israel, of course. But the *process* by which a very comprehensive system of injustice was codified—and you have the possibility of even liberal and progressive, and sometimes even moral individuals carrying out these immoral policies—makes it part of the system. As a person who practised before military courts many times, I occasionally encountered very progressive, very liberal, very ethical, moral, decent Jews carrying out their functions in these courts. Invariably they will tell you, 'we have full sympathy with you and with your clients. However, this is the law.'

A little anecdote to bring it out of the academic to the practical. A military commander, or a governor of a certain area has the authority to insist on administrative punishments, including the authority to imprison, to deport, to demolish a house, to restrict freedom of movement, to close institutions, etc., simply by giving an order that, in his opinion, it is necessary or required for the security of the area. Unlike in other oppressive regimes, Israel provides an avenue for redress when this happens: one can appeal the administrative order. In this case, let us say, they arrest my client for six months, which is renewable. As an attorney, I can appeal to an Appeals Board on behalf of an administrative detainee. I appear before the Appeals Board which says, 'What do you have to say.' Then I have to say, 'I have nothing to say! My client is innocent! Why are you putting him in prison?' The judge, in true neutrality, turns to the representative of the state, 'Well, what do you have to say?' and he says, 'What I have to say, what evidence and what arguments I have, I want to tell to you and you alone, in the absence of the Palestinian detainee and his attorney, so would you ask them to please step outside?' I protest vigorously, saying, 'This is unjust. Even in South Africa during its *apartheid* times this would not be allowed.' And the judge would say, 'I sympathise with you, but this is the law! It says that this hearing would be held in secret, and that evidence, as well as arguments, would be stated in your absence.' So I step outside; they whisper together for five minutes, I return and, 'Now what do you have to say?' he asks me!

The truth is that, if I do not like the decision, which invariably confirms the six-month detention order, I can, in theory, appeal, and go to the High Court, which brings us to the second interesting attribute of the system. The Israeli High Court of Justice plays an integral role in the system of the oppression of Palestinians, and in justifying the process by which it is done. One goes to the High Court, where an attorney is always welcome—in fact, the Israelis make a 'big deal' of the fact that Israel is the first country in the world to open its courts to the citizens of its occupied territories. So one goes to the High Court, and what does one have to say? One objects to the decision of the Appeals Committee! And the High Court will hear one out: 'What do you have to say?' 'This is unjust, this is unfair, this is contrary to international law, this is a violation of human rights.' *But it does not violate any specific Israeli law!* 'It is a violation of the Geneva Conventions, of which Israel is a signatory!' 'Yes, but the Geneva Conventions have not been *adopted* by the Knesset, so that while Israel may be obligated under international law to follow them, we as a local municipal court, have no authority to impose our will on the government. Only the Knesset can do that by enacting specific legislation incorporating the Geneva Conventions into their local law. Until that time, we cannot help you!'

Until quite recently, the Israeli High Court enjoyed a wonderful reputation throughout the world as being a very progressive, very learned bastion of jurisprudence, largely because most of its decisions were never translated! They remained in Hebrew, and almost all commentaries on the High Court were done by sympathetic individuals who quoted very selectively what they described. Hence, it was assumed among the international legal community that Israel was one of the Western democracies with a very vibrant and progressive legal tradition, and that the High Court acted as a watchdog over the government, preserving the rights of the oppressed, including the Palestinians from the Occupied

Territories. The High Court, then, plays a pivotal role in the systematic violation of human rights while pretending to act as a watchdog over the actions of the Israeli government.

Another aspect of the systematic nature of violations of human rights of Palestinians is the system of isolating different components of the oppressive structures within the Israeli establishment. What do I mean? It is necessary for the Zionist enterprise not only to fool the outside world as to what is happening, but also to defend the conscience of the average Israeli concerning what is happening. What is important is not only what the outside world thinks of Israel, but what Israelis themselves think of themselves and of their society. The way that is done is by isolating the different components of the process of oppression from one another and insulating the general public from what is happening.

Again, this is an example of the outrageous way torture takes place. The professional Shin Bet interrogator tortures the Palestinian in order to obtain his confession. It is very important to obtain confessions, because one wants to try the Palestinian in a regular court, and to convict him according to the burden of proof, which is carried by the prosecution, believe it or not! The individual torturer is completely isolated from the person who actually takes down the confession, and who later has to appear in court and testify that the confession was taken voluntarily. This 'scribe' sits in a separate office. He meets the Palestinian under slightly more comfortable circumstances, offers him a cup of coffee and a cigarette, and assures him that what he says will be written down carefully. If the Palestinian states he has nothing to write down, he will be sent back to the person who obtained the confession from him in the first place. This one who takes down the confession already has a memo of all the things that the torturer has obtained. He or she is also insulated and isolated from the prosecutor who gets all the material ready, prepares the charge sheet and presents it to the judge. The prosecutor is also isolated and insulated from the judge who needs to maintain his pristine objectivity and impartiality, and who will only rule on the basis of the evidence in front of him (i.e., the signed confession) and who is, in fact and truth, independent of any political pressure from any side that would be partial. Israelis would never allow anybody to interfere in the independence of their judiciary. They simply set their rules in such a way that the result which the judge will reach will, inevitably, be precisely what is wanted. Not to mention that these judges in the whole legal process, of course, also are isolated and insulated from the rest of the population.

This procedure is not unique to courts. It goes beyond the courts, but the Israeli law and courts play a central role in the process of violations of the human rights of Palestinians. Zoning and planning also play a very important role. The person who comes to demolish a Palestinian's house is very sympathetic. He will simply tell him that no one anywhere in the world is allowed to build without a licence or a permit, and no permit will be issued except in accordance with a proper town plan describing where the roads are going to be and where the schools and the high-rise housing is going to be. So if there is no town plan a licence cannot be procured. 'It is not because you are an Arab! Jews would not get a permit either without a town plan! And, Jews who build without a license would also have their home demolished.' However, Jews almost never build houses! The government builds for them, with American money of course, and then there is no need to deal with these issues. When there is a need for building permits and building plans and licences, they are all based on a global plan that has these elements already in place.

The curious thing is that in the State of Israel the Arab citizens—unlike Palestinian Arabs in the Occupied Territories Israeli Arabs are citizens of the state—who now constitute about 20 per cent of the population, are largely invisible. They really do not exist! In fact, in Hebrew, the word for 'person', or 'man', is 'Jew'! So even public opinion polls refer to *Jewish* public opinion; they consistently ignore and eliminate 20 per cent of the population. Dr Ian Lustick recently told me that Israel has a very serious problem now because of the existence of all sorts of Jews whose Judaism is suspect, like the Falashas (Ethiopians) and the new immigrants from the Soviet Union, 25-40 per cent of whom are not Jewish! How does one deal with public opinion polls that should reflect only the opinions of Jews with all these Jews whose Judaism is suspect? Right now, one of the ways they do it in public opinion polls is to refer to 'non-Arab populations', not even to 'the Jewish population'. That is how they do it! While they know who the Arabs are, they do not know who the Jews are! For the first time in history, because of the power, the privileges, and the status that are enjoyed by Jews in the State of Israel, it is now advantageous to be Jewish, now it is something that you try to be, to have your Jewishness acknowledged because there are financial, housing, job opportunities, residency, all privileges that come with being recognised as Jewish in the State of Israel.

All this takes place within the context of a state that pretends, both to itself and to the outside world, that it is a secular, democratic, open, modern, progressive society living in the 20th century. It tries very hard to maintain that image, both towards the outside world and towards its own population. It is a very difficult juggling act. A lot of sophistication, energy, ingenuity, and thinking goes into achieving clearly undemocratic, oppressive, racist, and exclusivist ends while maintaining an appearance of democracy, universalism, and openness.

For a long time we Palestinians helped in this process because we never challenged it. We knew the State of Israel to be racist; we did not have to challenge it on the basis of racism. We knew it to be oppressive and undemocratic; we never had to challenge and show the limits of the contrary claims. We knew there was nothing to be obtained in the High Court of Israel, so we never challenged it on the principles of justice on its own terms. These days, a major new reality is taking place. Precisely because of the overwhelming power of the State of Israel and the utter weakness of the Palestinian and Arab side, it has become possible for the State of Israel to be more blatant and more open about its true nature, particularly with the election of Benyamin Netanyahu. Netanyahu's was *not* a razor-thin victory: he got a 60 per cent majority of the *Jewish* vote, which is the only one that counts in Israel. Shimon Peres got only 40 per cent. With Netanyahu's election it became possible for Israelis to be more open and more blatant about their desire to keep all the Occupied Territories, and only sub-contract to the Palestinian National Authority certain undesirable functions. Incidentally, they think Palestinians can do these things much more effectively than they can because Palestinians do not have to deal with an Israeli High Court, or with a tradition that pretends to respect human rights. They expect Yasser Arafat and the Palestinian Authority to be more effective in oppressing their own people than Israel is because they do not have to live up to 'our scruples' and 'our high Western democratic liberal standards'.

This is now the situation. There is an open, or an increasingly open admission of the nature and the policies of the State of Israel. For people who work in human rights, this is a wonderful opportunity to become more effective in the struggle. For Christians, who have to deal with the basic moral, philosophical, and ideological issues, it is a new challenge. Now, for the first time, we can in fact have an audience as we make a genuine critique of the State of Israel itself, of the Zionist movement and of the ideology on which it was built, and the oppressive policies that have all along been directed towards the local population and their rights.

JEWISH FUNDAMENTALISM

Moshe Reiss

Fundamentalism is endemic to all three monotheistic religions—Judaism, Christianity and Islam—the three religions coming from 'Avraham Avinu', our father Abraham. That is perhaps because these religions have an other-worldly basis—that is, heaven, or, the next world—which gives its believers (or at least its extreme believers) an inner reality that differs from outer or secular reality.

What does a fundamentalist believe in? It is the belief that its adherents, its members have the single truth about the ultimate meaning of life. Almost as if they and *only* they have spoken directly to God and only they continue to speak for God. Despite the holy books telling us that all human beings are God's children, some seem to be more God's children than others; the rest are second class citizens in God's world.

Fundamentalism within Judaism comes in two different forms. One may be called *Haredi-ism* which is a view that Judaism, a religion more of law or deeds than of theology, has *fixed* laws or rules of behaviour; fixed many centuries ago. One of those fixed rules is passive Messianism. Passive Messianism assumes Jews live in exile until the coming of the Messiah. The second form of Jewish fundamentalism involves the active ideology of Messianism—that the State of Israel is the beginning of the Messianic state. This view is usually associated with 'Religious Zionism'.

This essay will present the most extreme versions and positions of Jewish fundamentalism. Very few Jews may accept the positions in the extreme that will be presented. But many more follow some of its precepts. Thus *Haredi-ism* as presented may not involve more than a few thousand or tens of thousands of believers, but the impact of *Haredi-ism* on the 'modern Orthodox', on the Chief Rabbinate, and the political parties of 'Shas' and the 'United Torah Party' is significant. Similarly the extreme position of the 'National Religious Party' and its *Gush Emunim* wing may also involve only a few thousand, or tens of thousands of believers, but the party is strongly influenced by these. All these are part of the coalition government of the State of Israel and the government is influenced by all three of these religious-political parties.[1]

[1] Ultra-orthodox and Religious Zionists each hold about 10 per cent of the seats in the Knesset.

One can be an observant Jew and a Zionist, and not be a 'Religious Zionist'. An observant Jew is not required to believe that the State of Israel is the dawn of a Messianic state as stated in a prayer proclaimed by the Chief Rabbinate: 'Our Father in Heaven, the Rock of Israel and her Redeemer, bless You the State of Israel, the beginning of the dawn of our redemption.'

Rather, an observant Jew can believe that the State of Israel is a state like other states. This was the belief set forth by Theodor Herzl who is the founding father of Zionism. He believed, as do other secular, moderate, traditional and observant Jews, that Zionism was and is a national movement to protect Jews from antisemitism.[2] This need was made blatantly clear by the *Shoah* and continues to this day.

What is most ironic about these two types of Jewish fundamentalism, is how opposed they are to each other. *Haredi-ism*, in its most extreme form is anti-Zionist, while the basis of 'Religious Zionism' is its pro-Zionist views. Most *Haredim* believe that the people of Israel are still in exile and that the children of Israel had no right to establish a Jewish state, and, further, the attempt to do so was evil. The National Religious Party sees the State of Israel as 'the dawn of our redemption'.

What is interesting about Judaism is that, as a whole, it has never been monolithic, that is, it has never been fundamentalist. But it has always had a problem with fundamentalist tendencies. Judaism has evolved through, and indeed has been strengthened by, intellectual conflict. In the Second Temple Period there were many varieties of Judaism. The Talmud makes clear that for man, there is no absolute truth; both Rabbi Shammai and Rabbi Hillel had the truth, although their truths were in direct conflict with each other. Both rabbis lived during the transition to the Common Era.

In the Middle Ages, the greatest Jewish scholar was Maimonides, who was born in Cordoba, Spain, and lived most of his life in Egypt and all of it under Muslim rule. He wrote some of his works in Arabic. There was enormous conflict between his rationalist philosophy and those of the fundamentalists of his day. He was a physician and philosopher, studying Aristotle through Arabic translators, and very learned in secular sciences.[3]

---

[2] Believing that the State of Israel is a normal state does not necessarily contradict the idea of the dawn of redemption. The fact that a Jewish state was born after almost 2,000 years, after the *Shoah*, and has survived five major wars can be seen as miraculous, if not redemptive. This need not deny that Israel was intended as a normal state and is so intended by most of its inhabitants.

[3] In 1985, the United Nations held an international conference celebrating the 850th anniversary of his birth, in Cordoba, Spain. Jewish, Christian, and Muslim scholars met to discuss his impact on their respective religions.

His books were burnt by Jewish fundamentalists. Yet he is considered today, even by fundamentalists, the greatest Jewish scholar since the Talmud.

At the end of the 18th century a conflict arose between the followers of Rabbi Eliyahu (Elijah), known as the Vilna Goan (Goan means 'great one'), and the new Jewish movement of piety called *Hasidism*. This movement became very popular among the poor, less educated masses of Jews. The Vilna Goan, in addition to being a great Jewish scholar, was also known for his knowledge of the secular sciences, and had books of mathematics translated into Hebrew and Yiddish, so that his followers could study them. The Vilna Goan was concerned about the superstition and lack of scholarship amongst the *Hasidim*. He burnt the books of *Hasidism* and excommunicated its followers.

Both Maimonides and the Vilna Goan are among the heroes of the *Haredi* world. Yet if either Maimonides or the Vilna Goan were resurrected and saw the degree to which the *Haredi* world rejects any knowledge of the secular world they would consider *Haredi-ism* as heresy to their views of Judaism.

Haredi-ism

In terms of the law, *Haredim* state that the law was established by Moses on Mount Sinai, never to be changed. This in spite of the fact that the Talmud is a series of books discussing the meaning and different interpretations of the law. Rabbi Hillel's interpretation of the law, in serious conflict with Rabbi Shammai, was accepted by the Talmud.

Rabbi Hillel was born in 65 BCE and died (c.) 10 CE. The Talmud tells us he had a love of humanity, was gentle, modest, compassionate to the poor and promoted justice for the oppressed. That is why his legal interpretations prevailed. In his teaching of Judaism Hillel said 'love peace, seek peace, love mankind and thus lead them to the law.' Two examples of his legal interpretations are the *shmita year* and gentile conversions.

In the *shmita year*, each seventh year (in the land of Israel), the land lies fallow, that is, agricultural land is not planted and debts are annulled. This law still applies today. It was meant to protect farmers and protect the land. In an urban environment (which already existed in Jerusalem at the turn into the Common Era) loans had a different purpose. If they were annulled no one would make a loan in the sixth year for fear of its not being paid. Rabbi Hillel established that a creditor could declare the loan due to the Sanhedrin (the Talmudic Rabbinical Academy) and the owner of the debt could then collect the loan. Rabbi Shammai opposed this as a legal sham. The Talmudic sages ruled in favour of Hillel.

During that time Gentile conversion to Judaism was also debated. According to the Talmud three Gentiles came to Rabbi Shammai, who told them all to leave his house. They came to Rabbi Hillel, who said to them, 'What is hateful to you, do not do to your neighbour: that is the whole *Torah*; the rest is commentary; now go study.' All three were eventually converted.

The House of Shammai was clearly more conservative than the House of Hillel. In the Talmud the sages ruled that 'he who observed the House of Shammai deserves death.'[4] The reason is that the Talmud as seen above did not foster the stringent interpretation, but, rather, the lenient interpretation of the law. *Haredi-ism* (and much of modern Orthodoxy) fosters the stringent interpretation, and can therefore be called anti-Talmudic.

An example of the power of the Halakhic community to interpret the law is a legend told in the Talmud. Rabbi Eliezer ben Hyrcanus, a colleague of Jochanan ben Zakai and teacher of Rabbi Akiva,[5] had an argument about a legal interpretation, but the other sages disagreed with him. He said, 'If I am right let the carob tree move a hundred cubits.' The carob tree moved one hundred cubits. The other sages said, 'No proof can be brought from a carob tree.' Rabbi Eliezer then said, 'Let the river go backward.' It did, and the sages said, 'No proof can be brought from a river.' Rabbi Eliezer then said, 'Let the walls of this study house tilt.' They did. The sages continued to ignore the miracles, and then Rabbi Eliezer said, 'Let God state that I am right.' A voice from heaven, known as a *Bat Kol*, attested to Rabbi Eliezer being right. Rabbi Joshua, the head of the Assembly, then said, 'The *Torah* is not in Heaven, we pay no attention to voices from heaven.' According to the Talmud, God laughed, saying, 'My sons have defeated me.' When Rabbi Eliezer refused to accept his defeat and continued to insist on his opinion he was excommunicated.[6] That the *Torah* is not to be interpreted in Heaven but on earth, by living human beings, is the moral of this story.

Another aspect of *Haredi* fundamentalism is their attitude towards

---

4 Babylonian Talmud *Berachot* 1a and Jerusalem Talmud *Berachot* 1:4.

5 Rabbi Yochanan ben Zakai began the Talmudic Academy after the destruction of the Second Temple, and Rabbi Akiva was its greatest sage.

6 Bialik, H N, Ravnitsky, Y H (eds.), (translated by W G Braude), *The Book of Legends*, Schocken Books, New York, 1992, p. 223.

exile and redemption. They believe that the Jewish people are in exile, even though living in Israel. Exile, in this case, means a state before the Messianic age, or at least a time without a Temple. The Temple's destruction in 70 CE began the current exile. There is only exile or redemption, and the latter can come only from God. Thus being in Israel, even in a state controlled by Jews, is irrelevant to exile. In metaphysical beliefs there is only good or evil; there are no greys in this world view. Nothing can change until God intervenes. Their belief is tied into a completely passive coming of the messianic age.[7]

Neturei Karta

The *Neturei Karta* (Guardians of the City)[8] is a small sect in Jerusalem that does not recognise the State of Israel and in fact believes it to be anti-God. They represent the most extreme version of *Haredi-ism* and are clearly anti-Zionist. Their prime ideology is passive Messianism. They see the State of Israel as an attempt towards Messianism and therefore demonise it. They are associated with the *Edah Haredit*[9] (many thousands of ultra-orthodox persons) in Israel, and with the Satmar Hasidic group in Brooklyn, New York. The Satmar community came from northeastern Hungary and were led for decades by Rabbi Joel Teitelbaum. He was a very pious scholar and a charismatic with a fundamentalist outlook. Prior to his death in 1981, he was the official Rabbi of *Edah Haredit*, his successor, Rabbi Moshe Teitelbaum, continuing in this role. He was known as an anti-Zionist in the early 1920s. He was saved by the Zionists from the Nazis and moved to Jerusalem in 1944. But he left in 1946 and moved his community to Williamsburg, a neighbourhood of Brooklyn, New York.

Rabbi Joel Teitelbaum was associated with the beginning of this

---

7 This view is known in the Talmud as the 'Three Oaths'. The 'Three Oaths', written after the destruction of the Second Temple and the disastrous Bar Kokhba rebellion, was a plea against zealotry. The two fundamentalist groups can be described as zealots. This view was almost universally held by Orthodox Jews at the beginning of the twentieth century. The *Shoah*, the establishment of the State of Israel, and the Six Day War changed that.

8 Founded by Amram Blau and Aharon Katzennelbogen, this political-religious group broke from the Agudah in 1939, when it became non-Zionist rather than anti-Zionist. The Agudah recognised the need to emigrate from Poland during the growth of Nazism. This required co-operating with the Zionists.

9 Founded in 1918, one of its principle beliefs is anti-Zionism and the non recognition of the State of Israel. Its major work is communal, dealing particularly with *Kashrut* and marriages. This requires it to cooperate with the state.

anti-Zionist movement in the 1920s. It began by opposing other ultra-orthodox groups which had agreed to associate with the Zionist movement. It condemned both secular studies and agricultural settlements in Palestine, the latter being considered by them as active Messianism and 'Satanic'. As a motto they converted the phrase in Zechariah, 'May the Lord who has chosen, rebuke you, O Satan' (Zech 3.2) to, 'May the Lord rebuke you, O Satan who chooses Jerusalem.' Thus those who choose to go to Jerusalem have chosen to associate with Satan. As Rabbi Joel Teitelbaum has stated in his book *Vayoel Moshe*:

> May the Lord rebuke Satan, for he [Satan] has chosen Jerusalem in order to better those who dwell there ... to seduce and corrupt the entire world wrapped in the mantle of Jerusalem's glory.[10]

The *Neturei Karta* believe that the State of Israel should not exist. The state is anti-Messianic. When the Messiah comes he will create a new spiritual and physical reality which will conform to *Halakhah* (Jewish law). And since the Messiah has not come, exile and suffering which are the result of Jewish sins, must continue. The *Neturei Karta* do not vote in Israeli elections, have their own schools and do not speak Hebrew, preferring Yiddish. They have called for the liquidation of the State of Israel. Immediately after President Nasser closed the Gulf of Aqaba in 1967, they stated:

> We have no connection with them [the Zionists] or with any of their affairs. We desire no benefit from them or through them, neither deliverance nor protection. Nor do we want collaboration with them.[11]

In fact they asked the United Nations to give them passports as residents of the International City of Jerusalem. As the Satmar Rabbi has written,

> The very idea of people of Israel achieving independence before the coming of the Messiah represents heresy against

---

[10] Frankel, J (ed.), *Jews and Messianism in the Modern Era*, Oxford University Press, Oxford, 1991, in chapter by Aviezer Ravitsky, p. 35.

[11] Leslie, J C, *The Rift in Israel*, Routledge and Kegan Paul, London, 1971, p. 59.

> the ways of the Lord, may He be blessed, for it is He alone who enslaves and redeems.[12]

The *Neturei Karta* stated in an advertisement in the New York Times on 27 May 1992:

> A. Only in Israel do Jews live in danger and insecurity.
>
> B. In Israel Jews suffer religious intolerance, oppression and persecution greater than anywhere else.
>
> C. Jews have not had a single day of peace under the Zionists.
>
> Furthermore the only dream [the Zionists have] realized is to destroy Judaism, their true goal being to change the identity, character and nature of the Jewish people, replacing the principles of the Jewish faith with atheism, materialism and chauvinism.

According to Aviezer Ravitsky, Rabbi Teitelbaum believed 'the holocaust and the establishment of the State of Israel [are] but a single continuous process: the final eruption of the forces of evil as a prelude to redemption.'[13] And, that is why the Jews were punished.

> [I]n our generation one need not look far for the sin responsible for our calamity ... The heretics have made all kinds of efforts to violate these adjurations [the Three Oaths], to go up by force and to seize sovereignty and freedom by themselves, before the appointed time ... [They] have lured the majority of the Jewish people into awful heresy, the like of which has not been seen since the world was created.[14]

Thus for the Satmar Rabbi, a survivor of Bergen-Belsen, the Holocaust is blamed on the Zionists. As he has stated, 'No force on earth shall move me from my stand, to accept the Zionist heresy, from which

---

12 Frankel, *Jews and ...*, Ravitsky, p. 52.
13 Frankel, *Jews and ...*, Ravitsky, p. 39.
14 Rabbi Teitelbaum, quoted in Frankel, *Jews and ...*, Ravitsky, p. 39.

the Merciful One must save us.'[15]

What is the basis of this theology? Firstly, they believe that the Jewish people are intended to be a holy people, different from other nations: 'We shall dwell alone' (Num 23.9). The Jews have not acted, and do not currently act as a holy people. Consequently they are in the age Moses predicted in Deuteronomy 32, the age when they rebel against God and are punished. Jewish exile is deserved. The only thing to do is study *Torah* and wait passively for the Messiah as demanded by the 'Three Oaths'. 'Whoever doubts that this redemption will come miraculously rejects the principal belief in the Torah.'[16]

Since the Jews are a metaphysical people, only metaphysical changes are acceptable. The State of Israel is a form of false Messianism. Anything done to further the coming of the Messianic age is not only counterproductive, but heretical. 'It is clear beyond all shadow of doubt that the buildings put up by the heretics will all be burnt to the ground by the Messiah.'[17] Any human action to bring about the Messianic age antagonised God and the gentile world. Victories by the State of Israel are caused by the devil. Only in the diaspora can Jews fulfil their role.[18]

Secondly, Zionism is anti-Judaism.

> The idea of a Jewish state is the great defilement and the profound heresy that the Zionists have introduced ... Zionism is basically the reverse of our belief and religious ideology. To become a Zionist means to conceive Jewry as something temporal and earthly, utterly divorced from all the divine connections, upon which the whole of belief is based.[19]

Zionism and the Jewish state are secular, and joining the secular world means rejecting the role of the holy people upon which Judaism is based. As Rabbi Amram Blau, the leader of *Neturei Karta* until his death, put it:

---

[15] Frankel, *Jews and* ..., Ravitsky, p. 59.

[16] Rabbi of Satmar, quoted in Simon, A, and M Friedman (eds.), *Religious Redemption and Politics in the Mid East*, SUNY, Albany, 1990, chapter by A Ravitsky, p. 14.

[17] Frankel, *Jews and* ..., Ravitsky, p. 60.

[18] Schnall, D, *Radical Dissent in Contemporary Israeli Politics*, Praeger, New York, 1979, p. 131.

[19] Domb, Yerahmiel, quoted in Simon and Friedman, *Religious Redemption* ..., Ravitsky, pp. 22, 52.

> *These* Zionists came to *our* Holy Land to build *their* national home and destroy religion and uprooted *our* holy *Torah* and *our* faith in *our* true salvation through the coming of the Messiah.[20]

The use of *these* and *their* for Zionists, and *our* for themselves makes it clear that the Zionists are no longer to be considered Jews. Rabbi Blau added that Zionism 'constituted the ultimate and absolute denial of all fundamentals of Jewish belief because Zionism is an attempt to replace Judaism.'[21] Joining the secular world, fighting the gentiles and protecting Jews are all against God.

> In all that pertains to redemption, the holy *Torah* forbids us to make the slightest effort to force the end, and whoever does so is in complete opposition to the true faith and has no portion in the *Torah* of Moshe.[22]

Thirdly, they are the remnant of the remnant. The Jewish people were always saved by the great righteous ones who saved the world, and they are part of that elite group. They compare themselves with that group which begins with the patriarchs, Moses and Jeremiah. In an advertisement in the *New York Times* on 21 June 1982, they declared that, just as when Jeremiah had pleaded with the king of Judea to surrender to Babylon as a repentance for Jewish sins, Jews continue to sin by creating the State of Israel instead of living among the Gentiles. Zionists are 'the proud reincarnation of the infamous hoodlums who were responsible for the genocide of the Jewish people at the time of the First Temple.'[23] They are very critical of other Orthodox Jews who have chosen to cooperate with the Zionist state. In referring to the *Agudah* (part of the United Torah Party) who have been part of government coalitions, the *Neturei Karta* said 'the petty *Agudah* clique placed itself at the disposal of Satan and its paid agents, destroying all the divisions, separating Orthodox Jewry from the Zionist heresy.'[24]

---

[20] Quoted in Simon and Friedman, *Religious Redemption ...*, Ravitsky, p. 5 (italics added).

[21] Quoted in Simon and Friedman, *Religious Redemption ...*, Ravitsky, p. 57.

[22] Simon and Friedman, *Religious Redemption ...*, Ravitsky, p. 57, quoted from Rabbi Yoel Teitelbaum's *Vayoel Moshe*—'Forcing the end' is a talmudic code name for bringing the Messiah.

[23] Domb, Y, *The Transformation*, Hachomo, Brooklyn, NY, 1958, p. 102.

[24] Domb, *The Transformation*, p. 102.

Fourthly, they claim, as noted above, that the 'Three Oaths' of the Talmud forbid the Jews to establish a state. 'Our salvation will not be a human salvation. When the time comes [He will] redeem us.' Thus, any attempt at active movement to establish a state or any form of even partial redemption is forbidden, and the Messianic age can come only directly from God. As Rabbi Teitelbaum wrote,

> Even if the Members of Knesset were righteous and holy men ... even if they were the talmudic sages, if they take the government and freedom in their own hands before the time came, they defile the holy Torah.[25]

While the *Neturei Karta,* the *Edah Haredit* and the *Satmar Hasidim*[26] account for only several tens of thousands of believers, their strict adherence to fixed Jewish law influences all ultra-Orthodox and many modern Orthodox. Their anti-Zionist and anti-secular attitude is accepted by many ultra-Orthodox (many more are non-Zionist rather than anti-Zionist), although by very few modern Orthodox. Their passivity in terms of the *Shoah* and the conflicts between Arabs and Israelis influences very few beyond their own believers.

Religious Zionism and *Gush Emunim*

Gush Emunim (Bloc of the Faithful), the settler movement associated with the National Religious Party (*MIFDAL* in Hebrew) believe there is a place between exile and full redemption. They see themselves as the true Zionists. 'We—and only we—are continuing the true Zionism.'[27] They see Israel as the beginning of redemption and 'the fulfillment of the Zionist vision'.[28]

The late Rabbi Zvi Yehuda Kook, their spiritual founding leader, said 'Our reality is a messianic reality'.[29] Even Rabbi Yehuda ben Nun, one of the moderate leaders has said, 'The exile has ... been abolished.'[30]

---

[25] Medding, P, *Israel State and Society*, Oxford University Press, Oxford, 1989, p. 244.

[26] The *Agudah* also accept these four beliefs.

[27] Aranoff, M, *Israeli Visions*, Transaction Press, New Brunswick, 1984, p. 85.

[28] Silberstein, L J, ed., *Jewish Fundamentalism in Comparative Perspective*, New York University, New York, 1993, chapter by Ehud Sprinzak, p. 117.

[29] Sprinzak, in Silberstein, *Jewish Fundamentalism* ..., p. 97.

[30] Berg, A, *What is a Jew?*, WJC, Eighth Plenum Assembly, January 1986, p. 3.

Since, clearly, full redemption had not been attained they are willing to accept what we would call partial redemption and *actively* work for full redemption.

Nineteen years after the establishment of the State of Israel there occurred an event that seemed to some as Messianic. Rabbi Zvi Yehuda Kook stated in May 1967, that the existence of Israel was an expression of redemption, and asked why Hebron, Shechem and Jericho and the west side of the Jordan River were not in Jewish hands. He stated that the land was holy forever. One month later, in the 1967 war, the Jewish state won those territories. Rav Kook defined in an article entitled, 'The State as the Embodiment of the Vision of Redemption', two types of redemption: a 'partial return' and a 'full return'. Partial return includes the ingathering of the exiles (the diaspora Jews) in the land of Israel and is a precondition for full return which is Redemption.

At the end of the 1967 war Rabbi Goren, then Chief Chaplain of the Israeli Armed Forces and later Chief Askenazi Rabbi of Israel, blew the *Shofar* (ram's horn) in front of the Western Wall—a symbolic Messianic act. The victory in the Six Day War reignited the flames of Messianism. Rabbi Goren said, 'The Messianic age is in this world, and things remain as they are, the only difference between them being that in Messianic time the kingdom will return to Israel.'[31] Given that the kingdom had returned to Israel and Jerusalem was controlled by the Jewish state, he was claiming that the Messianic state had arrived.

At the end of this war all of Jerusalem, Hebron with the graves of the Patriarchs and Matriarchs, and Judea and Samaria were in Jewish hands—a land almost as large as the Hasmonean Israel and with more independent power. As Rabbi Menachem Kasher wrote, 'On the basis of all this I cannot understand those who do not see this period as Redemption.'[32] Rabbis Kook, Goren and Kasher clearly saw the State of Israel after the Six Day War as a Messianic reality.

The first principle in the *Gush Emunim* theology is *redemption.* The present is the first stage of redemption. Many *Gush Emunim* activists were graduates of Rabbi Kook's *yeshiva* (Rabbinical Seminary) Mosav Ha'Rav Kook.[33] Rabbi Kook, the spiritual light of the *Gush Emunim*

---

[31] Sapperstein, M, *Essential Papers on Messianic Movements and Personalities in Jewish History*, New York University, New York, 1992, p. 493.

[32] Frankel, *Jews and ...*, chapter by Janet Aviad, 'The Messianism of Gush Emunim', p. 199.

[33] Named after Rabbi Zvi Yehuda Kook's father, Rabbi Abraham Yitzchak Ha'Levi Kook, the first Chief Askenazi Rabbi of Palestine, a great scholar and mystic who died in 1935.

movement, stated that, 'Re-establishment of Jewish sovereignty in Israel after two thousand years, the reappearance of *Torah* centers in Israel, the in-gathering of exiles, the rebuilding of Jerusalem, the settlement of the land, the blossoming of the desert, the miraculous victories in wars, and the *baal teshuva* [repentance] movement'[34] were all signs from God. In this theology Zionism is an agent of God preparing the Jews for redemption. Zionism was not designed to create a normal state (as Herzl, the founder of Zionism had hoped), but a holy state. This state expanded in 1967 because of the desire of God to bring redemption. Negotiating to give up this land is thus giving up on God and redemption.

The second principle of this theology is the *holiness of the land.* The 'Greater land of Israel' is the absolute property of the Jewish people, and both the land and the people are unconditionally holy. To quote Rabbi Zvi Yehuda Kook:

> All activities designed to transfer ownership of parts of Eretz Israel from hands of gentiles to those of the Jews come within the definition of the divine commandments to conquer the Land of Israel, *outweighing all commandments of the Torah.* This is borne out by the fact that *by definition* the *Torah* obligates us to implement this precept even to the point of war, which naturally entails risking the loss of life.[35]

On the other hand, Rabbi Avraham Yitzchak Ha'Levi Kook, the first Askenazi Chief Rabbi of Palestine and the father of Rabbi Zvi Yehuda Kook, stated that, 'It is not in the interest of Jacob [the Jewish people] to wield sovereignty when this entails wholesale bloodshed'.[36]

The third principle of *Gush Emunim* is that Zionism is Judaism. The State of Israel, the land of Israel and the people of Israel are connected as a holy state, a holy land and a holy people as defined in the *Torah.* The holy nation is not to be 'a nation like other nations', but, 'a light unto the nations'. The government of the State of Israel does not have the right to give up land; the land is a gift by God to the Jewish people forever. They reject Herzl and his colleagues' original Zionist ideology as a way of normalising Jewry.

---

[34] Kook, Rabbi T Y, *Torat Eretz Yisrael,* Ateret Cohanim, Jerusalem, 1991, pp. 252-53.

[35] Tomaschoff, A, ed., *Whose Homeland?,* Jewish Agency, Jerusalem, n.d., Rav Shlomo Aviner, 'Messianic Realism', p. 115.

[36] Tomaschoff, *Whose Homeland?,* from p. 105.

> Zionism has not come to solve the Jewish Problem by the establishment of a Jewish State, but is used, instead, by the High Providence as a tool in order to move Israel towards redemption. Its intrinsic direction is not the normalization of the people of Israel, in order to become a nation like other nations, but to become a holy people, a people of the living God, whose time is in Jerusalem and a king's temple at its centre.[37]

With their bond with the land metaphysical, *Gush Emunim* became a spiritual elite bringing forth the age of redemption. Its function was to save Zionism. Zionism is Jewish tradition, Jewish tradition's objective is redemption, and, thus, Judaism is Zionism. For *Gush Emunim* these values are higher than western values such as human rights and democracy. Rabbi Shlomo Aviner has stated that conquering the land is a 'Jewish Value', while democracy is not.[38] Moreover, Elyakim Ha'etzni, a secular *Gush* leader has stated that 'peace and democracy are a false messiah'.[39]

The current Rabbinical head of the National Religious Party, Rabbi Mordecai Eliyahu, surprisingly a Sephardic Rabbi and mystic, has a long history of religious fundamentalism. In 1983 (he was then the Chief Sephardic Rabbi of Israel) he stated that the Lebanon War was a holy war, and that the Lebanese city of Tyre was part of Greater Israel.[40] More recently, he has stated that given repentance, the murderer of Prime Minister Yitzchak Rabin, Yigal Amir, should be pardoned.

There is a small dovish wing of *Gush Emunim* based around Rabbi Yehuda Amital. Rabbi Amital is the head of a *yeshiva* in the West Bank. While he sees the Jewish people as being in the process of redemption, it must be done in a natural process: 'In a natural process there is diplomacy and strategy, as well as economic and social considerations that must be taken into account.'[41] 'If opportunities for a genuine and final peace with the Arabs materialize ... and we are faced with the choice of more Jews in the Land of Israel, with less Holy Land, or fewer Jews in the Land of Israel and more Holy Land under Jewish

---

37 Rabbi Yehuda Amital, later to become a dove, in Sprinzak, E, *Ascendance of Israel's Right*, Oxford University Press, Oxford, 1991, p. 116.

38 Sprinzak, E, *Gush Emunim*, AJC, NY, 1986, p. 12.

39 Ha'etzni, Elyakim, *The Shock of Withdrawal*, Dawn, Quebec, Montreal, 1987, p. 32.

40 Quoted in the English version of *Ha'aretz*, 12 April 1998.

41 *Jerusalem Post Magazine*, 29 October 1993, p. 4.

rule, we should choose the first option.'[42] He was suggesting that with peace more Jews would immigrate to Israel. His political party, *Meimad*, had been unable to win a seat in the Knesset.

Who are the *Gush* settlers? There are approximately 155,000 settlers in the Occupied Territories. The estimates of how many of them are observant appear to be 60 per cent. This is much higher than the estimated 20-25 per cent of the general Israeli population.[43] The settlers are young, 93 per cent under 45, compared to 35 per cent for the general population. They are better educated, 66 per cent with post high school education, compared to 13 per cent for the general population. They are mostly Askenazi, 82 per cent, compared to 40 per cent for the population in general.[44]

A group of 531 *Gush Emunim* settlers, surveyed as to their predominant motives for settling in the 'Gush', answered as follows:

1. 59 per cent said 'the desire to create a Jewish settlement presence in Judea and Samaria'.
2. 57 per cent said 'the *mitzva* [Jewish commandment] to settle the land of Israel'.
3. 49 per cent said 'desire to prevent a return of Arabs'.
4. 33 per cent said 'self interest such as improving quality of life, especially for their children'.[45]

The non-observant settlers, 40 per cent of the settlers, a much less studied group, came, presumably, because of economic incentives, combined with a desire to live in a more rural environment. This is not to deny that some of the secular settlers came for nationalistic reasons.

---

[42] Frankel, *Jews and ...*, Shavit, p. 110.

[43] In the *Jerusalem Report* (September 1993) Yossi Klein Halevi estimated the religious as 60 per cent. Some estimates of the Orthodox component of settlers are lower.

[44] Weisburd, David, *Jewish Settler Violence*, Pennsylvania University Press, Philadelphia, PA, 1989, p. 51. This study was done in 1989 when there were approximately 130,000 settlers. The correlation of better educated and upper classes being more traditionally ritualistically religious and believing in both life after death and satanic forces is documented in Glock, C Y and Rodney Stark, *Religion and Society in Tension*, Rand McNally, Chicago, Il. 1968, chs 10-11.

[45] Weisburd, *Jewish ...*, pp. 55, 57.

Conclusion

Fundamentalists have been defined as persons who believe they have the absolute direct word from God. Each of the three monotheistic faiths has a different set of traditions and rules, and different theologies about salvation and redemption. Conflicts for those with a fundamentalist view become obvious. Those who, in each religion, hold to more pluralistic views, that God spoke to different peoples in their own language and traditions, can respect each other. Fundamentalism is by definition the opposite of pluralistic. It is monistic: only the believers know God's word.

It is ironic that amongst Jews both *Haredi-ism* and *Gush Emunim* have a fundamentalist belief—that is, each knows the direct word of God—and each belief is the direct opposite of the other.[46] Hanan Porat (MK), a major spokesman of *Gush Emunim,* stated that 'those who would give up "Greater Israel" are profaning the name of God,'[47] and the Satmar Rabbi has stated that Zionism 'constituted the ultimate and absolute denial of all the fundamentals of Jewish belief'. One believes that Zionism is Judaism and the other that Zionism is a heresy and anti-God. What for *Gush Emunim* is the major event—the Six Day War—is irrelevant to *Haredi-ism.*

Fundamentalism of the *Haredi* type can never be defeated, because its proponents live in an inner reality. They are not concerned with the outside world. And, their passivity does not impact on the Arab-Israeli problem. They have no political ambitions. However, they do create an internal Jewish problem due to their influence on Jewish law. To the extent that they influence Orthodoxy in general, they aggravate the conflict between secular and observant Jews. The ultra-Orthodox have gained considerable power in the religious establishment, and in terms of Jewish law their power combines with the modern Orthodox. Examples of this cooperation are the issues of 'Who is a Jew?' and conversion. This is partly due to the political system in Israel that allows small parties to have substantial power in a coalition government. Since separation of religion and state is an unlikely event in the Jewish state, it is difficult to see how this problem can be resolved.

The National Religious Party and *Gush Emunim,* from the perspective of Arab-Israeli relations, are a different problem. Their messianic religious beliefs are held, to some degree, by tens, or a few

46 At the beginning of this century almost all Orthodox (and non-Orthodox) Rabbis were against Zionism, as being against the 'Three Oaths'.

47 O'Dea, Janet, *Forum 38,* 1978, p. 44.

hundreds of thousands of believers. They are active and aggressively political. Clearly, some believe in violating the laws of the State of Israel. The political system noted above gives them more political power than their numbers alone justify. In addition, there are secular nationalists who do not believe in their religious Messianism, but have developed a form of secular Messianism.[48]

These two types of fundamentalism come to Judaism from opposite poles of Jewish history. One, that exile is permanent until God brings the Messiah. The other, that we are living in 'the dawn of our redemption', and creating the future. They have some views in common. They both believe in the uniqueness of the Jewish people, its covenant with God, and that 'normalising' Jews and Judaism, the original basis of Zionism, is heretical. They both see the secular Israeli as the 'other'. They both emphasise Israel as a Jewish state rather than a democratic state. For both, the religion of Judaism is more important than the nation of Israel.

---

[48] This essay discusses religious fundamentalism. It is clear that there also exists a form of secular fundamentalism in Israel, in Northern Ireland and in the former Yugoslavia, among other places, that is related to, but independent, of religion.

CHRISTIAN ZIONISM IN SCANDINAVIA

Göran Gunner

Christian Zionism in Scandinavia embraces a variety of Christian organisations, churches, individuals and ideas expressing concern for Zionism and the State of Israel. I will restrict myself here to those aspects of Christian Zionism which associate the role of Israel with a predicted schedule of 'the plan of God', which is considered to reach its culmination at the end of time. These ideas are sometimes labelled 'fundamentalism' or 'Millennialism' both in the media and in academic research, while in the USA they are usually associated with Dispensationalism. These terms are less frequently used in Scandinavia, and people holding Christian Zionist positions seldom call themselves fundamentalists or dispensationalists, although they may use 'Christian Zionist'. I choose the example of Scandinavia, since it is most familiar to me, while at the same time intend to display an international pattern. I exclude the historical development, and will not differentiate between different theological positions, but try, rather, to establish a summary of the ideas in the air.

The concrete application of a Christian Zionist theology to the State of Israel

The geo-political agenda

When there are talks about borders in the Middle East Christian Zionists ask: What borders? The answer goes, 'the only interesting borders are the eternal borders set by God.' The present and the future are joined in a political interpretation of the borders. One map gives Israel the right to possess Jordan, the northern part of Saudi Arabia, Iraq down to the Gulf, most of Syria and all of Lebanon—even Egypt, including Cairo, is part of God's promise.[1] In that perspective, discussions about Hebron and Nablus

---

[1] Sören Teglund, *Israel-Guds egendomsfolk*, Ord & Tom, Borås, Sweden, p. 25.

are very far away. Instead, the question on the agenda is how Israel will get the rest. Concerning Jerusalem, the solution is of course clear. Ulf Ekman, one of the most outspoken Christian Zionists in Sweden today, insists that two flags will never fly over Jerusalem. There will be only one, that with the Star of David. And Jerusalem will survive until Jesus arrives, since Jesus needs it.[2] Such is a clear geo-political agenda, with a Middle East in the hand of a great, Greater Israel. And God resists any people which opposes the State of Israel and an Israeli Jerusalem.

Arabs and Islam as the enemy

Christian Zionism has always tried to identify the different players in the End Time in categories of good and evil. In the 1960s and 70s, the Arabs, Palestinians, and the Palestine Liberation Organisation were pictured as terrorists and the evil enemy of humankind and God. But both before and after, it has not been the political figures who have been used, but, rather, the religious. At the turn of the last century the Ottoman empire, identified as the declining Islamic power, was used as a sign of the imminent end of time. In the 1980s Islam was once again introduced as a super-enemy of Israel. The growing impact of Islam now became the satanic power used as a mythological construction of the enemy at the End Time. Concerning what is going to happen to the Arab population living in the area, one author has a solution. 'The Arabs accepting and actively working in favour of the programme of the PLO will be in the same situation as the people of Edom thousands of years ago. The people of Edom were the enemies of the Israelites and terrorised them, and since they hated the people of God they were exterminated.'[3] These Christian Zionists support the cleansing not only of Palestinians from Jerusalem, but of the majority of the population in the Middle East, as a means of implementing the geo-political aspirations of a Greater Israel.

All the Jews should go to Israel

Operation Jabotinsky was established by the Word of Life organisation to

---

[2] Ulf Ekman, *Israel-landet, folket, uppgiften. Studiehandledning*, Livets Ords förlag, Uppsala, p. 12.

[3] Teglund, *Israel-Guds ...*, p. 25.

persuade the Jews in the former Soviet republics to go to Israel. It runs the operation under the banner of 'a second Exodus'. One reads from a pamphlet: 'The second Exodus is here! The Word of God speaks about a second Exodus, that the Jews should be reassembled from the North to their own country. Now is a historical opening for the Jews from Russia. Hundreds of thousands have already emigrated to Israel. Operation Jabotinsky has the duty to help them home!'. Special 'fishing-teams' collect Jews for further transportation. The ship *Restoration* made the first four tours before summer 1996, and several trips every year are supposed to bring 150 to 200 persons each time. In one of the pamphlets about the operation an Israeli embassy employee is reported as saying, 'On behalf of the Israeli government I want to thank you for what you are doing in favour of us. It is thanks to persons like you the State of Israel can exist.'[4] Others like the late pastor Kjell Sjöberg have been very active in collecting money for Operation Odessa.[5] A bible centre in Bergen in Norway has a special meeting every second week where people are trained to go as 'fishermen' to the former Soviet Union. Through prayers and Jewish songs and dance they want to 'awaken' the Jews to go to Israel, which is their future.[6]

Support to the politicians in Israel

Every year a group of hundreds of Scandinavians travels to Israel for the celebration of the Feast of Tabernacles, organised by the International Christian Embassy in Jerusalem and its local office in Scandinavia. When the reports are given in Scandinavian languages it is not the encounter with the religious Jews, which is in the centre but that with the politicians of Israel. One finds both the former Prime Minister Yitzhak Rabin and the present one, Benyamin Netanyahu, as speakers, under the headline 'A strong Jewish state'.[7]

It is not the religious Jews who are put into focus, but the people who are supposed to have the control of the army and the power to bring the geo-political dreams of Christian Zionism into reality. Indeed one finds examples of a rather negative way of talking about modern Judaism.

---

4 *'Det andra Exodus âr hâr!'*, Pamphlet with no date, Livets Ords, Uppsala.

5 *Nyhetsbrev* December 1996 newsletter from Kjell Sjöberg.

6 Levende Ord Bibelsenter. Bergen, Norway. http://www.levendeord.no/information.html

7 *Budskapet från Jerusalem.* December, 1995. Published by the Christian Embassy, the Swedish Office.

The Norwegian Pentecostal author, Thoralf Gilbrant, describes Judaism as an amputated form of Israel's religion of revelation, or as the most tragic anachronism in the world.[8] Others are much more sensitive when talking about this issue, but, nevertheless, it is clear that religious Israel is blind and deaf and in need of Christ. My analysis of the End Time literature in Swedish has led to the conclusion that the End Time approach appears to be very pro-Israel in a nationalistic perspective, while being very much against Jewish religiosity.[9] At the same time, the interest in the political future of Israel is used as an instrument to provoke the coming of Christ and the millennium.

Important components in Christian Zionist theology in Scandinavia today

The millennium and the State of Israel

What about Armageddon and the coming nuclear war, and such? Traditional models concentrate on the battle of Armageddon and the Tribulation preceding the final catastrophe. That is the theology of Hal Lindsey and John Walvoord, and of their European echoes—Christian Zionists waiting for the final catastrophe. There is a good sale for such books translated into the different Scandinavian languages.

In a guide for students accompanying six tapes by the leader of the Word of Life, Ulf Ekman, there is a map of the End Time, followed by the basic model of Dispensationalism. At first Ekman's map looks like all such efforts to cover the whole of human history, from the creation to eternity. But something is missing in relation to the Second Coming of Christ. In the plan of God according to Ekman, there seems to be no wars, no tribulation, but, rather, a Jewish people saved as Christians in the millennium. This is of the utmost importance, since it solves a critical problem in traditional Armageddon-theology. In traditional End Time chronology, a pattern appears like the following:[10]

---

[8] Toralf Gilbrant, Tidens tecken. Del IV 1975, Den Kristna Bokringen, Uppsala, 1975, p. 90.

[9] Göran Gunner, *Nâr tiden tar slut. Motivförskjutningar I frikyrklig apokalyptisk tokning av det judiska folket och staten Israel.* Stockholm, 1996, p. 383. A translation of the title is 'When Time is Ending: Changing Emphases in Swedish Evangelical Apocalyptic Thinking concerning the Jewish People and the State of Israel'.

[10] Gunner, *Nâr tiden tar slut ...*, p. 384.

God's Offer	*The Jewish Reply*	*God's Counter-reply*
Old Testament Time		
The promise of Land		
Chosen—covenant	Apostasy—sin	God punishing the Jews Diaspora—suffering
New Testament Time		
The promise of Messiah		
The new covenant in Christ	Hardness of heart— Christ rejected	God punishing the Jews Diaspora—suffering
The Present Time		
The promise of Land		
The return to the Land	A covenant with the Antichrist	Tribulation for the Jews two-thirds destroyed The millennium

In Armageddon theology the world as well as the Jewish people were supposed to enter the most terrible time ever with the coming of the Antichrist and the destruction of land and people. After the battles, Christ would return to establish the Kingdom of God for one thousand years, the millennium. Then the prophecies of the Old Testament would be fulfilled. At the same time, this kind of interpretation understands the fulfilment as already existing through the present building up of the State of Israel. The question, then, appears to be, why should everything be fulfilled up to the present time just to be destroyed in the battles of the End Time? And, why, then, is there a need of a new fulfilment with the Second Coming of Christ? When Ekman excludes all the awful happenings as the tribulation for the Jewish people in the End Time, one can get the impression that the present State of Israel will simply continue up to the millennium. In other words, the millennium is already under construction.

This raises a new problem, of course: one does not really need the Second Coming of Christ either, since the prophecies relating to land and the State of Israel are already fulfilled. Without the destructive Armageddon theology the Christian Zionist dreams of the present-day Israel fit the pattern. If this tendency continues, it may end up in a theology which identifies the present State of Israel with the millennium. It will be more important than ever to support the expected geo-political fulfilment, cleansing the land of its people and bringing every Jew to Israel. The Christian Zionists are helping the State of Israel and God to prepare the End Times. Then there seems to be only one aspect left for the Second Coming of Christ. He will convert the Jews to Christianity and then take into his possession a land already prepared.

The secret code of the Bible

In the traditional apocalypticism in the Scandinavian countries speculation concerning the End Time has been an important factor. Years like 1897 and 1933 were predicted to be the last years of the earth and the beginning of the Great Tribulation. Since nothing happened in those years, the method of making calculations from the numbers in the Bible has more or less ceased in Scandinavia. But now in the footsteps of the Bible code breakers and Michael Drosnin's best seller, there has been a renewal in finding the hidden message of the Bible.[11]

Let me give you a couple of examples, familiar to those of you who have looked into the Bible code. Wars are prominent in Genesis 14. The secret message is found with the help of a computer counting characters in the biblical text. Take every sixth letter reading backwards in verse 6, and you are supposed to get the word 'activated'. Take every thirteenth letter forwards and you get 'Russian', and take every fifty-seventh letter backwards through verse 5 to 17 and you find 'scud'. The interpretation of the message from verse 5 to verse 17 is that on 18 January 1991 Russian Scud missiles from Iraq were activated against Israel.[12] This helps to give the reader the impression that the Gulf War was predicted already in Genesis. The booklet is published by an organisation whose object is to help Jews emigrate from the former Soviet Union to Israel. Two more examples are Ezekiel 37.5-38.8 and Gen 15.17. Picking up characters from Ezekiel 37.5-38.8, the author finds it predicted that the UN would vote in favour of the establishment of the Jewish state.

Genesis 15.17 reads 'When the sun had gone down and it was dark, a smoking fire pot and a flaming torch passed between these pieces.' If you look in the Hebrew text, ignore the last six letters and the spaces in between the words, and then count the next fifteen letters from left to right, the translation is, 'evil fire, gun, into Rabin'. You end up with a

---

[11] See, for example, 'Busting the Bible Code Breakers', in *Jerusalem Report*, 4 September, 1997.

[12] Walter Dittrich, *Koder I Bibeln. Numeriska Strukturer*, Insamlingsstiftelsen Shuv, Höllviken, 1996, p. 48.

hidden message about the killing of Rabin.[13] These kinds of calculations, of course, will once again focus on the prediction concerning the State of Israel. But it is no longer only the establishment of the state that is predicted in the Bible, but even the recent activities within the state, if only one reads it afterwards with the help of a computer counting characters. Once again there is biblical proof that God exists and knows what is going to happen in the State of Israel. The reader is assured that, to this very day, political development in Israel is related to the Bible.

It seems that in the Scandinavian countries the emphasis on the End Time as a catastrophe with nuclear wars and destruction will be toned down. Instead, more and more, the State of Israel will be understood as the fulfilment of the millennium, with all that that implies for the geo-political agenda, with Jerusalem at the centre, Islam as the enemy, and the return of all Jews to Israel. When Christ returns the millennium will already have been established. According to this interpretation, among the most important duties for a Christian is to support financially and politically the State of Israel and the restoration of the Jewish people.

Christian Zionism at different levels

The image of an iceberg helps one to understand the influence of Christian Zionism in Scandinavian society. At the top level, one finds Christian individuals or small groups with the support of Israel as their agenda, or one of the main focuses of their activities. They are active in media-publicity, issuing magazines and books, broadcasting on local radio stations, producing tapes, and now using the information technology media. It is a rather small group of individuals, often connected in different kinds of networks, and with a good deal of financial support. If one searches the words 'Christian' and 'Zionist' in the Scandinavian languages on the Internet, one frequently encounters the Word of Life (*Livets Ord*). The influence at this level on the Scandinavian market is restricted to the group of the already convinced. In relation to Church people and society in general they are rather marginalised.

At a second level, under the top of the iceberg, we find pastors of different denominations, journalists and lay-people. An important group here is the Christian tourists and pilgrims who go to Israel and get only the Zionist interpretation of the history and of contemporary society. Here

---

13 Hans-Holger Lorenzsonn, *Sodot. dolda Budskap I Bibeln,* Sodot, Munkfors, 1996, p. 34.

one finds ideas circulating which, among other subjects, depict the State of Israel as 'a miracle', and 'the Promised Land'. The number of individuals involved at this level seems to have diminished since the 1970s .

At the third level there is a broader grassroots acceptance of some of the ideas associated with Christian Zionism. Indeed, some of the people involved do not associate their ideas with Christian Zionism at all. Invariably their views are combined with other political, historical, emotional and religious concepts related to Israel and the Jewish people. For the individual at the grassroots level it is not always a reflected ideology, but, rather, a feeling built up over the years. Often this feeling is expressed through questions whenever other interpretations of the present situation in the Middle East are presented. The questions take the following form: 'But what about the prophecies? Is not Israel the only democracy in the Middle East? Do not the media just do PLO propaganda, instead of reporting the facts? But is not Israel right anyhow?' And, at the same time, more and more people listen to different opinions in order to get the answers to the questions.

In my view, the first level has changed dramatically in Scandinavia over the last hundred years. From being an important concern in many of the traditional Free Churches, Christian Zionism has moved to the agenda of individuals, para-church organisations, and to new US-inspired and imported Christian movements. As a result, at levels two and three, there has been a decrease in that kind of Christian Zionism which has apocalyptic and millennial connotations. Once again, it is important to stress that this kind of Christian Zionism is a tiny minority among the Churches today, and that its influence in society in general is very restricted.

What does God require?

The Christian Zionist theology exemplified in this presentation has created a hermeneutic adaptable to every new historical setting. In order to adapt the Bible to time and space, this kind of hermeneutics interprets the text to correspond with events in the surrounding society. In trying to keep abreast of political developments among the world powers and in the Middle East new interpretations will always surface. The result will not be revelation but, rather, confusion among different interpretations. When one takes time to expose these ideas in detail one finds an odd use of the Holy Scripture, as well as eccentric understandings of the past and the present.

It is important to expose the Christian Zionist hermeneutics. This includes examining the characteristic way a set of small text-units are deployed in a certain pattern, with one text used to support or comment on another, in an interplay between the past, the present and the future. Using mythical language, stories are produced which compare the building of the State of Israel to the desert flourishing, and insist that the hand of God is fighting for Israel in its wars, as well as portraying the Muslims as the enemy of Israel. The relevance and factual accuracy of the stories are of minor importance compared with the overall intention of using them to support the basic belief system.

It is important for the Church to give an ongoing interpretation of the present situation, taking into account the real geo-political context. The process started with the recognition of the existence of the Palestinian people. This was followed by a growing awareness of the humiliating conditions of the Palestinians under occupation, and of the severe problems following the peace process. Sensitivity to discrimination and the abuse of human rights has required the forms of Christian Zionism examined above to be interrogated. Awareness also of the situation of the Christian population in Jerusalem, as well as in the whole of the Middle East, has been an important factor in the matter. In this work the Church needs to develop a biblical theology, one giving a fair reading of both the Old and the New Testaments.

CHRISTIAN ZIONISM: A BRITISH PERSPECTIVE

Stephen R Sizer

At its simplest, Christian Zionism has been defined as 'Christian support for Zionism'.[1] Central to Christian Zionism is the belief in the abiding relevance of the promise God made to Abraham in Genesis 12.3, 'I will bless those who bless you, and whoever curses you I will curse; and all peoples on earth will be blessed through you.'[2]

Christian Zionists tend to see themselves as defenders of, and apologists for the Jewish people, and in particular, the State of Israel. This support involves opposing those deemed to be critical of, or hostile toward Israel. It is rare therefore to find Christian Zionists who feel a similar solidarity with the Palestinians.

The most well known and influential British Christian Zionist organisations include the Church's Ministry Among Jewish People, also known as The Israel Trust of the Anglican Church (CMJ or ITAC); Christian Friends of Israel (CFI); Intercessors For Britain (IFB); Prayer Friends of Israel (PFI) and the Council of Christians and Jews (CCJ). These are all part of an international coalition of Christian Zionist organisations which includes Bridges for Peace (BFP); The American Messianic Fellowship (AMF); The Messianic Jewish Alliance of America (MJAA); Jews for Jesus (JFJ); and, of course, the International Christian Embassy Jerusalem (ICEJ). These organisations are part of a broad coalition, which is shaping the content of the Christian Zionist agenda today.

Contemporary Christian leaders include the likes of Derek Prince,[3] David Pawson,[4] Lance Lambert,[5] Walter Riggans in Britain,[6] along with

---

1 Chapman, Colin, *Whose Promised Land, Israel or Palestine?*, Lion, Oxford, 1992 (rev. ed.), p. 277.

2 Richards, Rob, *Has God Finished with Israel?*, Monarch, Crowborough, 1994, pp. 177-78.

3 *The Last Word of the Middle East*, Derek Prince Ministries International, Fort Lauderdale, 1982; *The Destiny of Israel and the Church*, Word, Milton Keynes, 1992.

4 *Jerusalem—The Next 1,000 Years*, audio tape DP.1115, Anchor Recordings, Ashford.

5 *The Battle for Israel*, Kingsway, Eastbourne, 1975); *The Uniqueness of Israel*, Kingsway, Eastbourne, 1980.

6 *Israel and Zionism*, Handsell, London, 1988; *The Covenant with the Jews: What's So Unique About the Jewish People?*, Monarch, Tunbridge Wells, 1992.

Jerry Falwell,[7] Pat Robertson,[8] Hal Lindsey,[9] Mike Evans,[10] Charles Dyer,[11] and John Walvoord in the USA.[12] These writers have a considerable influence in popularising an apocalyptic pre-millennial eschatology and Zionist vision on the British Evangelical scene in particular.

That their teachings warrant the description 'Armageddon theology'[13] is evident from the provocative titles of some of their publications.[14] In offering a definition, Louis Hamada traces what he sees as the correlation between Jewish and Christian Zionism.

> The term Zionism refers to a political Jewish movement for the establishment of a national homeland in Palestine for the Jews that have been dispersed. On the other hand, a Christian Zionist is a person who is more interested in helping God fulfil His prophetic plan through the physical and political Israel, rather than helping Him fulfil His evangelistic plan through the Body of Christ.[15]

---

7 Simon, Merrill, *Jerry Falwell and the Jews.* Jonathan David, Middle Village, New York, 1984.

8 *The New Millennium, 10 Trends That Will Impact You and Your Family By The Year 2000,* Word, Dallas, 1990; *The Secret Kingdom: Your Path to Peace, Love and Financial Security,* Word, Dallas, 1992 (rev. ed.).

9 *The Late Great Planet Earth,* Lakeland, London, 1970; *The 1980's Countdown to Armageddon,* Bantam, New York, 1981; *Israel and the Last Days,* Harvest House Publishers, Eugene, Oregon, 1983; *The Road to Holocaust,* Bantam, New York, 1989; *Planet Earth 2000 A.D. Will Mankind Survive?,* Western Front, Palos Verdes, California, 1994; *The Final Battle,* Western Front, Palos Verdes, California, 1995.

10 *Israel, America's Key to Survival,* Haven, Plainfield, NJ, n.d.; *The Return,* Thomas Nelson, Nashville, 1986.

11 *The Rise of Babylon, Signs of the End Times,* Tyndale House, Wheaton, Ill, 1991; *World News and Biblical Prophecies,* Tyndale House, Wheaton, Ill, 1993.

12 *Israel in Prophecy,* Grand Rapids, Zondervan, 1962; *The Nations in Prophecy,* Grand Rapids, Zondervan, 1967; *The Rapture Question* (rev. ed.), Grand Rapids, Zondervan, 1979.

13 Wagner, Donald, *Anxious for Armageddon,* Herald Press, Scottdale, Pennsylvania, 1995.

14 Notably, Hal Lindsey, *The 1980's Countdown to Armageddon,* 1981; *The Road to Holocaust,* 1989; *The Final Battle,* 1995; Charles C Ryrie, *The Final Countdown,* Tyndale House, Wheaton, Ill, 1982; Mike Evans, *Israel, America's Key to Survival,* n.d; John F Walvoord, *Armageddon, Oil and the Middle East Crisis,* Zondervan, Grand Rapids, MI, Life Publishers, 1991; Dave Hunt, *Peace, Prosperity and the Coming Holocaust,* Harvest House, Eugene, Or, 1983.

15 Hamada, Louis Bahjat, *Understanding the Arab World,* Nelson, Nashville, 1990, p. 189.

CMJ, founded in 1809 under the name 'The London Society for Promoting Christianity amongst the Jews', was the first Christian Zionist organisation in Britain. The less accurate description of 'London Jews' Society' (LJS) eventually proved more popular.[16] At its inception LJS had a fourfold mission agenda.

> 1) declaring the Messiahship of Jesus to the Jew first and also to the non-Jew; 2) endeavouring to teach the Church its Jewish roots; 3) encouraging the physical restoration of the Jewish people to Eretz Israel - the Land of Israel; 4) encouraging the Hebrew Christian/Messianic Jewish movement.[17]

During the last century, in response to changing attitudes toward the Jews, LJS modified its name several times, first to 'Church Missions to Jews',[18] to 'The Church's Mission to the Jews', then, 'The Church's Ministry Among the Jews'[19], and finally, in 1995, to 'The Church's Ministry Among Jewish People.'[20] Their promotional literature now indicates a more subtle and less explicit three-fold strategy,

> The aims of CMJ are:
>
> Evangelism: To be workers with God in his continuing purpose for the Jewish people, both in Israel and world-wide, especially in seeking to lead them to faith in Jesus the Messiah as their only Saviour.
>
> Encouragement: Supporting Jewish believers in Jesus in all possible ways.
>
> Education: To help Christians to appreciate the biblical, Jewish roots of the Christian faith.[21]

---

[16] Stevens, George H, *Go, Tell My Brethren: A Short Popular History of Church Missions to Jews*, Olive Press, London, 1959, p. 13.

[17] Crombie, Kelvin, *For the Love of Zion: Christian Witness and the Restoration of Israel*, Hodder & Stoughton, London, 1991, p. 3.

[18] Stevens, *Go* ..., p. 13.

[19] Crombie, *For* ..., p. 260.

[20] Church's Ministry Among Jewish People (CMJ), *Shalom* 3, 1995, p. 1.

[21] CMJ, *Shalom* 3, 1994, p. 1.

This third aspect of their ministry was further modified in 1995 to emphasise not merely the Jewish roots of the Christian faith, but its living abiding relevance now, together with their concern, like that of the Council for Christians and Jews (CCJ), to confront anti-Semitism. The third 'aim' therefore now reads, 'To help Christians to appreciate the biblical, Jewish roots of the Christian faith and life. The concern to combat anti-Semitism.'[22]

Whether this justifies defending the State of Israel from criticism for its continued occupation of the West Bank and Gaza is a controversial and sensitive point within CMJ. Material obtained in 1990 from Emmanuel House in Jaffa indicates that the commitment of some members of CMJ leadership to 'restorationism', that is, the active encouraging of Jewish people to move to Eretz Israel, including the Occupied Territories, appears to remain an important, if not explicit or well publicised aspect of their ministry. Their leaflet explaining the ministry of Emmanuel House states,

> ITAC, as the London Jews Society is known today, has always believed, proclaimed and worked towards the return of the Jewish people to Zion. This policy is rooted in a firm belief in the message of biblical prophecy which has accurately foretold these things.[23]

In the 1996 Annual Report of CMJ, its General Director, Walter Riggans, explicitly and unequivocally identifies CMJ with restorationism and with support for the State of Israel.[24]

Not to be outdone by Christian Zionist organisations preoccupied with the fulfilment of biblical prophecy in Israel during what are regarded as the 'End Times', Riggans, under the section of the report, outlining 'CMJ Issues', and in the context of the primary tasks of evangelism and encouragement, writes,

> Within this focus we need to be aware that God's concern is with the Jewish people the world over. In our day there seems to be in some Christian circles a restriction of interest to the State of Israel and to the significance of various events

---

[22] CMJ, *Shalom* 3, 1996, p. 1.

[23] Israel Trust of the Anglican Church, *Immanuel House, Tel Aviv 1866-1990*, ITAC, Tel Aviv, 1990.

[24] The Church's Ministry Among Jewish People, *General Director's Annual Report 1996*, CMJ, St Albans, 1996.

> for the unfolding of Biblical prophecies relating to the end times. CMJ has always been at the forefront of teaching about God's restoration of the Jewish people to and in Israel, and we are continually excited by, and watchful of all that is happening. We are humbled by what the Lord is doing among Israeli believers. In other words, our prayerful interest in the State of Israel is as constant and committed as ever.[25]

Perhaps this is why Walter Riggans defines the term 'Christian Zionist' in an overtly political sense as '... any Christian who supports the Zionist aim of the sovereign State of Israel, its army, government, education etc.; but it can describe a Christian who claims to support the State of Israel for any reason.'[26]

In a 'Resource Pack' produced in 1996 for group study as well as to answer objections to the work of CMJ, material is included under the bold heading, 'The State of Israel: Why should we support it?'[27]

Christian Friends of Israel (CFI), likewise, insists on the unconditional necessity of 'Standing with Israel' and bringing blessing to her as a nation, though in their case, primarily through prayer and humanitarian projects rather than by evangelism.

> We believe the Lord Jesus is both Messiah of Israel and Saviour of the world; however, our stand alongside Israel is not conditional upon her acceptance of our belief. The Bible teaches that Israel (people, land, nation) has a Divinely ordained and glorious future, and that God has neither rejected nor replaced His Jewish people.[28]

The Council of Christians and Jews (CCJ) may also be regarded as a Zionist organisation. While prohibiting proselytism of Jews by Christians associated with CCJ, its members, nevertheless, show more concern to defend the actions of the Israeli Government than with the claims of Christ. For example, when Said Aburish's *The Forgotten Faithful* was published in 1993, Beryl Norman wrote an intemperate rebuttal in

---

[25] *General Director's Annual Report 1996*, CMJ, St Albans, 1996.

[26] Riggans, Walter, *Israel and Zionism*, 1988, p. 19.

[27] The Church's Ministry Among Jewish People, *Always be Prepared to Give an Answer Resource Pack*, CMJ, St Albans, 1996.

[28] Christian Friends of Israel, *Standing with Israel*, information leaflet, n.d

the *Church Times*, criticising him for being,

> part of a major campaign now being waged to win over Christians in the West to the Palestinian cause, and ensure that Israel loses Western Christian support.[29]

When invited to elaborate in correspondence, she did not substantiate these claims, but made further allegations. In response to a request for evidence she claimed that,

> Militant Palestinian groups—PLO, Hamas—are using the churches. It is very easy to identify this—same vocabulary, same phrases, same stories. Our friends in Israel see this at first hand.[30]

Of all the Christian Zionist organisations, the International Christian Embassy (ICEJ) is probably the most influential and controversial, having many supporters in the UK. It is significant that many of the staff working for the International Christian Embassy apparently worship at the Anglican, Christ Church, near the Jaffa Gate in Jerusalem, which, coincidentally, is the headquarters of the Church's Ministry Among Jewish People (CMJ) in Israel. Ray Lockhart, the vicar of Christ Church, when invited to comment on the work of ICEJ, refused to express any criticism of it.[31]

In what is a useful summary, Walter Riggans, General Director of CMJ, claims Christian Zionists generally agree on three cardinal beliefs, allowing for a wide diversity of views as to their theological significance eschatologically, as well as their implications for Christian practice.

> The return of Jews to the land in the last 100 years and the establishment of the State of Israel should be (or can be) interpreted as a fulfilment of Old Testament promises and prophecies concerning the land, or at the very least as signs of God's continuing mercy and faithfulness to the Jewish people. For many Christians today the greatest visible sign of God's faithfulness is the survival of the Jewish people.

---

[29] Norman, Beryl, 'The Churches in the Middle East', *Church Times*, 18 June 1993.
[30] Beryl Norman in correspondence, following her letter to the *Church Times*, 1993.
[31] Interview with Ray Lockhart, vicar of Christ Church, Jerusalem, 1994.

> God has preserved them, cared for them, directed them, against all the odds. And so, in a sense, the greatest sign of all is the State of Israel, and Jewish sovereignty over Eretz Israel; such is a classic Christian Zionist position ...
>
> The establishment of the State of Israel has special theological significance because of what it means for the Jews, or because of what it means in the sequence of events leading up to the turning of the Jewish people to their Messiah and the second coming of Christ.
>
> Christians should not only support the idea of a Jewish state, but (at least in general terms) support its policies ... In the most modest of ways I would suggest that Christians as Christians must give support in principle to the State of Israel as a sign of God's mercy and faithfulness, and as a biblical mark that God is very much at work in the world ...[32]

Karen Armstrong is not alone in tracing in Christian Zionism evidence of the legacy of the Crusades. Fundamentalists have, she claims, 'returned to a classical and extreme religious crusading.'[33] The Ruethers also see the danger of this kind of Christian Zionism in its 'dualistic, Manichaean view of global politics. America and Israel together against an evil world.'[34] Bishop Kenneth Cragg writes,

> It is so; God chose the Jews; the land is theirs by divine gift. These dicta cannot be questioned or resisted. They are final. Such verdicts come infallibly from Christian biblicists for whom Israel can do no wrong—thus fortified. But can such positivism, this unquestioning finality, be compatible with the integrity of the Prophets themselves? It certainly cannot square with the open peoplehood under God which is the crux of New Testament faith. Nor can it well be reconciled

---

32 Quoted in Chapman, *Whose*, p. 278.

33 Armstrong, Karen, *Holy War. The Crusades and their Impact on Today's World*, Macmillan, London, 1988, p. 377.

34 Ruether, Rosemary and Herman Ruether, *The Wrath of Jonah: The Crisis of Religious Nationalism in the Israeli-Palestinian Conflict*, Harper & Row, New York, 1989, p. 176.

> with the ethical demands central to law and election alike.[35]

Christian Zionists have aggressively imposed an aberrant expression of the Christian faith and an erroneous interpretation of the Bible which is subservient to the political agenda of the modern State of Israel.

> The Christian Zionist programme, with its elevation of modern political Zionism, provides the Christian with a world view where the gospel is identified with the ideology of success and militarism. It places its emphasis on events leading up to the end of history rather than living Christ's love and justice today.[36]

Christian Zionism has no place in the Middle East and should be repudiated by the Universal Church. It is 'a dangerous distortion' and a significant shift away from orthodox Christocentric expressions of the Christian faith.

> (This is) ... a fundamental disservice also to Jews who may be inspired to liberate themselves from discriminatory attitudes and thereby rediscover equality with the Palestinians with whom they are expected to live God's justice and peace in the Holy Land.[37]

Christian Zionism is a devious heresy and an unwelcome and alien intrusion into this culture, advocating an ethnocentric and nationalist political agenda running counter to the work of reconciliation, and patient witness among both Jews and Muslims.[38]

In the course of interviews I conducted with Palestinian clergymen during 1993 and 1994, one leading Anglican cleric said, 'Making God into a real estate agent is heart-breaking ... They are not preaching Jesus any more.' They are, in the words of another Palestinian clergyman,

---

[35] Cragg, Kenneth, *The Arab Christian. A History of the Middle East*, Mowbray, London, 1992, pp. 237-38.

[36] Middle East Council of Churches, *What is Western Fundamentalist Christian Zionism?*, MECC, Limassol, 1988, p. 13.

[37] Middle East Council of Churches, *What is ...*, preface.

[38] Middle East Council of Churches, *What is ...*, p. 1.

'instruments of destruction'. Another senior churchman was equally forthright,

> Their (i.e., Christian Zionists generally) presence here is quite offensive ... projecting themselves as really the Christians of the land ... with total disregard for the indigenous Christian community.

Similarly outspoken criticisms of the Israel Trust of the Anglican Church (ITAC) were made by another Palestinian Anglican clergyman I interviewed: 'CMJ are propagating Zionism rather than Christianity. It is working against the interests of the Anglican Church in Israel.'

Essentially, Christian Zionism fails to recognise the deep-seated problems that exist between Palestinians and Israelis; it distorts the Bible and marginalises the universal imperative of the Christian Gospel; it has grave political ramifications, and ultimately ignores the sentiments of the overwhelming majority of indigenous Christians.[39] It is a situation that many believe Israel exploits to her advantage, cynically welcoming Christian Zionists, as long as they remain docile and compliant with Israeli government policy. Consequently,

> Local Christians are caught in a degree of museumization ... They are aware of tourists who come in great volume from the West to savor holy places but who are, for the most part, blithely disinterested in the people who indwell them. The pain of the indifference is not eased insofar as the same tourism is subtly manipulated to make the case for the entire legitimacy of the statehood that regulates it.[40]

Cragg offers this astute critique of Christian Zionism,

> The overriding criteria of Christian perception have to be those of equal grace and common justice. From these there can be no proper exemption, however alleged or presumed. Chosenness cannot properly be either an ethnic exclusivism or a political facility.[41]

---

[39] Chapman, *Whose Promised Land ...*, p. 277.
[40] Cragg, *The Arab Christian ...*, p. 28.
[41] Cragg, *The Arab Christian ...*, p. 237.

Christian Zionism offers an uncritical endorsement of the Israeli political right, and, at the same time, shows an inexcusable lack of compassion for the Palestinian tragedy. In doing so it has legitimised their oppression in the name of the Gospel.

REAGAN AND BEGIN, BIBI AND JERRY: THE THEOPOLITICAL ALLIANCE OF THE LIKUD PARTY WITH THE AMERICAN CHRISTIAN 'RIGHT'

Don Wagner

When Israeli Prime Minister Benjamin Netanyahu arrived in Washington, DC on 20 January 1998, for what the press characterised as a 'showdown' with President Clinton over the dying Middle East peace process, he did a very strange thing. He went directly to meet with Clinton's opposition in the Christian 'right' where the Revd Jerry Falwell and over 1,000 fundamentalist Christians saluted Netanyahu as 'the Ronald Reagan of Israel'.[1]

By opting for a meeting with the Christian 'right' Netanyahu was making several bold political statements, including his 'Declaration of Independence' of sorts from Clinton's commitment to the Middle East peace process, known as the Oslo Accords. At the same time, the Israeli Prime Minister was consolidating his support in the Republican 'right', signalled by his meeting with Newt Gingrich the same evening. Revd Falwell pledged that he would contact over 200,000 Evangelical pastors, asking them to 'tell President Clinton to refrain from putting pressure on Israel,'[2] a theme Gingrich echoed at a press conference the next day. Netanyahu could now rest in relative comfort that he had control of the US Congress on Middle East policy.

As for the President, a strange coincidence occurred the following morning as news of his alleged affair with intern Monica Lewinski rendered the stalled Middle East peace process a poor side-show. President Clinton's press conference with Palestinian leader Yasser Arafat focused exclusively on the Lewinski caper. Three days after his arrival, Netanyahu left Washington, DC with a stronger hand than when he arrived, and the

---

1 *New York Times*, 20 January, 1998.

2 'Gingrich: Netanyahu Mistreated', Associated Press, 20 January 1998 (AP@WashingtonPost.com).

criticisms of the Clinton administration were all but forgotten.

The Netanyahu meeting with Revd Falwell and followers presents an interesting political and theological convergence that has a fascinating but relatively unknown history. A quick review of the history reminds us that the Netanyahu linkage with the Christian 'right' is completely consistent with Likud 's political strategy in the United States and patterns established by Netanyahu's mentor, Menachem Begin during the Clinton and Reagan administrations. The Netanyahu meeting was hardly a surprise. In fact, it was quite predictable. In the following presentation I will examine the Likud-Christian 'right' relationship in the United States, concentrating on its emergence during the Carter administration and its peak period under President Ronald Reagan. Then, we will turn to its resurgence during the Clinton Administration and the specific case of Likud cooperation with the Christian 'right' during the 'persecution of Christians' debate.

Back to the future

Christian fascination with 'Israel' and its prophetic role at the end of history has been part of Christianity since the days of Jesus and the early Church. Luke's account of the Ascension inserts such a question in the mouths of the Disciples just prior to Jesus' Ascension: 'Lord, is this the time when you will restore the Kingdom to Israel?' (Acts 1.6) This fascination is rooted in Jewish apocalyptic literature and was quite popular in 1st-century Palestine. We see hints of this eschatology in the book of Daniel, Zechariah 9-14, and various Apocryphal books.

Apocalyptic eschatology also shows up occasionally in the Gospels (Matt 24), the early Pauline letters (I Thess 5.1-11), and the Book of Revelation. While this model of eschatology did not dominate early Christianity it did surface at intervals, particularly in advance of a centennial year or during a crisis.

One version of this early eschatological thought is called 'historic premillennialism', which believed Jesus would return once the world had been evangelised, a task that would then lead to the establishment of his millennial kingdom. However, by the 18th century, another model of premillennial eschatology was emerging in England. It was rooted in three streams of British Christianity: the piety and literal hermeneutics of English Puritanism; a history of British fascination with Israel which viewed the British as the 'new Israel,' a theme that dates back at least to the Venerable Bede (7th century AD); and the type of eschatology that viewed biblical prophetic texts as having a literal, future fulfillment. Two English premillennialists were the forerunners of this movement: the Revd Thomas Brightman, who published the treatise *Apocalypsis Apocalypseos* in 1585[3], and Sir Henry Finch. Finch was a prominent lawyer and Member of Parliament who published his views in 1621, calling upon the British people and Parliament to support Jewish settlement in Palestine in order to fulfill biblical prophecy.[4] Initially, these perspectives were interpreted as support of the anti-monarchy movement and quickly fell into disfavour, particularly with the collapse of the Cromwell 'experiment'. However, the seeds of this theology ran deep in the British imagination and would lie dormant for only a season.

Following the American and French Revolutions, many Europeans felt insecure, sensing that the world was collapsing around them. Several millennial theologies emerged during the 1790s and continued for another fifty years, including various utopian movements, the Millerites (Seventh Day Adventists), and others. During this period one person emerged whose work popularised and systematised the millenarian themes while simultaneously developing a new school of thought called 'futurist premillennialism'. The Revd John Nelson Darby (1800-82), a renegade Anglican priest from Ireland, captured the spirit of the age and offered convincing biblical arguments for these ideas. Gradually, his sixty years of unceasing travel and preaching across the European continent and North America convinced a generation of Evangelical clergy and laity alike of his views. Darby's theology articulated the following novel features:

1. Biblical prophecies and much of scripture must be interpreted according to a literal and predictive hermeneutic.
2. The true Church will be removed from history in an event called the 'Rapture,' based on I Thessalonians 5.1-11, and Israel the nation will be restored as God's primary instrument.
3. Seven historical epochs or 'dispensations' were outlined according to which Christians should interpret history. Each epoch reflects a particular manner in which God deals with humanity, such as the present.

---

[3] *Apocalypsis Apocalypseos*, no publisher, London, 1585, is available in the British Museum.

[4] Finch, Sir Henry, *The World's Great Restauration or Calling of the Jewes*, Edward Griffin for William Bladen, London, 1621.

4. Dispensation of 'Grace' or its predecessor 'Law.' This hermeneutical method is often called 'Dispensationalism, ' or 'Premillennial Dispensationalism.'
5. The futurist premillenial view of history was decidedly pessimistic, pointing to the 'Rapture' of true believers prior to the 'Tribulation' and final battle at Armageddon. Christians are encouraged to study the 'signs' of the times so they will be able to anticipate Jesus' imminent return.[5]

Evangelical historian Timothy Weber summarises the futurist premillennial worldview and orientation toward history:

> Premillennialists reject popular notions of human progress and believe that history is a game that the righteous cannot win. For them, the historical process is a never ending battle between good and evil, whose course God has already conceded to the Devil. People may be redeemed in history but history itself is doomed. History's only hope lies in its own destruction ... At the end of the present age, the forces of evil will be marshaled by Satan's emissary, the Antichrist, who will attempt to destroy God's purposes. After an intense period of tribulation, Christ will return to earth, resurrect the righteous dead, defeat Antichrist and his legions at Armageddon, bind Satan, and establish his millennial rule.[6]

Darby brought these perspectives into the popular Bible and Prophecy Conference movement in the United States during the late 1870s-1890s, where premillennial dispensationalism became the dominant method of biblical interpretation and influenced a generation of Evangelical leaders, including the evangelist Dwight L Moody. Another early Darby disciple was William E Blackstone, who brought premillennial dispensationalism to millions of Americans in his national bestseller *Jesus is Coming* (1882). Blackstone is credited with organising the first Zionist lobbying effort in the United States in 1891, when he enlisted J P Morgan, John D Rockefeller,

---

[5] Darby, J, Nelson, *The Collected Writings of John Nelson Darby*, Volume I, Number 1, Kingston on Thames, Stow Hill Bible and Trust Depot, 1962, p. 94-96.

[6] Weber, T P, in *The Variety of American Evangelicalism*, Donald Dayton and Robert K. Johnston (eds), University of Tennessee Press, Knoxville, 1991, p. 6.

Charles B Scribner, and other financiers to underwrite a massive newspaper campaign requesting President Harrison to support the establishment of a Jewish state in Palestine.[7]

Similar efforts were underway in England, led by the Evangelical social reformer Lord Shaftesbury, who, like Blackstone, was so taken with Darby's eschatology that he translated it into a political agenda. These efforts are now regarded as seeds of the Christian Zionist movement, and they preceded Jewish Zionism by several years. Lord Shaftesbury is also credited with coining an early version of Zionist fathers Max Nordau's and Theodor Herzl's theme 'a land of no people for a people with no land.'[8] Also noteworthy is the fact that both Lord Arthur Balfour (author of the famous 'Balfour Declaration' of 2 November 1917) and Prime Minister David Lloyd George, the two most powerful persons in British foreign policy at the close of the war, were both raised in dispensationalist churches and remained committed to this view of the Bible and history.[9]

Developments since 1948

The establishment of the Jewish state in 1948, stimulated advocates of premillennial dispensationalism and gave it new momentum. To see the Jewish people restored as a nation was a sign that the clock of biblical prophecy was ticking and we were rapidly approaching the final events leading to the return of Jesus. During the Cold War era, dispensationalists readily interpreted the Soviet Union and its allies as the Antichrist, interpreting such passages as Ezekiel 38-39 as a prediction of an impending Soviet attack on Israel. Joining the Soviets were a Ten Member confederation, often interpreted as the European Union, based on the 'the beast' in Daniel 7.

When Israel captured Jerusalem in the war of 1967, dispensationalists were certain that the end was near. L Nelson Bell, Billy Graham's father-in-law and editor of the influential evangelical magazine,

---

[7] Sandeen, E, *The Roots of Fundamentalism*, University of Chicago Press, Chicago, 1970, pp. 19-21.

[8] Hyamson, A M, *Palestine Under the Mandate*, Methuen & Co. Ltd., London, 1950, pp. 10, 12.

[9] See Guedalla, P, *Napoleon and Palestine*, G Allen and Unwin, Ltd., London, 1925, pp. 48-49; and see also Christopher Sykes, *Two Studies in Virtue*, Alfred A Knopf, New York, 1953.

Christianity Today, wrote in his editorial of July, 1967: 'That for the first time in more than 2,000 years Jerusalem is now completely in the hands of the Jews gives the student of the Bible a thrill and a renewed faith in the accuracy and validity of the Bible.'[10]

By the early 1970s there were numerous books, films, and television specials that gave further popularity to the premillennial dispensationalist perspective. Authors such as Hal Lindsay made a virtual industry out of his volume *The Late Great Planet Earth*, which has sold over twenty five million copies, led to two films, a consulting business with a clientele that included several Members of Congress, the Pentagon, and later Ronald Reagan. During the late-1970s, the climate was ripe for an organised political venue.

With the arrival of the American Bicentennial at least five trends converged in the USA religious and political landscape that accelerated the rise of Christian Zionism. First, the fastest growing branch of North American Christianity was the conservative Evangelical and Charismatic movements, where premillennial dispensationalism was rooted. Mainline Protestant denominations and the Roman Catholic Church were facing declining budgets and attendance, a trend that has continued since the early 1960s. Second, a Southern Baptist Sunday School teacher was elected president of the United States in 1976, giving increased visibility and a degree of legitimacy to the once marginalised evangelical movement. *Time Magazine* declared 1976 as 'the year of the evangelical' and suddenly evangelicals were not only affirmed, but some were respected. Still, the mainstream media seemed confused by the various traditions and polarities within the complex movement, failing to distinguish charismatics from fundamental Baptists, or the diverse political and theological voices that were clamoring to claim the term 'Evangelical' for their particular viewpoint.

A third development concerned Israel and pro-Israel lobby organisations and networks in the United States. Since the War of 1967 and Israel's occupation of Arab lands, many Jewish organisations had been experiencing tension with the mainline Protestant, Eastern Orthodox, and Catholic communities. Jewish organisations and lobbies such as AIPAC (American Israel Political Affairs Committee) turned to the growing evangelical community for support, as Rabbi Marc Tannenbaum of the American Jewish Committee stated, the evangelical community is the largest and fastest growing block of pro-Jewish sentiment in this country.

---

[10] Bell, L Nelson, Editorial, *Christianity Today*, July 1967.

Since the 1967 War, the Jewish community has felt abandoned by Protestants, by groups clustered around the National Council of Churches, which, because of its sympathy with third world causes, gave the impression of support for the PLO. There was a vacuum in public support for Israel that began to be filled by the fundamentalists and evangelicals.[11]

Several Jewish organisations like AIPAC and the Anti-Defamation League (ADL) added staff to facilitate new relationships with evangelicals and fundamentalists. The Israeli Ministry of Tourism turned its attention toward the Bible Belt and viewed evangelicals as a major new market for Holy Land tours and revenue for Israel. The fourth factor that accelerated the emerging evangelical Christian Zionist movement's political agenda was the election of Menachem Begin as Israel's prime minister in May 1977. Prior to Begin's election, Israeli politics had been dominated by the secular Labour Party. Now a more right-wing ideological government came to power in Israel, dominated by hard-line military personalities such as Raphael Eitan and Ariel Sharon, plus the increasingly powerful settler movement and smaller Orthodox religious parties. Likud constituencies utilised the biblical names 'Judea and Samaria' for the West Bank and employed the 'divine argument' to justify its confiscation of Arab land for settlements (i.e., 'God had given the land exclusively to Jews and they have a divine "right" to settle anywhere in *Eretz Yisrael*'). The Christian 'right' welcomed the Likud leaders and the two bonded at the political and theological levels.

A fifth development may have been the primary catalyst that accelerated the Likud-Christian 'right' political alliance. When the evangelical President Jimmy Carter stated during a speech in March 1977 that he supported Palestinian human rights, including the 'right to a homeland', the Israeli lobby and Christian Zionists shifted into political overdrive. Previously, the Labour government had expressed its displeasure with the Carter administration's openness to a United Nations brokered International Conference on the Middle East conflict, based on UN Resolutions 242, 338 (essentially the exchange of Israeli occupied Arab land for peace and security arrangements). Likud came to power just two months after Carter's statement and immediately mobilised the broad evangelical community. Their strategy was simple: to split the evangelical and fundamentalist Christians from Carter's political base and simultaneously to rally support among conservative Christian Americans for Israel's opposition to the United Nations peace conference.

---

[11] *Washington Post*, 23 March 1981.

Within a matter of weeks, full-page advertisements appeared in major newspapers across the United States. The text stated in part: 'The time has come for evangelical Christians to affirm their belief in biblical prophecy and Israel's divine right to the land.' The text then shifted to target Soviet involvement in the UN International Conference: 'We are particularly troubled by the erosion of American support for Israel evident in the joint US-USSR statement.' Taking aim at Carter's recent statement, the text went on: 'We affirm as evangelicals our belief in the promised land to the Jewish people ... We would view with grave concern any effort to carve out of the Jewish homeland another nation or political entity.'[12] The advertisement was financed and coordinated from Jerusalem by the Institute for Holy Land Studies, an evangelical organisation with a Christian Zionist orientation. Several leading dispensationalist personalities signed it, including Dr Kenneth Kantzer of *Christianity Today* and Trinity Seminary (Deerfield, Il.), the singer Pat Boone, and Dallas Seminary president and dispensationalist theologian, Dr John Walvoord. The advertisement campaign was the first sign of a Likud-Evangelical Christian Zionist alliance engaging in a specific political strategy that was opposed to the policy of a standing US President and the State Department. Investigations by several Christian scholars failed to solve the source of funding for the expensive advertising strategy, but a former employee of the American Jewish Committee, Jerry Strober, who coordinated the campaign gave a clue when he told *Newsweek Magazine*: '(The Evangelicals) are Carter's constituency and he (had) better listen to them ... The real source of strength the Jews have in this country is from the evangelicals.'[13]

At times the new alliance proved to be uncomfortable for Jewish leaders, as when newly elected President of the Southern Baptist convention, Revd Bailey Smith, stated publicly that 'God does not hear the prayers of the Jews.' Within weeks Revd Smith was taken to Israel by the AJC and his views were 'corrected.'[14] While Christian Zionists and Jewish organisations agree on many levels, the deep-seated antisemitism in the Christian 'right' and enthusiasm for evangelising Jews remain unresolved issues.

---

[12] Advertisement: *The Christian Science Monitor*, 3 November 1977.

[13] Claibourne, W, 'Israelis Look on U.S. Evangelicals as Potent Ally', in *Washington Post*, 23 March 1981.

[14] Claibourne, W, 'Israelis Look ...'

Reagan and Begin

The 1980 election saw the Evangelical vote swing to Ronald Reagan who became president of the United States with the full support of major Jewish organisations, the pro-Israel lobby, and the Christian 'right.' Certainly, the Iran hostage crisis hurt Jimmy Carter more than any other factor, but his near total loss of the Evangelical vote played a significant role in his defeat. By 1980, Likud policy was aggressively represented on Capitol Hill by AIPAC but also within the Reagan administration itself. For example, when Israel decided to embark upon its controversial invasion of Lebanon in the spring of 1982, Begin sent Defence Minister Ariel Sharon to Washington to enlist the Reagan administration's support. By late May, Sharon was given the green light by Secretary of State Alexander Haig. Within days of the June 1982 invasion, full page advertisements appeared in the *New York Times* and other leading newspapers requesting evangelical support to Israel's invasion.

Prime Minister Begin developed a unique relationship with President Reagan and many fundamentalist Christian leaders, especially the Revd Jerry Falwell. As head of the largest lobby of the Christian 'right', Falwell and the Moral Majority had long been supporters of Israel on both the political and ideological levels. In 1979, according to Grace Halsell who interviewed Falwell in his Lynchburg, Virginia office, Israel rewarded him with the gift of a Lear Jet and honoured the televangelist with the prestigious Jabotinsky Award during an elaborate dinner ceremony in New York a year later.[15] In the spring of 1981, when Israel bombed Iraq's nuclear plant near Baghdad, Begin did not initially call President Reagan or anyone in the administration, but dialled Jerry Falwell and requested that 'he explain to the Christian public the reasons for the bombing.'[16] Clearly, the Israeli leadership had noted both the public relations and the political potential of the evangelical and fundamentalist 'right', and set in motion a defence of its actions. On 13 March 1985, while speaking to the conservative Rabbinical Assembly in Miami, Falwell pledged to 'Mobilize 70 million conservative Christians for Israel and against anti-Semitism,'[17] a theme echoed again in January 1998. Falwell is also credited with the conversion

---

[15] Halsell, G, *Prophecy and Politics*, Lawrence Hill & Company, Westport, Connecticut, 1986, p. 74.

[16] Halsell, G, *Prophecy and Politics*, pp. 75-76.

[17] Sawyer, K, 'Falwell Attempts to Mend Interfaith Fences', *Washington Post*, 4 April 1985, p. A-4.

of Senator Jesse Helms from an anti-Israeli position to becoming its most staunch ally, a matter worth considerable economic and political value as Helms went on to chair the important Senate Foreign Relations Committee.[18]

A regular feature of the Reagan White House was the series of seminars and briefings the administration gave to its Christian 'right' supporters. One example was the 19 March 1984 briefing by Reagan staff, the pro-Likud lobby (Americans for a Safe Israel and AIPAC), and State Department officials. Approximately 150 Christian fundamentalist leaders were invited to each event, reflecting the priority given to this constituency by the Reagan White House. The Christian participation was a virtual 'Who's Who' list of the Christian Zionist movement, including Hal Lindsay, televangelists Jimmy Swaggert, Jim and Tammy Bakker, Jerry Falwell, Pat Robertson, authors and activists Tim and Bev LeHaye, and political strategist Ed McAteer of the Religious Roundtable. The briefing was led by leaders from the Likud lobby in Washington, DC and top Reagan spokesmen such as J William Middendorf (head of the OAS) and Bud McFarlane, later of Iran-Contra fame. Quietly working in the background was Marine Colonel, Oliver North. The intimate Likud-Reagan Administration briefings reflected the unity of the two policies.[19]

Ronald Reagan himself was a committed Christian Zionist and his support for Israel had both strategic political and loosely articulated premillennial dispensationalist underpinnings. Reagan seemed to have a fascination with Israel's role at the end of history and often referred to it, both in private and on at least eight public occasions. One private instance was widely reported in the press that the president was engaged in a telephone conversation with Tom Dine, Executive Director of the Likud oriented Israeli lobby AIPAC, when Reagan said: 'You know, I turn back to your ancient prophets in the Old Testament and the signs foretelling Armageddon, and I find myself wondering if—if we're the generation that is going to see that come about. I don't know if you've noted any of these prophecies lately, but believe me, they certainly describe the times

---

[18] Senator Helms was outraged by Israel's 1982 invasion of Lebanon and was quoted in the *Washington Post* as saying: 'Shut down relations ... Just shut off relations.' After considerable AIPAC and Moral Majority financial support and politicking, Helms won a close Senate race for his North Carolina seat in 1984, and has been a staunch pro-Israel backer ever since. See Sol Stern, 'The Neo-Conning of the Jews', *The Village Voice*, 4 September 1984.

[19] Author's copy of the 19 March 1984 programme and invitation list from The White House, Washington, DC.

we're going through.' The remark was published in the *Jerusalem Post* and picked up across the country by papers subscribing to the Associated Press.[20] This stunning expression of Presidential intimacy with the chief lobbyist for a foreign government was 'benignly' garbed in dispensational Christian images, but the political overtones could not be missed.

The Netanyahu era

In May 1996, Benjamin Netanyahu narrowly defeated Shimon Peres, and the Likud Party returned to control the Knesset and the Prime Minister's office. During his years as Israel's representative at the United Nations and in other posts, Netanyahu had endeared himself to the Christian 'right', having been a regular speaker on the 'Prayer Breakfast for Israel' circuit and similar venues. He had learned from his Likud mentors, Menachem Begin and Yitzhak Shamir, that outside the US government itself, the Christian 'right' represented the largest potential political base for Israel and an untapped reservoir of financial support. Within a few months of the Israeli election, the Netanyahu government convened the Israel Christian Advocacy Council in conjunction with the Israeli Ministry of Tourism. Seventeen American evangelical and fundamentalist leaders were flown to Israel for a 21-26 October 1996 tour of the Holy Land, plus a conference at which they pledged support for what was essentially a Likud agenda. Included in the delegation were the President of the National Association of Evangelicals, Dr Don Argue; President of the National Religious Broadcasters, Dr Brandt Gustavson (an organisation that oversees approximately 90 per cent of the Christian radio and television broadcasting in North America); and Revd Donald Wildmon, President of the American Family Association, a popular fundamentalist crusader against the Hollywood film industry and major television networks. After the Evangelical leaders signed a pledge indicating their desire to insure that 'America never, never deserts Israel,' Dr Argue added: 'We are a people of the book first, and Israel is the land of the book. We represent forty nine denominations and some 50,000 congregations and we were taught at our mother's knee to love Israel.'[21]

Several members of the Advisory Council were involved in the pro-Israel advertisement in the *New York Times* on 10 April 1997,

[20] Jones, L, and G T Shepphard, *TSF Bulletin*, September-October, 1984.
[21] *United Methodist Review*, 29 November 1996.

'Christians Call for a United Jerusalem.' The advertisement may have been a direct response to a December 1996 *Times* advertisement by the Churches for Middle East Peace calling for a 'Shared Jerusalem'. The Christian Zionist advertisement made the bold claim that its signatories reach more than 100,000 Christians weekly and went on to call for evangelicals to support the Likud position on Jewish sovereignty over Jerusalem. Using several familiar themes of premillennial dispensationalism, the advertisement claimed that 'Jerusalem has been the spiritual and political capital of only the Jewish people for 3000 years.' It noted the 'biblical' claim as the basis of Israel's claim, citing support from Genesis 12.17, Leviticus 26.44-45, and Deuteronomy 7.7-8.The advertisement was signed by Pat Robertson of the Christian Broadcasting network; Ralph Reed, then Director of the Christian Coalition; Ed McAteer of the Religious Roundtable; and Revd Jerry Falwell, among others. Articulating one of Netanyahu's themes in anticipation of pressure from the Clinton administration, the advertisement asked that Israel 'not be pressured to concede on issues of Jerusalem in the final status negotiations with the Palestinians.'[22]

In an important new development, the Likud Party learned during 1997 that some American Jews were reducing their usual generous contributions to the Jewish National Fund and other pro-Israel agencies in the United States. Many in the influential Reformed and Conservative Jewish communities had cut back on their giving due in part to the increasing power of the Orthodox parties in Netanyahu's government and the 'second class status' assigned to non-Orthodox Jews in Israel and the United States. Likud then turned to the evangelical and fundamentalist Christian communities to offset the losses. One organisation that played a major role in fundraising was the International Fellowship of Christians and Jews, led by Rabbi Yechiel Eckstein of Chicago, which raised over $5 million for the UJA, almost entirely from Evangelicals and fundamentalists.[23] In a separate fundraising initiative, longtime friend of Israel and signatory of the 'Christians for a United Jerusalem' (CUJ) document, was the Revd John Hagee, Pastor of the Cornerstone Church in San Antonio, Texas (also the mailing address for CUJ). On 4 February 1998, Hagee called a press conference and announced his church was

---

22 'Christians Call for a United Jerusalem', Paid Advertisement, *The New York Times*, 18 April 1997.

23 *The Jerusalem Post* (Internet Version: http://www.jpost.com/News/Articles-7.htm), 13 November 1997.

giving over $1 million to Israel, and claimed the money will go to help resettle Jews from the former Soviet Union in the West Bank and Jerusalem (we might add, on exclusively Jewish settlements). Speaking from his dispensationalist perspective, Hagee stated: 'We feel like the coming of Soviet Jews to Israel is a fulfillment of biblical prophecy.' When asked if he realised his support of Israel's Likud policies were at cross purposes with those of the US government and possibly illegal, Hagee retorted: 'I am a Bible scholar and a theologian and from my perspective, the law of God transcends the law of the United States government and the US State Department.'[24]

During the autumn of 1997, with international pressure increasing on the Netanyahu administration from the United States and European governments, theprime minister's public relations specialists developed another strategy in cooperation with Christian Zionist organisations based in Jerusalem. The initial phase of the strategy appears to have been launched in a 22 October 1997 report on Israeli Radio (*Kol Yisrael*) News indicating the Palestinian National Authority was persecuting Christians. Two days later, the *Jerusalem Post* published an extensive article indicating a new Israeli Government report claiming that 'the few Christians remaining in PA-controlled areas are subjected to brutal and relentless persecution.' The article continued: 'The report says, "Christian cemeteries have been destroyed, monasteries have had their telephone lines cut, and there have been break-ins to convents."' According to the *Post* article, the Israeli report claimed the Palestinian Authority 'has taken control of the churches and is pressuring Christian leaders to serve as mouthpieces for Yasser Arafat and opponents of Israel.' Further, the report claimed that the authority was harassing 'Christian pastors and Muslim converts to Christianity.' It referred to 'one convert in the northern West Bank who was arrested by the PA Preventive Security agents and has been tortured since then in a PA prison.'[25] A month later US Congressman J C Watts (Republican, Oklahoma) reiterated the arguments in the *Washington Times*, blaming Arafat and the Palestinian Authority for the Christian exodus, and questioning the $307 million in grants from the United States.[26]

Palestinian Christian leaders were quick to respond. Bethlehem Mayor Hanna Nasser, a Christian, said: 'Our churches have complete

---

[24] Religious News Service, 6 February 1998.

[25] 'Christians Persecuted by PA', *The Jerusalem Post* (International Edition), 1 November 1997.

[26] Watts, J C, 'Yasser Arafat vs. Christians', *The Washington Times*, 4 December 1997.

freedom and I've never heard that they've been under pressure.' Lutheran Pastor Revd Dr Mitri Raheb of Bethlehem, challenged the Israeli report as pure propaganda, noting that when Bethlehem was under Israeli occupation his house was robbed in 1991 and his car stolen twice, but 'there have been no robberies since the Palestinian Authority has taken over. On the contrary, there is a greater sense of security now than there was under occupation.' As for the claim that cemeteries were vandalised, Revd Raheb stated that most incidents occurred when Israel controlled Bethlehem and were acts of Jewish settlers. He noted that recently one vandalisation incident occurred by Muslim and Christian youth, who were on drugs.[27]

During May 1998, a joint delegation of Evangelicals for Middle East Understanding and Open Doors International, sent a fourteen-member team to investigate the allegations. The delegation confirmed that the allegations of persecution by the Palestinian National Authority could not be substantiated. After interviewing over sixty spokespersons in Israel and the Palestinian territories, including a variety of Christian leaders, the Director of the Israeli Ministry of Religious Affairs in the Department of Christian Communities, Mr Uri Mor, and several Christian Zionist leaders, EMEU concluded:

> 1. there were isolated incidents of discrimination and increased tension between Christian and Muslim communities in certain areas, but there were no cases that could be characterized as persecution in the territories under the Palestinian National Authority; there were four cases of converts from Islam to Christianity who experienced pressure from their families, communities, and those who had criminal backgrounds received pressure from the Palestinian Authority, but the context and reasons for pressure cannot be construed as persecution;
> 2. some Christian Palestinians are concerned that if Islamic Law (*Shari'a*) becomes the law of the Palestinian areas, there may be significant restriction of religious freedom for Christians in the future, but quite the opposite is the case at present;
> 3. EMEU/Open Doors found 'disturbing indications

[27] Muna Hamzeh-Muhaisen, 'Christians in Bethlehem: Where is the Discrimination?' *Palestine Report*, 31 October 1997.

> of political motivations behind (the) recent publicity about Christian persecution.'[28]

On this point, the investigative team learned that the Christian Zionist group, the International Christian Embassy-Jerusalem, cooperated with the office of Israeli chief spokesman for the prime minister, David Bar-Ilan, to exaggerate accounts of Christians being persecuted and circulated it to the international press. In addition, a staff member of the United States consulate in Jerusalem interviewed Uri Mor, Director of the Department of Christian Communities Office for the Israeli government, who stated the report was intended to be an internal document, but Bar-Ilan's office leaked it to the Christian and secular media. Asked why the prime minister's office would do so, Mr Mor noted that Bar Ilan uses such information as his 'bread and butter' in the Israeli propaganda war against the Palestinian Authority.[29] Clearly, there was no attempt by either the Israeli government or the Christian Embassy to note the particular criminal status of those claiming to be persecuted, or to distinguish between understandable pressure from families or communities following a conversion. EMEU questioned the motives of both the Christian Embassy and the Israeli government, wondering if they were designed to discourage growing sympathy for Palestinian Christians while simultaneously seeking to influence the debate on persecution in the United States Congress.

EMEU added that the real issue is the decline of Christians throughout the Holy Land since Israel became a state in 1948 and later took control of Jerusalem, the West Bank, and Gaza Strip. The report concluded:

> EMEU found the situation in Israel and the Palestinian territories would be enormously improved by a swift and just peace settlement. If present conditions persist, both Israelis and the Palestinians will suffer while the flow of Christians out of the Holy Land is likely to continue ... The Christian community is in danger of diminishing to utter insignificance in the place of its birth. In coming years, will the only worshipers here be foreign visitors? This could happen if hopelessness drags on and there is not a just and

---

[28] Press Release: Evangelicals for Middle East Understanding, Jerusalem, 24 May 1998 (available from EMEU, 3225 W. Foster Avenue, Chicago, Illinois 60625).

[29] 'The Myth of Christian Persecution', *LAW—The Palestinian Society for the Protection of Human Rights and the Environment*, May 1998, p. 3.

durable peace for Israel and the Palestinians.[30]

Further, EMEU learned that on 22 May 1998 the Israeli Knesset passed the first of three readings of a strongly worded 'anti-missionary bill' that would have broad implications on evangelical activities in Israel, including publishing, broadcasting, mailings, or distributing materials. The new bill had the full support of Prime Minister Netanyahu and his cabinet, a matter that troubled several Christian Zionist organisations, which told EMEU a few days earlier that they had Netanyahu's guarantee that another anti-missionary bill would be 'buried.' While some Christian Zionists and other evangelicals are willing to trust Netanyahu to defeat the new legislation, others are not as certain. The new legislation, called the Pinchasi Bill (after the author, Knesset Member Raphael Pinchasi of the Orthodox Shas Party). complicates Netanyahu's relationship with Christian Zionists and may dampen the enthusiastic support of many evangelical and fundamentalist Christians for the Prime Minister.[31]

*

In his recent book,[32] the brilliant octogenarian and Oxford don, Bishop Kenneth Cragg, struggles with the tragic dynamic of how two victims, Palestinians and Jews, are trapped in an age old process: 'The victims on both sides of the Israeli-Palestinian divide are not merely casualties of a regional conflict but captives of an age-long story.' Cragg reflects on Robert Browning's poem 'Holy Cross Day', written to condemn the medieval Christian practice of requiring Jews to listen to sermons in September that remind them of being accomplices in the crucifixion:

> Ay, the children of the chosen race
> Shall carry and bring them to their place:
> In the land of the Lord shall lead the same,
> Bondsmen and handmaids. Who shall blame,
> When the slaves enslave, the oppressed ones o'er

---

30 EMEU Press Release ...

31 'Anti Missionary Bill Passes First Knesset Hurdle', *The Jerusalem Post*, 21 May 1998.

32 Cragg, Kenneth, *Palestine: The Prize and Price of Zion*, Cassell, London and Washington, 1997.

The oppressor triumph for evermore.

Cragg concludes: 'The poet recognised the human instinct but could not then know how it would miscarry.'[33]

[33] Cragg, Kenneth, *Palestine: The Prize ...*, pp. 105 -106.

CHRISTIAN-MUSLIM RELATIONS—PAST, PRESENT AND FUTURE

Rafiq Khoury

I look at the future of Muslim-Christian relations from a premeditated standpoint, which I hold firm and which I have no reason to hide. It is the stand of hope which does not disappoint those who have it (Romans 5.5). I present this vision as a witness more than as a researcher, and it comes in three parts. In part one, I consider the movement of history and mention some aspects of the experience of the relations between Christians and Muslims in the East in general. In part two I discuss more specifically the situation among the Palestinians as it relates to Christians. Against the background of this historical experience—and this is the subject of part three—I will point out some of the features of the future. I will present those features as a call for commitment, so that we may allow this genuine experience, which is exciting and promising, to continue its march in history, in spite of all the difficulties.

Christian-Muslim relations in the East in general

There is no doubt that the Palestinian experience of Muslim-Christian relations is unique. In order to enter into the details of the 'game' of Muslim-Christian relations in our history—we know that it is a complicated 'game'—we will deal with some of its components, which, in my opinion, make up the deep foundations of this experience, and the seeds of the future. There are five components.

The cultural partnership

The cultural factor plays an important, if not a crucial role in human relations, because it opens the way to integral interaction, and the fertilisation of relations between different groups. Both the Christians and the Muslims of the East belong to the same cultural roots, the Semitic root that remains a common denominator, in spite of the variety of expressions. It may be important to notice here that the Arab peninsula was the human reservoir which fed this part of the world with successive waves of population.

On the one hand, this cultural relationship partly explains the continuous tension that the local Christians in our region experienced with the Byzantines, in spite of the fact that both belonged to the same religion. On the other hand, it also explains the way those same Christians received the Muslims at the time of the Islamic conquest.

This cultural relationship resulted, naturally, in a rich cultural outcome. We should not hesitate to say that this co-operation should be recorded as a brilliant historical step on the part of the Christians of the region. Instead of remaining in a closed circle of their own, longing for the 'good old days' of their past glory, they took the initiative to participate in the process of developing the Arab-Islamic culture in all spheres of life. The Patriarchs of the Catholic Church of the East summarised this by saying:

> We [Muslims and Christians] draw on a single heritage of civilisation. Each of us has contributed to its formation according to his own genius. Our kinship of civilisation is our historical patrimony. Christians of the East are an inseparable and integral part of the cultural identity of Muslims. In the same way, Muslims of the East are an inseparable part of the cultural identity of Christians.[1]

We may add that this phenomenon was repeated in a different historical context during the Arab Awakening of the 19th century, in which Christians contributed a major share of the cultural heritage which remains an integral part that cannot be ignored in our modern Arabic culture.

The arabisation of the Churches of the East

The arabisation of the Eastern Christians was done so rapidly as a result

---

[1] The Council of the Patriarchs of the Catholic Church of the East, 'The Christian Presence in the East is a Witness and a Message', Easter 1992, p. 48 (Arabic).

of this close cultural relationship. The Arabic language became, as of the 7th century, the main language and communication tool of the common Semitic culture, without cancelling out the other languages. The Christians of the East adopted the Arabic language, together with their traditional languages, in their daily life, in their theology, spirituality, holy rites and sacraments. The Arab-Christian heritage is an amazing expression of this arabisation. This is what made the Catholic Patriarchs of the East say:

> The common opinion that claims that 'the Arabic language has refused to be Christianised, and Christianity has refused to be Arabised' is false in the light of all historical evidence.[2]

This cultural relationship, and what derived from it, opened the way to Arab Christianity to become as it is known to us today, namely an inseparable part of the Arab world.

The unity of eastern Christians around Arab culture

Christianity in the East has suffered a lot because of its internal splits and struggles, caused by differences in the respective cultural heritage and languages. Therefore, one may say without exaggeration that the Arab Islamic culture, along with its language, gave, and still gives Christians a factor for Christian unity which did not exist before. It is enough to mention that a trend of Christian thought emerged around the Arabic language and culture between the 8th and the 14th centuries, which overcame the denominational boundaries between the various Churches, and enabled them to communicate with each other in spite of their theological and doctrinal differences.

May I call to mind the testimony of Fr Samir Khalil who said in this respect:

> (I said above) that the cultural interaction between the various Christian groups in the Middle East became obvious, and the credit for this is due to the Arabic language—which has become common to all. In order to give an idea about this phenomenon, I picked some examples in the relations between the Nestorians and the Copts. I choose this case

2 'The Christian Presence ...', p. 29.

> because it has some identified differences. The two groups belong to two different theologies opposing each other completely, existing in two distant countries (Egypt and Iraq), belonging to two pre-existing and different cultures (Syrian and Coptic), and in spite of this an interaction took place between them, at least during the classical era of the Arabic culture.[3]

The author gives as an example a set of Nestorian laws, which were taken as the basis for the laws in a similar Coptic group, and were then adopted by the Maronite Church.[4] This emphasises the fact that, 'in spite of their theological difficulties, the Christians of the East spoke the same Arabic language, therefore, the doctrinal writings passed on from one group to another, and so, the educational and cultural relations among the Arab Christians came to be harmonised on an ongoing basis.'[5]

It is regrettable that in ecumenical circles there is but little care for this side of our heritage. These historical facts cause us to say that the ecumenical movement of the East cannot separate itself from the Muslim-Christian dialogue. Both are calling for each other to form two sides of the same movement.

Muslim-Christian dialogue

There is another aspect to this historical experience, which is not of less importance. It is the Muslim-Christian dialogue in the past. Muslim-Christian dialogue is not a recent phenomenon, but can be traced back to our early common beginnings, which is one of its outstanding characteristics. We must point out that Arab Christian thought developed through a relationship with Islam, with which Christians were in daily contact. We see here an important characteristic of this Arab Christian heritage. Fr Samir says, 'This is the only Christian theology which was thought of and was written through a basic relationship with another religion.'[6] Out of their daily relations both parties could not avoid asking

---

[3] Samir, S K, 'La tradition arabe chrétienne et la chrétienté de Terre Sainte', in *Christianity in the Holy Land*, edited by D-M A Jaeger, Jerusalem 1981, pp. 358-59.

[4] Samir, 'La tradition arabe chrétienne ...', p. 355.

[5] Samir, 'La tradition arabe chrétienne ...', p. 366.

[6] Samir, 'La tradition arabe chrétienne ...', p. 366.

each other for explanations of their respective religions. In this framework, let us look at the body of literature which reached us as a result of a dialogue between Muslims and Christians, concerning those subjects about which there was debate and discussion.

It is true that some of those writings were characterised by a poisoned and crooked style, but what interests us here is what may be called an atmosphere of chivalry in a number of those debates, conducted in an apologetic style, without the spirit of crooked debate. We may see behind those dialogues a hint of a broad and open atmosphere, of an eagerness for knowledge, seeking logic, away from extremism. The general atmosphere of broad-mindedness which prevailed at that time came as a result of open-minded caliphs and thinkers who were in constant communication with the other parties. This stimulated creative activity.

Difficulties in this experience

It would be naive and dishonest to try to hide the difficulties which are inherent in such an experience of inter-religious relations. This experience, spread over thirteen centuries, is a complex motif which cannot be without negative shadows, and these ought to be recorded to give a complete picture, especially as they have left their traces on the memory.

The atmosphere of tolerance which characterised the early centuries did not continue in a straight line, but rather included different periods which placed Christians of the East in difficult situations. When such procedures were the outcome of ill desires of rulers, the taxes imposed upon Christians became very heavy, to the extent that many Christians were pushed into conversion to Islam. It often happened that relations between the Muslims and the Byzantine empire reflected badly upon local Christians, so that any victory won by the Byzantines could be easily turned into pressure applied against the local Christians. In addition to this, we remember the humiliating conditions imposed upon Christians in terms of clothing, headdress, and names. Such conditions reached a peak during the reign of Caliph al-Hakim.[7]

Even in our own generation we experience other kinds of difficulties too: negative stands which at times go to the extreme—the taking of physical life (as in Egypt), the attacks carried out by extremists

---

[7] Issa, A O, *Les minorités chrétiennes de Terre Sainte à travers les siècles*, Jerusalem, 1976, pp. 129-35.

against Christian targets (as in Algeria), the massacres (on the basis of religious identity) carried out mutually in Lebanon, other persecutions met with in daily life (at work, etc.), and in incidents with this or that denomination, all of which cast a dark shadow over Muslim-Christian relations.

Christian-Muslim relations in Palestine

Muslim-Christian relations have their own characteristics in Palestine, due to some special conditions which prevailed in our history and in Palestinian society. We mention the following.

The strategic and religious character of Palestine

A closer look at Muslim-Christian relations in Palestine, cannot proceed without taking into consideration those strategic and religious aspects that are particular to Palestine. On the strategic side, it is to be noted that Palestine is located on a crossroads connecting three continents: Asia, Africa and Europe. Such a location makes Palestine a meeting-point, and we see this today, where the mix of cultures determines the kind of society we live in, whether we like it or not.

In addition to this strategic factor, there is the religious one as well. Palestine is the Holy Land for the three monotheistic religions, Judaism, Christianity and Islam. This stamps the Holy Land with its unique character in the field of inter-religious relations. The Holy Land is the place for an intensive religious life—with all of its places of worship, pilgrimages, ceremonies and calendars (where the religious factor may coincide with the national one), its symbols, and religious manifestations. In such a context the 'other' is sought and seen, not through imagination, but directly through the eye, and this reality enters slowly into the cultural heritage of the whole society, imparting to it (unconsciously at times), a special wisdom of life and tolerant co-existence. The Palestinian Declaration of Independence (Algiers 1988) knew how to put these ingredients together.

The early arabisation of Palestine

We should draw attention to a basic fact about Palestine. In the view of V

Monteil, it is the most arabised part of the Arab world.[8] The Christians of Palestine have a deep and spontaneous conviction that they are Palestinian Arabs. Arabism in its Palestinian context is an accepted and understood identity, without any doubts or problems. To Palestinian Christians this identity is a matter of fact, about which there can be no debate.

It is important to focus on this issue because of its importance in determining the special nature of Muslim-Christian relations in Palestine. Following this line of thought we may note that the Palestinian Christians in the modern age have never thought of having a separate political entity. Add to this the fact that all the attempts of outside elements to push the Palestinian Christians into establishing separate, or special political parties have failed. Likewise, all attempts by the Israeli occupation to set on fire an inter-religious conflict also have failed.

The Palestinian question

The Palestinian question, or tragedy, is very much alive, and is written with letters of blood in the heart of the wounded memory of the Palestinian people of modern times. We cannot possibly understand who these people are unless we take into account this long journey of suffering and struggle, aspirations and stresses, hopes and disappointments.

This 'desert journey' has helped give Muslim-Christian relations in Palestine a special flavour. The Muslims and the Christians of Palestine found themselves together on the long and tragic journey of the Palestinian people. They did not suffer because of each other, but rather with each other. As we know, suffering binds people together. They also did not struggle against each other, but rather carried on their struggles together. Struggle also binds people together. They share the same aspirations for the future, and work in the same 'workshop'.

The Palestinian experience

The Palestinian people were uprooted from their land and thrown on to different roads of the world to start their 'desert journey'. They became the new 'wandering Jews' of this world, the ones at whom the finger is

---

8 Monteil, V, *Les Arabes*, Paris 1957, p. 7.

pointed. This journey became a unique experience of the Palestinian people in the Middle East. We cannot separate this experience from their social outlook.

This experience has deepened their sense of national identity, so that they were classified as Palestinian, even by their fellow Arabs. In the course of their uprootedness, they came in contact with many different cultures, and found themselves always in the face of pluralism, which became rooted in their minds. Their suffering from different kinds of discrimination, oppression, and injustice has led to the development of a meaningful national solidarity. Through this 'desert journey' (in 'the forest of guns') they also learned the way of democracy, which opened the door to all sorts of political and ideological trends. This became a key factor, in my opinion, against any return to the old way, in the realm of the political education of the Palestinian people. It is in the framework of this rich and pluralistic experience that Muslim-Christian relations must be placed, and where the crossing of religious boundaries became an important part.

From experience to thinking

Sharing a common life together has a long history for Christians and Muslims, and this has inspired in the two parties a wisdom as to how to relate to one another which developed as a result of centuries of living as neighbours. If we pause to look at the Palestinian case, we find that this coexistence became a basis for thinking and analysis, especially since the 1967 war. It seems that this trend is very important, and must be expressed openly, because any experience which remains vague and poorly understood is weak unless it reaches our consciousness. But, this is what is taking place in Palestine on more than one level.

Problems in our experience

The history of Muslim-Christian relations in Palestine includes also some negative aspects, most of which have been caused by outside factors (i.e., the Crusades, interference of foreign powers, imperialism, protectorates, etc.). Internal factors, due to actions on the part of Muslims, include waves of persecution, discriminatory conditions during some periods of our history, the *dhimma* (protection) system, the pressures of the majority, and sectarianism. Problems for which Christians must take responsibility include the minority complex, the foreign element in the Churches and institutions at the level of the hierarchy up to recent times, and even nowadays, seeking the protection of foreign consulates during the Ottoman regime, and denominationalism. In addition to these problems, we must add the 'game' of majority-minority, which is well known in many of our societies.

Christian-Muslim relations: a vision for the future

The future of Muslim-Christian relations may be summarised under three main headings.

A promising future

We have said before that an optimistic outlook on the future is based on the deep roots of the past, on present conditions in the Arab world, and particularly within Palestinian society. We are in a dynamic situation, shaped by the course of our own journey through history. This progress forms an inseparable part of a deep heritage carried forward by both religious groups—separately and jointly. There are various historical, educational, social, political, and religious roots. Again, I quote from the message of the Catholic Patriarchs of the East:

> The experience of living together as we have lived over the years, is still firm in spite of all the obstacles and pitfalls. There are many positive values, sound reasons and a true empathy, binding Muslims and Christians together on all levels—civil and religious—for all classes of society. No matter what is said, and no matter what negative aspects there are (and it is natural to have such negative aspects) no one can deny the fact that Muslims and Christians in our Arab countries belong to one and the same homeland. They share the same destiny, their feelings and reactions are the same toward both global and local challenges.[9]

---

[9] The Council of the Patriarchs of the Catholic Church of the East, 'Together before God for the Sake of Man and Society.' Third Pastoral Letter, Christmas 1994, No. 21 (Arabic).

I add here to this Christian voice, that of the Muslim voices in Palestine, and they are many:

> The Christian existence in the Arab body is an integral one, and not a supplementary or secondary one. Together with them we are the makers of the same cultural history, which was, still is and shall continue to be, because we are all the inhabitants of one homeland.[10]

A future surrounded by challenges

The hope inherent in the future, and the will to get to it are not enough in order to create this future. The challenges which stand against it, make it fragile and easily broken, and so we need to face them with realism and creativity. Let look at some of these challenges in a questioning way, which may help us to move forward in our thinking.

The challenge of instability
I do not reveal something new when I say that this part of the world is going through a crisis in its growth. This places it in a situation of instability at all levels, political, economic, social, educational, religious, etc. In this period of transition, with its difficulties and its doubts, frustration is the norm in our region. We seem to be bowed down by so many difficulties, and it seems as if the world is moving toward a dead-end. In this part of the world, we are swinging between modernism and tradition, a fact which poses great problems.

Islamic-Christian relations cannot be separated from this wider question which cuts through all of society. These relations are influenced by the general atmosphere which pervades everything. The great danger inherent in this situation of crisis is extremism. When extremism takes hold, it ruins the comfortable atmosphere needed to promote community projects that benefit all members of society.

The challenge of otherness
The question of otherness is a current preoccupation, and rightfully so. The great movement which the whole world has undergone—the shifting

---

[10] Abed Al-Rahman, 'The Christian Being is an Organic Being in the Arab Body', in *Al-Liqa Magazine* 95/2, p. 72 (Arabic).

from a village culture to that of cities, the mixing and interaction of societies, the influence of modern transportation and global media networks—puts all human beings in continual relations with each other. In addition, we see that people are more and more aware of their respective identities. All of this has pushed the problematic question of otherness to centre-stage, where it remains—urgent and unsolved.

It should be noted in the framework of our own society, that the various religions, specifically Islam and Christianity, have their own particular outlook on each other. This outlook plays a big part in the development of their mutual relations, and, today, faces needs and events which demand a reappraisal of historical attitudes to our situation. The condition of *dhimma* would seem to be at the very heart of this problem of otherness, and Christian Arabs feel this in a sensitive way. Are we considered people of *dhimma* or nationals? Was the last word uttered on the subject of *dhimma*? Is there a way which takes into consideration the usual interpretation of the words of God in the Qur'an, and, at the same time, the realities of the current situation? Do the achievements of modern society have to be classed as antagonistic to mutual understanding, or do they invite us to look deeper into the question of the other, so that we may reach a solution that meets all the demands of the present? It seems that, to date, we have gone around in circles in our handling of this question. Can we go forward and achieve a breakthrough in this matter?

The problem of otherness poses additional general questions. Must we continue to see the 'other' only through the spectacles of our own doctrines? Can we start to see the 'others' as they see themselves? How can we improve our outlook toward religious 'others' in their otherness, and how can we handle this otherness well? How do we define ourselves in the midst of so many comparisons with the 'other', when the 'other' may be considered an enemy, a threat, or might even be totally negated. The 'other' could also be considered complementary, or simply different. It seems to me that these questions—which remain open—are at the very heart of the debate concerning the otherness of the 'other.'

The challenge of emigration

The symptom of emigration of Christians from the Arab world, especially from Palestine, is well known to all. Therefore, we would not deal with it here were it not for its effect on the future of Muslim-Christian relations. We may find ourselves, as some might believe, about to fight a lost war, for there are no soldiers to fight it, as the French saying goes. The situation is indeed perilous, but I do not share the pessimism of those who prophesy the death of the Christian body in Palestine and the Arab world, and I do not say this out of blind faith.

I mention this matter here because it is not just an internal problem for Christians. Rather it concerns all the religions of our region. It is not in the interest of anyone, neither Christian nor Muslim, that the Christian community become no more than a gaping wound in the Arab body. The absence of the Christian element would impoverish the Arab identity here. This is why Sheikh Najeeb El-Ja'bari says:

> It is the duty of Muslims to make the Christian existence in the Holy Land an Islamic problem, in addition to it being a Christian one—it must not be let go of.[11]

The challenge of education

This challenge concerns Christians. We have seen how Arab Christians experienced this inculturation in the past. Now we point out that this inculturation remains unsolved—it cannot be considered done with. It is on the agenda today with new emphasis, and in a condition of constant change, as it faces new demands. I believe that this area must be given fresh impetus, based on the experience of the past, and the requirements of the future. We must also find ways of bringing in new findings in the fields of theology, ceremony, and developments in spirituality, etc. The aim being always to expand and deepen our Christian faith, and make it real in the special cultural environment

Inculturation is a project that we ought to work on constantly to make it a more profound experience. In that way we may keep our place as an integral cell in the cultural body of the Arab world, and be a leaven in the bread, rather than a hair in the lump.

The political-religious challenge

The Arab East does not recognise boundaries between the political and the religious, and the debate around this subject is ongoing in the Arab world. At present, the national identity is gradually being replaced by the religious one on the political front. The Islamic groups may be considered pioneers of this trend since they have produced movements in society which can be said to derive from Islam. Such a project raises lots of

---

[11] *Al-Liqa Magazine* 95/2, p. 95.

questions, even fears and worries among the Christians of the Arab world. Will they be recognised for what they are, an inseparable part of society, or will they become a marginal group in the national life? Are they headed for a ghetto, or will they be fully-fledged citizens and members of this new society? Are they going to be merely tolerated, or fully integrated into the society? As you can see, this is no academic debate for the Christians of Palestine. It is rather a question that comes to the heart of their being.

The challenge of sectarianism

Arab society is deeply religious. Religious feelings continue to be the strongest and most sensitive ones in the Eastern soul. Certainly, this has its benefits, but it also has its dangers which must be taken seriously. Sectarianism is deeply rooted in history since very early times. It was at its height during the Ottoman rule and was enshrined in the Millet Law. It was later picked up by the imperialistic regimes according to the principle of 'divide and rule'. It nurtured sectarianism, and created lots of problems in the Arab world.

We know that the potential for sectarian trouble can arise on many occasions, especially during feasts and religious celebrations, and at times for minor reasons. All it needs is a misunderstanding between two persons; and if it happens that one is a Christian and the other a Muslim, we have an inter-religious dispute on our hands. It can lead to extreme, blind sectarian behaviour that can undermine stability in our society. In Palestine, sectarianism is rife because of the unstable conditions we are living in. Through the centuries, our societies developed a mechanism for resolving this type of conflict. We called it 'wisdom of life', but is it not time that we went deeper in this case, to get to the roots of sectarianism?

A future we build together

The future of Muslim-Christian relations may be seen from the vantage point of its fruits—both in the past and present. A good future of this kind does not come about by itself. It takes men and women who believe in it to foster its dynamics, in order to push it forward and turn it into a tangible reality. This is a task which demands our joint efforts. Only by working together can we make it happen. Here I would like to draw attention to some aspects of this joint effort, which demands commitment—both in thought and deed from both sides. At the same time we need to leave space for criticism and self-evaluation. We need more than ever before to have frank debate, as happens within the same family.

The religious discourse

I would like to refer once more to the pastoral message of the Eastern Catholic Patriarchs:

> Religious discourse has principles and literary rules. In itself it directs us to faith in God, and to the love of all his creatures regardless of their religious affiliation. But if discourse becomes an attack, and if it distorts the truth, then it may be harmful to all parties involved. Aggressive discourse is picked up by the Christian or Muslim in the street and gets turned into blind sectarianism, which opposes coexistence and its requirements. Some regretfully form the opinion that the safety of their belief is possible by giving a distorted view of other's beliefs and by attacking them. This is but shallow thinking, and can lead to picturing the other as an enemy. In the end it leads believers into disharmony and mutual animosity. This can prepare the way for that state of mind in which the physical or moral annihilation of the other can take place. Therefore discourse must be developed—by both groups—to take it away from the spirit of ill debate which will never convince the other, but has a negative effect on inter-personal and inter-religious relations.
>
> Therefore, we call upon Christian thinkers and theologians in our Arab world to develop a new vision which is just and fair to Islam without flattering it. We also call upon Christian educational institutions to introduce Islamics in their academic programs, in co-ordination with specialised teachers. We call upon the Muslim Ulama' and the Muslim educational institutions to come to an understanding of Christianity. If Christians are given the chance to learn what Muslims say about themselves, and Muslims hear what Christians are saying about themselves, then both may really get to know each other in a true, objective and mutual way. This is the kind of understanding which may tear down the walls of separation which stand between us, and create a suitable atmosphere for communication, co-operation and a continued seeking to achieve common goals.[12]

[12] The Council of the Patriarchs of the Catholic Church of the East, 'Together Before God ...', p. 26.

Religious discourse does not stop at the level of the scholar, but should reach into everyday language—at school, at home, in the media, in the mosque and church, etc. We should always ask whether our language encourages mutual coexistence or whether it increases sectarianism.

From texts to souls

When it comes to Muslim-Christian relations, we tend, in formal discourse, to be satisfied with the quoting of religious texts dealing with tolerance from Muslims, and verses on love from Christians. In such cases, each party tries to pull out its best texts. Perhaps it is time to move from the 'texts to the souls', as Maronite Patriarch Nasr Allah Boutros Sfeir always says. It is in the hearts that the future of Islamic-Christian relations will be decided. It is in the human heart that the course of relations in every human society is fixed. We are not being pessimistic when we say that the human heart is inclined towards violence. This is the kind of weakness that must be exposed in order for it to be defused. Entering into the complex game of relationships is at times devastating; but it is still a common urgent responsibility. It is in the heart that we face closed conditions such as prejudices, cruel sectarian attitudes, and inherited stereotypes. Here we must address the healing of memories. We know that the memories of both parties are overloaded with the remnants of the past. This prevents the establishment of fruitful relations with the other. Dealing with the depths of these negative memories, which control our behaviour, is a responsibility which we ought not to neglect.

Unless we know how to enter this complicated and dark area within our personal and collective selves, all those religious texts will then remain vague and useless—not being applied to our mutual relations in our daily lives. Entering the depths of the collective self opens the way for us to develop an identity which does not consider the religious other a threat to our own identity, nor denies that identity. We cannot take the path of the other, with the other, and for the sake of the other, unless we begin with the process of inner self-cleansing. It is at this level that we may find energy which releases our religious texts and liberates them. God knows how much we, here in the East, need to get out from the realm of 'being nice', which we often use to hide away from reality, in order to be able to get to the magnificent truth which sets us and the others free.

The culture of 'face'

Our culture as peoples of the East is that of the 'face'. It was said that the

Arab prophet was able to solve the most complicated problem over a cup of coffee. The personal and face-to-face getting together plays a major role in human relations. We get to recognise the face. This applies to Muslim-Christian relations also. This getting together humanises the other. Imam 'Ali said: 'People are enemies of the unknown.' Many of our negative stands will collapse if only we cross the threshold of our solitude—personal and collective—so that we may meet the other, away from our own masks and theirs.

On the practical level, channels of communication must be created at all levels of life, in schools, religious institutions, and in daily life, so that we may open the door to this kind of knowledge, to become acquainted and to understand the other.

Conclusion—together before God and humankind

To our regret, politics have occupied a great space in the field of Muslim-Christian relations, at the expense of relations on the religious and spiritual level.

To be present before the merciful God together may open our hearts to new and fruitful horizons which politics do not allow us to see. In this case, we shall not be on opposing fronts, but shall stand together before God who calls upon us to convert our hearts, and liberates us from our human desires which prevent us from taking a positive step towards the other. Discovering God is at the same time discovering the other in a new light, in purity and in the peace of heart and spirit. From this perspective we can say that our living together in harmony comes through the circle of our humble and sure standing before God, who calls us to be better Christians and better Muslims.

This standing before God cannot but lead into a commitment for the wellbeing of humankind especially those who are poor and suffering. It may just be that those very people would be the ones to reconcile us—through their poverty and suffering.

In the conclusion to the message of the Catholic Patriarchs of the East I find a testimony to this:

> We—Muslims and Christians—are not two fronts or opposing parties, but rather we are all stewards before God,

> and He is the Master of the Universe, and He is not owned by anyone. We are all of Him, from Him and for Him. We can never accept those whom God puts in our path unless we accept God in our life first. The more we discover God, the more we discover the sanctity of the human being.[13]

[13] The Council of the Patriarchs of the Catholic Church of the East, 'Together before God ...', p. 48.

JUBILEE: A RALLYING CRY FOR TODAY'S OPPRESSED

Jacob Milgrom

I was invited to participate in a 'Jewish-Christian Symposium on the Jubilee' sponsored by the World Council of Churches at the Ecumenical Institute, Bossey, Switzerland, 19-23 May 1996. There were 32 representatives from 15 countries, including India, Uganda, Brazil, the Philippines and Indonesia. I single out the third world nations because, firstly, I was enabled to feel, even vicariously, their people's pain and suffering and, secondly, I was witness to a vivid demonstration that their hopes for remedial action are expressed by the biblical jubilee.

The basic postulate of the jubilee is Leviticus 25.23-24: 'Furthermore, the land must not be sold beyond reclaim, for the land is mine; you are but resident aliens under my authority. Therefore, throughout the land you hold, you must provide redemption for the land.'

'Land' is here Canaan, the promised land; and 'you' refers to the people of Israel. They are to keep in mind that the owner of the land is God, and that they are only resident aliens; that is, God is the landlord and the Israelites are tenants. And the deity-landlord-owner has decreed that 'the land must not be sold beyond reclaim: each Israelite clan has been assigned a plot of land' (Numbers 26) that must always remain in its possession.[1] Even when it is sold it can always be reclaimed, a process called 'redemption', and every fiftieth year (jubilee), it must be restored to its original owner.

Cancellation of debts and return of forfeited land was also known in the ancient Near East.[2] It usually occurred when a king acceded to the throne. Its purpose was to 'prevent the collapse of the economy under too great a weight of private indebtedness.[3] However, it was generally

---

1 Milgrom, J, *The Book of Numbers*, Jewish Publication Society, Philadelphia, 1950, pp. 219, 480-82.

2 Weinfeld, M, 'The Sabbatical Year and Jubilee in the Pentateuchal Laws and their Ancient Near Eastern Background', in *The Laws in the Bible and its Environment*, ed. T. Veijola, Vandenhoeck & Ruprecht, Göttingen, 1990, pp. 39-62.

3 Edzard, D O, in *The Near East: Early Civilizations*, ed. J Bottero, *et al.*, trans. by R F Tannenbaum, Weidenfeld and Nicolson, London, 1965, chapters 2, 4, and 5, p. 225.

limited to the king's retainers,[4] and subject to his whim. The biblical jubilee, in contrast, was inexorably periodic and incumbent on every Israelite.

The jubilee has become the rallying cry for oppressed peoples today as did the exodus theme for their counterparts in previous decades. This time, however, they are not enslaved politically (except where colonial rulers have been replaced by their own), but shackled economically. The global market economy has generated unprecedented growth and prosperity, but not for them. The fact is that 20 per cent of the world's people possess 83 per cent of the wealth.[5] Moreover, three quarters of adjusting countries in sub-Sahara Africa have suffered declining per capita incomes, and in Latin America the declines were at least as bad.[6]

The impoverishment of the third world has brought attendant injustices. Relevant to the jubilee theme is the issue of global pollution, especially in the third world nations. The depletion of the rain forests in the interest of the timber and mining industries, for example, has caused irremediable losses to Costa Rica. Though it, singularly among Latin American countries, experienced significant economic growth between 1970 and 1990, the concomitant environmental decay in its soils and forests produced the loss of natural capital totalling 6 per cent of the gross domestic product of that period; in Indonesia the loss was 9 per cent.[7]

As a result, the debtor (third) world has issued the following demands to the creditor nations (who operate through the International Monetary Fund and similar agencies): 1) cancellation of their debts; 2) restitution of land and resources to their original owners; 3) cessation from pilfering natural resources and polluting them (one symposium paper cited Genesis 2.15b; God leased us the earth 'to work it and tend it', but not to despoil it); and 4) termination of economic slavery (e.g., the atrocious case in *democratic* India, cited in the introduction to Lev. 25.39-55)[8] by universally raising wages to a subsistence level.

The jubilee prescribing remission of debts, restoration of land, Sabbath rest for land and person, and release from economic servitude corresponds to all four demands. Obviously, their implementation would be met by large-scale resistance. Some demands would need to be modified. For example, as one symposium paper pointedly asked: Would not the

---

4 Bar-Maoz, Y, 'The "Misharum" Reform of King Ammisaduqa', in *Researches in Hebrew and Semitic Languages* (Hebrew), Bar-Ilan, Tel Aviv, 1980, pp. 40-74.

5 UN Human Development Report, United Nations, New York, 1993, p. 37.

6 UN Human Development Report, p. 45.

7 UN Human Development Report, p. 30.

8 Milgrom, J. *Leviticus 17:27,* Doubleday, New York, (forthcoming).

simultaneous remission of all debts inhibit creditors from lending at all?

Indeed, this is the problem that faced the outstanding spiritual authority of the 1st-century CE, Rabbi Hillel. He found that loans were not being made because of their automatic cancellation at the sabbatical year (Deuteronomy 15.1-2). As a solution, he issued an edict of Prosbul (Mishnah *Shebi'it* 10.3), a Greek legal term meaning 'before an assembly'. It circumvented the sabbatical by empowering the court, in place of the creditor, to collect the debt from the real property of the debtor if the bond were delivered to it in advance of the sabbatical year (Mishnah *Shebi'it* 10.2,4,6).[9]

Nonetheless, evidence can be adduced that countries employing some of the jubilee provisions have experienced spectacular economic growth rather than precipitous decline. For example, in just two years from 1952 to 1954, the percentage of South Korean farmers who owned their land instead of working as tenants jumped from 50 to 94. Something similar happened in Taiwan, another 'Asian Tiger'. Thus the jubilee laws, *mutatis mutandis*, offer a realistic blueprint for bridging the economic gap between the have and have-not nations, which otherwise portends political uprisings that can engulf the entire world.

In May 1996, Bossey, Switzerland, I witnessed the unfurling of the flag of jubilee.

For my Palestinian friends I offer this prayer of consolation and hope:

> For there is hope for a tree,
> if it is cut down, that it will sprout again,
> and that its shoots will not cease,
> Though its root grows old in the earth,
> and its stump dies in the ground,
> yet at the scent of water it will bud
> and put forth branches like a young plant (Job 14.7-9).

---

[9] For the range of rabbinic views, see Ch. Albeck, *Seder Zera'im* (Hebrew), Bialik Institute, Jerusalem, 1957, p. 383.

THE BOUNDARIES OF OUR DESTINY
A JEWISH REFLECTION ON THE BIBLICAL JUBILEE ON THE FIFTIETH ANNIVERSARY OF ISRAEL

Marc H Ellis

The journey of the Jewish people in the last fifty years has been astounding in its magnitude and significance. Where Jews were once weak, we are now powerful. Where Jews were once dispersed, we are now concentrated. Where Jews were once dependent on the whims of others, we are now independent. Where Jews once lacked a home, we now have a homeland.

Of course, all of these statements need qualification. Historically, Jews were not always weak nor are they all-powerful today; the Diaspora has shrunk considerably and the concentration of Jews has increased, but diverse Jewish communities exist within Israel and outside of it. Jews today feel at home in the West and in Israel, but the accusing images of those whom Jews have displaced remain. Can one feel at home when those who were once at home have been displaced?

Thus the journey from Auschwitz to Jerusalem is much more complicated than originally thought, and the narrative that joins the Holocaust and Israel which has evolved in that journey is deficient in many ways. The historic and continuing displacement of Palestinians remains before the Jewish people as the central question that accompanies this journey. On the fiftieth anniversary of Israel, the destruction of Palestine, which began with the founding of the state and continues today within the Oslo process, forces a revaluation of the last fifty years and indeed of the very direction of Jewish history.

The suffering of Palestinians has taken place within the shadow of the Holocaust. This suffering has been imposed by some who survived the Holocaust and by those who assert power in the name of the victims of the Holocaust. Palestinians have become, in a very real sense, the last victims of the Holocaust. Though the memorialisation of the Holocaust occurs as if Palestinians do not exist, and as if Jews are innocent of crimes against the Palestinian people, the accusing images remain: Palestinians do exist and have been wronged by those who claim the innocence of their own suffering, and the redemption of that suffering in the founding of Israel. For a people who claim memory as a distinctive aspect of their history, it is amazing that forgetfulness which has become a constitutive part of Jewish identity.

Do we fear that remembrance in its broader sense—in the suffering we experienced and the suffering we have caused—will make explicit the connection to a people whom we have rendered invisible, degraded, and displaced? Do we fear this remembrance will force a confession and a change of direction, so that a land conquered and divided, usurped and swallowed up, will one day be shared? Are we afraid that the boundaries we have drawn and defined in identity and geography are not the boundaries of our destiny?

Perhaps we fear that the fore-ordained boundaries have already changed, that in the oppression of the Palestinian people an unanticipated ending has come about and that the ending that Auschwitz proclaimed has already shifted in these intervening fifty years. Auschwitz proclaimed the reality of weakness and Europe. Palestinians proclaim the reality of Jewish power and Israel. Perhaps both Auschwitz and Israel are part of an ending that could not be predicted and can only be faced with a strength that comes from humility born of suffering and confession: that is, the end of Jewish history as we have known and inherited it.

This end is complicated, and there are prohibitions against even suggesting this most obvious occurrence. For if in suffering and victory, in sorrow and celebration, in humiliation and the accusing images against us, the end of Jewish history has been realised, how are we to proceed? If the boundaries of our destiny have indeed altered by actions against us and by actions we have taken—and this only in the last fifty years—is there any refuge from what history might bring to us in the next fifty years?

At the same time that the boundaries of Jewish destiny have shifted, a new Jewish exile has appeared, responding to both the cataclysm of the Holocaust and the oppression of the Palestinian people. One might say that this Jewish exilic community, in being faithful to both Jewish suffering and the oppression of Palestinians by Jews, is expanding the boundaries of Jewish destiny by embodying both events. The boundary they embody, the destiny they explore, comes within the Holocaust and the Palestinian catastrophe as a solidarity with the Palestinian people. At the end of Jewish history as we have known and inherited it, the boundaries of Jewish destiny are being defined by those Jews who have crossed over into a solidarity with the Palestinian people.

Language of justice/language of God

What is this solidarity? How can it be defined? What are the foundational elements of it? How can it be sustained? Are the redefined boundaries of Jewish destiny still Jewish, and in what way are they Jewish? Does solidarity with the Palestinian people mean the end of Jewish identity? Or if Jewish identity continues in this solidarity what will be its elements? What language can we use to speak of this solidarity? From what sources can this language come? Can we use biblical language? Can we invoke the language of God?

On the fiftieth year of the founding of Israel, the most obvious element of Jewish history and identity—indeed the most obvious language—to confront the injustices committed during these decades is found in the journey of the Jewish people. For the history itself, a history which has experienced injustice and suffering, and the identity that has emerged, which so often has focused on justice and compassion, has developed a language filled with concepts and metaphors that address suffering in bold ways. Paradoxically, it is this very same history, identity, and language that indicts contemporary Jewish life, and renders much of Jewish understanding remote from contemporary life, or even hypocritical in its use. Even more difficult is that this history is mobilised against its own understandings by being mobilised against the Palestinian people. In doing this, those Jews who take the lessons and language of Jewish history seriously and apply them in a time of Jewish empowerment are often rendered inarticulate and mute. If the entirety of Jewish history is mobilised against itself to further the goals of contemporary Jews, then those who carry with them the meaning of Jewish history are defined as something other than Jewish. At the same time, those who are in exile from the Jewish community precisely because of this situation often implicitly accept the definition of Jewishness that condemns them to exile. Therefore, those who carry the tradition in exile often see themselves against the Jewish community, or at least unable to articulate Jewishness because others have already done that, albeit in a way that the exile rejects.

Yet the inability to articulate Jewish terminology that issues from the deepest aspects of Jewish history poses a significant dilemma. Do those who have chosen exile instead of complicity with injustice cede the ground of Jewish identification to those who are complicit? This dilemma is further complicated by the use of Jewish history and language by forces of Jewish renewal which, while mouthing the need for justice, are in fact part of the system of oppression.

One thinks here of the group *Oz veShalom*, the Shalom Hartman Institute founded by David Hartman, and even the progressive journal *Tikkun*; all attempt to use the Jewish tradition to separate Jews from injustice by separating them from the occupation of Palestine. In their understanding, Jews are innocent and Israel is redemptive, and they remain so even with the injustice being perpetrated today. By eliminating that injustice, Jews and Israel, therefore, return to their previous reality, and continue on as if the separation of Jew and Palestinian, with borders that allow Palestinians a limited and dependent autonomy, is sufficient to redress the catastrophe that has befallen the Palestinians at the hands of the Jewish people. In this analysis, Palestinians remain peripheral to Jewish history, and the celebration of Jewish renewal can continue and even accelerate. Thus the language of Jewish history can be employed to reassert Jewish innocence and redemption as it discusses the force of justice in the Jewish tradition, while, at the same time, rendering Palestinians to a peripheral status not unlike the status Palestinians occupy in the minds and activities of those who actively oppress them. Can one say that the biblical language of the stranger so often applied to Palestinians by Jewish progressives as a way of protecting their status in the land has significant differences from those who see the Palestinian as a stranger without that protection? If Palestinians, actually indigenous to the land and the region, are seen, especially by European and American Jews, as strangers and foreigners, to be displaced or to be protected in their assigned status, then at the base of the language and conceptual understanding is a deception that can only change the ultimate destiny of Palestinians in the degree of their defeat. It is this confluence of Jewish militarism and renewal that makes the contemporary Jewish narrative so powerful, and also renders Jewish exiles so seemingly distant and inarticulate. To be involved in this debate between 'hawks' and 'doves', between the forces of Netanyahu and Peace Now, is intuitively understood by those in exile to be senseless.

The use of Jewish concepts and language can be considered only within a framework beyond the debate of Jewish militarism and renewal. This framework makes sense only if the victims of militarism and renewal are empowered to speak their story and their history as equals who have a right to be free in their own homeland, a homeland not confined to the outer reaches of what was once Palestine, or to a 'Jerusalem' that has never been part of that city. The appeal to Jewish history can be made only if Jewish and Palestinian history are now seen as joined on the way to a creation of a new history beyond the cycle of domination and defeat. The contextualisation of Jewish history and language changes both as they provide a way out of abstraction and complicity. To be sure, the boundaries of Jewish life are challenged with an expansion of vision that is complex and untested, but the history of the Holocaust and Israel has brought us here. To pretend that Jewish life exists somewhere else without this history, or somehow transcends the reality of this history, is a fantasy that allows power to triumph unrestrained.

What if elements of the Jewish tradition are invoked with a prospective and transformed communal orientation? What if those Jews in exile speak of the tradition, with Palestinians as active and equal participants, to help envision a shared future? Of course, that means listening to and being participants in Palestinian traditions which also project a future of inclusion and reciprocity. This calls for the contribution of particular histories and visions that include and transcend the particularities of the present. These particularities, explored in the hope of creating an equal and just future, then become vehicles for the expression of particularity *en route* to another identity that includes Jew and Palestinian, and transcends both. It is this formation of a new identity that allows the present division between Jew and Palestinian, a division that is accelerating in the Oslo era, to be reversed and overcome. The end of the cycle of violence comes into view when the land of Israel/Palestine is unified and when both peoples and the culture that grows from their integration share possibilities of life and responsibilities of citizenship.

One thinks here of various traditions within Jewish life that may contribute to this future. The first that comes to mind is the image of the jubilee, the biblical warrant for the redistribution of land and wealth in fifty year cycles. Here empowerment accumulated over five decades is counterpoised by the redistribution of power: the cycle of victory and defeat, wealth and poverty, rootedness and exile, is halted and a new vision is offered. While once divided into the haves and have nots, the land of Israel/Palestine would now be shared and its wealth equally distributed. The political life of both communities would be equalised and joined as if the lives and futures of both peoples depended on the consent and vision that could be generated within this new polity.

The biblical jubilee is complicated by its own history as an idea and by its contextualisation in Jewish history. Biblical scholars are almost unanimous in the opinion that the jubilee was probably never practised. And the idea itself was constructed in an exile that saw as its first priority the return to the land. Though a return to a land from which a people has been dispossessed is not problematic in itself, the cycle of displacement which began with the entry into the land in the first place and the subsequent exile, with now another return in mind, continues a process that injures. Return is hardly simple or without further harm, and the mobilisation of the exiled population required to induce a return often distorts aspects of the ideology used to mobilise a further uprooting. The return itself, in its organisation and power centres, is also complex, and the jubilee tradition was codified by a certain class within the exilic society, in this case the priests who had lost power in the dispersion, and some of the regulations found in the jubilee legislation are an assertion of priestly place and power in the coming return. At the same time, the theological warrants which grew up around the jubilee and give its divine warrant present difficulties because the return is tied to God and a destiny that has been given to the Jewish people. The natural right and desire to return is mandated, and those who now live in the land or those who seek to remain behind in their new home are defined as outside the will of God. Such a call to return, often couched in a stridency peculiar to monotheistic religions, can also become a call to internal and external violence.

Nonetheless the image of justice, the breaking of the cycle of power and dependency, wealth and poverty, the sense that perfection is unachievable, but injustice, when carried to extremes, is unacceptable, remain important parts of the Jewish tradition even, and especially, as it is being violated in a wholesale fashion today. It is this very violation and the haunting cost of the Jewish return, and in the context of the absolute need for a Palestinians' return to their own homeland without a further uprooting and dispossession of Jews or Palestinians, that makes relevant again this ancient tradition. In the fiftieth year of a continuing cycle of injustice, the need for return and a new definition of what return can and should mean, the need for a jubilee interpreted in the context of a new and shared history, is crucial. Can this image of justice embedded in the jubilee be implemented in the contemporary context as an end to suffering and injustice? Can a jubilee pronounced in the land today open a future beyond exile and return, return and exile? Can a jubilee move Jews and Palestinians beyond a dynamic which seems endless and only deepens the wounds and uprootedness of both peoples?

The boundaries of our destiny

The understanding of the jubilee in a new context, across borders and boundaries, is also a challenge to the three religions that arose in this area and have contributed many values and much violence to the world. In some ways, the Israeli-Palestinian conflict has little or nothing to do with religion *per se*, while in other ways the conflict and its resolution may help define the future of Judaism, Christianity, and Islam. For if none of these religions caused this contemporary struggle for land, place and power, all have been implicated in legitimating or delegitimating the various peoples and positions involved. For reasons of offence and defence, all three religions have been mobilised in assertion and quiet in complicity. There is no lack of commands from God to uproot and dispossess, at least as issued by the leaders of all three religions, and the calls for peace and justice have also issued from these leaders. Moreover the general and over-arching narrative that explains the victory and defeat of peoples in this conflict, as well as the hope that the defeated one day can become the victor, has also issued from these ancient traditions. Can these traditions be rescued from their own proclivity toward complicity? In rescuing these traditions, can the image of God also be rescued?

If we see rescue as restoration, as a restoration of innocence and origins, as if a history of complicity does not exist or can be transcended, then the rescue will simply be a continuation of what has been. However, the inclusion of those who have suffered under the 'redemption' of the victor means that the tradition itself continues, with foundational change incorporated into the very life of the tradition. Within this inclusion the restoration will look very much like the renovated holy sites in Hebron and Bethlehem, walled off, secured from ordinary life, separated for different religious communities, and where all who seek to worship are searched by soldiers of the state before they enter. As one report on the newly renovated Rachel's Tomb commented: 'The tomb's once tiny prayer area has been increased five-fold by the renovation. But many other changes are security related: the towering walls were erected to protect Jewish worshippers from stones, gasoline bombs and rubber bullets when Israeli soldiers and Palestinian rioters clash in adjacent Bethlehem.' In a revealing comment at the reopening of the tomb, Israeli Defence Minister Yitzhak Mordechai told the worshippers, 'We came here after 2,000 years of longing.' He spoke as Israeli soldiers with automatic rifles patrolled from nearby rooftops.

If restoration is the theme and foundational change is refused, the ancient longing will become the future pictured here. If the tomb is guarded by soldiers, if worship can only take place protected by the military, if the worship of God is literally sealed off from, and, at the same time, symbolises the reality of injustice, do these soldiers also guard God? Is God now restricted in Rachel's Tomb, like the worshippers? Does God wall off those who seek him to protect them from the injustice that has been perpetrated often in God's name? Or, is God at the checkpoint nearby, with those who are outside the walls, who need protection and justice from those who have returned to renovate and guard this shrine? It is more likely that those who experience and witness injustice without redress and are displaced in the name and promise of God will deny God or hesitate to name God because of what is done in God's name. A-theism will be the choice, an understandable one in light of the situation.

But across boundaries, in an enlarged sense of a joint destiny, the walls of Rachel's Tomb seem ridiculous and counterproductive to worship. Though a-theism would continue as the legacy of the past, a new theism might emerge that would allow the past to remain and be reinterpreted for the present. A common legacy could be affirmed even as a new identity, and hence a new legacy, develops. The question of justice in Judaism, Christianity and Islam is reintroduced, along with other secular understandings, to forge a path into the future. The jubilee arises, then, not as restoration, or even a call to particularity, but as a contribution among others to the healing of broken histories and to the joining of two communities. Perhaps God, too, is articulated again within this framework of justice and reconciliation. This God, which as yet does not exist, is a God who accompanies a journey rather than directs it, and contributes insights on the way rather than commanding from a distant and guarded place.

In this scenario, the jubilee functions as a confrontation with the victorious who pretend innocence. Further, it decentres the claims of an authoritarian God or priesthood, and shifts return and restoration to an inclusive justice that, while imperfect, promotes a society where justice and equality are the norm. This means a decentring of any one ethnic, religious, or cultural system and the promotion of diversity and integration so that elements of each community contribute to a public culture and politics defined beyond ethnicity and religiosity. Rather, the definition of the new society emerges from all these elements freely contributed, sifted through, and transformed in the outcome. Instead of religious certainty—the walled tombs in Hebron and Bethlehem—a diaspora sensibility of openness, availability, and hospitality forms. Recognising the diaspora in Israel/Palestine is to decentre the 'Holy Land.' Paradoxically, as with religiosity, this decentring opens the land to a renewed spirituality without militarisation. Those who come to sites like Rachel's Tomb will do so in the spirit of pilgrimage and openness to neighbour and to God. The secular life around these sites will continue and develop its own understandings of openness. This is part of the diaspora: the free choice of worship, the example of faith and secularity as deepening of both paths, and the discussion of the responsibilities of citizenship that bind both the religious and the secular.

Jerusalem, too, is in need of an expanding vision. Too often Jerusalem is seen in dichotomous ways—either ours or theirs, redeemed or unredeemed, the centre of salvation or pagan. Though the physical boundaries of Jerusalem have expanded under Israeli control this has represented a desire to conquer and use the city for Jews only. As the physical boundaries have expanded, the boundaries of memory and inclusion have constricted. Triumphal claims to Jerusalem narrow the vision even as victory is proclaimed as a fulfilment of destiny. But this destiny, claimed in such extraordinary ways, militarises symbols and excludes the ordinary life of Jews and Palestinians alike. To assert the extraordinary character of the city, ordinary goodness and hospitality are de-emphasised and derided. In a sense, these dichotomous understandings legitimate and then reinforce each other until militarisation is essential not only to protect the victor from the defeated, but to protect the victor from the haunting images of having to dispossess in order to achieve and maintain control. In the very heart of Jerusalem, historically and today, is a void where the victims of this 'salvation' cry out.

Can Jews drive their children to school in the morning for Orthodox religious education and also recognise that where these schools now stand was once another population now displaced? Can the classes in Talmud and Jewish history, the debates of the sages and the recalling of suffering, make sense if the revocation of Palestinian Jerusalem identity cards takes place even as the lessons are taught? This can only happen if the ordinary lives of Palestinians and Jews are subordinated to the extraordinary. But what if the centre of contemporary Jerusalem was seen as broken rather than salvific and shared in that brokenness, rather than divided by victory and defeat. What if the ordinary became the norm for decision, making the ordinary life of Jews and Palestinians central. This would mean the need to restore the ordinary, as the ordinary has been severely disrupted, and creating a new ordinary, where Jews and

Palestinians can live a life beyond the divisions of the present. Like the jubilee, restoring the ordinary would be prospective, envisioning a shared future rather than a romanticised past.

Since the jubilee represents an attempt to restore the ordinary as a vision of a shared future of justice and peace, why not begin in Jerusalem, on the fiftieth anniversary of Israel? As the centre of Israel/Palestine, broken in the cycle of occupation and dispossession, and in hope of creating an extraordinary achievement in the re-establishment of ordinary life, this could signal the start of a jubilee that extends to the whole of the land.

Of course, we realise that the opposite is occurring today and that the vision of Jerusalem as the broken middle of Israel/Palestine, rather than being implemented, is being destroyed. Therefore the jubilee is also distant and becoming more so every moment. There comes a time when the very will and capability of a people are so decimated that the vision becomes an abstraction, a pious hope rather a real alternative. On the fiftieth anniversary of Israel and the fifth year of Oslo, the hope is receding, perhaps beyond repair, at least in the ways that many have looked at the question in the past decade. The restoration of the ordinary in a future of equality and justice cannot come within the boundaries of either community alone, or within the two-state solution once seen as a legitimate and possible compromise. The vision of victory has been too successful, and there are little territory or resources left for this division to be efficacious in any manner. In this sense a chapter in Jewish and Palestinian history has come to an end. Today the struggle is within the larger entity called Israel that encompasses Israel and Palestine, Jew and Palestinian. Though some may find this an attempt to salvage something from defeat, it actually corresponds to the central issues of inclusion in Jewish history. For solidarity with the Palestinian people means a struggle for freedom of Jews and Palestinians in the whole of Israel/Palestine rather than an enforced, artificial, and unjust separation. The challenge of the jubilee, then, takes on a new urgency within the land for all who live and seek to live within the land. Ending one chapter in Jewish and Palestinian history is thus an invitation to deepen the struggle within the boundaries of a new destiny.

For those Jews and Palestinians who travel this path, and all those who seek to join them, the struggle continues and is intensified. Issues, and the limitations of our present boundaries, have become clearer, and the end of one chapter of history becomes the call to embark on a new one. In this struggle one is reminded of the call to be faithful to a vision beyond the present and to transcend the boundaries of the given. One wonders if God requires this sensibility, or if God is found in pursuing this path. The jubilee presents a vision of the world where God remains an open question, awaiting a time where the ordinary comes alive and where the walls of Rachel's Tomb are guarded by a hospitality that flourishes when land and life are shared.

PILGRIMAGE ALTERNATIVES

Häkan Sandvik

Traditional pilgrimage

Living in this land it is fascinating to witness different kinds of pilgrim-groups touring the Holy Land. It is a very colourful view. Everything from the Greek Orthodox pilgrims, walking very sincerely in their groups, wearing black clothes, to the Western pilgrims/tourists following their tour-leader and wearing hats or umbrellas of different colours, so the guide can recognise the group. There are the Muslim groups gathering especially during the month of Ramadan, and the Jewish groups gathering during their feasts, most visibly around the Western Wall. Each tradition and each part of the world has its own way of making pilgrimage, expressing its own spirituality.

In the Holy Land we can certainly witness that pilgrimage is an integral part of religion. The very fact that we believe there is another and better world somewhere, sometime, makes us long to go there. The pilgrimage gives an experience, a kind of taste of this other world. It might be an experience from our true origin, paradise, or from the times we believe our religion existed in its pure form and was not distorted as we might feel it is today. It might also be a foretaste of our destination as human beings—of Heaven. Mostly it is all at the same time. The architecture of the holy places is often formed to express 'the other world' of which we become a part while entering the holy place. For example, most Orthodox churches have a picture of heaven in the cupolas with Christ, the Pantokrator in the middle. Moreover, many Muslim holy places are built to illustrate paradise.

Seen from this purely spiritual perspective, the local people and the political situation in the surroundings of the holy places are of no interest at all. The pilgrimage is, on the contrary, a way of fleeing, for a while, from the mundane world with all its problems. But this kind of pilgrimage, which we meet in the old traditions with a long heritage of pilgrimage, is exclusively a religious matter. There is no guide, the role of the travel agency is minimal. These pilgrims are far from being tourists.

Pilgrims—tourists

For Christians with weaker pilgrimage traditions the situation is very different. Here the borderline between tourism and pilgrimage is very thin. This makes Western pilgrims very easy prey to manipulation, both politically and economically. Even if I want in no way to underestimate the value of the experience a normal Western pilgrimage tour gives, Western pilgrims usually stay in this mundane world during the pilgrimage also. To a large extent they are in the hands of an official guide and a travel agent, both with their specific agendas, which is hardly compatible with the main intent of pilgrimage.

The contradictions between the intent of the pilgrimage-group and the facilitators of the tour have been managed in a very eloquent way by the Israeli side. In some cases, even to the extent of changing the whole pattern of Christian pilgrimage. A part of the tour demonstrates to the pilgrims the development of the Promised Land by the Jews, making the desert bloom. To many groups the State of Israel is a sign of the Second Coming of Christ—the Messianic Kingdom, and the guides have nothing against supporting that view. It is easy to see why such a tour has to avoid meetings with local people. To talk to people on the street, either Jewish or Palestinian, would distort the picture in a threatening way.

I have been amazed while meeting different kinds of groups: how many feel more uncomfortable when I am talking about Israeli society, with all its social and political problems, than when I talk about the situation for the Palestinians, or the halting of the peace process. They know there is a problematic relationship between Israelis and Palestinians, but to hear that Israel is a normal society with a lot of economic and social problems, as well as disharmony within the society itself, does not belong to their picture of the 'Holy People'. Hearing this threatens their images. I am not talking only about Christian Zionist groups who view this land as the Promised Land exclusively for Jews. It is true of most Western pilgrims who usually have a kind of dream, an image of a Holy Land in a very romanticised way, which image the tours attempt to strengthen. Meeting local people, people on the streets, then threatens this image. Those who call themselves 'Friends of Israel' often turn out to be only 'Friends of their image of Israel'.

Theological patterns for alternative pilgrimage

I want to bring up two, as I see it, very important theological reasons for changing the pattern of pilgrimage to the Holy Land. A pilgrimage should challenge our theology and our faith, not merely confirm it. If a pilgrim returns home the same person as when he or she came here, the pilgrimage has failed its purpose.

'... what our hands have touched ...'

The most central Christian message is the Gospel of the Incarnation. Our Christian faith is not only about images or theoretical dogmas. The Gospel speaks about God becoming a human being in a very ordinary village in a very ordinary human setting: God becoming man sharing human conditions. St John repeatedly underlines the tangibility of our faith in his letters: 'We have seen ... we have heard ... we have touched ...' (1 John 1.1). What we are talking about is not a theory, but, rather, something we have experienced. A pilgrimage is not intended to confirm superficially our imaginations, but to introduce us to the realities of the Holy Land—people as well as sites—and, by meeting these realities, however disturbing they might be, to find Christ.

Let me give some examples. Most tourists and pilgrims are very disturbed by all the souvenir sellers. Wherever you go you have a line of souvenir sellers, often small boys, trying to push you to buy something you absolutely do not want. A visit to Bethlehem is often very disappointing. We do not meet the little quiet town of Bethlehem from our Christmas hymns. We meet the Star Hotel, the Good Shepherd's Souvenir Shop, the Christmas Tree Restaurant, to mention only a few. Everything seems so commercialised. It is not what we expected Bethlehem to be. But give it another thought! How was the situation in Bethlehem during the first Christmas Night? There was no quiet little town with angels flying around singing Christmas hymns. People had come to Bethlehem from all over the area for the census. It was a densely crowded town, with queues and deafening noise—Middle Eastern culture has never been very quiet. As it was at that time, so it is today: where people gather business people are present, and that is the most natural thing. There were certainly a lot of businessmen chasing the people visiting Bethlehem during the first Christmas Night.

The same idea can be transferred to the experience of the *Via Dolorosa.* There you wish to walk in meditation, silently and think about the suffering of Christ. But it was not that way when Jesus walked towards Golgotha. His last days took place during the time of Passover and we know that the population in Jerusalem increased at least sevenfold during the feast, which means heavy crowds and much commercialism. Excavations outside the Temple Mount have revealed souvenir shops from the Second Temple Period. When people gather people do business, it is a part of normal life, and it was in this very normal life that Jesus walked his *Via Dolorosa.* This perspective is very important to reflect on for a pilgrim, because meeting the reality brings us much closer to the holy event itself than the superficial images do.

I will give yet another example of meeting the 'origins'. I was leading a group of Palestinian youths who were supposed to become local guides. I gave them the text of Psalm 23 and asked them to find in it images and expressions from their own culture and the natural surroundings in which they live. First they did not understand at all what I was aiming at, but when I gave some very typical examples from the psalm illustrating the culture and nature in Palestine, they immediately added several examples of which I was not aware.

We can meet the Bible most vividly in the local culture, not only by reading a passage from the Bible at a heap of stones. When Jesus was talking to his disciples, they were not only using their ears but also their eyes, their noses, all their sensations. The surroundings were illustrations of what Jesus was teaching. Much of this historical context is still the living culture in the Holy Land today.

A final example. Most of the life of an ordinary family during the time of Jesus was concentrated on four matters: finding water, and preparing bread, oil and wine. The family which had access to water, bread, oil and wine had a good life. But to get this required a lot of work and struggle. Now, what is most holy in our traditional churches? It is the water—baptism, the bread and wine—the holy eucharist, the oil—the holy ointment; in other words, sacraments. So the most day-to-day matters, the most mundane, are at the same time the most holy in the Church. The struggle for water and land for cultivation is still today a very central issue for the people in the Holy Land.

' ... though the parts are many, they form one body ... '

As Christians we are parts of the body of Christ. Most religions have some kind of community image that plays a very significant role for the faithful, for example, the *umma* in Islam and the collective identity of the Jewish people. As Christians we go one step further. We say we are limbs of the living body of Christ. This has consequences also for our pilgrimage. Meeting local Christians during our pilgrimage enriches our understanding and experience of the world-wide Church. This is true wherever we travel. But it is especially true in the Holy Land, because a meeting with local Christians also means a meeting with our own roots. Taking part in a local worship, be it in an Orthodox, Catholic or Protestant church, we are experiencing traditions which in many ways are the origin of our own tradition. Our tradition has its root in them. As a matter of fact, we learn to know ourselves by meeting the local Christians and their traditions.

Celebrating the liturgy in an Orthodox church is fascinating, for, although we all have different ways of expression, we can still recognise our own liturgy. We feel that we are a branch of the tree of the Church, maybe far away from the root, but still receiving the same nutrition. Learning to know ourselves by meeting the local Christians, worshipping with them, learning from their lives, but also recognising that we are part of the same body of Christ—that is what I call a pilgrimage.

HER JUBILEE— A CHANCE TO CHANGE

Jean Zaru

One of the beautiful posters made by Palestinians for the Beijing Women's Conference in 1995 is of a painting of women walking, taking long strides, looking into the horizon. They do not seem to be bent down by their bodies' pain, anxiety and hurt, for they have started their journey to affirm life by upholding the ideals written in Arabic on the poster: justice, equality, and freedom. As Palestinians and as women, our struggle to achieve these ideals, which are essential for the protection of Human Rights, continues today. It has been a long struggle, waged on so many fronts. It has been a long walk, and a long road to freedom still lies ahead.

On the way, we often get tired, confused, frustrated and sometimes lose direction, or find ourselves at an impasse, or down a one-way lane, or at a no-entry sign, or even at a dead end. But this has not discouraged us from continuing our journey with others and for others. In fact, these difficulties have made the issues of the struggle even more clear, and revealed to us the inter-connectedness of unjust structures, the web of oppression, and the various struggles for liberation. The call for liberation is heard everywhere. It is not an empty slogan or a liturgical anthem. Rather, it is a cry, a cry from the heart, a cry out of humiliation and oppression, a cry for a new future—beginning now. Will our religious structures or our Churches hear the cry for liberation and suffer with those who suffer?

In January 1987, the Central Committee of the World Council of Churches designated the years 1988 to 1998 as the Ecumenical Decade of Churches in Solidarity with Women. The decision to highlight this issue for a ten-year period was in response to deep and growing concerns, from all over the world, regarding the situation of women in Church and society. The aims of the Decade are:

1. Empowering women to challenge oppressive structures in the global community, their country, and their Church;
2. Affirming in shared leadership and decision-making,

theology and spirituality, the decisive contribution women are already making in Churches and communities;

3. Giving visibility to women's perspectives and actions in the struggle for justice, peace, and the integrity of creation;
4. Enabling Churches to free themselves from teachings and practices that discriminate against women;
5. Encouraging Churches to take action in solidarity with women.

Many people had hoped that the United Nations Decade and the Churches' Decade in solidarity with women would lead to radical transformation of our societies and of the situation of women who suffer from poverty, economic exploitation, sexism, racism, and violence. However, the sad truth is that not much has changed. Today, most women face more difficult conditions than they did fifteen or twenty years ago. At the same time, there have been milestones along the way that have made a difference in the collective understanding that is yet to be put fully into practice.

Only Churches which have responded to the jubilee call and reordered their lives and relationships can dare to direct that call to the wider human community. Are the Churches ready to respond to the challenge of jubilee and respond to the call for the restoration of community in the one household of God? Central to the understanding of the biblical jubilee is the self-limitation of power exercised through the control over land, capital, labour, and women.

Violence in all its forms, including both direct and structural, is an expression of the uncontrolled excess of power which destroys relationships in human community. The commitment to work towards overcoming violence is also one of the challenges of the jubilee. Jubilee is not simply the search for justice. It is an attempt to provide a comprehensive vision during periods of transition in which justice is an essential element. The jubilee indicates a new beginning, and a chance to change economic, social, political, and cultural life, so that a new and just order may be introduced, creation be redeemed and wealth be equally distributed, and a window of hope be opened to the future. It is a pivotal alternative to the prevailing order of exclusion and marginalisation. It is the celebration of life-centred values in the midst of despair.

It is also significant in this regard to mention the resolution of the Parliament of World Religions which met on 27 August-4 September 1993 in Chicago, USA. The participants resolved:

> 1. To declare 1993-2003 as a decade of religions in solidarity with women, a decade in which religious communities shall strive to increase the participation of women in all areas of religious life, and in which the authentic voice of the religious women will occupy its proper place in the international arena; and
> 2. To encourage greater commitment to action, both in our respective communities and globally for adopting a standard of substantive justice and fairness towards all human beings under which all will have equal dignity, regardless of gender.

This statement is a sign of hope, but we should be aware too that religion, in both its progressive and reactionary forms, has entered into and shaped almost every major crisis in our world, and has influenced our daily lives as well. On the progressive side, there are movements toward the radical alliance with the poor and the oppressed. There are activist reform and peace movements. On the reactionary side, there is narrowness and chauvinism in every religious tradition which easily allies itself with chauvinistic national movements. Religion is both a problem wherein its structures of dominance have oppressed us as Palestinians and as women, and a solution where its vision of liberation and equality has generated powerful movements for political, social and economic change.

My life in the past three decades has been caught up in the question of human rights. I did not know that this was so, for we did not always give the name 'human rights' to the things about which we argued, or for which we struggled. Since then, I have learned that the struggle for justice is one struggle, and that an action taken to defend or strengthen human rights in one place is an action on behalf of people everywhere. I now understand that our global responsibilities and relationships have a local face, and no matter where we live we can work for human rights. The kinship we form as we do so is the prototype of a new community which knows no national, racial, or gender/sexual boundaries.

However, it has been the women's movement for liberation, both locally and globally, which has touched me most deeply and forced me to change. Women's roles and status lie at the heart of every society. Girl babies may not be buried alive as was the practice in the past, but even now parents in many countries welcome a baby boy more enthusiastically than a girl. We have so much work to do, to unlearn what we have learned and to look out from different windows, and yet it is not always that simple. Often I see too that women themselves reinforce structures of injustice in the way they educate and raise their families. Often they use their power to dominate and coerce, rather than utilise the resources of mutual empowering and cooperation. The former type of power is oppressive, and marginalises others from the centres of decision-making. However, power can be used in a constructive way so that one can control one's life and influence one's community to act justly.

Another shortcoming of the women's movement is that certain trends are imposed. For example, women who, out of choice, choose to be mothers and take care of the family, are often judged as if their vocation and self-worth is less. No one should impose on others their lifestyle or values; rather, we should struggle so that women will have equal opportunities to men and the freedom to choose.

Women in different paths of our society might be struggling to change different things at different times. The starving overworked woman without adequate living conditions might not be worried about sexist language, but it does not mean that, if we are at different stages, one issue is more important than another. All of us are on this journey for freedom with others and for others, so, rather than discrediting each others' struggles, we must join hands, enrich and inspire one another to bring about a true community where justice and righteousness (right relationships) reign, rather than transfer power and privilege from one group to another, for no one is free until we are all free.

On this journey of struggle to change for the better, to transform ourselves and our societies, we often experience fatigue—and many are burnt-out—unless we are sustained by a commitment and a spirituality that is deeper than the ethics of revolution alone. The act of recovering a source of being created in the image of God is, for women, a redemptive act. It is to reclaim one's lost wholeness and sense of self-worth.

Freedom is not a new theme in Christian theology. The Gospel itself is a message of liberation in Jesus Christ. It is good news to all people in every situation and in every place of internal and external oppression. The situations may vary but all of us want to be alive and free. The struggle begins in a woman's own heart, mind and actions as she learns to be pro-woman. But it must stretch around the world to all people—men, women, and children who are looking for freedom to shape their own futures and participate in the search for what it means to be children of God. For Palestinian women, the liberating words and actions of Jesus in relation to women become an inspiration and a guide for us in our struggle for the liberation of our own people and for humanity, both on the political level as well as on the social level. As in all societies, we Palestinian women have been cast into certain roles that have kept us subservient and out of decision-making circles. Women's work has not been considered equal to men's work. The ministries of women have been considered less important than the ministries of men.

Let us look at a few women of the New Testament. How did they minister? What was their self-image? How did Jesus respond to each of them? My own life experience leads me to remember the Samaritan woman who met Jesus at the well less than an hour's drive north of where I grew up and now live. She came in the heat of the day because her social position did not allow her to join the other women who drew water in the cool of the day. She was taken aback by Jesus' request for water. Her self-image was not a positive one. Yet knowing this, Jesus looked beyond her social status and accepted her ministry to him. In forgiving (or affirming) her, he opened for her new possibilities for living. Often today, we feel the burdens of the Samaritan woman's dilemma. We have to deal with so many things in our society. The hierarchical structures in the Church and in society are a hindrance to our own growth and involvement. The expectations that we feel from our families and friends become an overwhelming burden as we seek to be faithful to God's calling.

Another example is the story in Luke 15 of the lost coin. Very few verses in the chapter are devoted to the fact that the woman is seeking something. The woman's intention is observed. The status of women in society has contributed to overlooking the part which speaks about the woman herself, and thus the message of the story is obscured—that message of God's love seeking the lost. Although as women in Palestine, we are full participants in our national struggle, we are not fully recognised so as to become part of the decision-making bodies. The *Intifada* has changed some attitudes, but we have a long way to go. Women are organising at the grassroots level and are beginning to connect the national struggle with the women's struggle for liberation.

A last example for now is the story of Mary and Martha. I can relate to many aspects of this story. First of all, the story points to the relationships between two sisters. Family relationships are important to us. They form the basis of our Palestinian society. Secondly, the story reminds us of the gifts we have and the roles we play. Jesus reminds us that we are all unique individuals, and no matter who we are and what we do, we must be concerned about God's work and God's family. Women in our society are expected to do all the household and family tasks. If we want to be involved in other work, in the Church or society, we have to do this in addition to the expected work in our homes. Finally, the story of Mary and Martha brings out the ongoing tension that we all experience and can identify with—that of contemplation and activity. Activity without contemplation is empty. Contemplation without activity is dead.

We Palestinian women live and work in a very traditional society where the 'do's' and 'don'ts' for women are made very clear. Often our ministry depends on how well we follow the expectations of our own people. If we do not meet their expectations, our ministry is not validated or even taken seriously. Unfortunately most people cannot look beyond the superficial. So, if I have any truth to communicate, I have to be careful not to lose the respect of the community. So I live my life in my traditional society on the one hand, and in the ongoing, ever-changing world on the other.

The women of Palestine are often referred to as the 'glue of our society'. We are the ones who hold together our families, while our husbands, brothers, and sons are in prison, deported, wounded, or killed, or perhaps have migrated for economic or political reasons. As co-partners we continue to be involved critically in a (mostly) non-violent struggle. We continue to work, support and build for a new future, a future time when, through our liberation, all of the Middle East and all of humanity would be liberated. It is this hope that inspires us and leads us. It is this hope that will turn the sufferings into a new dawn for all humanity. It is this hope that allows us to see the image of God in everyone.

INTERNATIONAL MODELS OF PEACEMAKING

Samuel Rayan

Introduction

Peace is freedom from war and strife; freedom from conflict, disturbance, and disorder. It is a situation within a group of people in which no organised use or threat of violence takes place.[1] It is, however, more than what this negative definition suggests. Peace is the proper ordering of life, both personal and social. It is constituted by a web of right relationships among persons and communities, and by the resultant harmony, growth, development, well-being and prosperity. 'The protection and liberation of creation and the realisation of more justice among people is peace.'[2] Peace, then, is a social reality made visible in harmonious relationships between persons in the family or the local community, and between states and nations. It is 'love made visible in the world.'[3] *Shalom* comprises both material and spiritual conditions of well-being. It is linked to justice and righteousness and to the land's generous yield (Ps 85). *Shalom* belongs to being human, and describes the 'intactness', integrity and wholeness of a community and its well-being. Its essential elements are mutual responsibility and trust, and consequent security.[4] *Salam* sums up all the blessings one wishes for those one loves. It is heaven's welcome to the blessed. *Eirene,* along with righteousness and joy in the Holy Spirit, is the substance of the Reign of God. Orderly obedience to the law of God is our peace (St Augustine). Peace is *shanti:* tranquillity and fulfilment born of friendliness to all creatures; it is the highest good a *yogi* longs for, and a *rishi* wishes the world. Peace is *niravana*, the secure fullness of being to which the Buddha points. According to Tao-te Ching, peace entails simplicity and 'fewness' of desires; it entails refraining from acting against the grain; it is quiet activity in which no prejudice obstructs the Tao, the

---

1 Galtung, J, *Friedenforschung*, 1968, p. 531.

2 Duchrow, U and G Liedke, *Shalom*, World Council of Churches Press, Geneva, 1987/1989, p. 112.

3 Kownacki, M L, OSB, *Peace Is Our Calling*, Benet Press, Erie, PA, 1981, p. 168.

4 Duchrow and Liedke, *Shalom*, pp. 113-14.

way; and no desire leads astray. Peace is a creative process in which we are called to co-operate imaginatively.

'International' is taken to mean not only distinct 'nations' in the usual sense of the word (under covenant of the UN charter), but also distinct groups within a given nation, which have serious difficulties in relating in a friendly fashion.

Models of peace are patterns or shapes which peace and peace-keeping have taken in the course of history. Not all of them have borne real peace; not all of them are standards of excellence. But every sample could perhaps teach us something about peace making, how to approach the task, or how not to.

Models of peace

Some twenty, more or less distinct models may be described briefly. A few are rather negative, and may not be followed; others are more positive and can set us on a relevant quest. All of them have their source in history, sacred or secular.

1. *The Pax Romana model.* This refers to the pacification by force of most of Europe and parts of Africa and Asia by the Caesars. By 27 BC Augustus brought the civil war to an end. There followed, for the ruling class, a period of prosperity, security and cultural flowering. For the rest, the greater part of the empire, it was an armed peace, a violent peace, imposed by conquest and subjugation in order to facilitate exploitation. A peace that involved continual dispossession of peoples, endless tax hikes, and deep misery. A peace very much akin to the graveyard. Of this *pax*, Seneca said that 'whole tribes and peoples have been forced to change their habits.' It was, perhaps, to the *Pax Romana* that Jesus referred, when He said that the shape and the reality of the peace which the world (read: the empire) gave was different from the pattern of peace he was offering (John 14.27).[5]

Similar to this, and in fact emulous of it, have been the more recent *Pax Britannica, Pax Gallica, Pax Americana* and other colonial-imperialist schemes constructed with weapons and violence, and geared

[5] Duchrow and Liedke, *Shalom*, 125; Swaim, J C, *War, Peace and the Bible*, Orbis Books, New York, 1982/83, pp. 46-48.

to exploitation as required by their economic systems. The wars which these peace schemes have fought are many; the conflicts with which they have littered the world are numerous, and the destruction they have wrought is beyond words. Empires 'sought peace by mastering the world, grinding down all "lesser breeds", with legions tramping the streets ...'[6]

2. Another peace technique has been the *partitioning* of land among conflicting groups, and the setting up of new nations confronting each other, in place of one nation. Real problems are left unresolved. Big powers often resort to this way in order to ensure further conflicts, followed by profitable interventions and the sale of arms. One may recall the partitioning of the Indian subcontinent, of the Korean peninsula, of Vietnam, of Ireland, and the arbitrary chopping up of the African continent by the colonialist Congress of Berlin of 1878.

3. *Military intervention* has been another means employed to secure peace. This model contains a destructive contradiction which has stood out in sharp relief in the case of the Indian peace-keeping force in Sri Lanka in the 1980s. The peace imposed on Bosnia, too, is precarious. Its limited success comes, not from armed action but from the collaboration of some politically conscious people. The Indian and the Pakistani military tactics in Kashmir are a no-win engagement, tragic and wasteful, endlessly souring relationships.

4. *Balance of Power* is a fourth model. This is the classical instrumental approach to peace, and is not different from *arms control* and *disarmament*. The approach has its merits: it is equitable; it creates space for diversity, and helps prevent exploitation. But it has its limitations and demerits as well. The approach is dissociative, in the sense that the antagonists are still kept apart by prejudice, fear, hatred, and threat. In most cases, there is power but little balance, or only a precarious balance, a dynamic balance. And in the matter of an arms race, dynamic balance is contagious. According to Johan Galtung of the Oslo Peace Institute, 'Disarmament does not seem to be the road to peace, but peace may be the road to disarmament.' Conflicts must be resolved by parties themselves coming together (or being brought together) in new associative relationships.[7] In this field, little can be expected of governments. Governments will control

---

[6] Swaim, *War, Peace and the Bible*, pp. 46-48, 75-76.

[7] Galtung, *True Worlds*, The Free Press, New York, 1980, pp. 363-64.

only horizontal arms races, not vertical ones; and quantitative arms races, not qualitative ones. What they agree to limit or discard are dated weapons, and the agreements they make, usually, have the possibilities of cheating built into them.[8] Patricia Mische observes that disarmament is a 'political football'. It veils the development of new weapons, and not all nations have been eager to endorse it.[9]

5. An abstract model underlying the schemes described above finds expression in the old maxim, 'If you want peace, prepare for war' (*si vis pacem, para bellum*). Its modern version is *deterrence:* if you want peace, spread terror. The saying embodies a falsehood. History shows that those who prepared for war, got war. A 1980 computer study, reported in the US *Military Review,* found that since 650 BC there have been 1656 arms races, of which all but sixteen ended in war.[10] And those who took the sword perished by the sword.[11]

6. We are coming now to more positive patterns. One is the *ending of the feud system.* For centuries after the fall of the Roman empire, European peoples were oppressed by a system in which conflicts were settled by force of arms, rather than by legal processes. Unarmed peasants, merchants, and pilgrims often fell victims to blood feuds between warring kings and competing barons and their armed knights. The system was gradually tamed through institutions such as the *Peace of God* and the *Truce of God,* by which the Church restricted fighting, under pain of excommunication, to certain days and certain classes of people. It was finally banned by the development of an alternative to armed tyranny, namely, a juridical order under the nation-state. Today, however, we have 'a global feud system in which the rule of force too often prevails over the rule of law.' This situation lays bare deep-lying human under-development and immaturity, if not insanity and criminality. And we do not yet have a global juridical order and an effective global authority to settle disputes without sabre-rattling and savagery.[12]

7. In the last hundred years there have been three attempts at world

---

8 Galtung, *True Worlds,* p. 202.

9 Mische, P M, *Star Wars and the State of Our Souls,* Winston Press, Minnesota, 1984/85, p. 88.

10 Mische, *Star Wars and ...,* p. 92.

11 Swaim, *War, Peace and the Bible,* pp. 75-87.

12 Mische, *Star Wars and ...,* p. 82.

order which could ensure global peace.

The first was the *International Arbitration Tribunal*, set up after two peace conferences held in the Hague in 1899 and 1907. But it failed to secure arms reduction, and to create a new world order sufficient to avert the outbreak of the First World War. The main reason for this: no nation was ready to cede an iota of its sovereignty to a world body.

The second attempt was the *League of Nations* established after the First World War. Everybody's fear of investing some of its sovereignty in an international body left the League weak and unable to prevent the Nazi horror and the Hiroshima-Nagasaki terror.

The third attempt is the *United Nations Organization*. Once again the sovereignty issue has proved a stumbling block. The UN lacks real authority to stop aggression, to effect disarmament, and to intervene with a minimum of impartiality and fairness. When its resolutions are flouted by Israel and by Iraq, and when aggression is committed by both, the UN's responses are vastly different and quite revealing. And, more basically, the UN is structurally undemocratic, having been forged by men with a feudal-imperialist mindset and culture rather than with democratic experience and tradition. What is needed, then, is another attempt which could well have a better chance to serve the cause of peace. The situation now is more favourable than in 1945. For, in the first place, the Hiroshima pictures, and the reports of the effects of nuclear bombs on people are now available to the public, which also knows of the existence today of over 50,000 nuclear weapons, and which fears that there will be more of them, if things are left to the compulsions of an amoral science, and an amoral economics, in which people do not matter. The need of a new way of thinking about peace and security, therefore, is being felt and affirmed. In the second place, global economic dependence, compounded by growth in population, unemployment and ecological crises, render the future uncertain, and affect the security of everyone. Manifestly, the situation calls for a new global awareness and a corporate effort. And, thirdly, the infrastructure required for a global peace-system is now in place, in the shape of world communication, travel and technology.[13]

8. In fact, there already exist some credible *International Systems* which testify to great possibilities and are already playing a significant role in global co-operation. They are a sign of hope and a promise of peace. They have an essential peace content. Such are:

[13] Mische, *Star Wars and ...*, pp. 90-91.

1) The International Telegraphic Union, 1865
2) The Universal Postal Union, 1874
3) The International Red Cross, 1863/64
4) The Hague Tribunal/International Court of Justice
5) The World Health Organization
6) The International Labour Organization
7) The Organization of American States
8) The Food and Agricultural Organization
9) The World Meteorological Organization
10) The United Nations Development Programme
11) The United Nations Industrial Development Organization
12) The United Nations High Commission for Refugees
13) The United Nations Educational, Scientific and Cultural Organization, and
14) The United Nations Children Fund.

These represent 'an amazing trend in this century towards the development of global-level public policy and global systems to manage global problems.'[14]

9. *Magnanimity and freedom from greed* are peace patterns. These may be illustrated from Bible history:

Genesis 13 narrates the story of a strife between Abraham's herdsmen and Lot's. Both men were rich in flocks, herds and tents: 'The land could not support both of them dwelling together; for their possessions were so great that they could not dwell together' (Gen 13.5-6). Abraham was not keen on strife, 'for we are kinsmen'. They had to separate and occupy different regions, to their right and to their left. Abraham left the choice to Lot who preferred the well-watered Jordan valley. Abraham was content with the rest. And they lived in peace (Gen 13.1-12).

Around 850 BC the prophet Elisha saved Israel's king from many a trap laid for him by the king of Syria. He struck with blindness the Syrian army sent to capture him, and led it to Samaria. There the king of Israel was ready to slay them. The prophet intervened. 'You shall not slay them ... Set bread and water before them, that they may eat and drink and go to their master.' The historian then concludes: 'And the

[14] Mische, *Star Wars and ...*, pp. 102-103.

Syrians came no more on raids into the land of Israel.' A 'novel experiment in peacemaking'! (2 Kgs 6.11-23).[15]

That lesson was not lost on Israel. A little over a hundred years later, King Pekah of Israel (737-732 BC) attacked Judah and slew 120,000 in one day, and took 200,000 men, women, and children captive, and much spoil. As the army was bringing them all to Samaria, the prophet Oded stopped them, confronted them with the sin of slaughter and enslavement, and bade them send back the captives. Samaria's community officials saw the point. 'Oded's belief in kindness to enemies made sense to them. What they wanted was peace and security, and this appealed to them as a way to get it. So they returned the spoil to the captives and the captives to their homes.'[16] They took the captives, 'clothed them, gave them sandals, provided them with food and drink, and anointed them; and carrying all the feeble among them on asses they brought them to their kinfolk in Jericho' (2 Chr 28.1-15).

10. The *prophetic model* calls for revolutionary change in our outlook on life and life's direction. Unlearn war, give up its practice, and transform tools of death into implements of life. Go up to the mountain of the Lord, discover his law, learn his ways and walk in his paths. This implies and demands that we and all nations 'beat our swords into ploughshares and our spears into pruning hooks,' and that no 'nation shall ... lift up sword against nation, neither learn war anymore.' To do otherwise is to miss, reject, the light of the Lord and walk in darkness (Isa 2.3-5). Micah upholds an identical model and adds a positive picture of the peace that follows the transformation of swords and spears: then 'they shall sit every man under his vine and under his fig tree, and none shall make them afraid.' Profound transformation of the culture of weapons, fear and war will blossom into a culture of life, peaceful and happy (Mic 4.2-4).

11. From biblical history I would like to consider the *peace of Cyrus of Persia* (c. 585-528 BC). After conquering Media (550) and Lydia (547), Cyrus defeated the Greeks and drove east to the borders of India. In 539 he conquered Babylon, restored the cult of their chief god, Marduk, and in the following year issued an edict, of which two versions are given in the Hebrew Scriptures: Ezra 1.1-3 and 6.3-5. In it Cyrus (Kurush) attributes his victories to YHWH, God of Israel, and sets the Israelite captives in

---

[15] Swaim, *War, Peace and the Bible*, p. 10.

[16] Swaim, *War, Peace and the Bible*, p. 9.

Babylon free, permitting them to return to Judea and rebuild their temple, destroyed some fifty years earlier. Cyrus, too, was celebrating a jubilee and meeting its challenge by loving mercy and doing justice. The Bible greets this non-Israelite as God's anointed liberator (Messiah) and the elected shepherd of his people (Isa 44.28, 45.1-2; 41.1-3).

12. A little later, in the 3rd century BC, there reigned in India emperor Ashoka who expended multifaceted efforts to secure universal peace. After his bloody invasion of Kalinga, shocked by the slaughter of thousands of people, Ashoka renounced war and violence, sought reconciliation, and wanted all people to live unharmed, self-controlled, calm and gentle. He banned all fighting and killing, organised medical services for human beings and animals, promoted cultivation of useful herbs, planting of shade trees, and the digging of wells along highways to serve people as well as beasts. He directed local rulers to tour towns and villages and teach people the *dharma* (religion) of obedience to parents, generosity to priests, modesty in possessions, frugality in life, and complete *ahimsa*, refraining from hurting living things.[17]

13. The *Satyagraha model* of Gandhi (1869-1948). *Satyagraha* means truth-insistence, grasping the truth and clinging to it. Gandhi defined it as soul-force, the power born of truth and love and non-violent resistance to the force of brawn, iron and lies. He followed the Jain-Buddhist ideal of *ahimsa*, non-injury, and the New Testament call to return good for evil. Soul-force is superior to the force of arms. Gandhi said, 'I ask all lovers of communal peace to pray that the God of truth and love may give us both the right spirit and the right word, and may use us for the good of the dumb millions.' *Satyagraha*, a non-violent, loving, long-suffering, struggle marked Gandhi's work for communal harmony; it marked his relation to the British while fighting their colonial hold to the last. He provides us with a peace model rich in spirituality, in political wisdom, and human hope; a model which proved historically effective.

14. The *Vietnamese model* is different from, and yet similar to Gandhi's way of resisting tyranny and oppression. The Vietnamese masses, politically conscientised and mobilised, became militarily effective. Their guerrillas are directly violent. 'But,' Galtung remarks, 'by the way in which they are

---

[17] Parrinder, G, 'Peace', in Eliade, M, (ed.) *Encyclopaedia of Religion*, vol. 11, 1987, Macmillan, New York, pp. 221-224.

organized, in small decentralized units, based on "participation" with "equality", "justice", "equity" and "solidarity" present, they are also examples of what they stand for.'[18] 'Just as there is a basic compatibility between capitalistic growth and modern hierarchical technocratic military organization, there is also a basic compatibility between self-reliance as the basic mode of production and paramilitary-guerrilla-*satyagraha* forms of defence whereby a civilian population is mobilized and becomes less vulnerable and less clientalized through dependence on vertical military organizations that, in turn, depend on centre countries for military hardware and software through hierarchical "alliance" systems.'[19]

15. *Justice-truth peace models* reach us from Malaysia, Australia and South-Africa. In Malaysia some 60 per cent of the population are Malay and Muslim; the rest are Chinese, with a small proportion of Indians. Much of the trade was in Chinese hands. Conflict grew between the major communities and erupted in the 1969 riots. President Rahman's government looked into the issues with courage and honesty, and solved the problem by tackling with fairness the social and economic issues, and by providing education, job-training and proportional reservations, thus ensuring justice and paving the way for equality. Since then, Malaysia has been able to grow in peace as we described peace earlier.

A further example is found among the indigenous tribes of Australia, dispossessed of their land by European invaders and immigrants. They finally laid claim to their ancestral land and appealed to the constitution of the nation. The government and landholders maintained that what was occupied was *terra nullius*, a land without people, no man's land. Or, let proof of proprietorship be adduced. The court, however, directed the parties concerned to negotiate as equals. That process culminated in the new laws initiating a movement of just and peaceful settlement.

Another model speaks from South Africa, with Nelson Mandela, a symbol of an oppressed and long-suffering people, standing up for truth and justice as the only path to reconciliation and peace. The setting up of the *Truth and Reconciliation Commission* after the fall of the immoral *apartheid* regime is a pattern of peace with justice, without witch-hunting.

16. *People's movements and citizens' initiatives* are, perhaps, the most

---

[18] Galtung, J, *True Worlds*, p. 194.
[19] Galtung, J, *True Worlds*, p. 409.

significant and promising models of peacemaking. The *Indo-Pak People's Forum* may be cited as an example. Around mid-1992, some human rights activists, Indian and Pakistani, met in Vienna. They found the fifty-year-old 'dialogue' between the two countries to be too elitist, too secretive, and too much militarily determined. They decided to hold a people's convention on peace and democracy. Work started in March 1994. Some two dozen persons from both sides of the border offered to spend time and energy on this 'impractical idea'. On 9 September 1994, this core group met in Lahore, Pakistan, and founded the People's Forum. Three conventions followed: in Lahore, November 1994, in Delhi, February 1995, and in Calcutta, December 1996. The governments co-operated by issuing visas; the public gave enthusiastic support, expressed in the shape of volunteer work, the hosting of delegates and welcoming them with flowers, and the signing of resolutions. The discussions and resolutions focused on demilitarisation, religious tolerance, governance, the Kashmir issue and gender justice. The need was felt to challenge misconceived notions of patriotism and national security, and a call was made to outlaw war. A lamp has been lit. The flame has to be tended, and the light must be helped to spread.

A growing number of people, tired of waiting for governments to act, engage in people-to-people programmes aimed at building understanding across borders, or offer non-violent resistance to military moves and nuclear projects.[20] Peoples' movements counter concentration of power in national security bureaucracies which play their own games, or even 'play out their imperial fantasies at the peoples' expense.'[21]

People should not be understood in any restricted and partisan sense: to mean, for instance, only industrial workers (Marx-Lenin), or only peasants (Mao), or only students (Marcuse), or the elite (liberals). There are no exclusively predestined bearers of the new world, no elect of history. All can, and should be, motivated to act. There are tasks for everybody, though tasks and talents vary. Peace tasks are to be distributed democratically.[22] One may recall Mao's consistent emphasis that 'the people, and the people alone, are the motive force in the making of world history', and that 'the masses have boundless creative power'.[23]

Peoples' movement means that all centre-periphery formations

---

[20] Mische, *Star Wars and ...*, pp. 95-96.

[21] Barnet, R J, *Roots of War*, Penguin, 1971/1977, p. 339.

[22] Galtung, *True Worlds*, pp. 396, 416.

[23] Galtung, *True Worlds*, pp. 398-99.

are being fought and rejected, in favour of a world where 'each part is a centre', and all vertical divisions of labour in the production of goods, of knowledge, of politics are being subverted in favour of democracy. Peoples' self-reliance is a dynamic movement 'from the periphery to the periphery of/by the periphery, and not something done for it.'[24] 'Citizens' initiatives can be seen as a plurality of revolutions at the micro level'—in city blocks, in factories, in families; micro-revolutions similar to those that took place in 1968 in schools, universities, hospitals and even in institutes like the International Peace Research Institute in Oslo.[25]

17. There is yet another model which is universal, and underpins and enriches all the others, the *earth model*, or, the *cosmos model.* The decisions we now make for peace and against violence and war 'must be based not on illusions of power, or historical conflicts and struggles, but on a deep understanding of the evolutionary process and miraculous events that have brought us to this point.' They must be based on 'a profound knowledge of the longer stream of billions of years of cosmic and earthly history.'[26] We and the universe are part of a larger process. We belong within the universe. The universe is not a machine, but 'a living, organic, systemic, dynamic, intelligent, divine process of which we are a part.'[27] And the earth is a single cell in the universe, functioning in communion with the whole. The universe is one; the earth is one; the planets, animals, humans are all related, inter-related, interdependent; one family breathing one breath.[28]

That means we can survive and grow in humanity only to the degree that we guide our life towards communion and co-operation with our total human and transhuman environment. The universe functions as 'a co-operative community'. Only in such a relationship is life possible. We are challenged today to integral and conscious communion with the total earth-process, and to assumption of total responsibility for the next stage of evolution.[29] Violent competition will not civilise us; it will not even enable us to survive. 'The earth and the universe which have functioned all along as a unitive, co-operative integrity' are our teachers. 'The earth itself does not recognize national boundaries, ... sovereignty,

---

[24] Galtung, *True Worlds*, pp. 399-401.
[25] Galtung, *True Worlds*, p. 416.
[26] Mische, *Star Wars and ...*, pp. 113-16.
[27] Mische, *Star Wars and ...*, p. 114.
[28] Mische, *Star Wars and ...*, p. 116.
[29] Mische, *Star Wars and ...*, pp. 118-20, 124.

... security, apart from the security of the whole. Until we learn the lesson the earth (and our today's knowledge of it) reveals to us we will never be secure.'[30]

18. Finally, at the heart of all efforts to do justice and build peace, at the heart of all peoples' movements, and at the heart of the earth and its processes, there lives and throbs the *Jesus model*. Jesus is Prince of Peace, and the Reconciler of the world. He comes unarmed. He lives poor without possessions that would need defending. Seeing the world as God's beloved family, he promotes, by word and life, sharing of resources, forgiving of offences, and love for all including enemies. He identifies himself with the victims of all violence throughout history, and resists violence and shames it with non-violent endurance and measureless love. In him those who are far or estranged are brought together in love.

> For He is our Peace.
> He makes the two [Gentile and Jew] into one entity, and breaks down the barrier which keeps them apart, by destroying in his own person the hostility. He restores peace and creates a single new man [and woman], and through the cross reconciles them to God in One Body. He comes to bring good news of peace to those who are far off and those who are near (Eph 2.14-17).

In his Passion he expressed God's pain caused by the violence we vent on each other. In his Passion he made his own the hurt of the world, and so drew us all into his broken heart and there 'gifted' us to one another and to God as one Body, one Earth, one history of suffering and folly, one forgiven family, called to one blessed destiny. It is in living that truth and loving one another, in loving God in God's children that peace consists, and a human life worthy of the name is lived.

Conclusion

> The whole Earth is pressing for a creative solution to the present earth-threatening conflicts ...We are being challenged to re-shape our perceptions, attitudes, values,

[30] Mische, *Star Wars and ...*, pp. 125, 126.

> and images of the future. We are being challenged to re-vision the human.[31]
> The present war system is self-reinforcing and among the most ugly creations of humankind. It is symptomatic of the whole global and domestic system based on competition and domination and it is at the same time cause and effect (mainly effect) of this system.[32]

The primary task, then, is to deal creatively with the enormous tensions which afflict us and our planet; and to attend to elementary honesty and sincerity, avoiding double-speak, double-deal and deceit, not only in personal life, but in politics as well, and in all international relations. Such a committed and creative approach will point to the positive models we have been reviewing, and will lead us towards what Teilhard de Chardin and Thomas Berry call 'a supreme achievement of a planetary order of magnitude', namely, that global human unity towards which all earthly developments are implicitly directed from the beginning.[33]

---

[31] Mische, *Star Wars and ...*, p. 130.
[32] Galtung, J, *True Worlds*, p. 199.
[33] Mische, *Star Wars and ...*, p. 129.

IN SEARCH OF PEACE: A SOUTH AFRICAN CONTEXT

Madipoane Masenya

In the heyday of *apartheid*, years typified by hate, enmity and the gross violations of human rights, we in South Africa watched days go by in anticipation; sometimes patiently, sometimes not. Each day was greeted by unique, albeit common activities. These were days typified by police guns and police dogs, all aimed at silencing the voice of the oppressed; days in which human blood flowed on a regular basis, blood of the innocent and that of the guilty. Days in which the value accorded to human life dwindled.

Most of us wondered if South Africa would ever taste a moment of peace (*salam, shalom*), not a peace in the sense of *Pax Romana* (a system of domination), but in the sense of *salam/shalom* (incorporating a design of living together).[1] Some got so disillusioned that they decided to leave the country, their class and race affording them that luxury.

As most of us know, the struggle was basically due to the minority group of people (whites) wanting to preserve their domination over the majority (blacks) because they considered themselves more human than the others. A struggle ensued, caused by those dispossessed of their land wanting to reclaim what legitimately belonged to them. In a nutshell, those were days of war. 'Peace' was achieved at the barrel of a gun.

In the light of this history, it is no wonder that people have referred to our first democratic elections of 1994 as 'miracle elections', basically because, on the whole, they were peaceful. It is no wonder that the world has regarded South Africa as one of the most notable examples of peace-loving countries. Mandela was right when he argued:

> Time and again the prophets of doom have been confounded by the capacity and determination of South Africans to solve their own problems and to realize their shared vision of a united, peaceful and prosperous country.[2]

---

1 See Huber, W, 'Justice, Peace and the Integrity of Creation: A Challenge for Ecumenical Theology', in *Scriptura* 24(1988): 1-16, p. 5.

2 Mandela, N R (speech), in Aneez, S, 'Mandela Magic for Truth Group', *Cape Times*, 14 February, 1996, p. 2.

Some religious observers have seen the intervention of God in South African affairs. The unbanning of political organisations, the release of political prisoners, including Nelson Mandela, the first democratic elections, and the Government of National Unity are but a few reasons for this. Though it would be an exaggeration to argue that the aforementioned activities took place without trouble, we may argue that, on the whole, the transition from *apartheid* to democracy, coercion to freedom, alienation to co-operation, took place smoothly and peacefully.

This paper will focus on two aspects of the transition which, in my view, contributed greatly to the present state of affairs.

The Mandela magic/government

Nelson Madiba Mandela is one of the most mysterious figures in South African political history. Maluleke regards him as a significant 'institution' and 'symbol' for the promotion of national unity and reconciliation. He notes that, 'Ever since his ascent to power, Nelson Mandela has done one thing with single-mindedness and resolute consistency; and that is the business of promoting national unity and reconciliation.'[3]

His activities, particularly his commitment to national reconciliation and unity (peace), have prompted some to regard him as a messiah sent by God. His generosity in dealing peacefully with all, including those who perpetrated crimes in the past, have prompted others to think that he is going to the other extreme. He has advocated peace both nationally and internationally. In his inauguration speech he remarked:

> We must therefore act together as a united people, for national reconciliation, for nation building, for the birth of a new world. Let there be justice for all. Let there be peace for all. Let there be work, bread, water and salt for all.[4]

His last remark is worthy of note because he seems to acknowledge that peace, or complete peace, may not be achieved if some

---

[3] Maluleke, T S, 'Truth, National Unity and Reconciliation in South Africa: Aspects of an emerging Agenda', in *Missionalia* 25(1997): 59-86, p. 62.

[4] Mandela, N R, 'Address by the President, Mr Nelson R Mandela at his Inauguration in Pretoria', *A Time To Build* (a booklet of speeches), 1994, p. 3.

are still disadvantaged economically,[5] whilst others have everything they need.

In his address to the United Nations General Assembly, Nelson Mandela challenged the organisation to work for the establishment of a new world order. According to him, the following four elements will need to be knit together in order to fashion the new universal reality: democracy, peace, prosperity and interdependence. He observed:

> The great challenge of our age to the United Nations Organization is to answer the question: given the interdependence of the nations of the world, what is it that we can and must do to ensure that democracy, peace, prosperity and interdependence prevail everywhere?[6]

In his speech to the meeting of the joint houses of the Congress of the United States of America, he remarked about South Africa: 'At the end, the bloodletting stopped. At the end, goodwill prevailed. At the end, the overwhelming majority, both black and white, decided to invest in peace.'[7]

The present constitution affirms the rights of everyone, and, in that way, it becomes a significant and enriching deviation from the *apartheid* one, with its one-sidedness. I quote the following lines:

> Everyone is equal before the law and has the right to equal protection and benefit of the law.
>
> The state may not unfairly discriminate directly or indirectly against anyone on one or more grounds, including race, gender, sex, pregnancy, marital status, ethnic and social origin, colour, sexual orientation, age, disability, religion, conscience, belief, culture, language and birth.

---

5 See also Maluleke, T S, 'Dealing lightly with the Wound of my People: The Truth and Reconcilliation Commission in Theological Perspective', in *Missionalia* 25, 1997, pp. 3, 324-43.

6 Mandala, N R, 'Address by the President, Mr Nelson R Mandela at the OAU Meeting at Tunisia', *A Time to Build,* 1994, p. 6.

7 'Invest in Peace: Address by the President of the Republic of South Africa, Mr Nelson Mandela to the Joint Houses of the United States of America', 1994, p.15.

> Everyone has inherent dignity and the right to have their dignity respected and protected.[8]

On the whole, therefore, the constitution affirms that there is unity in diversity. Our country is characterised by people of divergent races, cultures, languages, sexes, creeds, ethnic identities, and so forth. The affirmation of the dignity of each human being is extremely welcome in a situation where the humanity of many of us, was trampled upon. In the apartheid years, difference, particularly difference from the dominant groups, was viewed not as a blessing but as a curse.

Goduka is right when she argues that diversity is as old as humanity, and that South Africa has historically been a diverse country: 'However, after the European invasion, and the systems of colonisation and apartheid, the diverse nature of humanity was exploited, denied, and undermined by the establishment of the norm.'[9]

She continues to argue that in Europe, the West and in South Africa, the norm is white, male, heterosexual, Christian, middle-aged, healthy, able-bodied, and having access to wealth and political power. Anyone outside the norm is regarded as deficient, and therefore inferior. Under the new constitution, the norm has been replaced by the affirmation of unity and diversity as reflected in the Bill of Human Rights.

The Introduction to the Truth and Reconciliation Commission is one of the indications that the Mandela government is committed to peace. This commission was established by the Promotion of National Unity and Reconciliation Act of July 1995. We need to understand that act in the context of the underlying project to achieve national unity and reconciliation. This project developed from the 'negotiated settlement'—note that instead of opting for war, the political parties concerned opted for negotiations or peace—to the interim constitution and finally to the new constitution. The whole project, with its attendant processes, is based on the realisation that whereas in the past, South Africa was a deeply divided society typified by strife, conflict, untold suffering and injustice, the country now needs a future founded on the recognition of human rights, democracy and peaceful co-existence for all South Africans.[10]

---

8 The Constitution of the Republic of South Africa, 1996, i.e., Act 108 of 1996:7.

9 Goduka, N, 'A Manual to Empower Educators to Affirm Diversity', Unpublished paper, 1995, Pretoria, p. 1.

10 Statutes of the Republic of South Africa—Constitutional Law, Promotion of National Unity and Reconciliation Act, No. 34, 1995, p. 801.

Basic to the whole truth and reconciliation process is the pursuance of 'national reconciliation' rather than vengeance or justice in the judicial sense of the word.[11] Some of the objectives of the Promotion of National Unity and Reconciliation Act are:

1. To investigate as fully as possible the nature, activities and extent of gross violations of human rights committed during the period from 1 March 1960 to the cut-off date contemplated in the constitution, coming from the conflicts of the past.
2. The granting of amnesty to people who make full disclosure of all the relevant facts related to acts associated with a political objective committed in the cause of the conflicts of the past.
3. Affording the victims an opportunity to relate the violations they suffered.
4. Taking of measures aimed at granting reparation and rehabilitation and restoration and civil dignity of victims of violations of human rights.
5. Report to the nation about such violations and victims.
6. To provide for the establishment of the Truth and Reconciliation Committee.

Even though the Truth and Reconciliation Committee is limited in power and is a process, rather than a final product as yet, it shows the Mandela government's commitment to peace.

The government at present is working on the Reconstruction and Development Programme, which aims at redressing the imbalances caused by the previous regimes. A few examples of its intentions will suffice:

—The empowerment of women.
—The improvement of the quality of life of those who have been neglected by the previous systems. This includes programmes geared at providing housing to the homeless, running water to those who have had none, the improvement of the quality of education of those who were deprived of such before.

---

[11] Maluleke, 'Truth, National Unity ...', p. 60.

Though one has not exhausted the many activities which reveal the commitment of the government to peace in South Africa, one trusts that what we have discussed sheds light on the question.

The Concept of *botho/ubuntu*

One other factor which in my view has contributed to a peaceful co-existence of those who were formerly enemies of each other in South Africa is the African concept of *botho/ubuntu* (humanness). It has been to the benefit of the whole country that in South Africa, this quality is possessed by the victims of the previous regimes—African South Africans; hence the peace prevailing in the land.

The Northern Sotho proverb *Motho ke motho ka batho* literally means, 'A human being is a human being because of other human beings'. It highlights the interdependence of human beings with other human beings: 'because you are what you are because of what I am'.[12] It means that one's humanity is defined, complemented and enhanced by the humanity of others.[13] The concept *ubuntu/botho* implies a fundamental respect for human nature.[14] African humanism is typified by the following norms and values: justice, respect for person and property, tolerance, compassion, sensitivity to the aged, the handicapped and the less privileged, reliability, and so forth.[15]

Due to this God-given gift of ours, we were able to look beyond the unjust practices of our enemies to see in them human beings, who, like ourselves, have been created in the image of God. Our *botho* gave us the desire to want to reach out to them, with the understanding that together, irrespective of our differences, we form one same humanity. That, however, should not imply that those who do not possess this quality should take advantage of those who do by exploiting the latter.

As a similar humanity, we should strive for *botho* (humanness/humanity), since not one of us can hope to exist meaningfully without the other. The words of Mogoba are worthy of note: 'Wherever people are

---

[12] See also Mbiti, J S, *African Religions and Philosophy*, Heinemann, Oxford, 1989.

[13] Mosoma, D, 'Restitution/Reparation: A Commitment to Peace and Justice', in *Journal of Black Theology in South Africa*, 1991, pp. 23-32, p. 26.

[14] Teffo, J, 'Ubuntu/Botho is How to Live!', in *City Press*, 25 June, 1995, p. 14.

[15] Teffo, 'Ubuntu/Botho ...', p. 14; see also Mogoba, S, 'Committed to Peace', in Villa-Vicencio, C (ed.), *The Spirit of Hope: Conversations on Politics, Religion and Values*, Skotaville, Braamfontein, 1991, pp. 187-97, p. 195.

struggling to regain their humanity or to promote the human cause, I believe that God is at work.'[16]

The aforementioned proverb highlights the corporate mentality of Africans. If all of us South Africans can embrace this valuable collective mentality, we will be successful in our search for peace.

The picture given in the above paragraphs about peace in South Africa is a rosy one indeed. Has South Africa achieved peace? The following arguments will reveal that the answer to the question is a resounding 'no'. Some political parties, for example, contend that as long as the land has not been returned to its legitimate owners, we cannot speak about peace, justice and reconciliation. The words of Mosoma regarding the significance of the jubilee event for social construction are worthy of note:

> It was not a simple call for emancipation without corresponding appropriate structural innovation. To be sure, political emancipation without corresponding economic well-being embodied in the land is a fraud ... The jubilee makes political power and economic justice inextricably bound together. That is to say, any false dichotomy between the two realities is not acceptable.[17]

Mosoma goes on to argue that the whites in South Africa should admit their role in the dispossession of blacks from their land. Such truth will free them and enable them to realise and accept that land restitution is a form of justice which participates in the enhancement of the wholeness of life—this, according to him, is 'justice that breaks the stronghold of economic and political dependency and provides a future characterised by jubilee and celebration of life.'[18]

Regarding the Truth and Reconciliation Commission, some sceptical observers fear that if the Commission is not monitored, it 'may deal rather lightly with the deep wounds of God's people.'[19]

Some view the policy of affirmative action as marginalising the white minority. Some are wondering what is to become of the country should Mandela step down or die. Another significant concern may be

---

[16] Mogoba, 'Committed to Peace', p. 195.
[17] Mosoma, 'Restitution/Reparation ...', p. 29.
[18] Mosoma, 'Restitution/Reparation ...', p. 31.
[19] Maluleke, 'Dealing lightly ...', p. 341.

raised: if other sections of society (for example, women, the poor, the physically challenged, to name but three) are still marginalised, would it be fair to speak about peace? As Maluleke notes:

> There is neither historical nor compelling proof that human rights campaigns, nation building exercises, excellent constitutions or very civil societies have led to the extermination of racism, sexism and poverty.[20]

These are some of the valuable concerns raised concerning the state of affairs in the country. Concerns like this reveal that South Africa, like many other countries, has not attained peace yet; it is still in search of peace. We must, however, give the country credit for its commitment to peace.

In conclusion, I wish to remark on Jesus, the New Testament model of peace. Jesus Christ is the Prince of Peace, Jesus, the '...Christ who is the herald of Jubilee, messenger and enactor of liberation.'[21]

In Christ humans are assisted in having peace with their Maker and with one another. The type of peace offered by Christ is one which accommodates all; it shows no partiality. It reminds us that 'the conquering of enmity is a far better way to attain peace that is to the benefit of all the people of South Africa (of the world), than victory over the enemy'.[22]

Martin Luther King Jr also wrote:

> We never get rid of an enemy by meeting hate with hate; we get rid of an enemy by getting rid of enmity. By its very nature, hate destroys and tears down; by its very nature, love creates and builds up.[23]

Christ's mission of reconciliation reminds humanity of its responsibility to make peace with God, with fellow human beings (refer to the concept of *botho* above) and with nature. It would be a good idea if each of us could make sure that we do not return to dust before having fulfilled this precious divine purpose for our lives—being peacemakers.

---

20 Maluleke, 'Truth, National Unity ...', p. 80.

21 Ringe, S H, 'The Biblical Jubilee: A Strategy of Hope in Times of Crisis', unpublished paper, Washington, 1996, p. 10.

22 De Villiers, E, 'Peace Conceptions in South Africa in the Light of the Biblical Concept of Peace', in *Scriptura* 28, 1989, pp. 24-40 (brackets mine).

23 King Jr, Martin Luther, *Strength to Love*, Fortress Press, Philadelphia, 1986, p. 54.

INTERNATIONAL MODELS OF PEACE MAKING—NORTHERN IRELAND

Nicholas Frayling

Britain and Ireland are bound together by geography, shared language and shared Christian faith, but they have been in virtually continuous conflict for eight centuries. The focus of that conflict for the last eighty years has been Northern Ireland, a small province in the north-east of the island, covering just six counties.

The border was arbitrarily drawn by a British government to ensure a perpetual majority of unionists, who would be sympathetic to British rule in Ireland, and who owed loyalty to the British crown, and for the most part, to the Protestant reformed religion. Not even in the minds of its founders was Northern Ireland considered a viable political entity. It was created out of expediency, and like all such creatures, it was inherently unstable from the beginning. It could not be otherwise, because the Catholic minority—mainly nationalist or republican in sympathy—were denied equality under the law. The Northern Ireland state was itself an unjust creation, and it institutionalised injustice for more than one-third of its people.

Although much progress has been made in righting particular injustices, and although most parties are at present engaged in a peace process, under the guidance of an independent chairperson, the weight of history remains largely unaddressed, and threatens to crush the fragile hopes for peace which ordinary people of both traditions so movingly and continually express. I am an Englishman, a priest in the national Church, who has been working for nearly fifteen years in Liverpool—a city which was changed for ever by Irish immigration in the last century, and which, in the earlier part of this century, became a seedbed of sectarian and political strife. This has been substantially overcome by courageous religious leadership, and the willingness by all sorts of people to look at history afresh and see what new lessons can be learned from it.

Britain and Ireland are imprisoned by unhealed memories and the weight of history. Because they have been addressed only in a partisan and sectarian manner, they continue to provide the rationale for murder and mayhem in the present. Thus, when a British diplomat was murdered in Dublin, an Irishman was able to say to me, as if it were the most natural comment in the world, 'This would not have happened if it wasn't for the Hunger', referring to the great potato famine of the 19th century, and the neglect of the Irish people by the British government of the time. Similarly, a northern unionist said, 'There's no such thing as history here. There are facts, and our facts will never be the same as their facts.' In so far as our understanding of history is always culturally determined, it is hard to argue with either point of view, but, it does not take us very far.

As an Englishman, I have to be aware of certain stark realities in relation to the island of Ireland:

> We (that is, my nation) invaded Ireland, and fought our own battles there.
> We robbed the Irish people of their language and their literature, and attempted to rob them of their Church.
> We colonised Ireland with foreigners, and persecuted the Irish people when they would not conform to our religion.
> We drove the Roman Catholics into exile and killed thousands of men, women and children; and we invoked God as our justification.
> We failed to feed a starving people whose country was politically part of our own, leaving millions to die or emigrate without hope.
> We degraded the Irish people by caricaturing them in the British press and media.
> When they protested, we met violence with violence.

These atrocities were not confined to the native Irish. When it suited our purpose, we planted the land with Protestants, took advantage of their loyalty and industry, allowed them to die in unparalleled numbers for us in two world wars, and then told them we no longer needed them.

It is a fateful legacy which my country has bequeathed to the peoples of Ireland. How is it to be addressed? Maya Angelou has written:

> History, despite its wrenching pain
> Cannot be unlived, but if faced
> With courage need not be lived again.[1]

---

[1] Angelou, M, *On the pulse of morning.* Poem for the Inauguration of the President of the United States of America, New York, Random House, 1993.

That is the key, to face history with courage. It is very difficult. South Africa has given the world a particular model for addressing historical pain with courage, but in Ireland, there is as yet no consensus of the need for such truth-telling. Indeed, there is considerable resistance to the scriptural truth, 'There is no fear in love—perfect love casts out fear'—and even more, the following verse, 'If a person says he loves God while hating his neighbour, that person is a liar' (1 John 4.18,20).

Archbishop Robert Runcie has said:

> It is in understanding that healing comes. Those who do not wish to look at the past or understand the past or heal our memories are the sort of people who become easy victims of fatal lies and suspicions about other people in the present.[2]

Even more pointedly, President Richard von Weizsäcker, the president of Germany, spoke in 1985, on the 40th anniversary of the ending of the Holocaust (that unspeakable atrocity which so often gets in the way of rational debate on the theme of justice with our Jewish sisters and brothers):

> Whoever closes his eyes to the past becomes blind to the present. Whoever does not wish to remember inhumanity becomes susceptible to the dangers of new infection.[3]

It is vitally important for all who would call themselves peacemakers to take this on board, because it is an understandable facet of human nature, when confronted by pain—distant in time or very near—to say that we have to *forgive and forget.* Indeed, many in Northern Ireland have said this, and, faced with some of the excesses to which I have referred, that is not surprising. But it is misguided, both in terms of human psychology and of Christian theology. The way to move forward in circumstances of lasting pain or deep resentment is, not to forgive and forget (even if that were possible) but, to *remember and repent.* This is much harder, but certainly more creative.

---

[2] Runcie, Robert, Sermon on the 50th Anniversary of the Liberation of the Channel Islands, Guernsey, 1995 (unpublished).

[3] Von Weizsäcker, Richard, Speech to the *Bundestag* of the Federal Republic of Germany, 8 May 1985, quoted by Donald W Shriver, *An Ethic for Enemies*, Oxford University Press, New York, 1995, p. 110.

Repentance is the sort of theological notion which people like me are apt to talk about at conferences, but I have already suggested that it is a basic feature of human experience that you cannot have true reconciliation, be that personal or institutional, without sorrow and penitence, or if you prefer, apology and symbolic restitution. If we repent, others may choose to offer forgiveness—that is a matter for them—but it is not the main object. The repentance is important for its own sake and ours. Put even more basically, in the British/Irish context, there have been atrocities on all sides: violence begets violence, and blood will have blood, as the Bible graphically tells us, but somebody has to make the first move. The onus for that first move is on the nation or people who hold political power, and on whom the weight of history hangs most heavily.

Can repentance have a corporate as well as an individual reference? I believe it can, and this is persuasively argued by Donald Shriver in his important book *Ethic for Enemies.*[4] The truth is, since 1945 there have been numerous examples of honest apology in national and international affairs. Shriver discusses Russia, Poland, Germany, Israel, the Czech Republic, South Africa, to which I would add, in greater detail, four more recent examples, much nearer home for me as an Englishman.

1. President Mary Robinson of Ireland, speaking last year on the 150th anniversary of the Great Famine, acknowledged that apologies do not come easily to the lips of politicians, but added, 'I cannot tell you how much a sincere expression of regret would mean.' Prime Minister Tony Blair uttered such an expression just a matter of days after the general election in Britain.
2. The second example concerns the controversy which surrounded our queen's recent visit to India: whether she should go to Amritsar, and so, whether she should express regret for a terrible massacre there in 1919. In discounting any sort of apology, an official spokesman said there is no precedent for such an apology. But that is not true. The queen issued a fulsome apology four years ago to the Maori people of New Zealand for the breaking of solemn land treaties entered into in the reign of Queen Victoria. An opportunity was missed in India.
3. Much more up to date still, four months ago the Roman Catholic bishops of France issued a profound apology to the Jewish people for the Church's failure to speak out against the persecution of the Jews in 1940-44. The official Jewish response is instructive: 'If the seriousness of the error is

---

[4] Shriver, D, *Ethic for Enemies: Forgiveness in Politics*, Oxford University Press, Oxford, 1995

not admitted, everything becomes possible. The same circumstances might arise today, and no one would do anything about it.'

4. Finally, in Northern Ireland the British government has announced a fresh enquiry into a particularly terrible event known as Bloody Sunday, when 14 unarmed civilians were shot by British soldiers 26 years ago. It is highly likely that this will lead to some form of apology.

Sorrow and penitence, although they are the business of the theologian, clearly have a wider and more worldly relevance. They are valuable in their own right. More to the point, they provide a means, and sometimes the only means, to break an inherent pattern of evil and make possible new freedom of action. Furthermore, since sorrow and penitence presuppose humility, they are of particular benefit to the person or institution which offers them. Whatever else may be said about the South African experience, the fact is that South Africa has much to teach us. When the will for reconciliation is strong enough, when political leaders have the grace to feel, and the courage to express real humility and magnanimity, when God raises up religious leaders for whom concepts of justice are not an idea but an imperative, then it becomes possible to sit down and discuss the unthinkable with those to whom one has hitherto regarded as unspeakable.

South Africa is proceeding on the premise—not without risk, certainly—that honesty can only heal, and that history can be addressed with courage. Whether the present talks in Northern Ireland can summon the courage—yes, and the grace—to act on this conviction remains to be seen. If not, the truth of inherited pain and resentment will once again be regarded as potential weapons, to be decommissioned along with others, seemingly but deceptively more dangerous. This session is entitled 'International Models of Peacemaking'. I should have liked to give you a comprehensive overview of what is happening in the peace talks in Northern Ireland. I do not feel able to do so because, after several months, progress has been painfully slow, several smaller parties refuse to participate (or have been excluded), and the largest Unionist group will not engage in direct dialogue with Sinn Fein the Republican delegation. We simply do not know what is happening, though the courage and determination of the British and Irish governments to address real issues is not in doubt.

But for us as well as for them, the question is surely this: What does human society require in order to recover from past evil and injustice, and reach towards new shared experience in the future, free from fear? Surely it requires that hostility and a thirst for vengeance be set aside.

Repentance is only the beginning of that process, but it can make possible the first glimmering of trust without which no society can be at ease with itself.

The theme of this conference, Jubilee, the challenge of which is to live out God's justice and generosity in our lives and in the life of our nation. It is a very tough idea, the notion that justice might be restored to all who had experienced injustice, that God would set right all that had gone wrong in the life of a people. I speak as a Christian priest, and therefore reflect on these themes, as Jesus himself did when he spoke in the synagogue in Nazareth, echoing Isaiah's words of liberation. At the centre of the teachings of Jesus of Nazareth was forgiveness and tolerance, though it was balanced by a firm denunciation of injustice, oppression and particularly hypocrisy. He did not speak of the virtue of peace-loving or peace-seeking. 'Blessed are the peace-*makers*' is not the same thing at all.

I have been struck by some words of a secular Jewish philosopher, Hannah Arendt:

> The discoverer of the role of forgiveness in the realm of human affairs was Jesus of Nazareth. The fact that he made this discovery in a religious context and articulated it in religious language is no reason to take it any less seriously in a strictly secular sense.[5]

The Britain/Northern Ireland/Ireland problem is one of the very many conflicts around the world—indeed, just one in the alphabet of human misery from Algeria to Zaire—but for an Englishman it has to be the most tragic of all, for it is eight centuries old, and it concerns the very people to whom we are most closely related in the ways I described. There has to be a better way than has so far been found to set about the process of reconciliation between the peoples of our islands. Others here will already have made connections with the situations which confront them, and most obviously that which surrounds us here where we are meeting.

I do not imagine anybody here is familiar with the writings of Alice Stopford Green, a 19th century Irish writer. Her words are powerful and moving. She is referring to the Irish, but you will wish to make your own connections:

---

[5] Arendt, H, *The Human Condition: A Study of the Central Conditions Facing Modern Man*, Doubleday & Company, New York, 1959, pp. 214-15.

> To them has been meted out the second death—the lot feared beyond all else by men of honour. They have been buried by the false hands of strangers in the deep pit of contempt, reproach and forgetfulness—an unmerited grave of silence and shame.[6]

Politics and peace processes, even when conducted with integrity and the best of intentions, can take us so far and further. True and lasting reconciliation depends upon something deeper and even more demanding. As Naim Ateek has reminded us, the only way to peace is through the door of justice. That has to involve repentance for the past, and a new sense of trust for the future. It makes possible the discussion of all kinds of hurts. It opens up the possibility of forgiveness, from which reparation and new beginnings can flow.

Northern Ireland seems a very long way from Palestine in more senses than merely geographical, but it raises issues which are central to the biblical theme of jubilee. Jubilee is about restorative justice, addressing the causes of conflict, rather than tinkering with consequences. Whether the peace processes that are now in progress with regard to the particular conflicts will summon the courage to address the unhealed wounds of centuries remains to be seen. If so, there may be grounds for optimism as well as hope. If not, the present fragile peace will turn once again to bitter grief.

---

[6] Green, A Stopford, *The Making of Ireland and its Undoing*, quoted by David Corkery in *The Hidden Ireland* (first published 1924), Gill and MacMillan Ltd, Dublin, 1967, 1989, p. 285.

A VISION FOR PEACE: THINKING THE UNTHINKABLE

Hanan Ashrawi

It is a great pleasure and a great honour to be here. I feel a great sense of involvement that we are all here, not to think the unthinkable, but to challenge the *status quo* and the complacency that exists. I express my deep gratitude to *Sabeel*, to the organisers and all the people who have worked to make this a success. In particular, I want to thank Revd Naim Ateek, whose heroic efforts and unceasing work are much appreciated. His work embodies the constant search for justice and litigation that we all believe in.

I come to you today not as a politician. I do not think that any Palestinian who has a choice would choose to be a politician; sometimes we have politics pressed upon us. I have always said that we Palestinians are political beings because everything around us is permeated with politics. Decisions have been taken on our behalf, and so, in a sense, we have had to intervene. But, allow me to use my more academic garb in order to present my own vision, something not new or unique, but, perhaps, something which needs to be reiterated. I was very pleased with the title of this session, because a vision for peace could provide a starting point to challenge the thinkable, and to think the unthinkable. The key terms here are vision, peace, and 'unthinkability'. To have a vision we do not need to think about only utopian views or unrealistic idealism. What is essential is not to be a captive to the past, or a hostage to the present, but to transcend the pain of the moment and be able to project ahead. We must look at what ought to be and not only at what is, employ a sense of creativity and imagination with boldness, courage, candour, and honesty. These are essential criteria for visionaries, even beyond a sense of inspiration.

So what is peace? I do not claim that we can define peace today, but at least we know, having been the victims of the absence of peace all our lives, that peace is a state of being and of commitment. It is an active pursuit. It is a basic human right. It is not a gift bestowed on the weak by the strong. It is not a privilege. I believe that peace is a right, and, therefore, should be pursued. It is not a patronage, nor is it an exploitation of the weakness of the underdog. It cannot be brought about by coercion, intimidation, blackmail, or pressure. Nor can peace be attained by military or non-peaceful means. The means and the end have to be the same. Otherwise we could end up with a temporary ceasefire, with a truce, or with capitulation, at worst, with pacification and appeasement which are certainly temporary. As you all know, and as the theme of this conference has reiterated, peace is the essential component of justice, and cannot be a preparation for future conflicts, and therefore should embody the solutions to the causes of the conflict.

And what is unthinkable? Given the current status of affairs, given the fact that we are all victims of the arrogance of power, at all levels, whether in Palestine or elsewhere (threatening the people of Iraq, or other disenfranchised people), these kinds of conditions make the thought of a just peace almost unthinkable. But again it is relative, because, until recently, the prospect of peace between Palestinians and Israelis, or Arabs and Israelis, was considered unthinkable. People who even presumed to present an agenda for peace were considered to be unrealistic and thinking the unthinkable.

The Palestinian-Israeli conflict is one of the most complex, multi-dimensional conflicts in history. It has always contained an historical dimension, a cultural, geographical, political, and human dimension. But it also has a personal, a spiritual, and even an existential dimension. Therefore, it is one of the most difficult conflicts to resolve, and cannot be resolved partially. In a solution, I believe, we need several basic constituents or requirements of this vision of peace. First, we must make sure that in solving this conflict, in striving to achieve peace, we use the politics of parity, of morality. I know that in this jaded age of cynicism it is not really fashionable or trendy to talk about moral politics. Yet, I still believe that it is the dimension of moral politics which is essential to the pursuit of peace, while we are living right now the rule of power politics, the politics of power and domination.

Second, we must always keep the centrality of the human being, the human factor, as the means and the end of our peace endeavours. It is not in the service of the few, but in the empowerment of the human being. We have to talk about the politics of inclusion, rather than of exclusion, exclusive or exclusivity. We cannot adopt double standards for peace: all people are deserving and worthy of peace. We cannot have it that some are somehow more worthy of peace, of justice, or of freedom than others. We cannot put the stakes in relative terms. At the same time, we see ourselves within a clash of two narratives, and nothing is more obvious than the silent clash of the last fifty years, a half-century, a jubilee, in which there is an Israeli narrative being presented, and a Palestinian narrative which has stubbornly been excluded. I feel it is essential that the Palestinian narrative be put forth and be heard with courage and with candour.

We must also avoid absolutism because God does not take sides in geo-political conflicts. If we start with extremist absolutist ideologies we cannot achieve any compromise or reconciliation. Any attempt to employ ideology, which is what we are seeing now, is not a means of resolving conflicts, or of achieving peace. We see ourselves here in a situation of what I call a time warp. You have those victims who have had the courage and the confidence to seek a just peace. Then you have the conquerors who are resorting to the equation of absolutism and ideology. We see ourselves in a time warp, where the language we thought we had overcome or superseded is being revived in a way to exclude the rights of others. In discussing ideology versus radicalism, I do not believe that pragmatism can undermine the legality of rights. Being pragmatic does not mean abandoning the legal basis and the most fundamental rights of either side, particularly those of the Palestinians which have been denied. Therefore, all those calls for the Palestinians to be pragmatic are really a euphemism to abandon some of their most basic rights. We have to be very clear and forthright in distinguishing between pragmatism and realism, and between an appearance to the basic rights that should be the foundations of any future peace. This is what makes the difference between compromise and surrender.

The issue of mutual recognition goes along with the politics of inclusion. We must not accept the distortion of our narrative in order to be accepted. We must not accept the forced adoption of a vision of a discourse determined by the priorities of others. Recognition means the full recognition of this narrative. If it means that we have to adopt an alien version, then it means we are betraying ourselves in order to appease others, and that is a sure recipe for future conflict. Also, we will not, and we cannot, accept the rewriting of our history to adapt it to another version. We must not renounce our history, even though I always call not to be captives to history. We cannot change our history for the sake of a contemporary reality. We have to be true to our own legacy, to our own history, not to rewrite it for the sake of appeasement, or to be in line with a contemporary disequilibrium of power.

Also, there has to be an admission of injustice and a recognition of guilt. As long as the world refuses to admit that a deep, historical, collective injustice has been inflicted on the Palestinian people, we will be perceived, not as the victims, but as the perpetrators. It has to happen. I use the example of a Jewish Israeli who once told me that one reason why they cannot believe us when we say we want peace is because, if someone did to them what they did to us, they would not forgive and forget. Another Jewish Israeli said that if they would admit that a great historical injustice was done to the Palestinian people they would be self-negated. That is why I say that there is room here for mutual affirmation, rather than mutual negation. We will not negate ourselves in order to suit the needs of others. Therefore, this type of recognition, not just as a catharsis, but to prepare the grounds for genuine reconciliation is absolutely essential, because nobody has a monopoly on pain. Pain cannot be used to justify the infliction of suffering on others. I will not do unto others what was done unto me. We all have to be very careful about achieving this new equilibrium in which an admission of injustice and a recognition of guilt would prepare the foundations to move ahead without using pain and suffering as a club to punish others.

Also, we have to have the courage to address and to solve secular issues in a comprehensive and holistic way. Peace is not selective and fragmentary. We have to deal with the source of grievances, with the cause of injustice. Peace can never be cosmetic, and we should have the courage to lay open the central issues: Jerusalem, the land, boundaries, and self-determination. Recognition of the Palestinian right to self-determination is essential for this historical reconciliation. One flaw in the current peace process is that the paradigm always excludes the complicated factors, and goes to the simplest and most pragmatic steps. There is a failure to understand that in this paradigm the excluded factors are the sources of decision-making and self-determination among the Palestinians. So, if you exclude Jerusalem, issues of sovereignty, the recognition of identity, you cannot achieve peace. Neither can it be achieved by just giving functional goals and tasks, here and there, and isolated reservations, and calling that peace. We have to unravel all the constituents of the conflict, not in an abstract way, even though we understand the multi-dimensional, complex nature of the conflict. We have to move systematically, based on legality, with a serious political process, and refuse imposed taboos. Jerusalem is not a taboo. It is an issue that can be solved on the basis of international law and the legality of rights. If we deal with it only as a celestial city, we can never live in it as a terrestrial city.

We have to deal with the realities on the ground. A peace process is not an abstraction. It has to be translated effectively into behaviour, into realities that are tangible and complete. It cannot be left only at the political level. It has to be within the people, and it has to govern the behaviour of all sides. That is why we say you need the mindsets and the attitudes that are conducive to peace, reinforced by action, by praxis. We also have to go back to the basic principles.

I remember years ago in the 80s when they were asking us how we were calling for peace, we said, 'We are not calling for just any peace, we have foundations for peace.' We said the basic principles for peace should be mutuality, parity, and reciprocity. Now, we are in the middle of this big talk about reciprocity, and this imbalance of power. We forget that parity is the basic ingredient for reciprocity and mutuality. The principle of sharing is essential, because this is the principle that could govern the way we live in this land, whether we share life as two, separate states, or as one non-sectarian, or secular, democratic state. But so long as there is an insistence on exclusive possession, then there will never be peace. The principle of sharing has to be translated into actual practice, particularly when it comes to Jerusalem and the land. We have accepted the fact that Jerusalem can be two capitals for two states.

We must not accept excessive self-flagellation or even the disfigurement of the Palestinian psyche or ethos to serve the needs of others. We must maintain our own internal integrity; we must strive for democracy, for human rights, for the rule of law. We have always maintained that self-inflicted wounds are much more painful than those inflicted by others. We cannot, in any way, rationalise or justify our own internal shortcomings, excesses and violations, and we cannot, conversely, adopt the tactics, the discourse, or the methods of the adversary. And, no, we are not in the employ of the Israeli security, whereby we safeguard the security of Israelis, and ignore the rights and security of Palestinians. There has to be an integrity to our vision of authenticity, identity and rights, as a definition of our own source of value, which is not dictated by others, or by temporary conditions.

My value is not determined by how much I am served by others, but by how much I can serve the interests of my own people and humanity. This is intrinsic; it is not functional. I do not get approval or approbation, or a pat on the back from the Israelis, as long as I fulfil their requirements or their tests, and they certainly are attempting, and have succeeded in many ways, to place the Palestinians on a perpetual test of good behaviour. We are always on probation. We have to legislate by other peoples' standards and requirements—whether we fulfil their definition of compliance—while we have our own definition of our identity that is the source of legitimacy and the source of authority. Any leadership gains its legitimacy or strength, its authority, from its own people, not from external sources. No matter how much the Israelis or Americans approve of us, if we are not true to the rights and needs of our own people, if we are not held accountable by our own people, we do not have any legitimacy. And it is not bestowed by others. Therefore, this type of intrinsic, internal legitimacy is essential. That is why democracy and human rights are essential.

We must not be swayed, we must not allow ourselves to distort our own democracy, or violate our own rights in order to get external legitimacy. We must not confuse the means with the end, the process with the objective. There is a process that is fraught, but there is an objective called peace, and if the process is floundering, it does not mean that peace is a negative objective. To me it is absolutely miraculous that the Palestinian people have maintained, on the whole, a vast and strong majority in favour of peace, given the fact that this process has inflicted so much pain, suffering, and victimisation. I think that this is a sign of strong national and human maturity. We must maintain our collective contacts, keep our sights set on the goal, and not be apologetic or defensive about peace, because only the strong, only the confident, can bring peace.

Also, we have to have the courage to say 'no' when 'no' is needed. Peace is expansive and liberating, and cannot exist against a background where it is achieved at the cost of diminishing one partner or another. We must not accept being diminished by it, and we will not stand humiliated. I think that our generation has had a very painful legacy of conflict, of dispossession and dispersion, on the one hand, and exile or occupation, on the other. I believe that we are entrusted with giving the future generations a legacy not only that they can live with, but that they can defend and perpetuate. That is why I always agree that peace is a collective responsibility, and in our case particularly.

Moreover, peace is not just a bi-lateral issue. It is not just a Palestinian-Israeli question. The Palestinian tragedy was an international creation, and, therefore, there is an international responsibility to find a solution. That is why it is not just bi-lateral and subject to the imbalance of power. The Palestinian identity must be recognised, must be redeemed, and must be exercised. If we do not have two states, we will have one democratic state. One other thing must be kept in mind. We as the victims are the source of the legitimacy of Israel. The whole world may recognise Israel, but only the Palestinians can legitimise Israel. That is why peace has to be a genuine process of healing and redemption. I believe that in this day there are those who make history, and those who are victims of it.

We have to intervene to be the shapers of history in order to have the courage not to accept being victims of our history. I am confident that we will attain the unthinkable, because I have tremendous confidence in the will of a people that had been slated for eradication, to drop out of the recognition of history. But our will was never defeated, never broken, whether under occupation, or in exile. Together we shall get there.

A VISION FOR PEACE: THINKING THE UNTHINKABLE

Azmi Bishara

I do not know why we insist on thinking about the unthinkable. However, since we like to do it, let me remind you of Wittgenstein's injunction: that which one cannot think about, one cannot speak about. Nevertheless, we certainly do talk about the unspeakable. However, I prefer to speak about the thinkable, in the sense of what ought to be made possible, and what must be achieved, and discard the unspeakable. I will try to delineate the principles of a possible just peace as I see them.

There are only two 'thinkable' (in the normative sense of the word) and 'possible' options for a genuine peace in this period. When I use the word 'peace' I mean it in the normative sense, which should include justice. We Palestinians could, for example, continue to live as we do today; this is thinkable, but normatively unacceptable. I consider it unthinkable to accept an unjust peace, using a critical interpretation of Hegel's, 'what exists is reasonable' to mean: what is reasonable is worthy of existence. *Apartheid* is not reasonable; it is unthinkable and should not exist.

I believe that there are two possible, reasonable and, thus, thinkable options for peace in this period: the national option granted equally to two peoples with the right of self-determination; and the bi-national option. In my opinion, there are no other options. The Israelis believe there are other options, and that is why the reality looks as it does. The national Palestinian option is the statehood option. It is not an ancient one, as the Jewish-Israeli statehood option is not ancient either. Zionism, the movement that attempted towards the end of the 19th century to create Jewish nationalism, did not take off, and did not evolve from an existing Jewish nation, but from the need to create a Jewish nation. The need was not always there, however.

People did not always regard themselves as nations—the 18th-century middle classes and national intelligentsia created nationality, nation, and nationalism under particular circumstances. They did not create the concept of nation out of nothing, but from existing elements of ethnicity, religion, etc. They added to these elements, however, a new component that did not exist before—national culture, national history and memory, and, above all, national yearning for sovereignty. Establishing a nation, i.e., a state according to the concepts of 19th-century Europe, was the Zionist solution to the question of antisemitism. According to the Zionist doctrine, Jews should become a nation, and not just a religion. This is why Orthodox Jews were very hostile to the Zionists. Religious Jews were anti-Zionist because they thought that Zionism was an interference with the work of God. According to Orthodox Jewry, Jews were supposed to belong to a holy community. Zionists believed that Jews should form a nation in the modern sense of the word. What the Zionists failed to do was separate their nation from religion, as European and Arab national movements did. And because the Zionist Jewish nation is only a secularised Jewish community, the entry ticket is still conversion.

Arab nationalism separated the concept of Arab nation from the nation of Islam; it became one Arab nation, regardless of religion. Jewish nationalism never succeeded in doing that. The Jewish nation and the Jewish religion supposedly overlap, and we live in the contradictions of this notion, for this is the source of Israel's inability to separate state and religion.

I think we will live in this contradiction for a long time to come, however, and when I posit a 'national option' I do not mean the Zionist contradiction. I mean the fact—and I want to start with the 'other' if you do not mind, rather than with ourselves—that in the last 100 years a Jewish nationality emerged in Palestine. It emerged in an illegitimate way, but it emerged nonetheless. I call it Hebrew nationality; it is a Jewish-Israeli nationality that exists in Palestine. It does not and cannot exist in the whole world, and it is still in the process of formation, much like all modern 'nationalisms'. There is no such thing as a Jewish nation in the modern sense of the concept of nation, but there is a Jewish-Israeli nationality. The Jewish nationality in Palestine emerged, but it emerged on the ruins of our modern project, our Arab-Palestinian project.

There is no conflict between the national rights of the Palestinians and the national rights of Jews to Palestine, because there were no historical national rights to Palestine. In biblical times, there were no nations. In Europe and the Middle East, nations are a product of the 19th century. So, there were no conflicts over historical rights on Palestine. Western modernity, however, confronted the Palestinians with one huge colonial project that they could not, and were not supposed to be able to decipher. They could not tell who was a victim in Europe and who was not, in order to understand the special character of Zionism. They could not, they should not, and they would not, do that. To them Zionism was a colonial project, and Palestine was an Arab country. We cannot read the conflict retroactively as a conflict between historical rights. It was a conflict between native people and a colonialist movement that considered itself a national liberation movement.

Palestinian political nationalism, exactly like Syrian, Lebanese, and many other 'nationalisms', emerged later. Until 1948 the Palestinians conceived 'Palestine' in the framework of Arab unity. That is why, after the occupation of Palestine in 1948, the only doctrine we, as Palestinians, had in mind was the 'return', and what we call 'the doctrine of liberation'. Palestine should be liberated from colonialism. The misery and the tragedy lies in the fact that this colonial issue emerged at exactly the same time that other Third World nationalities were liberated, i.e., at the time of de-colonisation. Maybe this is one of the reasons why Palestinian liberation was a symbol in the Third World, as in the Arab world. Occupied Palestine was one of the few remnants of colonialism. Perhaps the reason why Palestine was colonised, when other nationalities were achieving independence, was that it was the only nationality whose national cause mingled with the Jewish question, which was a European issue, rather than an Arab one. The Jewish question was never an Arab one. The Palestinian issue eventually turned into an international issue. Many people wonder why the world has such an interest in us Palestinians. In fact, it does not: the object of international interest is the Jewish question.

Only after 1967 did an organised Palestinian nationalism emerge asking for statehood. Until then the Palestinians spoke about liberating Palestine from Zionist colonialism. Statehood was not in the movement's lexicon. The Palestinian national option, meaning sovereignty, is a post-1967 notion. After 1967, and only then, can we start thinking about the struggle as a conflict between two national options. One emerged, Israeli—whether it is legitimate or illegitimate is inconsequential. The other, Palestinian, leads the doctrine of liberation towards the doctrine of statehood in a part of Palestine. The fact that a Palestinian state was symbolically declared in 1988 is in itself not so important. What was symbolically important is the fact that it was declared on the principle of partition. The Israelis would like to neglect it. But when the PLO declared the Palestinian state in Algeria, it was on the principle of the partition of Palestine. The partition was accepted, but it was a partition between two national options, between two states.

In accepting the Oslo accords what the Israelis, including leftist Zionists and the Labour Party, had in mind was a kind of demographic separation, rather than two national options. And that is why many of our friends confuse the principle of demographic separation with that of two national options. They believe that left-wing Zionism is pursuing a Palestinian state in the West Bank and Gaza. When we speak about the partition of Palestine—let us ignore borders for a moment, and speak about principles—we are speaking about two states, two national options, and two separate sovereignties. This is very different from the separation of two demographic groups, because one can separate two demographic groups only in an *apartheid* system. To separate two demographic groups, one does not actually need two states. Clearly, the principle of demographic separation is not the principle of two states or two national options.

What is being implemented on the ground in Palestine is an *apartheid* system. We know only one in the world. Derrida once wrote that all the languages of the world refused to host it by translating it—and the word in all languages remained *apartheid.* Its essence could be summarised in one sentence: demographic separation, with one group having sovereignty, while the other does not. This is what the Israelis imagined under separation, or partition. What is now being built on the ground—on the ruins of our state option—that which was created after 1967, is a Bantustan system—the Bantustanisation of Palestine.

In the aftermath of the Gulf War, and due to reasons that I cannot analyse right now, the Palestinian leadership accepted the conditions imposed by Israel in the Oslo accords. They gave the peace process a chance. I think the majority of Palestinians, the vast majority, thought it was the only option open to them after the Gulf War, with the *Intifada* deadlocked, and with the collapse of the Soviet Bloc. After these events, they wanted to give the peace process a chance, and, understandably, they confused the recognition of the PLO with Israeli acceptance of Palestinian sovereignty—understandably, because the PLO represented the dream of sovereignty. It is a classic and tragic example of confusing the method with the goal.

But something happened which is very interesting to point out. Of course, I do not like to say we were warned before it happened. It is this. Not one nationality in the Third World would have won independence, if independence had to be derived from the balance of power with the colonial power. Not one. Neither Algeria, nor Vietnam, nor anyone else. The balance of power with the colonial power does not and cannot produce independence in the Third World. Independence after the Second World War happened not only because people revolted, but also because economic and moral powers in the colonial country prevented that colonial country from using all of its power. Without moral and economic constraints on the colonial country's power, not one colony would have won independence. A sense of justice, of relative justice, had to be involved in the realities of both sides.

The Israelis, including the people who created Oslo, thought that the historical compromise was the recognition of the PLO. With this fact we need to elucidate what the balance of power dictates. The balance of power in Palestine dictates *apartheid.* It does not dictate a Palestinian state. If there are no moral constraints on Israel's power, and if there are no moral elements to the peace process, the outcome of the process will not even be a relative justice. If justice is not a factor in Israeli and American public opinion, in Arab struggle and pressure, a Palestinian state will not emerge. The Palestinians cannot with their own power impose a Palestinian state on Israel. What will happen is what I previously called the normatively unthinkable: an *apartheid* system will emerge. However, if the Palestinian national option were to be exhausted, the Palestinian people would not simply accept *apartheid*, but would demand another option, based on the principle of equality. Then the bi-national option would emerge. If not two states, then one state, for both people. There can be no thinkable situation when one people has a state and the other has only autonomy.

Maybe here is where we reach the unthinkable for some, but certainly the thinkable for me, namely, a bi-national state. The Palestinians, the Palestinian elite, and the Israelis, needless to say, still cling to the national option. They want it; they want their own state. But if this generation fails to deliver it to the next generation, the next generation may not believe in the national option. The next generation may request equality. Equality in one civic entity with two nationalities within its framework. Many issues could be settled in such a framework, including the refugee question. Some Arab friends understood bi-nationalism to be a call for annexation, and they misinterpreted my intention. Bi-nationalism includes in it the existence of a national entity. Annexation is only a politically rhetorical challenge to the Israelis, who neither want to annex nor withdraw from the territories.

We need to remember that there are many narratives in our history. One of them, the dominant one, is that we started out as a refugee movement, not as an 'Occupied Territories' movement. The issue of return was the main thread. The United Nations recognised the Palestinian problem as a refugee problem before it recognised it as a national problem. Our refugees are still in Lebanon. The Palestinians in Lebanon live much worse than we do here. We want them to come back, but they cannot come back to Israel. In a two-state solution, Israel will remain a Jewish state, but the bi-national option will give serious consideration to the refugees. The settlements must be dismantled in a national option because they contradict national sovereignty. They cannot remain as a colonial power for two generations. If Jews want to be able to live near their holy sites they cannot be settlers, but must become the citizens of a bi-national state. This is the only way the Palestinians can let them be here: they cannot remain as colonisers.

Israel is digging the grave of the Zionist national option. In fact, it is unwittingly creating the infrastructure of a future bi-national option. There are only two options based on equality, but which, at the same time, take into consideration the existence of two national entities: the national (two states, two nations), or, the bi-national (two nations in one state with equal citizenship). In the bi-national option both people have the freedom to move, and the freedom to build. Not just one people. The irony is that the most efficient method used by Israel to bury its own national option has been its own settlements.

SPIRITUAL RESOURCES FOR PEACE—A VISION FOR PEACE

Michel Sabbah

Introduction

Sabeel, the Palestinian Liberation Theology movement, organised this three-day conference around the theme *The Challenge of Jubilee: What Does God Require?* In so doing, they challenged us to wrestle with this important question in numerous ways. For those of us who are Christian, we are meeting now in the land of the jubilee, and in Bethlehem itself, the city of the jubilee, where our Lord Jesus Christ was born. We stand at the threshold of remembrance and celebration of the mystery of the Incarnation of the Word of God, our Lord Jesus Christ.

But this theme also focuses attention on the current reality in the Holy Land, a reality which is shaped by the conflicting narratives of two peoples. The past fifty years recall two different stories, one for Israeli Jews and one for Palestinians. This year, in April 1998, the State of Israel will celebrate fifty years of statehood—a jubilee. At the same time, the Palestinian people will remember and commemorate fifty years of dispossession and tragedy, *Al-Nakba.*

These years have been marked by on-going conflict, tension and fears between the two peoples. And after fifty years of struggle, both of us, Israelis and Palestinians alike, have to confess that neither one of us has won peace. Both of us are still engaged in the same fight to realise a total and just peace, one which will acknowledge both the State of Israel as well as the human dignity of the Palestinian people and their right to establish their own state.

The *Sabeel* Centre, in their invitation to this event, also reminded us that 'it is timely for faith communities whose roots are in the jubilee vision to discover anew the responsibilities that God has entrusted to us as we work for the establishment of justice and peace today ... in the daily realities of life in occupied Palestine and in Israel.'

The first day of this meeting was convened under the theme 'remembrance and forgiveness', inviting us to the love of our neighbours and to acts of mercy. The second day focused on the concepts of 'truth and justice', inviting us to do justice, and today, the third day, we gather to reflect on the issues of 'liberation and healing', inviting us to walk humbly with God and to find in this humility a vision for peace.

To walk humbly, indeed, means to walk *with* God. The strong and the proud bear in themselves the permanent threat of going far from God. That is the meaning of the proclamation in the hymn of praise of the Virgin Mary thanking God for His grace towards her. She says:

> My soul praises the greatness of the Lord
> He has routed the arrogant of heart.
> He has pulled down princes from their thrones and raised high the lowly (Luke 1.46, 51-52).

So, a vision of peace starts with humility before God, with the vision of God's presence in our history. It is a presence which we do not always understand and one which often leaves many questions unanswered. Yet, from the various episodes in our history, certain issues of faith remain constant: we must try to understand them. We must not lose hope in God. There is a necessity to search constantly for new ways to move beyond our broken human attempts at living together.

Therefore, the reading and recalling of our history both invite us to acknowledge and to learn from our failures. In so doing, we open ourselves to the possibility of discovering new ways to move forward, new ways to win peace. Our reading of history should not motivate us to defeat the enemy. These new ways, then, cannot merely be new political or military movements. No, they must be focused primarily on new ways of being righteous and just with ourselves *and* with our brothers and sisters. As Pope John Paul II expressed it in his 1998 World Day Peace Message, 'Peace for all of us comes from justice of each one of us.' In such a framework, the only true objective of any struggle should be to win peace, and if this is our aim, then, and only then, will our enemies return to us as brothers and sisters. Then, and only then, will they be as God created and intended them to be.

As the Holy Father went on to say, 'The Jubilee is a time for which believers are devoted in a special way to God, the Lord of history. It is a reminder to all of the radical dependence of the creature on the Creator. In the biblical tradition, it was also a time for freeing slaves, for returning land to its rightful owner, for forgiving debts, thus restoring the conditions of equality willed by God among all the members of the people. It is therefore a special time for seeking justice which leads to peace.'

Foundations for our hope: justice with peace

'Justice goes hand in hand with peace and is permanently and actively linked to peace.' Justice and peace seek the good of one and all, and, for this reason, they demand order and truth. When either one is threatened, both falter. When justice is disregarded, peace is also in jeopardy. All of us—as beings created by God—are called to live in justice and to work for peace. When we give ourselves to acts of justice we are moved from acts of revenge towards acts of reconciliation. Justice, at its deepest level, is rooted in love. This love finds its most significant expression in mercy, and it is mercy which enables us to move from being enemies toward becoming neighbours.

As expressed in the Universal Declaration of Human Rights, justice is the 'recognition of the inherent dignity and of the equal and inalienable rights of all members of the human family'. This recognition is the foundation of freedom and peace in the world. This important declaration does not permit any state, group or person the right to engage in activities or actions which are aimed at the destruction of the rights and freedoms of others. It is a tragic fact that today this provision is still being violated blatantly through oppression, conflict and corruption. These words apply to our region today, both here as lived by Israelis and Palestinians, and in Iraq, where the United Nations are right now directly involved in situations which could lead to tragedy and the violation of human rights.

A vision of peace in our land, or in any land, must be based, firstly, upon our relations with God, with his mystery and presence in our own history. Secondly, it is based upon a set of relations among people, between the international community and our land, between the two peoples of the land, between the three religions of the land, and, finally, between the Churches of the world and the Church of Jerusalem.

The international community and our land

Unlike any other place in the world, our land has a special relationship to the three monotheistic religions and, consequently, a special relationship with all the followers of those traditions. Our land, therefore, is holy to many of the peoples of the earth. This reality has shaped the destiny of our land. Since the beginning of the Palestinian-Israeli conflict, the situation here has never been left to its own fate or to its two peoples. The international community has always intervened and played a decisive role in the various episodes of the history of this conflict. It has also recognised the rights of both peoples through various decisions. However, in the application of those decisions, the international community has not been a non-partisan adjudicator. In fact, until today, when international frameworks have called for significant changes in Israeli policies, it has refrained from intervening. Yet, in nearby Iraq, the international community has been willing to intervene, both through war and sanctions. In this land, neither has been used to enforce international resolutions. Is the difference in the measures used due to a difference in interests? The international community cannot claim to have a vision for peace, or hope to reach any just peace so long as this double standard is openly practised.

Human conscience cannot be silenced. No matter what, it will always echo the voice of God which has no armies, no military power, but contains nonetheless the invincible power of the spirit.

Relations among Israelis and Palestinians on the religious level

This relation is built upon the common vision of one God who is Creator of all, who gave the same human dignity to Palestinians and Israelis. It is this relationship which is the foundation for equality in human responsibilities and human rights. It is this relationship which establishes that no one is called to be superior or inferior to another.

Therefore, according to our main vision of God's revelation in this land, Muslim and Christian Palestinians and Jewish Israelis are brothers, equally created by God, loved by him and called to the same salvation. Jews, Muslims and Christians, each practising his or her own faith, are the subject of mutual love and respect. All of us are a part of the mystery of God's will in the mystery of the salvation of humankind. Election was for the Jews, but that election was for the salvation of *all* peoples of the earth. According to our Christian knowledge and revelation, all humankind is sharing the same loving call of God, one that is open to all peoples. Salvation comes through the Incarnation of His Eternal Word, our Lord Jesus Christ.

These religious realities are to be seen clearly in order to be respected for what they are and for the positive potentialities they have in our common fight for peace. They cannot be used in order to deprive any person of any of his or her rights. They cannot be a support for political claims. They can only be a support for the common quest for justice and peace. God's love calls us to more love and more justice and more peace. It is not a call for more military power, for more death, for more humiliations or more human violation of God's dignity in his creatures. Military or political power which seeks support for its action in religious foundations reduces God to our limited and sinful ways. This process assigns God the place of any soldier in the field. Religion must remain the refuge for all, where the warrior can rediscover his own human dignity in order to discover the human dignity of the adversary. Then, with this common discovery, justice for each can be better seen and better guaranteed.

Due to historical facts, Judaism has a particular relation to the West in general, and to Western Christianity in particular. This relation was one of persecution of Jews by the Christian West. This particular relationship of former persecutions helps to explain the assistance or the alliance of Western Christians with the Jewish people today. This often leads to a confusion between Judaism as a religion and Israel as a Jewish state. Therefore, this special relationship, when applied to the political realities which form part of our present day, often leads to misunderstanding. A vision of peace necessitates the clarification of this relation and its influence on the political conflict between Israelis and Palestinians.

Relations among Muslims and Christians

A global vision for peace also presupposes sound relations within the context of the whole Palestinian people, between Christians and Muslims alike. In any family or household, an ongoing effort is made to keep everything in order, attempting to keep out any strange spirit or disallowing any foreigner to sow seeds of dissension. Due to our different spiritual visions and orientations, many substantial differences can exist in the same house. This calls for co-ordination, and applies to the Palestinian vision also.

It is normally expressed that Muslims and Christians are brothers, and therefore, no dialogue is needed. Rather, it is quite the opposite. Because we are brothers, we have much to say to each other. Because we have different spiritual visions, we need to share our common spiritual riches.

Sometimes, it is also said, and some want it so, that Christians are living under and between two pressures, that of Muslims and Jews. The expression is inaccurate. In reality, like any other Christian group in the world, Palestinian Christians belong to their people. Here, they are Palestinians, just as the Muslims are Palestinians. They belong to their people, and therefore, they are not in the middle or between two pressures. They share the strengths and the weaknesses of their people.

At Christmas 1994, the seven Catholic Patriarchs of the East published their third common letter on the *Relations between Christians and Muslims.* They said, 'with Muslims we live in one country, and together we have a common homeland. Our common relations had in the past seen both difficult and easy days. Today, also, we have good days and difficult days. So it will be in the future. Our vocation does not consist in escaping from the milieu where God wants us to be. Our vocation does not consist in being Christians anywhere else in the world, but in being Christians in our Arab and Muslim countries. Here is where God wants us to be the witnesses of His Son and Eternal Word, Our Lord Jesus Christ. We are called to a difficult life and we have to accept the call.'

Together, as Christians and Muslims, we have to face the same challenges and share in all services. Therefore, we see the image of God in all, Muslims and Christians. We have to educate ourselves in order to find spiritual solidarity. This means that when we pray we cannot come before God alone or isolated, with our own adoration or petition or preoccupation. Before God, we have to bear in our spirit and in our hearts our Muslim and Christian brothers and sisters, their hopes and preoccupations.

The role of Christians

Our role as Christians in this land is to strive together towards more unity and co-ordination in our witness which is built on the same revelation of God through his Word, a word incarnate here in this city of Bethlehem. Our role is to shed the light of divine presence on all our lived realities. As we struggle for peace, we must attempt to see the truth and act according to it, with the abnegation and dedication required for the building of peace. As we seek to be more faithful to God, we draw nearer to the light of the Revelation in Christ. The more deliberately we attempt to live according to this light, the more we can build a true peace which is needed by all.

The second basic vision in the Christian witness is love. Love is the main and unique commandment given to us by our Lord Jesus Christ: 'I give you a new commandment: love one another; you must love one another just as I have loved you' (John 13.34). Love, here, means imitating God who loves all his creatures. When those creatures go astray and sin, God is patient. But God also requires them to come back, to repent and to convert. Love consists in seeing the image of God in the other and in believing that God is our common Father. This means that my dignity and the dignity of my brother and sister is the same and equal. As God requires repentance from me, so do I require it from my brother who violated my dignity and rights. Therefore, love can never mean a renunciation of rights. It is rather a spiritual strength which makes a person, and a people, stronger to speak and to act for dignity and the rights of all.

A vision of peace for Jerusalem

In conclusion, and for peace with justice to exist in this land, the relationship must be co-ordinated, accepted and commonly shared in respect of Jerusalem, the City of Peace and Reconciliation. This may well be the biggest challenge in our own spiritual and political lives in this land of two peoples and three religions.

Jerusalem must have a permanent stability, so that it will no longer be a source of war. The city must have a status which allows it to embrace its five essential and interwoven components: two peoples and three religions. No one should remain outside Jerusalem. All five components—Israelis and Palestinians, Jews, Christians and Muslims—should feel themselves equally at home in Jerusalem, equally sharing the same rights and responsibilities. Will we be able to give to Jerusalem this shared status which will make it a city of peace and reconciliation? I hope so.

I began my speech by quoting the invitation of the *Sabeel* leaders, 'it is timely for faith communities whose roots are in the jubilee vision to discover anew the responsibilities that God has entrusted to us as we work for the establishment of justice and peace today ... in the daily realities of life in occupied Palestine and Israel.' The Churches of this land, all of us indeed, are rooted in the jubilee vision. Therefore, we bear a responsibility in the process of healing and building a new society and a new set of relations among all the inhabitants of this land. The Churches of the world, due to their special relation to Jerusalem, the Mother Church, also share this responsibility.

Liberation and healing start with the vision of God's presence in our history. In this common vision, God commands us to continue to build despite all sufferings and losses. We are called to do so because God builds with us, and because 'the spirit of hope is at work in the world' (Pope John Paul II, in his 1998 World Day Peace Message). With God, we believe and work.

SPIRITUAL RESOURCES FOR PEACE

Edmond Browning

I would like to offer a prayer. This comes from our Church's *Book of Common Prayer*, and it is a prayer that has greatly affected me. It is called, 'For the Human Family'. Let us pray:

> Oh God, you made us in your own image and redeemed us through Jesus your Son: look with compassion on the whole human family; take away our arrogance and hatred which infect our hearts; break down the walls that separate us; unite us in bonds of love; and work through our struggle and confusion to accomplish your purpose on earth, that, in your good time, all nations and races may serve you in harmony around your heavenly throne; through Jesus Christ our Lord. Amen.[1]

I feel especially privileged to have been asked to speak on the subject of 'Spiritual Resources for Peace'. I do not know if any of you feel or understand the pressure that comes when you are the last speaker on the programme! The last few days I have listened to speaker after speaker, and I have thought to myself after each one is finished, 'Well, I have lost about three paragraphs!' And whether they claimed or disclaimed having a religious viewpoint, I think that each speaker had countless religious/spirit-directed values. Some even made it a point to say they are not speaking from a religious standpoint, but then turned right around and talked about religious values that are apparent in the situation. So I have to say that in a real spirit of humility I bring you the thoughts about our common witness and possibly some of the other values needed to undergird that witness.

I would like to begin by saying that Christian witness is not about expressing a 'liberal' viewpoint. Nor is being in prayer the prerogative of

---

[1] *The Book of Common Prayer*, Episcopal Church, Kingsport Press, New York, 1977, p. 815.

a 'conservative' point of view. In the United States, my Church, the Episcopal Church, has sometimes been called the Republican Party in prayer, and, at other times, the Democratic Party in legislative session. Of course, the Church, wherever it is, cannot maintain its integrity when it is aligned with any political ideologies. Faith transcends politics. And because that is so, I believe with all my heart that true peace for Palestinians and Israelis may best come from spiritual leadership from the three faith groups common to this region. And I would like to witness personally tonight and say thank God that *Sabeel* exists, for I think that in a real manner, they acknowledge and are implementing that truth in the search that they are helping all of us take. I want to pay tribute to all of those who have worked so diligently during the past couple of years to make preparation for this meeting that is just about to end, and I want to say that I think that it is going to have a kind of effect that will exist far beyond the walls of this university. I want to express my appreciation especially to Naim Ateek, for all he has done to give leadership to this cause.

So let me share with you the values that I believe must undergird any kind of witness for peace and justice. And let me speak about these values by sharing a couple of experiences.

Soon after becoming Presiding Bishop of the Episcopal Church I was at our cathedral in Buffalo, New York, for Ash Wednesday, where I had been asked to preach. That was followed by the imposition of ashes and the eucharist. A light lunch followed the service, and then I was asked to participate in a question and answer period. And people liked news from the presiding bishop. There was a man sitting there in a coat and tie who said, 'What do you think the greatest sin the Churches face today?' And I thought to myself, 'He must be a seminarian!' I had never been asked that question before, so I was taken aback a little bit, and I do not know about you, but sometimes we are caught in situations like that in which we wish we were somewhere else. But all of a sudden things began to come before me in a very short moment of time that helped to form an answer, and all of a sudden in my mind I was standing on the roadside looking into a community called 'Crossroads' which is a community just outside of Cape Town. I think it is one of the most beautiful cities in all of the world. We were 21 miles out of Cape Town, and we were looking at this community where the blacks were forced to live when *apartheid* was in its depth of denigration of humanity. You could see human waste lying all over the road.

Suddenly the scene changed and I was standing on the West Bank. And I saw the same sense of depravity and dehumanisation. And at both of those times I asked myself, 'Does anybody care?' And then I was taken quickly to San Francisco and I was walking through a couple of wards of patients suffering from AIDS, and I saw that their suffering, plus their families suffering, plus their loved ones suffering, and I asked myself the question, 'Does anybody care?'

And then suddenly I was on a reservation of Native Americans, and I saw the poverty that existed, and I was told that on that reservation and the other reservations in the country, there is the highest teenage suicide rate in the whole United States. And I asked myself, 'Does anybody care?'

And then I was sitting back in New York City, taken by the speaker of the Diocese of New York to certain hotels that had been set aside for the homeless. Hotels that were rat-infested, where children had nothing to do and would play in the halls, where drugs were sold, and I asked myself, 'Does anybody care?'

And suddenly I knew what I had to say to the young man. I said to him, 'Sir, I believe that the greatest sin that the Church has to face today is the sin of apathy, the sin of not caring.'

I know that during this conference there have been a lot of comments about the United States' electoral body and the public apathy. There have been all kinds of reasons given as to why Americans respond the way they respond. One major comment that was made pointed to our guilt that response was made to Israel in such lavish ways. Another was that this was just the way in which we respond to those we feel a desire to be uplifted. When we look at the United States' participation on the Israeli-Palestinian deadlock—the oppressed and oppression—it may not be because we are trying to appease our guilt, but that we are so apathetic to the real struggle that we do not sense or feel the collective pain, the injustice, the dehumanising of people.

I want to say to you that I think the majority of the people of the United States are apathetic to the Palestinian-Israeli situation. And to those Americans who are here today, if we do not understand that and take that back with us in terms of trying to build the kind of communication with our people about what is *really* happening here, then nothing is going to happen. And I mean that with all my heart.

In December 1990, my wife Patti and I joined thirteen other Church leaders and came to the Middle East to identify in solidarity with Church people, with Muslims and Jews, our abhorrence of the possibility of war in the Persian Gulf, and our desire to join in the search for peace. One third of the group came here, to Palestine and Israel, one third went to

Syria, and one third went to Baghdad. There is so much I could tell you about that. What I want to tell you is that we went into one museum in Baghdad in which there was a whole room of Palestinian art, and one of the most moving pieces we saw was one showing Jesus overlooking Jerusalem weeping. If Jesus exhibited any value it was certainly compassion —if the statement on the banner behind me, from Luke 4.17-18 and from Isaiah, says anything about his ministry it says that he entered into the sufferings of people, he entered the struggles of people, he entered into their fears and anxieties. His compassion was complete. It was not just empathetic, but it was a compassion that led him to action, which led, finally, to his own death. And I want to suggest to you this evening that I think that it is that kind of compassion, if you will, that is going to turn the apathy of this world to the suffering of the world. It can be that kind of compassion that will make a difference, and it is that kind of value that we need for one of our spiritual discourses to carry out the task that we have been given.

I once heard compassion being defined in a twofold manner. One is that compassion is being at the side of a river pulling out those who seemed to be drowning because of the rocks and the raging water. And, at the same time, compassion is going up to the head of the river to see why rocks were being thrown in. Compassion is an action that speaks to the right and wrong that exists in society. It seeks to do justice, as this conference has been talking about. To be a part of this conference, to understand the injustices committed, to experience the refusal to see the possibility of partnership in God's gift of land and resources, and to weep over it is not enough. *Real compassion is a calling to work to right the wrong.* Jesus did not just weep over Jerusalem. He gave—he gives his life for the sake of it.

Another value that I think is absolutely necessary in terms of resources that work for equality is again the love that has been here during the course of our time together. And that is the work of reconciliation.

In 1975, the worst earthquake up to that time in the history of humankind occurred in Guatemala. I was asked to go down to Guatemala and see what the Episcopal Church's response was to the tragedy. More men, women, and children lost their lives in seventeen seconds than in the five major battles of the Second World War. I had never been in a situation before where you could see death everywhere. Not only could you see death, but you could touch death and smell death everywhere. Death was so real that it was almost incredible. And in a matter of two to three days, this young priest said to me, 'Bishop, would you mind if I had an opportunity to talk to you for a few minutes.' And I said, 'Of course, let us sit down under the tree.' So we sat down and talked for a few moments, and he began to cry, and said, 'My only daughter of a family of three, was killed in this earthquake. And I tell you, I had never felt such loss in my life. The strangest thing is, because of that loss, I have begun to feel more one with my people than I ever felt before as a pastor. Their loss is my loss, and their brokenness is my brokenness, and their sorrow is my sorrow.' And I thought many times that that was probably one of the most meaningful theological statements that I had ever heard in my life. He was reconciled with his brothers and sisters in a way that possibly could never happen in any other way. Is it possible—and I propose this question to you—is it possible to hope that, in humility, out of the brokennesses in others, that in our brokennesses we can share the brokenness that exists in all of us? Is that possible? I want to suggest that it is possible, and it is the way to real reconciliation.

I want to raise another value which is so often swept aside in the heat of ideological fervour, and that is the value of pacifism. To all of us who struggle with this value, we are confronted by Jesus, who went to his death as a pacifist. I can never forget my visits to the Hiroshima peace memorial, to the Arizona memorial in Hawaii, to the Holocaust memorial here, to the memorial for the 236,000 who lost their lives in the battle of Okinawa. And I have to say to you parenthetically, that my experience in the room of the photo exhibit is not unlike my experience at those memorials. I would like to say that that photo exhibit is the beginning of a memorial to the Palestinian people. It would be wonderful if that memorial could be extended in such a way that we could be challenged humanly to the greatest level of pacifism, the pacifism of Christ.

Dear friends, I have to say that the Gulf War still weighs heavily upon me. I do not think I ever felt worse than the night the war started in Iraq. And no one will ever convince me that there was any other purpose to that war other than to defend a cheap supply of oil. And the so-called collateral damage against civilian populations with the use of weapons of mass destruction violates any semblance of just war criteria, let alone its affront to pacifism. And the continuing suffering of the civilian population under international sanctions, including the documented deaths of over half a million children since the end of that war, lies as a legacy of that effort, not to mention the US military personnel who today suffer from chemicals used against them. I am no admirer of Saddam Hussein. But my heart was and is broken for the Iraqi people. They, for us as people of faith, are children of God. I have no regret for my opposition to the war and to this present threat. The use of smart bombs is not very smart—in fact it is downright criminal. In this awful moment, I again see the image of the pacifist Jesus.

The two most noted pacifists of this century have shown that non-violence overcomes the most vicious circumstances. They were, of course, Gandhi and Martin Luther King, Jr. And they, like Jesus, gave their lives to the cause of justice for all people. Like Jesus, they may have appeared to have lost, but as events unfolded in the wake of their deaths, they were recognised as having transformed their generations. The spiritual power of non-violence is a tool for us that can never be underestimated.

The value that accompanied Gandhi and King and defined the very being of Jesus was *love*. This, of course, is our greatest value. And it is not offered as an option, but as a commandment for the work we are about. It is the spiritual gift which we hold up to the world.

We see these values through the eyes of Jesus, but they are embraced by all three Abrahamic faiths. And I think religion gets into trouble when we lose sight of these common values and embrace extremist or militant causes or greed for power. Sometimes our religions turn these values upside down and replace them with values of intolerance, judgmentalism, fear, ignorance, violence, fanaticism, even hate. These distorted values are the real enemy of the peace process. We have to remind ourselves and the world continually of the true values that shape our spiritual beings.

Dear friends, several years ago, I lost my cross, which was given to me by my diocese when I was made a bishop. There was another bishop who on his deathbed asked his children if they would give this cross, which I now wear, to me, saying, 'Tell him that he is to continue to be the hands and the heart and the arms of the constant Christ. To help to bring peace to the world for which Christ died.'

And I would say to each and every one of you, that if baptism means anything, it means that we are called to this task of being the hands and the heart and the arms of the constant Christ. So doing justice is not an option. It comes from our spiritual agenda, not from a political agenda. And if we leave this conference with that commitment, we might make a difference in our ministry to seek peace in this place. And that is my prayer and my hope for all of us.

CONFERENCE STATEMENT
Third International *Sabeel* Conference
The Challenge of Jubilee: What Does God Require?
10-15 February, 1998
Bethlehem University

At the invitation of *Sabeel* Ecumenical Liberation Theology Center and its local and international partners, more than 900 people (Christians, Muslims and Jews) from diverse parts of the world gathered in Bethlehem from 10-15 February 1998 to stand in solidarity and proclaim the challenge of jubilee. They came to discern God's call for them as peacemakers promoting justice for all people.

Most participants in the conference travelled throughout the Holy Land, before and after the formal proceedings, encountering local people and places in the Galilee, Gaza, Hebron and Jerusalem. The participants were outraged and horrified at the level of oppression and brutality of the Israeli occupation as they walked the contextual *Via Dolorosa* of the Palestinian people.

Nineteen ninety-eight commemorates the fiftieth year of the dispossession of the Palestinian people, on the one hand, and the establishment of the State of Israel, on the other. While Israelis are planning festive celebrations to mark victories and accomplishments, Palestinians who continue to struggle for the cause of justice, peace and liberation find themselves in the midst of a profoundly stalemated 'peace process' with a deeply frustrated hope for liberation.

Inspired by the biblical theme of jubilee, participants worshipped and prayed together as they were inspired by the challenge of God's word, 'to proclaim liberty to all the land's inhabitants' (Leviticus 25.10). 'What does God require but to do justice, to love mercy, and to walk humbly with God' (Micah 6.8). 'The Spirit of the Lord is upon me ... to preach good news to the poor ... to let the oppressed go free ...' (Luke 4.18-19).

The challenge is to practise perpetual jubilee and to articulate a new vision for peace, justice, security, and coexistence that satisfies the deepest needs of all God's people, rather than a solution based on military might and on a 'balance of power', which inevitably favours the strong and allows for racism, oppression, and discrimination against the weak.

This vision requires:

—The admission by the Israeli government that injustice has been inflicted on the Palestinian people.
—The return of all Arab and Palestinian lands occupied in 1967.
—The release of all Palestinian prisoners and detainees.
—The return home of all refugees and those who were expelled.
—The compensation of Palestinians for all damages done during the last fifty years of their dispossession.
—The guarantee of free access for Palestinians to Jerusalem and the cessation of all measures used to empty Jerusalem of its Palestinian population.
—The guarantee of full and equal rights to the Palestinians inside Israel.
—The compliance of Israel with all relevant UN resolutions.
—The challenging of all governments and in particular the United States and its allies for their continuing political, economic and moral support of the Israeli occupation.
—The lifting of sanctions and the removal of the threat of military intervention against the suffering people of Iraq.

The benefits of God's jubilee are for all the inhabitants of this land, Israelis and Palestinians, Muslims, Jews and Christians. The promise fulfilled will be for a life of true peace with lasting security for all people of the region.

14 February 1998